D0204087

Research in Therapeutic Recreation: Concepts and Methods

Editors

Marjorie J. Malkin and Christine Z. Howe

Research in Therapeutic Recreation: Concepts and Methods

Editors

Marjorie J. Malkin and Christine Z. Howe

Venture Publishing, Inc.
State College, PA

Copyright © 1993
Venture Publishing, Inc.

No part of the material protected by this copyright notice may be reproduced or utilized in any form by any means, electronic or mechanical, including photocopying, recording, or by any information storage and retrieval system, without written permission from the copyright owner.

Printed in the United States of America

Library of Congress Cataloging in Publication Data
Editors: Marjorie J. Malkin & Christine Z. Howe
         Research in Therapeutic Recreation: Concepts and Methods

Production: Bonnie Godbey
Printing and Binding: Thomson-Shore, Inc.
Manuscript Editing/Graphics: Naomi Q. Gallagher

Library of Congress Catalogue Card Number 92-63340
ISBN 0-910251-53-3

10 9 8 7 6 5 4 3 2 1

Memorial Library
Mars Hill College
Mars Hill, N. C.

Dedication

I would like to dedicate this text to my family, particularly my husband Keith Peterson, son Daniel Klotz, my parents Charlotte and Jacob Malkin, and my sister, Elaine Malkin. They have remained consistently supportive of my various endeavors, academic and otherwise.

M. J. M.

This book is dedicated to my former graduate students at the University of Georgia and the University of Illinois at Urbana-Champaign, many of whom are now colleagues, and Dr. H. Douglas Sessoms, Professor and past Chair of the Curriculum in Leisure Studies and Recreation administration at the University of North Carolina at Chapel Hill. These individuals especially inspire me by their quest for knowledge. They amaze me with their continuing desire to ask the "hard" questions and search for the most elusive answers, their strength and candor in discussing the stumbles along the paths followed in their searches, and their openness of mind to new pathways for understanding.

C. Z. H.

15.8
432 m

940902

TABLE OF CONTENTS

CHAPTER 4
PSYCHOLOGICAL PERSPECTIVES FOR THERAPEUTIC RECREATION RESEARCH: THE PSYCHOLOGY OF ENJOYMENT

CHAPTER 5
COLLABORATIVE RESEARCH: BRIDGING THE GAP BETWEEN PRACTITIONERS AND RESEARCHERS/EDUCATORS

CHAPTER 6
ETHICAL CONSIDERATIONS FOR THERAPEUTIC RECREATION RESEARCH: A CALL FOR GUIDELINES

CHAPTER 13
THE ANALYSIS OF SUBJECTIVE INFORMATION:
A PROCESS FOR PERSPECTIVE-TAKING

CHAPTER 14
CONFIRMING, INTERPRETING AND REPORTING
NATURALISTIC RESEARCH FINDINGS

Acknowledgements

Thanks are due, first and foremost, to Dr. John Allen, Chair of the Department of Recreation at Southern Illinois University, Carbondale, for his support, and to my colleagues and students for their encouragement and forbearance. The insightful and efficient editing of Chris Howe is also much appreciated. The support of the American Therapeutic Recreation Association (ATRA) Board was invaluable in this endeavor. Thanks also to all chapter authors including contributing members of the ATRA Research Committee, and to Bonnie Godbey of Venture Publishing, Inc. Finally, thanks are due to Linda Patrick and her staff at the SIU College of Education Support Center for manuscript preparation, and to Robert Cashon and Suzanne Vincent, editorial aides.

M. J. M.
SIU, Carbondale

Coediting a book with many chapters presents opportunities that are different from writing one alone, including stretching me and testing my sense of humor. This process enabled me to finally learn to use all of the features of our high-tech telephones for numerous long-distance phone calls to people who (just like me) are rarely in their offices on the first try. I have also developed personal relationships with the overnight letter carrier, photocopier, printer, and word processing software due to too much practice at drafting and redrafting. I have planted a tree, bronzed my recycling bin and vowed to never kick the copier again because it, as with other machines, responds better to someone who actually follows the directions for use than someone who resorts to violence.

Especially and on a serious note, I want to deeply thank Marjie Malkin for her great mind, inviting me to do this with her, and persevering; each of our chapter authors for their grace, enthusiasm, and commitment; the ATRA membership and their representatives for making this book possible; Bonnie Godbey and the personnel at Venture, for their cooperation and savvy; Joe Balog, Chair of the Department of Health Science/Recreation and Leisure Studies at SUNY Brockport in Recreation and Leisure Studies, for his support of efforts such as this; Ann Rancourt, Coordinator of the Program in Recreation and Leisure Studies, for providing the human and technological resources needed; and my colleague Dave Jewell, Professor of Recreation and Leisure Studies, who along with Ann, was there for me day-to-day.

C. Z. H.
SUNY Brockport

Foreword

This publication represents another contribution by the American Therapeutic Recreation Association to afford developing and practicing professionals resources for the delivery of quality services. *Research in Therapeutic Recreation: Concepts and Methods* is an effort to bridge the gap between the recreational therapy practitioner and the researcher. The book emphasizes the need to apply a diversity of methods to examine our theoretical foundations as well as demonstrate the efficacy of therapeutic recreation service delivery.

Throughout the text, the contributors reiterate the need to advance a research agenda for therapeutic recreation. The 1991 Temple University project on the efficacy of therapeutic recreation as a treatment modality brought to light the current state of the field. The verified critical deficiency of efficacy research in therapeutic recreation was a notable outcome of the project. This outcome also set the stage to recall the need for a strong research agenda in the field. At the heart of the agenda is the development of a set of values that embrace the desire and skills to be consumers of research and participants in the research process.

This text makes the case for quality research while offering an understanding of the research process and methods used in the exercise of field research. Practitioners at all levels must accept a role in the research initiative for the field and for the advancement of distinctive services to the consumer.

The American Therapeutic Recreation Association has accepted a role in confronting the research imperative for therapeutic recreation. *Research in Therapeutic Recreation: Concepts and Methods* is part of that commitment for action. This publication will be the first of many projects designed to address the critical research needs of the field. It is hoped that this effort will facilitate collaborative efforts between practitioners and researchers in demonstrating the efficacy of our services.

The American Therapeutic Recreation Association would like to extend special appreciation to Venture Publishing and Ms. Bonnie Godbey for their role in supporting these essential initiatives. The future depends upon an aggressive schedule of activities to demonstrate the value of therapeutic recreation services. It is the cooperative efforts of committed professionals and agencies that will have an impact.

Thomas K. Skalko, Ph.D., C.T.R.S.
ATRA President 1992-1993

Note From ATRA Board Liaison

In the past, research was much maligned and even feared by those who did not understand it. To the credit of our profession, research today is becoming accepted as a valuable means to expand the body of knowledge that underlies practice in recreational therapy. *Research in Therapeutic Recreation: Concepts and Methods* helps us to more fully understand and appreciate research by examining and explaining issues specifically related to research in recreation therapy.

This much needed work, written by recreational therapy researchers, can facilitate the movement of research into the mainstream of clinical practice. The book provides a comprehensive introduction to recreational therapy research for undergraduates, graduate students and practitioners. Students are offered an extensive overview of issues related to both quantitative and qualitative research methods. Practitioners will find the book to be a valuable resource for utilizing existing research findings and for conducting studies in clinical settings.

As Liaison to the Research and Publication Committees for the Board of Directors of the American Therapeutic Recreation Association (ATRA), on behalf of the Board I wish to acknowledge and thank all of those who have contributed to *Research in Therapeutic Recreation: Concepts and Methods*. The writing and production of the book was a large task that could have only been accomplished by the tireless efforts of those ATRA members who unselfishly gave of themselves so that the rest of us might benefit.

David R. Austin, Ph.D.
ATRA Board Liaison
Professor of Recreation
Indiana University, Bloomington, IN

Preface

This book had its origins in a series of presentations which occurred at the 1990 ATRA Annual Conference in Kansas City. These workshops involved both "qualitative" and "quantitative" research methods. Originally, two booklets were planned based on these conference sessions. Well, the project certainly grew, but hopefully not like Topsy! Increasing interest on the part of therapeutic recreation (TR) professionals in understanding and conducting research led to the expansion of this project.

As coeditors, it was our intent to assemble a group of forward-looking, highly-qualified chapter contributors. We invited a sampling of authors whom we recognized for their involvement with consumers (persons with disabilities/differing abilities) as either professionals in the field, educators, or researchers. They also possess methodological expertise and substantive knowledge of therapeutic recreation (TR) programs and services. As the biographical sketches evidence, we were more than able to meet our intent. We are struck by and thankful for the richness and diversity of talent attracted. We are challenged by the ideas and questions each of the authors has put forth and we are enheartened by the regard for humanity that is inherent in those ideas and questions.

More practically, it was our job to put an order to the chapters that at least we thought was logical and to encourage consistency among our writers. We have attempted to provide consistency without uniformity as there are some aspects to each chapter that are unique; not only in terms of content, but in terms of the best format to express that content. So, for example, in some chapters questions are embedded in the narrative, whereas in others, discussion questions or case studies appear at the end of the chapter.

Realizing that each author is a recognized expert in his or her subject matter, we felt the need to be equally respectful of the communication style of the author. Therefore, the relatively light touch of our editorial hand means that some persons may find selected chapters to read a little more easily than others, especially at first glance. However, whether the content and vocabulary are new or familiar, and whether the sentence structure is simple or complex, at second reading, the richness of the material will become self-evident.

As the coeditors, we, of course, hope that each chapter will be given a careful examination. Because we think of research as an active and vital process, we want to encourage reading about research to be an active and vital process, too. In future years we hope to find marked-up, well worn copies of this book in used bookstores, and in the offices of therapeutic recreation specialists (TRSs) as well as on the bookshelves of educators and students. We invite each reader to have a dialogue with each chapter, to correspond with us with their questions and concerns.

Each chapter is intended to contribute theoretically, methodologically, or substantively to the text section, as well as to the book as a whole. In particular, within sections II (Malkin) and III (Howe), each editor has made efforts to ensure continuity and communication with and between authors.

We have also tried to make this collection of chapters reasonably coherent so that the book as a whole may stand alone, especially for the reader who is a practicing professional in the field. However, we suspect that the best use of this book may be as a complement to a "full-blown" (and likely non-TR specific or even recreation and leisure specific) research methods text. We believe that our most important contribution is in being TR specific. Thus, our authors have tried to use examples and illustrations that relate inquiry to TR constructs, problems, processes, settings, or participants. By the way, when you see I, us, we, or our, that typically refers to the coeditors or the chapter authors. When you see investigative therapeutic recreation specialist (investigative TRS), that means you, our readers.

We are also obligated to consider the use of our language in terms of both population and paradigm. Words have power in their denotative and connotative meanings. In accordance with the ideal of using the least labeling terminology in reference to those people most commonly served by TRSs, we have tried to always put the person first, before the disability/differing ability. We have tried to eliminate phrases and phrasing that are patronizing euphemisms or limiting descriptors in order to emphasize and remind ourselves of the humanity and inalienable equality of those whom we investigate. After all, it is the consumers or participants who voluntarily cooperate with investigators to answer their questions. Without this cooperation the research could/should not be done, or certainly would not be done as well. Throughout the text, the emphasis is on such a "person-first" empowerment of program and research participants, and on nonbiased, nonsexist research approaches. The term "research participants" is used in several chapters in lieu of the more conventional "subjects" or "respondents" because it connotes a reciprocal relationship between the investigator and the persons cooperating with the investigation. "Research participants" implies enfranchisement, respect for the dignity of individuals, sensitivity to contextual concerns, and an unwillingness to think of or treat people as mere objects of inquiry.

Further, debate continues regarding the terminology of research (or for that matter, the definition of research). One author's paradigm is another author's heresy. One writer's call for consistency in the use of vocabulary is another's alarm for small-mindedness at best or the restriction of free association at worst. Should we be "free" to define something such as therapeutic recreation or positivistic research in any way we want to or should we strive for some commonly held definitions of these terms? Or, are these even questions that we should be asking? If only to minimize vagueness, ambiguity, and confusion (if not controversy), with the recognition that this is not the definitive statement of the meaning of all terms, the index of terms at the end of the text includes **bold** face references to indicate to readers the preferred definitions of key research terms within the text. By providing investigative TRSs with these highlighted definitions, we do not presume that there is only one single, correct definition for all of the terms listed. Rather, we are offering an easily accessible, reasonable plausible set of definitions that may be workable for our readers. We believe that the concept and process of research in TR is evolving and that the language used to do it and communicate about it must be dynamic, as well. Our goal is to provide investigative TRSs with a *reference point* as they travel on their journey through research.

Another purpose of this book is to "demystify" the research process by removing "research" from the sometimes exclusionary appearing, jargon-using, narrowly-focused domain of the "Paper Chase." By making research more accessible to the student and the practitioner, research should become more understood and applied to professional practice. Education about research terminology, design, implications, and applications is a two-way street. There must be dialogue and it must be a participatory, open experience among *all* TR professionals and students. Explication and understanding of research results, application, and collaboration are all necessary to this process.

The book is composed of three multi-chapter sections and a fourth single-chapter section whose "conclusions" we hope to challenge you to become an *investigative therapeutic specialist*, stimulate you to prove or disprove the points made, and serve as an inspiration for further inquiry. Section I, the Introduction, contains six chapters that introduce and provide an overview of the research process. Topics for Section I include: issues and needs in TR research, paradigmatic schemes, theoretical bases for TR research, practitioner/educator collaboration, and ethical issues. Section II covers positivistic research approaches, including survey and experimental studies, clinical or field trials, innovative (single-subject) research methodology, and issues of validity and reliability. Section III's chapters explicate naturalistic research approaches. Contents include discussion of selected qualitative research methods. Finally, in Section IV, efficacy studies in TR are analyzed with implications about the state-of-the-art in TR research and future needs.

Section I—Introduction

The purpose of this section is to introduce some basic concepts, needs, and issues related to research in therapeutic recreation. Also, theoretical and ethical issues are presented.

Within Chapter 1, coeditor Malkin explores key issues and needs in TR research as revealed by a review of the literature primarily from the past decade. The philosophical bases for TR research and social factors affecting the TR research process are examined. Recent developments in health care practice and research are analyzed to determine possible future directions for TR research.

Bullock, in Chapter 2, presents an analysis of two research paradigms: the positivistic and the naturalistic (interpretive). This chapter sets the stage for the core text sections (II and III) which further discuss these research paradigms. Bullock states that the research process is undertaken both to examine practice and to advance the intellectual development of the field.

Chapter 3, by Ellis offers a considered opinion on the degree to which recreation, leisure, and therapeutic recreation is a "science" or an "art" and the legitimacy of its research base. The chapter is an honest and candid appraisal of the research community and what they are all about from someone who is not only a member, but one of the strongest advocates of doing right by both consumers and the body of knowledge in recreation, leisure, and TR.

In Chapter 4, authors Dattilo and Kleiber analyze prevailing theories of self-determination, intrinsic motivation, social reactance, and learned helplessness as they pertain to a psychological perspective for therapeutic recreation research. They focus on the concept of enjoyment as crucial to an understanding of the socio-psychological basis for TR research.

Within Chapter 5, contributors Savell, Huston, and Malkin explore issues of "researcher/practitioner" collaboration and present a model for practitioner-initiated research. Far too often investigations fail to leave the drawing board due to lack of time, fear of the "unknown" research process, lack of energy, lack of computer resources, and about a dozen other viable reasons. This chapter offers a step-by-step model for collaborative research which uses the resources and abilities of both practitioners and educators/researchers.

In Chapter 6, Stumbo explores ethical considerations for TR research. Although there are codes of ethics in existence, Stumbo indicates to us that they primarily address the conduct of TR practice. There is a void in terms of guidelines for ethical research conduct for TR professionals who study individuals with disabilities. This void has resulted in some instances which at best are problematic and cause for concern, and at worst unethical and damaging to research participants. Stumbo presents convincing evidence that formal ethical standards for the conduct of research in TR **must** be established.

Issues and Needs in Therapeutic Recreation Research
Marjorie J. Malkin

A 1990 survey of the educational interests of members of the American Therapeutic Recreation Association (ATRA) indicated many research related needs involving therapeutic recreation curricula and continuing professional education. Specifically ranked as moderately to extremely important were the following items: client and program evaluation; assessment instrument development; practitioner (involvement with) research; educator/practitioner dialogue; the application of research results from TR studies and related disciplines; the importance of research to the TR profession; and applied research methodologies (J. Kaufman, personal communication, May, 1991). The development of this text on research concepts and methods in TR is, in part, a response to these stated needs and interests.

Further, the crucial importance of research has been acknowledged by many professionals. Despite the dual origins of the TR profession in hospital recreation and in the parks and recreation (leisure service) field, the vast majority of certified TRSs (C.T.R.S.) who have completed the National Council for TR Certification (NCTRC) examination are employed in clinical settings (*NCTRC Newsletter*, 1992 April/May). Therefore, current trends and developments in the health care industry influence the TR profession and its research to a great extent.

Russoniello states (1991) that the need to substantiate claims that recreational therapy "is an efficacious treatment ... is critical to the survival of the profession" (p. 1). Do TRSs indeed provide "treatments that bring about physiological and psychological change which ... ameliorates disease and dysfunction" (Russoniello, 1991, p. 1)? This author further points to the recent expenditure by the U.S. Department of Education in awarding a substantial grant to Temple University.

The grant was specifically to explore the efficacy of TR. Such an expenditure documents the importance of research and to some extent legitimates the profession.

What is Research?

Although there are volumes of classic and contemporary research texts written from a variety of ideological and disciplinary perspectives, **research** may be defined generically, and in very elementary terms, as the systematic collection of information about a particular subject. Research is a "diligent and systematic inquiry into a subject in order to discover or revise facts, theories, etc." (Webster's, 1991, p. 1145). Such an inquiry is aimed at the discovery and interpretation of facts; the revision of accepted theories in the light of new facts; and practical application of such theories (Webster's, 1984, p. 1002). The following chapters of this text describe and explain the concepts underlying such investigations in the field of therapeutic recreation, the techniques used in collecting and analyzing such information, and some accepted interpretations and applications of such research.

Research may be categorized in many ways. Pure research (basic or theoretical) has been contrasted with applied (action or practical). Research may be categorized by the techniques or methods employed, contrasting, for example, quantitative (expressed in mathematical terms) with qualitative (nonmathematical), or obtrusive with nonobtrusive techniques. Research can be framed in terms of its setting (field or laboratory). The larger concept of research paradigm (positivistic or naturalistic/interpretive) is discussed by Bullock in Chapter 2. Throughout the text there is discussion and clarification of some of these terms and issues. Readers need to be aware of the topical areas or categories, and the varied terminology used to describe them.

One of the primary aims of this text is to narrow the alleged "**researcher/practitioner gap**" in terms of knowledge about and conduct of research. Kraus and Allen (1987) believe that the arbitrary classification of research as either applied (practical) or basic (theoretical) may be responsible, in part, for such a research "gap" and for the lack of collaborative research efforts. They state (1987, p. xvi) that "even highly conceptual studies may have important practical implications, and . . . applied studies may be based on sound theory and may contribute significantly to an understanding of the field." They further contend that evaluation is a form of research, with practical or applied purposes. Research can have practical implications! Kraus and Allen (1987) identify some roles of research in recreation and leisure services in general; roles which can be extrapolated to TR. These are: to improve or apply new professional techniques and practices; to understand the experiences and needs of participants; to develop more effective programs; to measure specific outcomes; and to document the value and effectiveness of agencies and programs. Finally, these authors reiterate the critical need to document both the value and effectiveness of services in an era of increased demand for accountability coupled with budgetary constraints.

Philosophical Bases of Therapeutic Recreation Research

In many systems of philosophy, epistemology is believed to precede ontology. In other words, the theory of knowledge is believed to determine how people know "reality," and it examines the validity of such knowledge. Ontology refers to the nature of being, or what exists. Phenomenologists point out the primary role of human consciousness and awareness in the learning process. These issues of epistemology and ontology are discussed further in Chapter 2.

Philosophical issues and concerns as they affect TR have been addressed by Sylvester (1989), Peterson (1989), and in the text edited by Sylvester and others entitled the *Philosophy of Therapeutic Recreation: Ideas and Issues* (1987). Readers are referred to these sources, as a sound and explicit philosophical or conceptual base is crucial for the process of research in this, or any field. Sylvester (1989) offers the example of the guidance counseling field, which was preoccupied with immediate issues of practice rather than the development of theory. "Consequently, the field was not prepared to mold an intellectual foundation capable of supporting a body of knowledge" (p. 7). Furthermore such "[e]difices unfortified by legitimate philosophical constructs and valid theoretical knowledge decay and crumble under the pressure of critical analysis and external evaluation" (Sylvester, 1989, p. 7). Within the foreword to the 1987 text, Sylvester decries the attention to technique within TR, rather than to conceptual and ethical understanding. Hemingway (citing Mobily, 1985b) emphasizes that "a sound philosophy should not only guide practice but also give direction to research" (1987, p. 3). Hemingway further urges expanded philosophical inquiry "to illuminate the fundamentally value based nature of therapeutic recreation" (1987, p. 3). Readers of this text are encouraged to broaden their knowledge about such philosophical issues, and researchers are cautioned about the risks of continuing to conduct empirical research without an adequate conceptual or theoretical basis, as well as the need for all parties to become aware of issues of definition, values, and ethics.

Definition and philosophy determine research outlooks and approaches. However, there is currently no clear consensus as to the definition of TR, and the field is still "a profession in transition" (Compton, 1989). Historically, and to the present, much controversy or "cacophony" (Shank,

1987) has surrounded the issue of defining **therapeutic recreation**. This text certainly cannot offer a resolution of this situation. However, reference to some key issues and discussions of this topic is in order.

Historically, most TRSs are aware of the development of the NTRS **"leisurability" model** in the early 1980s. Crawford decries the lack of a scientific basis for the profession, as "the 'leisure ability model' is in large measure a service philosophy . . . that remains invalidated in many service settings and for many disability groups" (1991, p. 394). Many experts in the field feel that the model is lacking in two ways. First, the model encompasses "recreation participation," or the mere provision of recreation opportunities for individuals with disabilities, which is believed by many to comprise a separate endeavor called special recreation. Austin states that this approach "does not constitute a therapeutic approach because it does not involve purposeful intervention aimed at accomplishing specific treatment or rehabilitation objectives (Austin, 1991a, p. 15). Second, critics find that a focus on increasing independent *leisure* functioning is limiting. Such concerns were among those that led to the founding of ATRA, and the development of the ATRA definition statement. It specifies that:

> Therapeutic Recreation is the provision of Treatment Services and the provision of Recreation Services to persons with illnesses or disabling conditions. The primary purposes of Treatment Services which are often referred to as Recreational Therapy, are to restore, remediate or rehabilitate in order to improve functioning and independence, as well as reduce or eliminate the effects of illness or disability. The primary purposes of Recreational Services are to provide recreation resources and opportunities in order to improve health and well-being. (ATRA, 1990, p. 1)

This definition includes the goals of increased independence and function, as well as improved health and well-being.

Is the primary goal of TR to increase leisure functioning, or is it to improve health and quality of life? Readers are urged to undertake further study of these issues. Discussions and analyses are provided by Sylvester (1987), Austin (1991a), and Austin (1991b). Sylvester (1987) reviews the relationships among health, leisure, and happiness. He refers to previous definitions of recreational or leisure activity as "both a means of achieving and an integral part of health" (p. 76). He proposes leisure as the *goal* of TR, and describes leisure as the "opportunity for the celebration of freedom in activities enjoyed for their own sake" (Sylvester, 1986, cited in Sylvester, 1987). Austin (1991) also stresses the importance of the concepts of recreation and leisure in defining TR. Finally, Austin's (1991b) Health Protection/ Health Promotion model of TR is explicated, a view of TR that is compatible with ATRA's definition. Both emphasize health and wellness. Due to the large proportion of C.T.R.S.s employed in clinical settings, there recently has been increased emphasis in the field upon recreational therapy, as is consistent with ATRA's and Austin's definitions and philosophy.

Can these two definitional approaches, "leisure versus therapy," be reconciled? These and other definitions of TR include in some manner recreation and leisure's involvement in improving *quality of life* for the TR participant. Definitional issues are explored within this text. Specifically in Chapter 4, Dattilo and Kleiber analyze the relevance of the concept of enjoyment and related psychological constructs to TR. In Chapter 3, Ellis critiques the "scientific" basis of the historically related fields of TR, recreation, and leisure studies. Finally, readers are urged to study the suggested integration of the two primary definitional approaches (leisure and therapy) within Chapter 15 by Shank, Kinney, and Coyle.

Certainly TR is evolving, and there is a great deal of uncertainty as to the direction in which the field will go. As investigative TRSs, and as consumers of research literature, the importance of clearly stating issues of definition is apparent. Researchers *must* be explicit and clear in denoting definitions and theories underlying *each* research endeavor, and such definitions and theoretical bases must be stated clearly in every research report.

Finally, on a broader scale, investigative TRSs should be aware of developments in terms of the philosophy and theory of science which may affect TR research. Simplistically, the physics of Newton lead to a science which was linear, ordered, and determined. The relativistic physics which followed opened the door to a variety of nonlinear perspectives. What will developments such as the possibly unpredictable nature of quarks, the nature and study of "virtual reality," and concepts such as "fuzzy logic" imply for TR in the future?

Social Trends Affecting Research in Therapeutic Recreation

Therapeutic recreation practice is affected by changes in many social arenas, including government, the economy, family, education, corrections, and as noted above, the health care system where the majority of C.T.R.S.s practice. Therefore the impact of changes in health care is highlighted first.

The Health Care Crisis

The "**Health Care Crisis**" is getting cover page notice in the popular media (cf. *Time*, Nov. 25, 1991). The crisis is described as the high cost of health care and the lack of availability of medical insurance coverage to millions of Americans. The shortage of physicians in many areas, excess numbers of hospitals, inefficiency, fraud, and fear of malpractice are other aspects of this crisis (Cronin, Dolan, & Gorey, 1991). Ethical issues are also involved in the reexamination of the health care system.

It is urged that all such issues be discussed openly if "medicine as a profession hopes to regain the humanism that many feel has been lost in an era of rampant technological health care" (Conwell & Caine, 1991, pp. 1100-1). These authors note the related debate about allocating limited health resources to persons who are terminally ill. The importance of ethical issues, such as withholding treatment within a research protocol, or providing "experimental" treatments to clients in therapeutic recreation programs is discussed by Stumbo in Chapter 6.

Other current health care developments also are relevant to TR research. The U.S. Department of Health and Human Services has instituted a Center for Medical Effectiveness Research. As indicated by a Public Health publication in November 1990, the purpose of this Agency for Health Care Policy and Research (AHCPR), which was established in 1989 by PL 101-239, is to enhance the "quality and appropriateness of health care services and access to such services" (p. 1). This agency is responsible for developing and updating clinically relevant, voluntary guidelines for the practice of health care, including allied health professions. The research base of the various allied health professions must be enhanced, and clinical guidelines developed "through a multidisciplinary patient-centered, outcome oriented process" (Public Health Service, 1990, p. 2). Such practice guidelines are but one component of AHCPR's Medical Treatment Effectiveness program (MEDTEP), which also includes effectiveness and outcome research, data base development, and the dissemination of research findings and guidelines (Public Health Service, 1990). Allied health workshops were convened, as of July, 1990, to develop guidelines and to examine the role of allied health professionals in MEDTEP activities. Notably, recreational therapy was *not* included in the original list of allied health professions invited to participate, but ATRA has initiated liaisons with this group (T. Skalko, personal communication, December 29, 1991). Participants in the first workshop stressed the importance of basing clinical guidelines on research rather than solely on clinical consensus.

Raskin and Maklan (1991), when describing the MEDTEP components, report that the activities of this program are correlated with the Health Care Financing Administration (HCFA), the Public Health Service, and the National Institute of Health (NIH). Patient outcome studies include the large-scale Patient Outcomes Research Team (PORT) projects. These authors point out the primary goal of improving the quality of health care, and the secondary emphasis on cost control. PORTs share methodology and solutions through Inter-PORT work groups. Future discussions and results will be shared with the research community. Such large group efforts, collaboration, and cooperation may be models for investigative TRSs, who as members of an interdisciplinary research team will, we hope, become involved in PORTs in increasing numbers.

However, the impact of these federal agencies and large grants should be carefully evaluated. The keynote speaker at the September, 1991 conference on the benefits of TR in rehabilitation (hosted by Temple University) stated that the "outcomes that the discipline intends to achieve and can demonstrate actually achieving, must be outcomes that are valued by third party payers" (Coyle, Kinney, & Shank, 1992, p. 5). Investigators are cautioned that while grants and financial support for programs may be ensured by such an orientation, there is a question as to whether it is in the best interest of the profession to allow research priorities and desired outcomes of practice to be dictated by outside parties, particularly third party payers. Some potential "prostitution" of practice and research may be the unfortunate result.

Other Health Care Trends

The recent focus of the health care system upon wellness, health, and prevention can provide another constructive basis for TR practice and research. This emphasis is exemplified by the publication of a task force charged with formulating national health objectives for the year 2000 entitled *Healthy People 2000: Citizens Chart the Course* (Stoto et al., 1990). Readers are urged to investigate this book, which covers many topics relevant to TR practice and research, including the benefits of recreation in improving health and wellness. The focus of the text is on health promotion and disease prevention. TRSs should take a proactive role in comprehensively investigating the benefits of TR in health promotion.

Other External Influences on Therapeutic Recreation

Other external forces shaping TR are addressed by Crawford (1991). He considers economic, social, and political trends to be macro-trends that affect human services in general, and TR in particular. Crawford notes the economic constraints caused by the taxpayer "revolution" and the declines in funding coupled with trends toward deinstitutionalization, mainstreaming, and normalization. He points out that these have caused increased demand for services especially for community reintegration, transitional programs, half-way houses, etc. The problems, such as homelessness, which result from unfunded deinstitutionalization must be addressed by the TR profession. Hull (1987, cited in Crawford, 1991) also awakens readers to the potential impact of prison overcrowding on TR services and practice.

In the political arena, the effects of the Americans with Disabilities Act of 1990 (PL 101-336) upon TR practice and research are still to be determined. The Act affects transportation, employment, and programming, but most of the recreation-related discussion to date surrounds community (special recreation) programming for persons who are differently abled.

Family changes include divorce, single parenthood, demise of the nuclear family, the recent trend back to marriage and monogamy, intergenerational activities, cross-generational families, and homelessness, just to name a few. The present day awareness of the need to include TR in family programming (DeSalvatore, 1989; Malkin, Phillips, & Chumbler, 1991) may lead to increased attention to family issues within TR research protocols.

Within the public educational system, the expected impact of the Education for all Handicapped Children's Act (PL 94-142) has not materialized. This act called for the education of all "handicapped" children and the inclusion of TR as a support service. PL 94-142 was reauthorized and renamed Individuals with Disabilities Education Act (IDEA) in 1991. Readers are encouraged to refer to Bullock (1989), as he discusses the key issues surrounding the implementation of TR in special education. Research is needed to investigate the benefits of TR intervention in this crucial area.

The recent financial crisis in higher education may affect therapeutic recreation research in several ways. The higher educational system educates researchers, helps to set the agenda for much research, and conducts many of these studies. Financial exigencies may lead to a lack of funding for recreation or TR faculty or departments. Currently, some programs are having difficulty in demonstrating centrality to the mission of universities, or in competing for declining grant resources. Furthermore, external grant funding trends appear to be supporting service projects, rather than pure research (J. Allen, personal communication, May, 1992). Fewer numbers of departments offering a doctorate and declining numbers of doctoral students in TR may lead to a shortage of highly skilled researchers and educators (Compton, 1989a). Reorganization and realignment of departments within universities may affect the amount and type of research conducted. The realignment of TR departments or faculty may either strengthen (or possibly weaken) the TR research base. Due to the shifting organization and alignment of recreation and TR faculty, it may be difficult to set a unified research agenda for TR on a national basis.

Developments in computer technology, such as laptop and notebook size units as well as supercomputers, parallel networks, and computerized communication networks may affect TR practice and research procedures. Improved technology may affect the generation and analysis of data, as well as methods of collaboration and dissemination of research results.

A final social trend to be touched on is a heightened sense of internationalization. Therapeutic recreation, while developed primarily in the United States, is expanding into the international arena, as indicated by higher education programs (cf. in Canada, Australia, and New Zealand), and international conferences and publications (e.g., Albarrán, 1989; Hitzhusen (Ed.), 1990, *Global Therapeutic Recreation I*). Researchers must avoid an ethnocentric outlook, just as much as they must be aware of their other biases. Researchers must be aware of the gender, ethnic, cultural, and racial differences which exist among TR consumers, as well as the similarities. Researchers must address the previous lack of attention or acknowledgment of "minority" groups within the reported TR research (S. Middleton, personal communication, September 20, 1991). Readers are referred to the *Publication Manual of the American Psychological Association* (1983, pp. 43-49) for a discussion of ethnic and sexist bias in research design and interpretation, and of strategies for avoiding such biases in the language chosen to report research.

The Research Controversy

As this era of limited financial support continues to constrain the research community, there are additional issues and pressures which have emerged and are appearing on the front covers of national news magazines (cf. *Time* August 26, 1991, "Science under Siege: Tight money, blunders and scandal plague America's researchers"). Underfinancing, errors, and unethical behavior each contributes to problems, such as the appearance of incompetence, and fraud particularly in medically related research. Weekly headlines reveal picketing and lobbying efforts that demand increased funding for needs such as AIDS research. Other controversial issues include the dangers of silicone breast implants, the adequacy of testing drugs such as Halcion, and the lack of research on cancers that primarily affect women.

Difficulties in other fields have increased public skepticism, including the Times Beach dioxin uncertainty and the Hubble telescope failure, as well as the disputed cold fusion claims (Jaroff, 1991). Jaroff (1991) also cites fraudulent studies, misuse of funds, "pro-life" restrictions on fetal cell transplant research, animal rights activities, and the debates over genetic engineering as possible impediments to legitimate scientific research. The result, according to Jaroff's analysis, is diminished public confidence in science and research, and a feeling that "society" should take a more active role in managing the research process.

Tolcher (1991) identifies other possible distorting effects which result when research procedures are not clarified, partial results are revealed, or misleading wording implies results not actually obtained in research studies. "Precise carefully worded conclusions are required when controversial topics are being examined, so that we do not unknowingly enlarge therapies that are costly and whose benefits are unproved" (Tolcher p. 1103). Such clarity is an absolute necessity whether research is controversial or not.

Therapeutic Recreation Research Needs

Since the early 1980s, there has been increased attention in the literature to research in therapeutic recreation and research methodology. Throughout that decade, discussion of these two topics intensified. This began in 1983 with a special issue of *Therapeutic Recreation Journal* on research methodology, articles by Mannell (1983) and Hunter (1983) on methodology, and articles by Morris and Finch (1983) on multivariate hypothesis testing. Selected issues and needs raised by these and succeeding writers are reported as follows and categorized by their main focus. Readers are also referred to Compton (1989), who in the chapter on "Research Initiatives in Therapeutic Recreation," provides his insights on the research issues in TR. Compton presents his own historical perspective and discusses preparedness of professionals to conduct research. He also cites works by Iso-Ahola and Witt in assembling a list of 10 key ingredients necessary to improve the prospects of research in TR. Such issues and needs as identified in the literature are presented first in the discussion below. Then the current state of research in TR and prospects for the future are addressed.

Overall Perceptions of Research in Therapeutic Recreation

There is a persistent perception in the literature of an overall lack of research in the field of TR. Reasons cited are: the lack of valid research and systematic research efforts (Schleien & Yermatoff, 1983); a shortage of reported research on leisure behaviors of individuals with disabilities (Iso-Ahola, 1988); a lack of systematic research, as in a piecemeal or shotgun approach (Bullock, McGuire, & Barch, 1984); and the need to base services on substantive research (Witt, 1988b). Further, Crawford (1991) discusses the scientific basis of TR and concludes that the "body of knowledge has overall a very uneven base" (p. 394). Crawford also states that the "claims of the TR profession for client growth are based in large measure on philosophical models and clinical subjectivity" (p. 394). McCormick, Scott, & Dattilo (1991) agree with the absence of a systematic research tradition in TR, and refer to Witt's 1988 analysis of the slow progression of the knowledge base from the social philosophy stage, through the stage of social empiricism to the social analysis phase (see Chapter 3 of this text).

The perceived lack of meaningful research is reported widely. Patterson reiterates this deficiency in a December, 1991 Illinois Therapeutic Recreation Society section report as one of a number of "new hot and complicated issues" (p. 21). This is not a new issue, but it is a very common perception of the state of the art in TR research.

Lack of Quality Research in Therapeutic Recreation

Reynolds and O'Morrow wrote in 1985 that TR research efforts have not become fully defined "in terms of methodology, content, and philosophical direction" (p. 176). The paucity of research on the efficacy of TR interventions has been noted by many (Aguilar et al., 1987 cited in Compton, 1989; Ellis, 1989; Hemingway, 1987). (For a thorough review of this issue see Chapter 15). Aguilar (1990) expressed concern over the lack of clinical research in TR and the need to engage in both clinical and community-based efficacy research. "The lack of applied and action research that validates the effectiveness of the TR process as a client change agent in residential, clinical, and community settings remains the number one research priority of the field" (Crawford, 1991, p. 394). Hemingway notes in this regard that "a body of empirical research supporting the efficacy of therapeutic recreation has . . . been slow to emerge" (1987, p. 3).

Methodological Issues

The need to employ a variety of research methods and the lack of such variety in the past is noted (Aguilar et al., 1987, cited in Compton 1989; Ellis, 1989; Rickards, 1985). Overreliance on the survey method is reported by Iso-Ahola (1988) and by McCormick, Scott, and Dattilo (1991).

The dearth of experimental research was noted (Bullock, McGuire, & Barch, 1984; Iso-Ahola, 1988; MacNeil, 1988; Mannell, 1983). Ellis and Witt (1983) concur that research efforts to date have been largely descriptive and correlational. Those experimental studies that do exist have been mostly quasi-experimental, as the option of not treating a referral in a control group is ethically questionable (Rawson & McIntosh, 1991; Reynolds & O'Morrow, 1985).

Other writers call for the use of a variety of research methods. These include qualitative research methods (Bullock, 1983); "inquiries in art, philosophy, observation, technology and history as well as science" (Ellis, 1989, p. 91); and use of the case study, historical, empirical, and naturalistic methodologies (Compton, 1989).

Other methodological problems noted include shotgun approaches, lack of systematic research programs, lack of replication or expansion studies (Aguilar et al., 1987 cited in Compton 1989; Iso-Ahola, 1988; Witt, 1988a; Witt, 1998b), a shortage of valid and reliable assessment tools to evaluate client outcomes, the inadequate numbers of subjects, and problems obtaining agency cooperation (Reynolds & O'Morrow, 1985). Witt (1988a) also lists problems with assessment instruments, data collection techniques, and sample selection.

Uneven Focus Upon Selected Participant Groups

The uneven focus of research upon particular disabilities or groups of individuals from certain diagnostic categories stems from a number of problems. These include the frequency of empirical studies on persons with mental retardation and the infrequency of studying other groups (Iso-Ahola, 1988; McCormick, Scott, & Dattilo, 1991; Schleien & Yermakoff, 1983), the dearth of information on leisure and aging (MacNeil, 1988), and the lack of focus upon various ethnic and racial groups (MacNeil, 1988; S. Middleton, personal communication, September 20, 1991).

Readers are referred to an April, 1992 issue of *Leisure Today* which features overlooked or excluded groups in recreation and related fields. Such groups may be excluded not only on the basis of race, ethnicity, or class, but due to sexual orientation, "class, employment status, medical history, or other arbitrary characteristics" (Raymond, Ego, & Woodard, 1992, p. 2). Therapeutic recreators should be aware of such biases or hidden conditions. These include prejudice against individuals with AIDS/HIV, survivors of abuse or post traumatic stress syndrome, those with other stress-related illnesses, displaced or homeless people, and persons whose sexual orientation is not heterosexual.

The "Practitioner Researcher Gap"

The lack of cooperation and communication between researchers (who are largely academicians) and practitioners has been noted (Aguilar et al., 1987, cited in Compton 1989; Reynolds and O'Morrow, 1985; Rickards, 1985; Schleien & Yermatoff, 1983; Witt, 1988b). Such writers stress the need for increased collaboration and particularly state that the *value* of research must be understood by all (Witt, 1988b). Bullock, McGuire, and Barch (1984) found that over 90% of practitioners they surveyed felt research was somewhat or very important, were keeping up with current research, and were willing to work cooperatively with researchers (for further discussion of this issue see Chapter 5 by Savell, Huston, and Malkin).

Lack of Research Skills

Improved communication and participation in research by students and practitioners, as well as educators, is needed along with adequate training in research concepts and methods. Such preparation is essential to enable TRSs to become literate consumers of research results, as well as producers of such research. Aguilar et al. (1987, cited in Compton, 1989) note the generally poor research preparation in TR. Witt (1988b) calls for expanded education and focus on research and research skills. He notes that TR graduates at all levels need to be able to understand and to apply research findings. Morris and Finch, as early as 1983, emphasized the need for TR researchers and research consumers to increase their awareness of appropriate statistical analysis procedures.

Lack of Dissemination of Research Findings

The lack of outlets to disseminate the results of TR research, both inside and outside of the TR literature, has been noted by Aguilar et al., 1987 cited in Compton (1989); Iso-Ahola (1988); MacNeil (1988); and Schleien and Yermatoff (1983). Iso-Ahola (1988) called for the establishment of a journal focusing entirely upon TR research several years ago.

Lack of Theoretical Basis

As mentioned earlier, the lack of a solid conceptual, philosophical, or theoretical basis for TR, and consequently for much of TR research, is emphasized by Crawford (1991); Rickards (1985); Sylvester (1987); and Witt (1988a). The lack of a conceptual basis for research studies is addressed in Chapter 15 of this text. The overall lack of a philosophical or conceptual basis for the field of TR and for research has been reported by Hemingway (1987) and Sylvester (1987), and for TR research by Crawford (1991). Rickards (1985) writes that "research needs to address the theoretical foundations of therapeutic recreation" (p. 19). Rickards decries research which is conducted merely to justify services or for administrative purposes

Lack of Funding and Support

The lack of funds, facilities, and personnel to conduct research in TR is cited (Compton, 1989; Witt, 1988). These writers blame federal cut-backs that have resulted in a lack of funds for training, demonstration projects, and research. The absence of proper laboratories for TR research is pointed out, as is the scarcity of sources for funds to support efficacy research in TR.

Suggestions for the Future of TR Research

Based on a review of developments in TR research and earlier works by Compton, Iso-Ahola, and Witt, Compton (1989b, p. 434-435) indicated ten key ingredients for the future support of research in TR. These suggestions are of merit, and are reiterated as follows:

1. creating a pool of funds for research in TR[;]
2. training and re-training practitioners and educators in research and statistical methods[;]
3. requiring research competencies at the undergraduate level
4. demanding improvement in the research competence of graduate students with prestigious certification for those able to pass an examination[;]
5. establishing working agreements between universities and clinical and community settings to conduct research[;]
6. articulating a national research agenda and funding those who work on problems identified in the plan[;]
7. encouraging the submission of more grants to federal, state and private entities[;]
8. establishing a national training and dissemination center for research in TR[;]
9. publishing materials that link research findings to practice [; and]
10. ensure that each continuing education program offered to therapeutic recreation professionals has a research component.

Further suggestions are offered by Aguilar et al. (1987, cited in Compton, 1989) for state research networks; by Reynolds and O'Morrow (1985) for the employment of research specialists full-time in terminal-degree granting recreation curriculums; by Iso-Ahola (1988) who urges the establishment of a national research fund; and by Witt (1988b) citing Compton, who supports a national conference in research priorities, specialized laboratories, clinical consortia, the expansion of current periodicals, and longitudinal studies. Witt concludes, despite an awareness of the problems and barriers encountered in TR research, that there has been an increase in the exploration of the philosophical basis for TR, and increased interest in TR research. He cites the growth of research articles in *Therapeutic Recreation Journal (TRJ)* from 33% in 1978-80 to 58% in 1984-86 (Witt, 1988b). (See also Witt, 1988a, and Chapter 15 of this text for an evaluation of the volume of TR research articles).

In terms of both the quality and variety of research methods used, progress is evident, including the focus on this topic in a 1989 special *TRJ* issue on Innovative Research Strategies. This issue features innovative approaches such as social validation, experience sampling, and applied philosophy. Qualitative methods and naturalistic studies have been reported in the literature with increased frequency.

Writers have emphasized the importance of using the developing technology of computers and electronic communications (Compton, 1989) and of sophisticated orthotic and prosthetic devices within TR research (Crawford, 1991). Crawford also urges that TRSs move from a reactive to a proactive stance in terms of developing and testing modern technology.

McCormick, Scott, and Dattilo (1991) find that the anxiety among TRSs about conducting research may be the result of a "lack of knowledge of research principles" (p. 79). Their article, coupled with Dattilo, McCormick, and Scott (1991) in *The Annual in Therapeutic Recreation,* as well as this text on research in TR, may do much to address this concern. McCormick et al., Dattilo et al., and the authors of this text aim to demonstrate the relationships between theoretical paradigms and research methods.

Conducting quality research in TR is essential to ensure the flourishing of the field beyond mere survival. Several indications of increased awareness of this need are: the attention and resources devoted to the 1991 conference sponsored by Temple University on Efficacy Research in TR (see Ch. 15); the increased concern with collaborative research efforts (Kunstler & Kennedy, 1992) based on the professional priority on efficacy research (and the need to involve students, practitioners and educators in this process); and the increasing emphasis of professional organizations on research in their respective newsletters. For example, in a recent newsletter from Therapeutic Recreators for Recovery (*TRR*), O'Dea-Evans' (1992, p. 1) President's message lists ten priorities for action by therapeutic recreators to ensure the survival of TR. These items are as follows, and all ten focus on *research*:

1. Read and collect effectiveness research (inside and outside TR).
2. Develop Quality Assurance plans that collect effectiveness data.
3. Investigate your facility's policy on human subject research.
4. Develop questions on leisure functioning to include on your facilities follow-up surveys or your own department survey.
5. Volunteer your agency as a site for Graduate and Doctoral student research.
6. Find a research mentor.
7. Develop a research project for your agency.
8. Take a research methods or statistics class.
9. Publish your results.
10. Set a goal with a deadline to complete at least one item on this list.

As stated earlier, there has been some progress regarding these concerns. The ATRA research committee has redefined its mission to include facilitating research projects, encouraging practitioner/educator collaboration, disseminating and applying research findings, and promoting education concerning research techniques (Malkin, 1992). In terms of funding, ATRA has established the ATRA Foundation, a nonprofit association to benefit research and other professional objectives. The number and quality of journals in TR continue to increase. The Temple University efficacy conference was supported by a substantial federal grant. Research institutes, tracks, and sessions are appearing in national, regional, and state TR-related conferences with increased regularity. International journals and conferences in TR are developing. While signs of progress are welcome, investigative TRSs are encouraged to take the previous problems and deficiencies in TR research seriously. TR professionals and students must do their part to address some of the identified concerns and suggestions in order to increase their own research literacy, and to become active contributing participants in the development and utilization of quality research in therapeutic recreation. Such a focus on research is necessary to ensure the continued development of the TR profession both as a valued service and as a treatment intervention.

Individual efforts in contributing to the research process are important; however, Compton urges the creation of a federation to "optimize resources and increase a power base" (1989, p. 497). He encourages the formation of a collective organization to amass membership of all related organizations, hence providing political support for research, as well as for training and programs. Such political action and cooperation *indeed* are vital in competing for diminishing human service and health care resources (Compton, 1989).

Discussion Questions

1. Discuss the importance of theory and definition to therapeutic recreation research. Investigate two or three published research reports to determine if definitions of key terms and the theoretical bases for the study are explicitly stated. Are relationships between such concepts and the research study logically presented?
2. Discuss suggestions/solutions for narrowing the researcher/practitioner gap in TR. What are some means to enable practitioners to play a more active role in promoting research in TR?
3. What are key internal trends in TR which affect research? What is the relative importance of external factors discussed in this chapter which may affect TR research? Can you identify additional factors, both internal and external to the profession, which may inhibit or promote TR research?
4. Witt has diagrammed the following inhibitors to TR research: Discuss these factors and their interrelationships. Can you add any additional factors to this diagram?

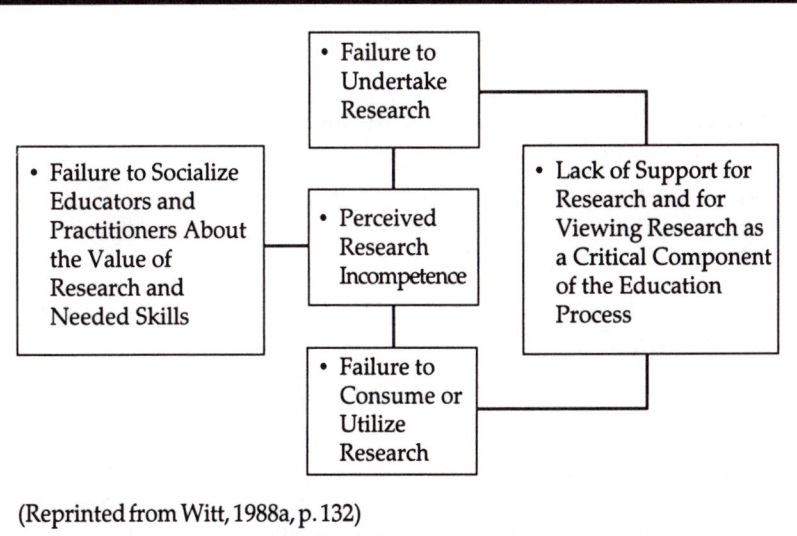

(Reprinted from Witt, 1988a, p. 132)

5. In a manner similar to Witt's diagram, create a diagram of factors *supporting* or *promoting* research in TR based on the information in this chapter and additional sources.

References

Agency for Health Care Policy and Research. (1990, November). *Allied health perspectives on guideline development*. Rockville, MD: Department of Health and Human Services (Public Health Service).

Aguilar, T. E. (1990). Guest editor's comments. *Therapeutic Recreation Journal, 24*(4), 7.

Albarrán, M. A. (1989). International issues in therapeutic recreation: A Latin American perspective. In D. M. Compton (Ed.), *Issues in therapeutic recreation: A profession in transition* (pp. 463-477). Champaign, IL: Sagamore.

American Psychological Association (1983). *Publication manual of the American Psychological Association* (3rd ed.). Washington, DC: Author.

American Therapeutic Recreation Association (1990, March). *ATRA Code of Ethics*, p. 1. Hattiesburg, MS: Author.

Austin, D. R. (1991a). Introduction and overview. In D. R. Austin, & M. E. Crawford (Eds.), *Therapeutic recreation: An introduction* (pp. 1-29). Englewood Cliffs, NJ: Prentice-Hall.

Austin, D. R. (1991b). *Therapeutic recreation: Processes and techniques* (2nd ed.). Champaign, IL: Sagamore.

Bullock, C. C. (1983). Qualitative research in therapeutic recreation. *Therapeutic Recreation Journal, 17*(4), 36-43.

Bullock, C. C. (1989). Therapeutic recreation in special education. In D. M. Compton (Ed.), *Issues in therapeutic recreation: A profession in transition* (pp. 373-384). Champaign, IL: Sagamore.

Bullock, C. C., McGuire, E. M., & Barch, E. M. (1984). *Therapeutic Recreation Journal, 18*(3), 17-24.

Castro, J. (1991, November 25). Condition: Critical. *Time, The Weekly Magazine, 138*(21), pp. 34-40, 42.

Compton, D. M. (1989a). Epilogue: On shaping a future for therapeutic recreation. In D. M. Compton (Ed.), *Issues in therapeutic recreation: A profession in transition* (pp. 483-500). Champaign, IL: Sagamore.

Compton, D. M. (1989b). Research initiatives in therapeutic recreation. In D. M. Compton (Ed.), *Issues in therapeutic recreation: A profession in transition* (pp. 427-444). Champaign, IL: Sagamore.

Conwell, Y., & Caine, E. D. (1991, October 10). Rational suicide and the right to die: Reality and myth. *The New England Journal of Medicine, 325*(15), 1100-1103.

Coyle, K., Kinney, T., & Shank, J. (1992, January/February). Benefits of therapeutic recreation: A consensus view. *ATRA Newsletter, 8*(1), p. 5.

Crawford, M. E. (1991). Trends and issues. In D. R. Austin, & M. E. Crawford (Eds.), *Therapeutic recreation: An introduction* (pp. 389-408). Englewood Cliffs, NJ: Prentice-Hall.

Dattilo, J., McCormick, B., & Scott, D. (1991). Answering questions about therapeutic recreation part II; choosing research methods. *Annual in Therapeutic Recreation, 2,* 85-95.

DeSalvatore, H. G. (1989). Therapeutic recreators as family therapists: Working with families on a children's psychiatric unit. *Therapeutic Recreation Journal, 23*(2), 23-29.

Ellis, G. (1989). Guest Editor's Comments. *Therapeutic Recreation Journal, 23*(4), 8-9.

Ellis, G., & Witt, P. A. (1983). Improving research designs in therapeutic recreation. *Therapeutic Recreation Journal, 17*(4), 27-35.

Gorman, C. (1991, August 26). The double take on dioxin. *Time, The Weekly News Magazine, 138*(8), p. 52.

Hemingway, J. L. (1987). Building a philosophic defense of therapeutic recreation: The case of distributive justice. In C. Sylvester, J. L. Hemingway, R. Howe-Murphy, K. Mobily, & S. Shank, (Eds.), *Philosophy of therapeutic recreation: Ideas and issues,* pp. 1-16. Alexandria, VA: National Recreation and Park Association.

Hitzhusen, G. L., & Gitgstad, J. R. (1990). *Global therapeutic recreation I: Selected papers from the 1st international symposium on therapeutic recreation.* Columbia, MO: University of Missouri-Columbia.

Hunter, I. R. (1983). Methodological issues in therapeutic recreation research. *Therapeutic Recreation Journal, 17*(2), 23-32.

Iso-Ahola, S. E. (1988). Research in therapeutic recreation. *Therapeutic Recreation Journal, 22*(1), 7-13.

Jaroff, L. (1991, August 26). Crisis in the labs. *Time, the Weekly Newsmagazine, 138*(8), pp. 44-51.

Kunstler, R., & Kennedy, D. W. (1992, Winter). A cooperative model for conducting efficacy researching therapeutic recreation. *The Voice.* New York State Recreation and Park Society, Inc., pp. 32-33, 51.

Kraus, R., & Allen, L. (1987). *Research and evaluation in recreation, parks and leisure studies.* Columbus, OH: Publishing Horizons.

MacNeil, R. D. (1988). Leisure programs and services for older adults: Past, present and future research. *Therapeutic Recreation Journal, 22*(1), 24-35.

Malkin, M. J. (1992, January/February). ATRA's Research Committee redefines mission. *ATRA Newsletter, 8*(1), p. 6.

Malkin, M. J., Phillips, R. W., & Chumber, J. A. (1991). The Family Lab: An interdisciplinary family leisure education program. *Annual in Therapeutic Recreation, 2*, 25-36.

Mannell, R. C. (1983). Research methodology in therapeutic recreation. *Therapeutic Recreation Journal, 17*(4), 9-16.

McCormick, B., Scott, D., & Dattilo, J. (1991). Answering questions about therapeutic recreation Part I: Formulating research questions. *Annual in Therapeutic Recreation, 2*, 78-84.

Morris, H. H., & Finch, H. A. (1983). A heuristic guide to multivariate hypothesis testing with application to research in therapeutic recreation. *Therapeutic Recreation Journal, 17*(4), 44-53.

NCTRC Newsletter (1992, April/May). NCTRC exam results. Spring Valley, NY: Author.

O'Dea-Evans, P. (1992, Spring). President's message. *Therapeutic Recreators for Recovery Newsletter*, p. 1.

Patterson, R. (1991, December). IPRA section reports: ITRS revises, extends its strategic plan; ends year with a healthy balance. *Leisure Review, 8*(6), p. 21.

Peterson, C. A. (1989). The dilemma of philosophy. In D. M. Compton (Ed.), *Issues in therapeutic recreation: A profession in transition* (pp. 21-33). Champaign, IL: Sagamore.

Raskin, I. E., & Maklan, C. W. (1991, June). *Medical treatment effectiveness research: A view from inside the Agency for Health Care Policy and Research.* Rockville, MD: Agency for Health Care Policy and Research (AHCPR program note), U. S. Department of Health and Human Services (Public Health Service).

Raymond, L. P., Ego, M., & Woodard, M. (1992, April). Guest editorial. *Leisure Today (Journal of Physical Education, Recreation and Dance)*, p. 2.

Reynolds, R. P., & O'Morrow, G. S. (1985). Scientific Inquiry: The foundation for professional development. In R. P. Reynolds, & G. S. O'Morrow, *Problems, issues and concepts in therapeutic recreation* (pp. 174-198). Englewood Cliffs, NJ: Prentice-Hall.

Rickards, W. H. (1985). Perspectives on therapeutic recreation research: Opening the black box, *Therapeutic Recreation Journal, 19*(2), 15-23.

Russoniello, C. (1991, November/December). President's message. *The ATRA Newsletter, 7*(6), p. 1-2.

Schlein, S. J., & Yermakoff, N. (1983). Data-based research in therapeutic recreation: State of the art. *Therapeutic Recreation Journal, 17*(4), 17-26.

Shank, P. (1987). Therapeutic recreation philosophy: A state of cacophony. In C. Sylvester et al. (Eds.), *Philosophy of therapeutic recreation: Ideas and issues* (pp. 27-40). Alexandria, VA: National Recreation and Park Association.

Stoto, M. A., Behrens, R., & Rosemont, C. (1990). *Healthy people 2000: Citizens chart the course.* Washington, DC: National Academy Press.

Sylvester, C. (1987). Therapeutic recreation and the end of leisure. In C. Sylvester et al. (Eds.), *Philosophy of therapeutic recreation: Ideas and issues,* (p. 76-89). Alexandria, VA: National Recreation and Park Association.

Sylvester, C. D. (1989). Impressions of the intellectual past and future of therapeutic recreation: Implications for professionalization. In D. M. Compton (Ed.), *Issues in therapeutic recreation: A profession in transition* (pp. 1-20). Champaign, IL: Sagamore.

Sylvester, C., Hemingway, J. L., Howe-Murphy, R., Mobily, K., & Shank, P. A. (Eds.) (1987). *Philosophy of therapeutic recreation: Ideas and issues.* Alexandria, VA: NRPA.

Tolcher, A. W. (1991, October 10). Letter to the Editor. *The New England Journal of Medicine, 325*(15), p. 1103.

Webster's college dictionary. (1991). New York, NY: Random House.

Webster's ninth new collegiate dictionary. (1984). Springfield, MA: Merriam-Webster.

Witt, P. A. (1988a). Leisure programs and services for special populations: Past, present, and future research. In L. A. Barnett (Ed.), *Research about leisure: Past, present, and future* (pp. 127-139). Champaign, IL: Sagamore.

Witt, P. A. (1988b). Therapeutic recreation research: Past, present and future. *Therapeutic Recreation Journal, 22*(1), 14-23.

Witt, P. A. (1989). Final thoughts. *Therapeutic Recreation Journal, 23*(4), 7.

Ways of Knowing: The Naturalistic and Positivistic Perspectives on Research
Charles C. Bullock

Research in therapeutic recreation is the systematic process of inquiry undertaken to examine the practice as well as to advance the intellectual development of the field. Research is conducted because people seek specific information about the efficacy of a particular intervention, or because they are generally curious about some aspect of their field. Researchers have questions which guide their inquiry. Research questions emanate from the researcher's interests. What to study is bounded only by a researcher's creativity.

To have **systematic inquiry**, it is essential that the question(s) be determined before the method(s) are chosen. An often heard phrase from both novice and unfortunately, seasoned researchers is something like, "I think I'll do a survey . . . " or "I want to make sure that I use a pre-post design." In both of these cases, the would-be researchers have decided how to conduct their research before they have articulated what it is that they are going to study. *What* to study (the questions) must precede *how* to study it (methodology). This is an axiom of research that is universally accepted even though it is not always followed. An axiom that is far less universally understood is the relationship of the research question to the research perspective (also referred to as the research paradigm). This chapter looks at two perspectives of research which are important to understand before a researcher formulates questions to *do* research.

There is no one way to do research. However, there are two major research perspectives within which most modern research is conducted. These perspectives are referred to as the **naturalistic** (sometimes referred to as interpretive, phenomenological, or constructivistic) and the **positivistic** (sometimes referred to as rationalistic and also including post-positivistic) perspectives. This chapter compares the two perspectives ontologically, epistemologically, and methodologically so that therapeutic recreation specialists can become good researchers as well as good consumers of research. This chapter sets the stage for the more detailed presentation of each perspective in Sections II and III of this book. It concludes with implications for therapeutic recreation practitioners and researchers.

Doing Research

Research answers questions about and substantiates the hypotheses about a field. Research is systematic inquiry. Research is a very individualistic enterprise. There are about as many ways to *do* research as there are people to do it. The way research is conducted depends as much on who a person is as where his or her disciplinary training was received. Certainly one's education influences the way a person conducts research. If a person trains with a survey researcher, the student investigator probably will graduate with good survey research skills. Similarly, if the student is taught research by an instructor who conducts little or no research yet was *assigned* to teach the research course, the student probably will end up with few research skills and little interest in research.

Long before being taught (socialized into) a particular way of doing research, a student is socialized into a particular way of knowing, a particular way of looking at and understanding the world in which he or she lives. The way a person knows or views the world and understands its relationships and interrelationships will likely dictate the perspective from which research questions are asked and research is conducted. Therefore before embarking on any research, it is important for a researcher to consciously acknowledge the world view or perspective within which he or she is operating, rather than accepting at face value the perspective embraced by his or her research mentor. This first step is very important but often is ignored.

Ways of Knowing: Philosophical Bases

The way a person knows, the way a person understands social reality is referred to as ontological and epistemological perspectives. A person's particular ontological and epistemological perspectives have been received and internalized as a result of the sum of the person's life experiences. There exist a multiplicity of ways that a person understands the world and these ways are constantly changing. A person's ontological and epistemological perspective is relatively well established by the time he or she is a young adult; however, it can and does change throughout one's life course as a result of innumerable and unpredictable life experiences. It should be noted, however, that the way a person looks at, and understands the world, once internalized, becomes part of who that person is and that the self may not change dramatically over the life course. It is necessary to understand the meanings of ontology and epistemology as they relate to the two research perspectives. Simply stated, **ontology** is the science of being or reality ... the nature of the "knowable." It is the nature of the social world. A person may have a realistic or a relativistic ontological perspective. **Epistemology** is science of the grounds of knowledge ... the nature of the relationship between the "knower" (the inquirer) and the "known" (or knowable). It encompasses how one identifies problems, seeks answers, and holds beliefs about how one gets information. A person may have an objective or a subjective epistemological perspective. (Guba, 1990). It is these two philosophical bases that lead researchers in TR to ask certain questions and to ask them in certain ways. They are the starting points or the givens that determine what inquiry is and how it is practiced. They cannot be proved or disproved in any fundamental sense. **They are the values, or the basic belief systems, or the paradigms within which people operate**. In a sense, they represent who people are and how people understand the world around them. The next section examines basic differences between the ontological and epistemological bases of both positivistic and naturalistic perspectives. In this section, it will become clearer how one's *way of knowing* (one's ontology and epistemology) differ in the two research perspectives.

Basic Tenets of the Positivistic Perspective

Since the time of Descartes (1596-1650), researchers have mainly focused on a perspective that has come to be known as **positivism**. The basic belief system of positivism is rooted in a realist ontology. A realist believes in the existence of a reality driven by immutable natural laws and that the business of science is to discover the *true* nature of reality and how it *truly* works. As such, the ultimate goal of science is to predict and control natural phenomena in the world (Guba, 1990,). According to Cook and Campbell (1979), this purist, *naive* realism has been modified by what they describe as critical realism which recognizes that even though there is a real world driven by real natural causes, it is impossible for humans truly to perceive it with their imperfect sensory and intellectual mechanisms. Yet, it is still a basic tenet of any form of realist ontology (and therefore positivism) that reality is *out there* and can be understood.

Objectivity is the cornerstone of the way (epistemology) the realist understands the immutable reality that is *out there*. To truly understand the reality that is *out there*, the human researcher must step outside of himself or herself in order not to be biased. It is both possible and essential for the researcher to adopt a distinct, noninteractive posture. By maintaining objectivity, values as *biasing* and *confounding* factors are thereby automatically excluded from influencing the outcomes. According to Guba: "The inquirer, so to speak, must stand behind a thick wall of one-way glass, observing nature as 'she does her own thing' " (1990, p. 19). Critical realists of course mitigate this position somewhat. They recognize that objectivity cannot be achieved in any absolute sense; however, they hold objectivity as the *regulatory ideal* and contend that it can be achieved *relatively completely* (Zukav, 1979).

Basic Tenets of the Naturalistic Perspective

The naturalistic (also referred to as the interpretive or phenomenological) perspective is in opposition to the positivistic perspective. The naturalistic social scientist understands the world very differently than the postitivist. He or she understands knowledge as the outcome or consequence of human activity rather than as an entity that is *out there* to be discovered. Knowledge is a human construction which by definition is never certifiable as ultimately true. Rather, it is always changing and forever problematic. Therefore, the **naturalistic perspective** takes an ontological position of relativism, which is to say that realities (not reality) exist in the form of multiple mental constructions that are socially and experientially based, local and specific, and dependent for their form and content on the persons who hold them. To the naturalistic researcher, realities exist only in people's minds and therefore cannot be understood as true realities that are determined by immutable natural laws.

Since realities are emergent social constructions, objectivity is not useful or even desirable epistemologically to the naturalist (relativist). Rather, subjectivity is sought. Relativists do not believe that reality can be frozen and understood. As such, from the naturalistic perspective, the researcher and the research objects become one. It is not necessary to differentiate between ontology and epistemology since what can be known and the individual who comes to know it are fused into a coherent whole (Guba, 1990). The subjective experience of the researcher (rather than objectivity) is what leads the researcher to an understanding of the realities under study. The findings are literally the *creation* of the process of interaction between the researcher and the research participants.

Comparison of the Two Perspectives

The foregoing philosophical distinctions form the philosophical basis for the research questions asked, the methods chosen, and the process of actually conducting and completing research. This section examines the differences in the two perspectives in relation to research design and process, research question(s), data collection and analysis, and data presentation.

The Research Design and Process

The way that research is designed and conducted differs depending on the particular perspective from which one is working. The research process will proceed more smoothly if the researcher recognizes and acknowledges his or her research perspective. This is often not done. Confusion results because he or she may be coming philosophically from a relativist ontology (a naturalistic perspective), but for one reason or another is trying to ask questions and conduct research from a realist ontological and epistemological (positivistic) perspective. It is nearly impossible for one's brain to do that. It is like thinking the world is round and flat at the same time. It is contradictory to think both ways simultaneously. A realist ontologically will therefore be more comfortable within a positivist perspective and a relativist will be more comfortable operating within the naturalist perspective.

The design and process of research is quite different in each perspective. For ease in understanding the differences in conducting research from these differing perspectives or ways of knowing, the processes are shown diagrammatically in Figure 2.1, page 30. Figure 2.1 should be used as a reference as the chapter proceeds to explain further the research implications of the two perspectives.

Working within a positivist perspective, a researcher uses deduction and *a priori* (preestablished) theory. For example, a positivist may predict a certain type of change as a result of involvement in a TR intervention based on the preestablished attribution theory or the theory of learned helplessness. The naturalistic inquirer, on the other hand, approaches research through induction. Rather than beginning with a theory, the naturalistic researcher seeks an emerging propositional or theoretical understanding which is grounded in the real lives and real worlds of the persons and the phenomenon being studied. This is referred to as **grounded theory** or inductive theory which is developed relative to a substantive area. In grounded theory, theory is the end point rather than the starting point. The creation of theory is based on observation rather than deduction (Glaser & Strauss, 1967).

The positivist meticulously attempts to control for variance so as to remain objective and not to contaminate the study, while the naturalist seeks out variation in an attempt to understand the phenomenon under study in its many and varied forms. The positivist determines exact methodology before beginning the data collection. The naturalist, on the other hand, rethinks methodology throughout the study and may adjust the methodology to better understand the phenomenon being studied. Such changes are necessary for the naturalistic inquirer to understand the emerging concepts and propositions, but are unallowable within a positivist framework.

For the positivist, subject selection is predetermined and fixed to comply to the canons of rigor of the perspective. On the other hand, the naturalist chooses research participants who will provide greater insight into

Figure 2.1
The Research Perspectives

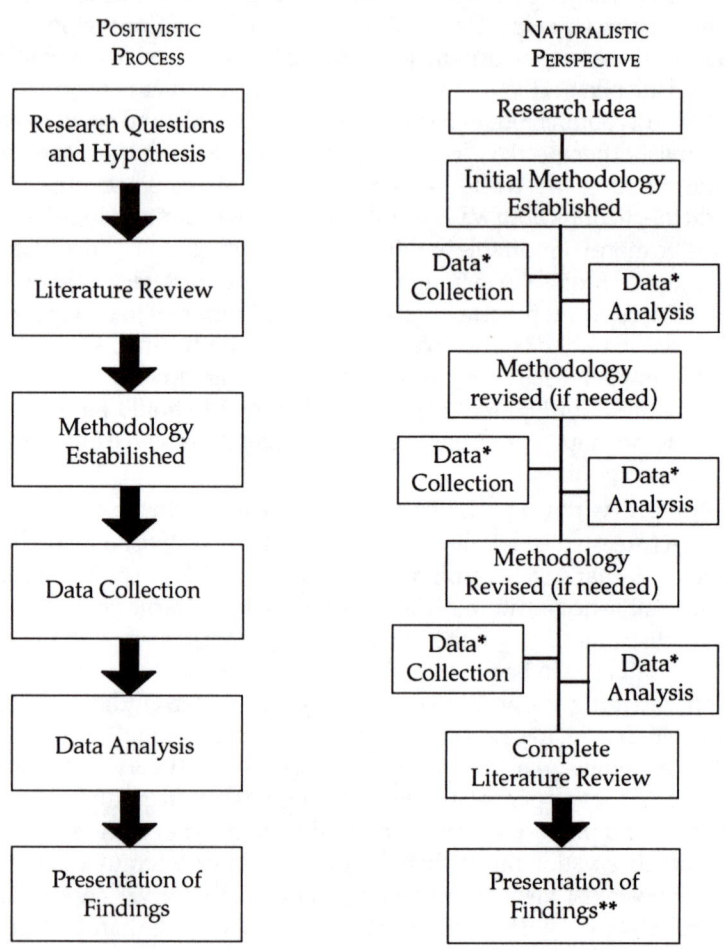

POSITIVISTIC PROCESS

NATURALISTIC PERSPECTIVE

* Data Collection (repeated as many times as needed)
   Data Analysis (repeated as many times as needed)

**Delineation of propositions and/or theories which have emerged

the phenomenon being studied and as such are not preset or fixed. In the positivist paradigm, data collection is also preset and once the data are collected, they are analyzed in accordance with the established research design. In the naturalistic paradigm, a data collection period is not predetermined. Rather, data are collected and analyzed throughout the research process. Ongoing analysis suggests the inclusion of new/different research participants as well as the collection of additional or different data. For the naturalist, the process of data collection and analysis is cyclical or recursive. For the positivist, it is a serial process. See Figure 2.2 for a comparison of the two research perspectives.

Figure 2.2
Comparison of Positivistic and Naturalistic Perspectives

POSITIVISTIC	NATURALISTIC
1. Research hypotheses	Research ideas
2. Predetermined design	Emerging design
3. Objectivity	Subjectivity
4. Theory testing	Theory generation
5. One shot data collection	Ongoing data collection
6. Probability sampling	Nonprobability sampling
7. Serial/linear analysis	Recursive/cyclical analysis
8. Controlled settings	Real world settings
9. Deduction	Induction

The Research Question and Hypotheses

Before any study can begin there must be a research question or research topic. This is true for both perspectives. However, the way the questions are posed differ greatly from one perspective to the other.

In the positivist perspective, with its realistic and rationalistic basis, questions are carefully crafted so that they can be *operationalized*. They are pieces of a pie rather than the entire pie. That is, they are finite. Questions are stated in such a way that they can managed within the rationalistic world view. The research question cannot be open ended because the object is to study reality as it exists *out there*. The more tightly the question can be framed, the better the positivistic study can be conducted. The positivist strives for explanation of cause and effect, prediction, and control. The postitivist divides a phenomenon into parts that can be isolated and categorized so that they can be studied. The research question must be stated in such a way that it can be tested, and the hypotheses verified. Clarity in the beginning is necessary to ensure that the study proceeds to a discovery of truth which can be generalized to other similar settings and situations. The **hypotheses** which emanate from the research question serve to further focus and direct the study.

An example of a research question and subsequent hypotheses from a positivistic perspective is:

> The purpose of this study is to determine the impact of an instructional approach incorporating self-control techniques as compared to an approach which provides encouragement and verbal praise, on decision-making in leisure of adolescents who are mildly mentally retarded. Specifically, the following hypotheses will be tested during this study:
>
> H1: Subjects will demonstrate higher levels of independent self-instruction towards decision-making during scenarios which require decision-making in leisure upon the introduction of self-instruction training as compared to the introduction of decision-making training incorporating encouragement and verbal praise.
>
> H2: During a follow-up probe three and one half months after the decision-making intervention has been withdrawn, subjects will continue to display increased levels of independent self-instruction towards decision-making when presented with scenarios in which decision-making in leisure is necessary.

In this study, the research question and hypotheses are tightly framed. The positivist has spent much time initially formulating questions and hypotheses. The testing of hypotheses becomes what guides the study. From this point forward, the data are collected in relation to the stated hypotheses and these hypotheses serve as the guiding principles of the inquiry. An adage which characterizes the importance of the research question from the positivistic perspective is, "How will you know when you get there if you don't know where you are going?" The researcher arduously conceptualizes and designs the study. Precision in the formulation of the question and hypotheses is a must for the positivist. Many people function more effectively with the positivist's structure and clear direction.

In contrast, the naturalistic investigator starts from a much less defined position. Rather than a tightly defined research question, there is a research area or phenomenon which is to be studied. This is consistent with a relativist position which views the world as an emerging production containing multiple realities which are constructed by the individuals interacting in it. To tightly structure a research question is to operate from a realist perspective which does not acknowledge the multiple and emergent nature of reality as understood by the relativist.

A word of warning is necessary. A less defined question is not a shortcut. It is simply a different starting point. The bulk of the work for the naturalist comes not in the beginning but emerges throughout the study as the researcher spends much time focusing and refocusing the inquiry and emerging propositions. This perspective must be systematic and rigorous even though it may appear *loose*.

The naturalist's initial lack of structure can be problematic for some people, causing the researchers to abandon their study because they did not understand fully the extent to which they would be involved as the study progressed. They may not really realize the extent to which ongoing data analysis leads to additional data sources and data collection. Rather than moving through a sequential research process, the naturalist repeats steps or adds steps (see Figure 2.1) in an attempt to create structure as the study progresses. The structure of a sequential research process simply is not available to the naturalist.

An example of a research question from a naturalistic perspective might be:

> I am interested in understanding the process of teaching deci-sion-making in leisure to high school students who have mild mental retardation. What are the techniques used to teach decision-making in leisure? What is really being taught—decision-making or a special kind of decision-making relative to leisure? Is it leisure or recreation about which we are talking? Is there a difference to the students? What do the students think they are being taught? How do students feel about what they are being taught?

The same research content (decision-making in leisure) is intentionally used to show the difference in starting points. It is clear that this is a much less precise question or more accurately, series of questions. Questions are stated so as not to begin with *a priori* assumptions about what is happening in settings which teach decision-making in leisure. Compare this to the previous question stated from a positivist perspective. The positivist strictly adheres to a succinct question and a set of corresponding hypotheses. The naturalist's question, on the other hand, is intended to be open ended in recognition that the world contains socially constructed multiple realities which the researcher must come to understand from his or her own subjective experience as researcher as well as from the perspective of the participants whom he or she will study. The positivist question charts a predetermined course which suggests methods and data sources to be used. The naturalistic question provides a direction for data collection and data sources but is intentionally less specific so as not to limit methods or sources.

Methodology: Data Collection and Analysis

Little ideological compatibility exists between the positivistic and naturalistic perspectives, but there may be overlap between research methods and techniques (Henderson, 1991, p. 22). There is confusion about this. The difference between research perspectives is not one of qualitative versus quantitative. Qualitative and quantitative refer to methods. Quantitative methods yield discrete, presumably easily measurable information that can be interpreted through the use of numbers/statistics. Examples include close ended or structured interviews, paper and pencil tests, and the like. Qualitative methods yield general descriptive information and seek concepts, insights, and understandings. Examples include open ended interviews, unstructured observations, and the like. See Figure 2.3 for a comparison of quantitative and qualitative methods.

Figure 2.3
Comparison of Quantitative and Qualitative Methods

QUANTITATIVE	QUALITATIVE
1. Objective	Subjective
2. Numeric	Non-numeric
3. Statistical analysis	Nonstatistical analysis
4. Large Ns*	Small Ns
5. Structured data collection	Open ended data collection
6. Tables/graphs for results	Narrative for results

* One notable exception is single-subject research design.

It is imprecise to talk about quantitative and qualitative research *per se*, although these terms have been commonly used in the literature. Rather, it is more precise and in line with contemporary language to discuss positivistic or naturalistic research within which either quantitative and qualitative methods are used. The differences in research perspectives are differences in world views which may suggest, but not dictate, differences in research methods.

It is true that certain methods lend themselves to a particular research perspective, but it is inaccurate to equate quantitative methods with positivistic studies and qualitative methods with naturalistic inquiries. Some researchers believe that any method can be used within any perspective. The guiding principle, whatever the perspective, is to choose methods which can best answer the research questions posed. For example, if a positivistic study seeks to determine the effects of a specific intervention, a pretest/posttest experimental design which uses valid and reliable research instruments might be the most appropriate methodology. If the study is framed from a naturalistic perspective in which initial data collection and analysis lead to additional data sources and data collection, observation or in-depth, open-ended interviewing might be the most appropriate methodology (see Figure 2.3).

Increasingly, investigators from both perspectives are advocating the use of **multiple methods** or **triangulation** (Denzin, 1978) to understand more fully the phenomenon under study. For example, in a positivistic study, triangulation would be achieved if structured behavioral observation (a quantitative method) and/or a content analysis of therapist's notes (a qualitative method) were used to augment the pretest/posttest data collected. In a naturalistic inquiry, triangulation would be using both unstructured observation (a qualitative method) and in-depth, open-ended interviewing (also a qualitative method).

A positivist researcher chooses subjects or respondents early in the study. For example, to respond to the decision-making question and hypotheses posed earlier, a positivistic chooses subjects from a predetermined sampling frame. The subjects may be chosen randomly to maintain objectivity and to conform to the standards of research practice followed by positivistic researchers. Methods are also selected early in the study. The positivist may choose to use structured behavioral observation for this single subject experimental design study. This method is considered a quantitative method, and it seems appropriate to answer the question posed.

Once the data sources and data collection techniques are chosen and used, the research design is set. To change methods or to change subjects during the study introduces bias and is a threat to the objectivity of the positivistic study. As shown in Figure 2.1, the research process from a positivist perspective is serial and moves from question to hypothesis to data collection to data analysis to presentation. There is no doubling back. There is no allowance for changing one's mind if it is realized that the methods chosen are not providing the best data to answer the question posed. A positivist researcher deals with this by conducting replication studies or extensions of studies in an effort to understand more fully the phenomenon being studied.

Within a positivistic perspective, which is structured and predetermined, many of the methods chosen will be quantitative (see Figure 2.3). Quantitative data based on rational, numeric findings fit most easily ontologically and epistemologically into the positivist paradigm. Quantitative data are analyzed statistically in order to provide **hard data** which indicate relative strength and predictive value. Qualitative data on the other hand, provide **soft data** which focus on explanations of symbolic meanings and often do not fit as easily into the positivist paradigm.

As can be seen from Figure 2.3, qualitative methods are subjective, non-numeric, and open-ended. It is for this reason that qualitative methods are used so widely within the naturalistic perspective. From the naturalistic perspective, neither data sources nor data collection techniques are preset and unchangeable. Rather, data sources and techniques are open and include any and all sources and techniques which further illuminate the phenomenon under study. Data analysis necessarily occurs throughout the data collection process. It is a recursive process (Howe, 1991) which is designed so that additional data and sources can be used as they become relevant to the study. Data collection is not done within a specified and predetermined time frame. Rather, it is done as long as needed to thoroughly explicate the phenomenon being studied. Data analysis suggests emerging themes, concepts, or propositions and as such directs the ongoing data collection. Consider the decision-making questions posed from a naturalistic perspective which were described earlier. Such a study might use unstructured observations within the classroom, along with open-ended interviews of students, teachers, and the TRS. The naturalistic researcher may observe both structured sessions as well as related classroom interactions in an attempt to understand the phenomenon of teaching decision-making in leisure. He or she may use any or all of these data sources and data collection techniques as long as they provide useful information. Most important, the main data collection instrument is the researcher whose skills at understanding from the perspective of the people and phenomena being studied cannot be underestimated. The naturalistic inquirer's subjective involvement and experience in the investigation form the cornerstone of this type of research and are consistent with a relativistic ontology and epistemology.

Ongoing data analysis is integral to the interpretive or naturalistic process. As in the positivist perspective, data can be analyzed in a variety of ways depending on the methods used. Because qualitative methods are usually used in naturalistic research, a brief review of some data analysis techniques is offered here. These and other analytic techniques are detailed by Glancy in Chapter 13 of this text. Three examples of qualitative analysis techniques include: enumeration (Miles & Huberman, 1984), the constant comparison technique of content analysis (Glaser & Strauss, 1967), and clustering (Miles & Huberman, 1984). **Enumeration** is counting the frequency of a unit of analysis. The frequency indicates the strength of the presence of the term or the phrase. **Constant comparison** distills **emic** (subject generated) or **etic** (investigator generated) patterns of responses or clusters of behavioral categories. Constant comparison is used also to compare information obtained from observations, interviews, question-naires, or existing documents in order to cross check among data collection methods. **Clustering** is used when the information obtained is unanticipated and is hard to place into typologies. Clustering, as a means of grouping emergent or unanticipated data, enables the placement of such data into categories of information that have similar patterns or characteristics, *or* it enables the development of new categories (Howe, 1991).

Data Presentation

The end point of any scientific inquiry is presentation of the findings or results to interested audiences. The outcomes are quite different depending on the perspective from which the researcher is working. The focus of the final product must be consistent with the perspective.

The positivist focuses on answering specific research questions or testing hypotheses and confirming theory. He or she is careful to describe the methodology used to give credence to the findings. The positivist goes to great lengths to show the objectivity of the study. He or she orders the presentation in relation to the hypotheses being tested and the theory being confirmed. He or she presents tables and graphs to explain the statistical/linear analysis. There is usually a section in which *hard data* results are presented and another section in which these results are discussed. The researcher will attempt to demonstrate the generalizability of the findings assuming that the canons of research established within the positivist perspective are followed.

The outcome of the naturalistic investigation is quite different. The researcher focuses on explaining, developing patterns, and discovering theory grounded in the lives and interactions of the people studied. He or she *thickly* describes and creates for the reader *the sense of having been there* (Guba & Lincoln, 1981, p. 149). He or she moves from the less structured research idea to a clearer explication of the phenomenon which was intentionally not operationalized at the beginning of the research. The naturalistic researcher makes no claims beyond the limits of the subjects who are studied, but thoroughly describes his or her understanding and interpretation of the phenomenon, so that others may understand the same or similar phenomena within their own contexts. Like the positivist, the naturalist ends with nearly as many additional questions as he or she began with. Yet, in both studies, the researchers are true to the ontological and epistemological bases of the perspective within which they operated ensuring credible findings regardless of the perspective.

Summary and Implications
for Therapeutic Recreation

The two research perspectives as discussed here are very different. In fact, in the opinion of this author, these perspectives are mutually exclusive. One cannot combine the two, and one cannot operate out of both perspectives at the same time. One cannot at the same time believe that the world is both round and flat. One cannot both control and introduce/allow variation nor can one set method and then change method at the same time. One cannot believe that theory can be confirmed and generated at the same time (Guba, 1985). These are opposite ways of thinking and knowing. Little possibility exists for mixing of the perspectives although it has been attempted with the outcome of creating a great deal of philosophical confusion (Henderson, 1991).

Whatever the ontological and epistemological perspectives within which the researcher feels most comfortable, it is important to understand the differences between the naturalistic and the positivistic perspectives. It is important to remember that research, although it is not always acknowledged, is *always* conducted within a particular world view which has been described as the research perspective. It is also important to remember that there is a difference between method and perspective, and that method does not define perspective; rather, that methods are chosen to answer a particular research question irrespective of the perspective from which the query is posed.

The perspective from which one operates makes little difference if the therapeutic recreator, as an individual, is not an active participant in the research enterprise. Whether one is an academic or a practitioner, whether one is a researcher, collaborator, or a consumer of research, to be a responsible professional, one must be an *active* participant in the research enterprise. Every professional discipline needs this level of involvement.

Research is sorely needed in the field of therapeutic recreation. It is needed to substantiate the contentions which are made about the efficacy of this field. It is needed to understand the processes of the interventions which are used. It is needed to convince administrators and funders as well as to satisfy consumers of TR services. Investigative TRSs have to ask the *hard* questions as well as the *easy* ones. That is, all concerned have to look discern cost-benefit of the service and not just the benefit. Individuals have to look at the differences and similarities between the TR field and other related fields. Research teams have to stand ready to explore problems of the field. Investigators have to study the various meanings and implications of words like *recreation, leisure, therapy,* and *treatment*. At the same time, TRSs must understand that today's findings may not even be relevant by the time they are published or otherwise disseminated. Economic, social, political, cultural, and other forces are changing the meanings of much of what is known; and, in order for the TR field to remain viable, TRSs must be active participants in, and consumers of good research.

Research can expand the boundaries of any field. There are different ways of knowing among TRSs. For that reason, it is valuable for TR to have research conducted from both perspectives to broaden and deepen the body of knowledge in TR. Systematic, scientific inquiry, from whichever perspective, can suggest new ways of *doing* therapeutic recreation. TRSs must be competent in this enterprise so that they can help the field to be continually responsive to the needs of persons with disabilities in a variety of circumstances and settings.

In the following two sections of this book, readers are provided with the knowledge to help them understand and/or participate in both the naturalistic and the positivistic research perspectives. Each perspective is explained procedurally and processually so that investigative TRSs can understand more fully and be prepared to conduct research in therapeutic recreation.

Discussion Questions

1. Explain ontology and epistemology. Why are these concepts important and at what point in a study should they be considered?
2. How does the research process from a positivistic perspective differ from the process from a naturalistic perspective?
3. Are quantitative methods exclusively associated with positivistic research, and qualitative with naturalistic? Explain.
4. Can a researcher conduct research from two different perspectives at the same time? That is, can the same researcher answer the same research question using two different perspectives? Can the same researcher operate within one perspective for one study and within another perspective for a different study? Explain your response using examples for clarification.
5. Which research perspective most closely fits who you are? Explain your choice giving personal examples for support. Then, from that perspective, pose two research questions/topics which you feel are most crucial to therapeutic recreation.

References

Cook, T., & Campbell, D. (1979). *Quasi-experimentation: Design and analysis issues for field settings*. Chicago, IL: Rand McNally.

Denzin, N. K. (1978). *The research act*, (2nd ed.). New York, NY: McGraw Hill.

Glaser, B. G., & Strauss, A. (1967). *The discovery of grounded theory: Strategies for qualitative research*. Chicago, IL: Aldine.

Guba, E. G. (1985). The context of emergent paradigm research. In Y. Lincoln (Ed.), *Organizational theory and inquiry*. Beverly Hills, CA: Sage.

Guba, E. G. (1990). The alternative paradigm dialog. In E. G. Guba, (Ed.), *The Paradigm Dialog*. Newbury Park, CA: Sage.

Guba, E. G., & Lincoln, Y. S. (1981). *Effective evaluation*. San Francisco, CA: Jossey-Bass.

Henderson, K. A. (1991). *Dimensions of choice: A qualitative approach to recreation, parks, and leisure research*. State College, PA: Venture.

Howe, C. Z. (1985). Possibilities for using a qualitative research approach in the sociological study of leisure. *Leisure Studies, 10*(1), 49-62.

Howe, C. Z. (1991). Considerations when using phenomenology in leisure inquiry: Beliefs, methods, and analysis in naturalistic research. *Journal of Leisure Research, 17*(3), 212-224.

Miles, M. B., & Huberman, A. M. (1984). *Qualitative data analysis: A sourcebook of new methods*. Beverly Hills, CA: Sage.

Zukav, G. (1979). *The dancing Wu-Li masters*. New York, NY: Bantam.

Suggested Readings

Anderson, S. C., & Hultsman, J. T. (1988, October). *Epistemological problems with the positivistic study of leisure perceptions: The need for grounded theory.* Paper presented at the Leisure Research Symposium at the annual meeting of the National Recreation and Park Association, Indianapolis, IN.

Berger, P. L., & Luckman, T. (1967). *The social construction of reality.* New York, NY: Anchor Books.

Bullock, C. C. (1983). Qualitative research in therapeutic recreation. *Therapeutic Recreation Journal, 17*(4), 36-43.

Bullock, C. C. (1988). Interpretive lines of action of mentally retarded children in mainstreamed play settings. *Symbolic Interaction, 9,* 145-172.

Cook, T. (1983). Quasi-experimentation: Its ontology, epistemology, and methodology. In G. Morgan (Ed.), *Beyond method: Strategies for social research* (pp. 74-94). Beverly Hills, CA: Sage.

Chenery, M. F., & Russell, R. V. (1987). Responsive evaluation: An application of naturalistic inquiry to recreation evaluation. *Journal of Park and Recreation Administration, 5*(4), 30-38.

Davis, F. (1973). The Martian and the convert: Ontological polarities in social research. *Urban Life and Culture, 2*(3), 333-342.

Kuhn, T. S. (1970). *The structure of scientific revolutions* (2nd ed.). Chicago, IL: The University of Chicago Press.

Mobily, K. (1985, October). *Thoughts on a reconstruction of leisure research.* Paper presented at the Leisure Research Symposium at the annual meeting of the National Recreation and Park Association, Dallas, TX.

Smith, J. K. (1983). *Quantitative verses qualitative research:* An attempt to clarify the issues. *Educational Researcher, 12*(3), 6-13.

Smith, J. K., & Heshusius, L. (1986). Closing down the conversation: The end of the quantitative-qualitative debate among educational inquirers. *Educational Researcher, 15*(1), 4-12.

Taylor, S. J., & Bogdan, R. (1984). *Introduction to qualitative research methods: The search for meaning* (2nd ed.). New York, NY: Wiley.

Znaniecki, F. (1934). *The method of sociology.* New York, NY: Farrow and Rinehart.

The Status of Recreation, Leisure, and Therapeutic Recreation as a Developing Science[1]
Gary D. Ellis

The 1986 annual meeting of the Utah Academy of Science, Arts, and Letters was a significant milestone in the history of the scholarly study of health, physical education, and recreation in the state of Utah. The Academy is the oldest and most prestigious organization of university professors in Utah. The 1986 meeting was especially significant because, for the first time, faculty members from health, physical education, and recreation were invited to participate in this forum for discussion, dialogue, and debate among members of the Academy. The invitation suggested that health, physical education, and recreation had become recognized as legitimate and important scientific disciplines that added an important new dimension to the Academy. Despite the increasing problems of overspecialization and difficulties in identifying a core of common knowledge that binds health, physical education, and recreation, it seems noteworthy that colleagues from the arts and sciences observed significant progress in the development of the health, physical education, and recreation disciplines.

Despite the obvious reason to be pleased with the Academy's positive evaluation of this progress, it is important to remember that the most meaningful evaluations of progress are internal; those that come from within. The university and clinical research environments in which Academy members work seem to be preoccupied, even obsessed, with evaluation.

1. Author's Note: This chapter is based on a presentation made at the 1986 meeting of the Utah Academy of Science, Arts, and Letters in Cedar City, Utah. The original version of the chapter is published in *Encyclia*, Volume 63, 1986, pp. 115-125. The chapter is reprinted here in revised form with the permission of the Utah Academy of Science, Arts, and Letters. The author was invited to submit the paper in order to expose it to a wider audience.

As a result, in the eyes of members of the Academy, the validity of the statement concerning self-evaluation is likely evident. Through retention, promotion, and tenure reviews; accreditation visitations; graduate school reviews; and countless other evaluative processes, academics are constantly enamored of such questions as: How many articles did you publish this term? Of what quality were they? How much grant money did you raise? What presentations and speeches have you made during the last year? Do you prepare adequately for the courses you teach? What were your students' reactions to your classes last term?

Educators often seem to spend so much time evaluating and receiving feedback from evaluations that not enough time remains to complete basic responsibilities in teaching, research, and service delivery. Yet, through it all, faculty inherently know that they are their own best critics. Perhaps it can be boldly suggested that the members of a discipline's evaluation of themselves is the evaluation which truly makes the difference and truly matters.

It is in this spirit that this chapter is a self-evaluation of the status of recreation, leisure, and therapeutic recreation as a developing science. Although the Academy has seen fit to include recreation and leisure faculty among its membership, a critical self-evaluation seems to be in order. There is a story that Arthur Haley had on a wall in his office a picture of a turtle resting on top of a fence post. Passers-by who inquired about the picture were told that it served to remind Haley that people who are elevated to greater heights always have much help getting there. The central question posed in this chapter is whether recreation and leisure studies is a science that has earned its membership in organizations like the Academy. Or is its presence in that organization a result of significant "help" from scholars in the related disciplines of health and physical education which have made greater progress?

Science in Recreation, Leisure, and Therapeutic Recreation

What are some characteristics that establish a field of study as a science? Once this question is answered, one may evaluate the extent to which recreation has achieved the status of being a science. Then one may examine the prospects and problems encountered as recreation, therapeutic recreation, and leisure studies emerge as a developing science.

The question, "What is a science?" has been addressed by philosophers and scholars from other disciplines for hundreds of years. As with most ideas worthy of contemplation and dialogue, a myriad of possible answers to that question exists. This chapter is limited to discussing four views on the meaning of science. These include the view of the general public and the views of three social scientists whose ideas on the topic are both interesting and instructive.

Science: The Public's View

Consider the view of the general public on the meaning of science. Their view is of utmost importance because the public pays the taxes which support many of the endeavors of the people in the recreation, leisure, and TR field. Further, the public is ultimately who should benefit from the endeavors of the practitioners of the field. Unfortunately, there appears to be no evidence that the general public views the study of recreation, leisure, and therapeutic recreation—or health and physical education either—as legitimate sciences. Rather, the general public seems to associate "science" with the physical and life sciences: biology, chemistry, physics, medicine, and related disciplines. The public seems to define science as a complex and esoteric body of knowledge that is constantly growing and that generates knowledge that directly affects the quality of human life. It is uncertain that the general public believes that the discipline of recreation has developed knowledge that directly impacts on the quality of life of people, both with and without disabilities.

For example, at a poster session at a national conference, we presented a summary of a study of relationships among different mental imagery strategies, state of consciousness, and the bowling performance of beginning bowlers. During the session, an interested and well-meaning public school teacher approached us and asked if imagery "worked." In the stereotypical style of the social scientist, we began to formulate a response in terms of such phrases as "under certain conditions" and "several studies have shown...." The teacher abruptly cut us off. "Don't give me that stuff," he said, "I just want to know whether or not it works."

His statement pointed to a major difference between the social and physical sciences, at least in the wise eyes of the general public. Although enormous mysteries still exist in the physical sciences and the public remains tolerant of these uncertainties, answers to many important questions have been found. A sound body of scientific knowledge underlies the technology which has produced such marvels and tragedies of the modern world as microwave ovens, television, radio, artificial hearts, thermostats, and chemical and nuclear weapons. The physical sciences have moved far beyond elementary questions and are addressing increasingly complex problems that regularly find their way to newspaper headlines and evening news broadcasts. By contrast, those of us who might be considered "leisure scientists" are unable to provide definitive answers to the seemingly most elementary of questions of social science. Does imagery affect bowling performance via its effects on state of consciousness? What specific instructional techniques most effectively promote leisure education outcomes? How might a therapeutic recreation specialist facilitate the generalization of consumers' perceptions of self-efficacy across different activities and roles? How can TRSs motivate people to participate? The science and technology of recreation, leisure studies, and therapeutic recreation has not generated definitive answers to questions such as these. In fact, the science and technology of leisure and TR is only at the early stages of searching for answers to these social scientific questions.

Science: Three Social Scientists' Views

In contrast to the view of the general public concerning what constitutes a science is the view of people within the social sciences. In 1980, Iso-Ahola provided an insightful account of the evolution of the social sciences, based on Hollander's (1971) work. Reviewing and interpreting Hollander's position, Iso-Ahola (1980) remarked that social sciences follow a fairly predictable developmental sequence. At birth, a new social science enters into a period which Hollander refers to as an era of "**social philosophy**." That era is marked by intense speculation about the meaning, value, and purpose of the concepts which are of concern to the discipline. Prominent writers during a social philosophy period tend to either be philosophers, eloquent speakers, exceptional logicians, or artists in the use of words. Collection of data for empirical validation of any tentative theories that emerge from this speculation, however, is not undertaken. The emphasis is on dialogue, logic, and rhetoric rather than empirical research.

Few people would argue that the recreation, leisure, and therapeutic recreation discipline has not experienced a period of social philosophy. Any graduate of a recreation curriculum who has been exposed to the problems of defining play, recreation, and leisure has had a taste of the dominant form of intellectual activity during the social philosophy era. Many of the statements and definitions concerning leisure and related terms that emerged from the social philosophy era were founded in the writers' interpretations of early philosophers; perhaps most notably the critical idealism of Plato and Aristotelian realism. Without belaboring the point, the influence of these philosophical schools of thought can be observed in the following definitions of leisure.

Murphy (1974) reviewed philosophical perspectives of leisure including the classical definition of leisure as a condition or state of being—a condition of the soul which is divided from time. Leisure is "an act of aesthetic, psychological, religious and philosophical contemplation" (Gray, 1971, cited in Murphy, 1974, p. 23). More recently from a psychological perspective "leisure means to be engaged in an activity performed for its own sake, to do something which gives one pleasure and satisfaction . . . to be oneself, to express one's talents, one's capacities, one's potentials" (Neulinger, 1974, cited in Murphy, 1974, p. 30).

While definitions such as these are useful in helping to establish broad parameters of the field of study and they continue to be topics of endless discussion in undergraduate (and sometimes graduate) courses in recreation and leisure, they are insufficient in the eyes of a society that demands scientific verification and technological application.

Social Empiricism

Following social philosophy, the next stage in the development of the social sciences is called **social empiricism** (Hollander, 1971; Iso-Ahola, 1980). During the social empiricism era, increased recognition of the importance of empirical documentation is present. The broad, sweeping statements of the social philosophers, however, provide little guidance to data collection efforts. As a result, the data that are gathered tend to be used for describing the *status quo* rather than for explanation and understanding. In other words, little effort to identify causal structures among variables is undertaken. Consequently, no significant gains are made in understanding relationships among variables that are essential for the emergence of an applied technology of the discipline. Rather, the focus of research is on describing distributions of individual, superficial variables that are presumed to be readily observable and easily measured.

An example of research from the social empiricism phase in the development of leisure and therapeutic recreation is the numerous investigations of recreation activity participation preferences. These studies were valuable in that they demonstrated that leisure could be a topic of empirical research, yet they contributed very little—if anything—to the development of a scientific knowledge base in recreation and leisure. The continuing use of ill-conceived and poorly constructed "home-made" leisure interest inventories so frequently used in TR for "assessment" is clearly a lingering artifact from the social empiricism phase of the discipline's development. Consistent with the research from that era, such instruments may indeed provide a quantitative summary that is in some way representative of something that individuals like to do in their free time. Unfortunately, the instruments provide no evidence of such important behavioral concerns as: setting-related preferences, social group preferences, motives, needs, constraints, independence, developmental level, or centrality of an activity to one's definition of self or well-being. In short, at their very best, these homegrown instruments measure trivial, superficial variables that have little to do with consumers' levels of functioning, their quality of life, or the role and significance of leisure in their lives. Such instruments are outmoded remnants of an earlier stage of this discipline's intellectual development.

Social Analysis

In the 1980s, the recreation, leisure, and therapeutic recreation discipline seemed to enter into a period of transition from social empiricism to an era of social analysis. This transition is still underway. **Social analysis** is characterized by an attempt to understand the underlying structure of human behavior by exploring why people behave as they do. Social analysis requires rigorous investigations into relationships among complex variables related to personal meaning and definition, such as values, attitudes, personality dispositions, and beliefs. Research within the social analysis framework is characterized by controlled investigations that uncover relationships among variables by tests of scientific theories about human behavior. It is through understanding these relationships that a technology may emerge and investigative TRSs may begin to provide satisfactory answers to questions such as those about motivating consumers, ensuring that perceptions of self-efficacy generalize, and about methods of engineering that optimize experiences for clients, park visitors, and other consumers of leisure services. As Iso-Ahola (1980) put it, as people begin to understand relationships between variables, it becomes increasingly evident to leisure and TR professionals that it is better to know how to best facilitate social interaction and feelings of competence during a game of volleyball rather than knowing where most players put the net afterwards.

Recent research in recreation, therapeutic recreation, and leisure studies is indeed consistent with this social analysis philosophy. Review and integrative papers that have the potential to lead to theory development are being published with increasing frequency. Complex studies seeking to "tease out" hidden relationships among variables are now the norm in the leading journals that publish research in these areas. The level of sophistication and the complex procedures for identifying these relationships are quite bewildering to those faculty members and professionals who completed their formal education during the periods of social philosophy and social empiricism. To quote a folk hero of the '60s, Bob Dylan, "the times, they are a-changing."

Another Social Scientist's View

Hollander's discussion of social philosophy, social empiricism, and social analysis is one of many ideas of what the social sciences are and how they evolve. Another view was presented by Privette (1983). Privette delineated three components of a science: content, technology, and systematic organization of knowledge. How does the recreation, leisure, and therapeutic recreation discipline fare according to these standards?

In terms of content, this discipline has not yet arrived. Rather than proactively identifying the parameters of its concern, the discipline seems to fluctuate reactively according to what topics are in vogue at a given point in time. During the 1960s the focus was on public sector parks and recreation. Since that time, a variety of topics surfaced, floundered, or vanished altogether. Among the many topics that have been examined and are now rarely the focus of rigorous inquiry are: activity substitutability, leisure education, leisure counseling, activity analysis, applications of attribution theory, neurolinguistic programming, rights of people who have disabilities, and wellness. Looming on the horizon seem to be questions related to tourism, consumerism, entrepreneurship, and leisure self-efficacy.

Rather than building a knowledge base by systematically examining the common dimensions of leisure behavior across topics, investigators in the discipline approach questions and problems in a childlike manner. They play enthusiastically with new topics for a while, become bored with those topics, and then move quickly on to other interests and activities as newer and perhaps more lucrative social concerns arise. Leisure and TR investigators also seem to follow scholars in other disciplines as *they* pave the way on new questions, problems, and topics. This is not to say that follow-up studies or applying the theories of other disciplines to this one is bad. However, those should not be the only efforts of leisure and TR inquiry. Leisure and TR investigators also need to take the lead in understanding the leisure phenomenon and claim it as their unique area of focus and contribution.

Perhaps, true to the analogy, the discipline is so young that the dilettante level of exploration of the environment is appropriate. With time, a definitive content of the discipline of recreation, leisure, and therapeutic recreation may emerge.

Technology is another component of a science (Privette, 1983). Technology involves innovation, problem-solving, and translating scientific knowledge into practical applications. In 1985, one leading scholar, Mannell, noted that an implied goal of leisure research is the eventual emergence of leisure "experience engineers," who are able to design social and physical environments that repeatedly create positive leisure experiences for people. Although researchers are beginning to identify some factors that seem to affect the quality of people's experiences and some people (with little formal preparation in counseling) are professing to be "leisure counselors," a definitive technology of recreation, leisure, and therapeutic recreation seems, at this point, to be many years away. Also, many behaviors that appear to reliably produce pleasureful experiences in modern society, including television, books, sex, and alcohol and other drugs, have not been particularly prominent foci of leisure research. If a technology of recreation and leisure is to emerge, it is likely that studies of a wide range of behaviors and environmental contingencies that reliably produce certain experiential states will be needed. Ultimately, of course, it will become necessary to not only learn about various forms of behavior that produce pleasant, relaxing, and arousing states of consciousness, but to distinguish between behaviors that are hedonistic and dysfunctional and those that are virtuous and functional in terms of human growth, development, and well-being.

In addition to content and technology, Privette (1983) stated that the systematic organization of knowledge is essential to a science. This, also, seems to be an area which is in need of attention by recreation and leisure professionals. The status of the knowledge base of the young discipline was summarized by Mobily (1984, p. 1) as follows:

> Repeatedly, I have been confronted with little or no framework to guide my research efforts. Where are our theories? Where is the literature to guide hypotheses? How do I know what to expect or predict? In short, where is our body of knowledge? 'How to' materials with oversimplified solutions dominate the market. It appears that we know but do not understand. . .

Mobily also declares that progress toward the development of a systematic organization of knowledge depends not on the collection of additional data bases, but rather on the development theory to account for complex leisure phenomena.

Self-evaluations are often more critical than evaluations of others. The views of the general public and three [perhaps representative] social scientists, as understood by this author, lead to the belief that recreation, therapeutic recreation, and leisure have not achieved the status of being a science. Rather, this young discipline may be in an important era of transition; it is an adolescent, sometimes reaching longingly back to its childhood, but usually hurtling toward adulthood, independence, and scholarly recognition. In this developmental process, certain obstacles will have to be overcome, but the prospects for growth and development appear to be exceptionally bright. What may be some of the obstacles, problems, and prospects of recreation, leisure, and therapeutic recreation as a developing science?

Problems and Prospects[2]

There are four major problems which must be overcome in the developmental process: (1) a dearth of theory; (2) a major gap between leisure researchers and practitioners; (3) lack of quality measurement tools; and (4) the threat of "professionalization." A concentrated effort is needed to ensure that these problems are overcome.

It could very well be that the dearth of theory is the reason that such a great diversity of topics have been studied by leisure or TR researchers. The scope of these topics has been so broad that only a few "research programs" designed to build a body of knowledge in a particular area are identifiable.

---

2. Coeditors' Note: We hope that the readers will find the challenges first posed in 1986 to be equally as provocative now. Ellis' thoughtful critique gives all of us pause to examine ourselves in our educational, researcher, practitioner, and advocate roles.

Researchers might justifiably be accused of running in all directions, studying a little of everything, but not much of anything. The diversity of topics which have been investigated is evident from examining the six very general categories into which research topics in only one subdiscipline (therapeutic recreation) were categorized in a published content analysis (Schleien & Yermakoff, 1983): (1) leisure needs, preferences, pattern, and attitudes; (2) effects/values of recreation; (3) community integration; (4) skill acquisition; (5) teaching strategies; and (6) program evaluation.

It is significant to note not only the breadth of these topics, but that their classification system was based on logical groupings rather than on theoretical structures. In other disciplines theory serves as a basis for both research and practice. In the physical sciences, both science and technology are guided by complex theories, such as those involving subatomic particles. Humankind's ability to explore the universe apparently is based in part on the development of theory surrounding the idea that space—such as that which separates one person from another—is bent.

In psychology, research and practice are based on a number of theoretical positions: behaviorism, dynamic/psychoanalytic theories, gestalt theory, etc. No analogous theories currently exist to explain leisure and to provide guidance to research and practice in recreation and therapeutic recreation. In the absence of theory, peoples' efforts lack focus and direction and such research, despite its enormous complexity, seems woefully shallow. The situation is reminiscent of the "Patricia Hearst Burgers" of the '70s. If one looks beneath the bun, one finds no patty. Theory development is a critical need facing leisure and therapeutic recreation investigators at the present time.

A problem related to the need for theory is the need for increased quality in measurement instruments and procedures. In a review of major assessment instruments in TR, Howe (1984) commented that most of the instruments were greatly lacking in terms of conceptualization and reliability and validity data. The situation is not better in other subdisciplines. The science of a discipline can proceed no more rapidly than the availability of quality tools for measuring the variables that are of critical interest to that discipline (Nunnally, 1978). Recreation, therapeutic recreation, and leisure cannot fully develop as a science until major variables are conceptualized within clear theoretical foundations and more adequate measurement procedures are developed.

Relationships Between Researchers and Practitioners

A second major problem that recreation, leisure, and therapeutic recreation professionals must overcome is the gap between research and practice. Although this is the topic of Chapter 5 it is briefly mentioned here. At the heart of this gap there seems to be a fundamental misunderstanding of the purpose of recreation, leisure, and therapeutic recreation science. Many individuals, both practitioners and educators, have been on the "firing line" during the last few years. Perhaps beginning with the social attitude that spawned Proposition 13 in California in the 1970s, parks, recreation, and therapeutic recreation personnel have been challenged to provide specific evidence of efficiency and accountability in service delivery. Mistaking science for technology, practitioners increasingly turned to the scientific community for a justification for leisure services and for a defensible underpinning for the services that they provide.

Unfortunately, researchers in leisure and therapeutic recreation had little to offer practitioners in terms of insight on day-to-day operations. Researchers were and still are struggling with the difficult period of transition between social empiricism and social analysis. Their challenge at this point was to begin to develop insight into infinitely complex recreation-related phenomena and how those phenomena relate to such important concerns as quality of life and rehabilitation. Many researchers had limited interest in designing studies primarily to provide specific technological advice to practitioners. Even when the interest was present, the lack of available definitive knowledge on which to provide technological advice was not.

Observing that almost all of the prominent researchers in this discipline are from related disciplines (e.g., forestry, sociology, geography, business, and psychology) recreation and TR practitioners reasoned that these individuals had little understanding of the recreation, leisure, and TR discipline and that this lack of understanding was the source of the apparent disinterest of the research community in addressing practical problems. New, highly specialized journals emerged, which were designed to meet the needs of practitioners in specific areas of leisure service delivery. This overspecialization was supported by the National Recreation and Park Association, which discontinued the functions of the office of its Director of Research during this period. The fundamental problem, however, was that practitioners were confusing science, which seeks to explain phenomena that may or may not have an immediate "applied" consequence, with technology, which seeks to solve applied problems and create improvements through innovation.

Ultimately, this confusion between science and technology has contributed to the fragmentation of the discipline at a time in which unity is the greatest need. Practitioners (understandably) tend to give their attention mainly to action research and to the journals that seem to be most directly related to their particular range of interest. Social scientists, on the other hand, fail to nurture working relationships with practitioners that might give birth to needed technology and innovation by merging scientific knowledge and theory with practice. As Witt (1984, p. 60) observed, "the result is a further splintering of the discipline into disparate entities with little to say to each other and little understanding of the theoretical base and applications to practice which hold [the discipline] together." This gap between research and practice must be eliminated for future progress to be made. Strategies to do this are proposed in Chapter 5.

The Dangers of Continued Professionalization

Finally, the professionalization of recreation may be a significant threat to the continued scientific development of the discipline. Currently, efforts are underway to extend certification and licensure procedures for practitioners. Comprehensive accreditation procedures for higher education programs are already well in place. Professionalization appears to promote a separatism of knowledge and an emphasis on "how to" rather than the more basic questions of "what" and "why." Most importantly professionalism seems to promote the unjustifiable position that a scientific knowledge base and a technology of recreation, leisure, and therapeutic recreation already exists. This false sense of security evidently encourages educators, who should know better, to channel precious energy into providing shallow answers rather than into theory development, scientific research, and searching for solutions to fundamental questions that may ultimately have implications for practice.

Sufficient Cause for Optimism

With these problems and challenges in mind, what may be the prospects for development? First of all, underlying the previous criticism is a strong belief that the discipline will overcome the aforementioned challenges. This optimism is based in part on the new breed of scientists that is emerging. Emerging leaders in this discipline are no longer social philosophers spouting rhetoric. Instead they are individuals who are well schooled in the concepts and methods of scientific research. Superficial theses and dissertations which were the norm during the social empiricism age are becoming increasingly rare. There are very impressive graduate students and young faculty members throughout the country. In general, they are curious and inquisitive. They seem to thrive on complexity and the unknown. With the future in their hands, there is good reason to be optimistic.

Another reason for optimism is that exciting new methods of research are being developed. Investigators are beginning to look beyond the mechanistic and reductionist models of social science research. Future research will involve more studies within the transactional model, taking into account important time, sequence, and contextual variables (Altman & Rogoff, 1986). Technologies for studies of this nature are available and results of a few studies that are consistent with the transactional model have already been reported (cf. Csikszentmihalyi & Kubey, 1981; Larson & Csikszentmihalyi, 1983).

Concluding Remarks

In conclusion, this "self-evaluation" of the status of recreation, leisure, and therapeutic recreation as a developing science would be incomplete if a degree of reflection on a fundamental premise of this chapter was not included. That premise is that it is desirable for recreation, therapeutic recreation, and leisure to develop as a science.[3] Perhaps, for example, recreation, therapeutic recreation, and leisure studies might develop more as an *art* than as a science. By nature, leisure and recreation seem to be phenomena which are as well-suited to artistic inquiry as to scientific scrutiny. Contemporary views are that leisure is an emotion, feeling, or state of mind. It is assumed to be a highly individualized phenomenon which is perceived differently by different people. The role of emotions is central to artistic inquiry. Science strives for emotional neutrality. Art seeks to explicate and understand; science to explain and control. The ultimate aim of science is truth, which implies singularity of vision and absolutes. Art, on the other hand, strives for meaning and allows for diverse interpretation and relativism (Borg, 1983, p. 28). Leisure and recreation, in many ways, seem to be better suited to artistic inquiry than scientific inquiry.

Finally, the limitations of science need to be addressed. One of the more eloquent statements of these limitations was provided by the philosopher, Will Durant (1961):

> Science wishes to resolve the whole into parts, the organism into organs, the obscure into the known. It does not inquire into the values and ideal possibilities of things, nor into their total and final significance; it is content to show their present actuality and operation, it narrows its gaze resolutely to the nature and process of things as they are. Science tells us how to heal and how to kill; it reduces the death rate in retail and then kills us wholesale in war ... only wisdom can tell us when to heal and when to kill. (p. xxvii)

As the scientific development of recreation, leisure, and therapeutic recreation continues to unfold, individuals must keep in mind that science is only one tool that provides one way of knowing. Other approaches to knowing are of equal and greater value. Science, without concurrent cultivation of other ways of knowing, would certainly prove to be insufficient. The ultimate goal must be wisdom.

---

3. Coeditors' Note: We would qualify the use of the word science to "positivistic" science, but are retaining Ellis' original language which paints science in broad strokes to contrast with art.

Discussion Questions

1. Recount in your own words the public's view of science in general and how the physical and social sciences are differentiated. Identify the challenges to recreation, leisure, and therapeutic recreation professionals in helping the public to come to an improved understanding of science especially as science relates to the TR field.

2. Compare and contrast Hollander's three eras in the evolution of social science: social philosophy, social empiricism, and social analysis. Select which era you believe recreation, leisure, and TR research is in and provide a rationale for your belief. Then consider how your selection addresses the four major developmental problems proposed in this chapter: inadequately developed theory, practitioner-researcher gap, poor instrumentation, and "professionalization."

3. Reference is made to the need to investigate the quality of the leisure or recreative experience, with indicators of quality including affect/affective states. How does this challenge fit with the ideas of "other ways of knowing" or the "artistic" investigation of recreation, TR, and leisure studies?

References

Altman, I., & Rogoff, B. (1986). World views in psychology: Trait, interactional, organismic, and transactional perspectives. In D. Stokols, & I. Altman (Eds.). *Handbook of environmental psychology*. New York, NY: John Wiley.

Borg, W. (1983). *Educational research: An introduction*. New York, NY: Longman,.

Csikszentmihalyi, M., & Kubey, R. (1981). Television and the rest of life: A systematic comparison of subjective experience. *Public Opinion Quarterly, 45,* 317-328.

Durant, W. (1961). *The story of philosophy*. New York, NY: Washington Square Press.

Hollander, E. P. (1976). *Principles and methods of social psychology* (2nd ed.). New York, NY: Oxford University Press.

Howe, C. Z. (1984). Leisure assessment instrumentation in therapeutic recreation. *Therapeutic Recreation Journal, 18*(2), 14-24.

Iso-Ahola, S. E. (1980). *The social psychology of leisure and recreation*. Dubuque, IA: Brown.

Larson, R., & Csikszentmihalyi, M. (1983). The experience sampling methodology. In H. T. Reis (Ed.), *Naturalistic approaches to studying social interaction*. San Francisco, CA: Jossey-Bass.

Mannell, R. C. (1985). The "psychologization" of leisure services. In T. Goodale, & P. Witt (Eds.), *Recreation and leisure: Issues in an era of change*. State College, PA: Venture.

Mobily, K. E. (1984). The state of leisure research: Ten miles from nowhere. *Leisure Commentary and Practice, 3*(5), 1-3.

Murphy, J. F. (1974). *Concepts of leisure* (2nd ed.). Englewood Cliffs, NJ: Prentice-Hall.

Nunnally, J. (1978). *Psychometric theory*. New York, NY: McGraw-Hill, Inc .

Privette, G. (1983). Peak experience, peak performance, and flow: A comparative analysis of positive human experiences. *Journal of Personality and Social Psychology, 45,* 1361-1368.

Schleien, S. J., & Yermakoff, N. (1983). Data based research in therapeutic recreation: State of the art. *Therapeutic Recreation Journal, 17*(4), 17-26.

Witt, P. A. (1984, May). Research in transition. *Parks & Recreation,* pp. 60-64.

Psychological Perspectives for Therapeutic Recreation Research: The Psychology of Enjoyment
John Dattilo and Douglas A. Kleiber

Psychology has devoted itself in large part to defining internal and external conditions that liberate and constrain behavior. This includes the study of self-determination, intrinsic motivation, social reactance, and learned helplessness. The prevailing theories that address these matters are the subject of this chapter. Before considering them, however, it is important to ask a question of purpose. What is the significance of these theories for therapeutic recreation? Or to put it another way, what is the task of TR for which these theories are most relevant? We believe that a purpose not only of TR, but of leisure services in general is to engender *enjoyment.* For whatever additional benefits enjoyment may bring, it is, *in and of itself,* a major rationale for the provision of leisure services. Leisure professionals seek to identify the factors that interfere with and prohibit enjoyment, those that facilitate enjoyment, and other benefits that accrue to people who enjoy themselves. However, the nature of enjoyment itself has not always been made clear. Enjoyment is associated in the literature with recreation (Shivers, 1981), with leisure (Gunter, 1987; Mobily, 1989; Roadburg, 1983; Shaw, 1985), and with therapeutic recreation specifically (Dattilo & Barnett, 1985; Francis, 1991; Shary & Iso-Ahola, 1990), but its inherent characteristics are rarely articulated.

The work by Csikszentmihalyi (1975, 1982, 1985a, 1985b, 1990) and his associates (Csikszentmihalyi & Csikszentmihalyi, 1988) on *optimal experience* offers a useful starting point for this examination and for further consideration of psychological perspectives on therapeutic recreation. Using various methods including interviews, surveys, and experience sampling, these investigators have studied the qualities of subjective experience that people have when they are doing what they want to do most and loving it. By examining the experiences of dancers, rock climbers, writers, basketball players, as well as artists, surgeons and others who love their work, these investigations have isolated characteristics of enjoyment, or what is referred to more technically as **optimal experience**. The studies show that the experience of **enjoyment** is distinguishable from **pleasure**, the latter being the result of satisfying basic biological drives such as hunger, thirst, sex, and sufficient stimulation. Enjoyment is the experience derived from investing one's attention in action patterns that are intrinsically motivating. The activity is often so compelling in and of itself that one becomes deeply absorbed in it and loses consciousness of self and awareness of time. The word used to describe the subjective quality of this optimal experience—often by actors themselves—is *flow*. The sense of movement that this word implies is created by the merging of action and awareness around the challenges provided by an activity and the feedback that defines a person's capability to meet those challenges. While many activities can create this optimal experience, any given activity must become more challenging, in keeping with expanding skills, to maintain the experience. So unlike pleasure, enjoyment is consistent with concentration, effort, and a sense of control and competence. Enjoyment is often used colloquially as the equivalent of *fun*, or simple positive affect, but it is used here, as Csikszentmihalyi and others have, to reflect a considerable degree of psychological involvement as well.

An activity is assumed to be enjoyable, then, when one continues with it for no apparent reason beyond the activity itself. We say that such an activity is "intrinsically motivated." However, it is in the subjective experience of the activity that the factors producing this sustained interest are revealed. From the research of Csikszentmihalyi and others it is clear that concentration, effort, and a sense of control and competence are all critical aspects of the experience of enjoyment, and thus, it is these factors that must be understood and managed by the TRS if enjoyment is to be facilitated (see Figure 4.1).

There are some indications that individuals are inherently, even genetically, different in their ability to generate optimal experience, or flow-type enjoyment, for themselves (Kleiber & Dirkin, 1985). Csikszentmihalyi (1975) describes an **autotelic personality**, wherein the appropriation of self-generated, enjoyable action patterns seems to be most common. However, he adds that such patterns can be taught and environments arranged to make such experiences more common. While there are other agendas for TRSs, teaching people to generate optimal experience and establishing environments conducive to flow is especially important (Ellis, Witt, & Aguilar, 1983; Voelkl & Birkel, 1988). Creating conditions that enhance concentration, effort, and a sense of control and competence, while promoting freedom of choice and the expression of preference, is the engineering of enjoyment. However, to do this, it is necessary to understand the psychology of **self-determination** and the factors that interfere with it. The theories associated

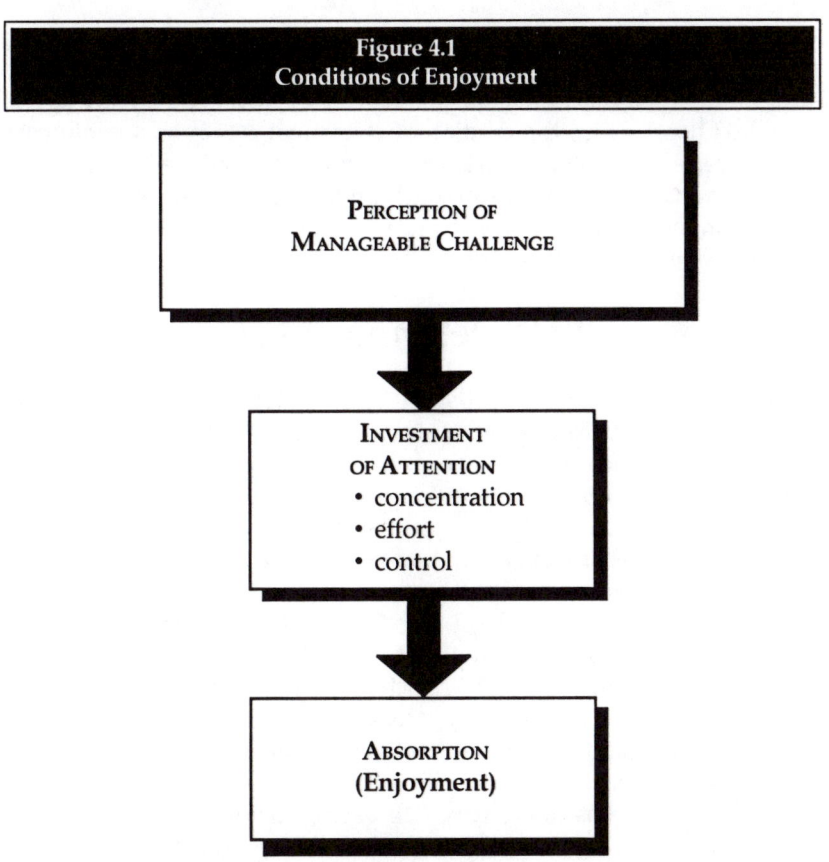

Figure 4.1
Conditions of Enjoyment

PERCEPTION OF
MANAGEABLE CHALLENGE

INVESTMENT
OF ATTENTION
• concentration
• effort
• control

ABSORPTION
(Enjoyment)

with self-determination, and the factors interfering with it, provide us with valuable information for developing strategies to enhance concentration, effort, and a sense of control and competence, thereby fostering enjoyment. Murray (1988, p. 156)[1] supported this approach when he asked and answered the following question:

> How can social policy facilitate human enjoyment if that enjoyment is intimately linked to the exercise of competence in the face of challenge? The immediately obvious and the unthreatening answer is that social policy must facilitate the acquisition of competence by all its citizens—an answer that, among other things, can be translated into a call for better educational programs so that people will become more competent.

---

1. Reprinted by permission of Simon & Schuster, Inc. from *In pursuit of happiness and good government*, by C. Murray (Copyright 1988 by Cox, & Murray, Inc.). New York, NY.

Also worth noting by way of introduction, is that while enjoyment is sufficient in itself, as the culmination of intervention and as an indicator of the acquisition of self-determination, it is also a *precipitating* experience as it is described here. Thus, the creation of enjoyment serves as a reinforcing experience, leading a person on to greater challenges and to higher levels of self-determination. As enjoyment comes under one's own power, it offers an orientation for making the most of one's circumstances, and enhancing the quality of one's life.

Self-Determination

In the early 20th century most psychologists believed that all motivation occurred in response to physiological needs (Deci & Ryan, 1985). However, by the 1950s, psychologists came to recognize various psychological factors as very influential in human motivation. One particular psychological factor, perceived control, received increasing attention from the 1960s to the present. This trend is based on the assumption that a sense of psychological well-being is augmented by a belief that one has some degree of control over personal events (Leary & Miller, 1986). For people receiving TR services, a sense of control is particularly important in establishing self-determination.

Deci (1980) asserted that self-determination involves the flexibility and ability to choose options and to adjust to situations when only one option is available. Cognition, affect, and motivation mediate self-determination. Limitations placed on an individual's self-determination result from environmental and unconscious forces. Self-determination reflects the interaction between freedom and constraint. When self-determination is achieved, increases in learning and perceptions of competence occur. Conversely, the experience of a lack of self-determination occurs when an individual fails to consider various options, or does not adjust to the situation when only one option is available.

Motivation and Perceived Causality

Individuals who are self-determining are internally motivated (Neulinger, 1981). If people believe in the relationship between their behavior and outcomes and understand that they are the initiators of behavior, they have **internal causality** (Deci, 1980), and feel responsible for the consequences of their actions. If people feel that events that affect them result generally from influences outside their control, they have **external causality**.

Automated behaviors are those that were initially within the realm of volitional responding or choice, but have since become controlled by some mechanized process. Behaviors become automated when they are "overlearned" through repetition (e.g., walking or driving a car). People who exhibit a predominance of automated behaviors are externally motivated and cease to feel responsible for such behavior. When individuals believe that a relationship exists between behavior and outcomes, but conclude that outcomes (e.g., chemical dependence and obesity) are the *cause* of behaviors (e.g., abuse of drugs and overeating) rather than the result of these behaviors, they have external causality. A kind of competency (e.g., ability to handle stress in a situation) may be perceived as a result of these "automated" behaviors. People abusing drugs or overeating may report that the activity relaxes them and relieves stress. However, Deci (1980) warns that:

> The capacity for mindless responding is an interesting double edged sword. On the one hand it is extraordinarily important, for it frees one's attention and will for new concerns. On the other hand, it also interferes with one's self-determination, for nonchosen behaviors may become rigid and difficult to change (p. 59).

There are some behaviors that cannot become self-determined. Behaviors that are fully determined by physical and physiological principles are motivated directly by environmental requirements (e.g., reflexes and instincts). When people exhibit these behaviors they are said to have impersonal causality (Deci, 1980, p. 128). Individuals possess impersonal causality if they believe that their responses and associated outcomes are independent. While impersonal causality is characteristic of reflexive behavior, when it is generalized to potentially controllable behaviors it becomes maladaptive. Perceptions of incompetence and helplessness occur among individuals with an impersonal causality, resulting in limited motivation to exhibit instrumental behavior. The perception of a person possessing impersonal causality was illustrated by an individual speaking to Deci: "I've lost the desire to make choices. I feel like I'll exist as long as my body holds out but I won't participate" (Deci, 1980, p. 128). Many TRSs have heard similar words from would-be participants when encouraging them to try to learn a new leisure skill or participate in a recreation activity.

Intrinsic Motivation

Deci and Ryan (1985) concluded that self-determination is associated with **intrinsic motivation**. Motivation that is intrinsic energizes behavior and results in feelings of autonomy. Performance of the behavior does not require external rewards or control. The experiences of interest, enjoyment, and excitement provide reinforcement for such behaviors. Once again, we recognize that these are the experiences most often associated with leisure, recreation, and the desired results of TR Interventions.

People who are intrinsically motivated will seek challenges that are commensurate with their competencies; they will avoid those situations that are too easy or too difficult. Intrinsic motivation is reflected in the process of seeking optimal incongruities within the environment and then reducing these incongruities. Individuals who are intrinsically motivated in certain situations are more likely to learn, adapt, and grow in competencies that characterize development. However, intrinsic motivation is vulnerable to influences from environmental forces.

Environmental Considerations

There is a continuous interaction between people's evaluation of the environment and their motivation. The environment can encourage self-determination by being responsive and informational, or the environment can discourage self-determination through controlling and capricious responses to behaviors. An environment is responsive and informational if it reacts to a person's initiatives, provides data about the person's competence, and encourages further action. A responsive and informational environment fosters intrinsic motivation and internal causality. The result of this is self-determined behavior. Similarly, events involving choice and positive feedback provide information to the person thereby enhancing self-determination. For example, Maughan and Ellis (1991) demonstrated that administration of praise and persuasion for performance accomplishments associated with a video game enhanced the efficacy judgments of adolescents residing at a private psychiatric hospital.

Although a controlling environment does not respond to people's initiatives, it does demand behaviors from individuals. When an environment directs and controls people, they often experience extrinsic motivation, external causality, and automatic behaviors. The presence of rewards, deadlines, and surveillance that pressures people toward specific outcomes tends to undermine intrinsic motivation, promote extrinsic compliance or defiance, and inhibit enjoyment. Deci and Ryan (1985) noted that:

> Research has substantiated that extrinsic rewards and controls can affect people's experience of self-determination. In such cases, the events will induce a shift in the perceived locus of causality from internal to external, a decrement in intrinsic motivation for the target behavior, less persistence at the activity in the absence of external contingencies, and less interest in and enjoyment of the activity. (p. 57)

Studies by Lepper and Greene (1978), among others, have demonstrated such effects. Typically, children are *playing* at some activity such as drawing and then experimenters offer to pay the children for these drawings. *Productivity* increases some while rewards are offered (the children draw more). However, when rewards are withdrawn, children show less interest in the activity than they did before the rewards were offered and less when children were not offered rewards at all. Referred to as the **over-justification effect,** such studies show that intrinsic motivation can be undermined by extrinsic rewards.

Some individuals experience environments that do not respond to their initiatives. As a result, outcomes are perceived to be unrelated to their behaviors. In this type of an environment, contingencies (the relationship between an action and associated consequences) are not clear and cannot be mastered by the individual. According to Deci (1980), capricious environments that contain negative feedback and noncontingencies tend to erode all forms of motivation, result in impersonal causality, and stifle instrumental behavior. For example, when TRSs provide nonspecific praise or criticism to people with disabilities as they attempt to learn a new leisure skill without regard to the effectiveness of their responses, TRSs will inhibit, rather than stimulate, learning and a desire to master the skill. Participants will have difficulty determining the efficacy of their actions when TRSs fail to provide them with specific informational feedback.

Individual Differences

Stable psychological orientations influence the ability to exhibit self-determining behaviors. People who have an orientation characterized by autonomy tend to select or interpret events as informational. For instance, a woman with a physical disability may attempt to paint using a newly constructed hand brace. If the person's orientation was characterized by autonomy, she may attribute praise for her improved art work to the adaptations she has made. In contrast, other people consistently select or interpret events as controlling their behaviors. These people believe the praise of another is required in order for them to continue painting. Rather than promoting self-determination, adoption of the latter orientation results in behavior perceived not to be within their control. In addition, people who have an impersonal orientation tend to experience situations as beyond their control. Often, they lack motivation to exhibit any behaviors. The question for researchers and TRSs alike, is: how resistant are such dispositions to change? While this question will be considered again shortly, the malleability of such "stable" characteristics has great implications for therapeutic recreation intervention and treatment.

In summary, self-determination is necessary for the optimal experience of enjoyment. It makes effort and the investment of attention worthwhile for a person, and these are the factors that bring about enjoyable involvement. This experience serves in turn to develop competence thereby reinforcing self-determination (see Figure 4.2, page 64). Having considered enjoyment and self-determination, we now turn our attention to those theories, reactance and learned helplessness, that establish the difficulties experienced by some individuals in achieving self-determination. These difficulties often result in the failure to experience enjoyment.

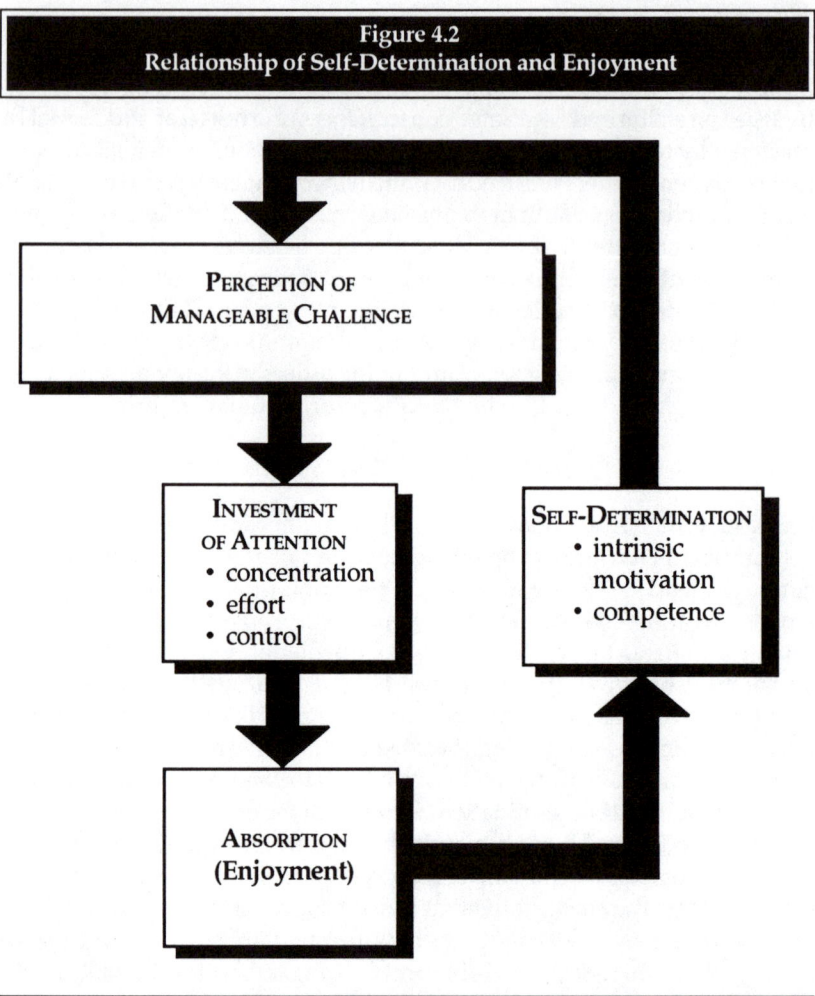

Figure 4.2
Relationship of Self-Determination and Enjoyment

PERCEPTION OF
MANAGEABLE CHALLENGE

INVESTMENT
OF ATTENTION
• concentration
• effort
• control

SELF-DETERMINATION
• intrinsic
  motivation
• competence

ABSORPTION
(Enjoyment)

Psychological Reactance and Learned Helplessness

Brehm (1977) asserted that the experience of **freedom** involves a set of behaviors that requires pertinent physical and psychological skills. In addition, individuals must have the knowledge and understanding to enable them to make a choice in order to experience freedom. Behaviors that are free include only those acts that are realistically possible for the individual.

According to Brehm, given a set of free behaviors, *reactance* will occur when any of these behaviors is eliminated or threatened with extinction. **Reactance** is a motivational state directed toward reestablishing free behaviors that are eliminated or threatened. The occurrence of psychological reactance increases the desirability of the eliminated or threatened behavior; that is, the behavior becomes more attractive to the individual. For instance, when a person is about to select one recreation activity from among several alternatives that are all attractive (e.g., swimming, dancing, and reading), elimination of one alternative (e.g., swimming) will result in that activity becoming more attractive and desirable.

A person who experiences reactance will be motivated to remove the threat to the free behavior or regain the lost free behavior. When reactance occurs there is an increased tendency to engage in the threatened free behavior, engage in behaviors that imply continued engagement in free behaviors, and encourage other people of similar abilities and status to engage in threatened or eliminated behaviors. For example, a person playing a basketball game is told by a TRS to stop yelling obscenities. The individual may continue or even accelerate the use of obscenities, may reduce the use of obscenities but increase physical aggression, or may encourage other players to use obscenities.

Magnitude of Reactance

The magnitude of reactance of a person is influenced by the degree of importance the person places on the free behavior that has been threatened or eliminated. Importance is a direct function of the person's perception of the unique value that the behavior has for satisfying the individual's needs. Uniqueness involves the degree to which no other behavior in the individual's repertoire could satisfy the same need.

The importance of the eliminated or threatened free behavior, compared to the importance of other free behaviors, also influences the magnitude of reactance. Therefore, existing opportunities available to an individual, at a specific time in a given situation, will influence the importance of the free behavior and, in turn, affect the magnitude of the person's reactance to the threat of elimination of the free behavior. The greater the proportion of free behaviors eliminated or threatened with elimination, the greater the magnitude of reactance. The proportion of free behaviors is influential in two ways: (a) the number of free behaviors presented to the individual, and (b) the number of behaviors eliminated or threatened. As the number of free behaviors available decreases and number of free behaviors eliminated or threatened increases the degree of psychological reactance will become greater.

Many individuals with disabilities have limited leisure repertoires resulting in few free behaviors. As a result, the elimination or threat of elimination of these free behaviors will initially produce reactance. As environmental conditions (e.g., architectural barriers or negative attitudes) limit free behaviors, people with disabilities will tend to experience reactance rather than enjoyment. However, if the environmental conditions that limit free behavior persist over time, individuals will eventually relinquish that freedom.

Relinquishing Freedom

When people expect to influence a certain outcome, but find their control and freedom jeopardized, initially they exert more effort to establish control (reactance). However, Wortman and Brehm (1975) reported that the perception of helplessness will occur if people become convinced that further attempts will not produce an outcome. Leary and Miller (1986) explained that people find it difficult to assess their ability to control a situation when they first encounter events that are troublesome for them to control. Often, people initially assume that the cause of difficulty is unstable and specific to the situation. Therefore, they increase their attempts to exert control. That is, they feel that their failure may be related to factors that could change the next time they try (e.g., the difficulty of the recreation activity, people associated with the activity, their luck, the amount of effort and concentration they expend). However, if they are still unable to gain control after repeated attempts to do so, they may begin to assume the outcome is uncontrollable and will experience helplessness.

A person will eventually relinquish the desire for freedom when reestablishment of freedom proves impossible. The length of time required for individuals to abdicate their belief that they have freedom to engage in the eliminated or threatened free behavior depends, in part, on the certainty of elimination. The more apparent the inability to experience the free behavior becomes, the more readily the person will give up that freedom. Given the unequivocal elimination of an important freedom, an initial demonstration of a sharp increase in the desire to engage in the eliminated behavior will occur (Wortman & Brehm, 1975). Eventual surrendering of freedom will follow. The surrendering is equivalent to the condition referred to as *learned helplessness*.

Learned Helplessness

Seligman and colleagues first used the phrase "learned helplessness" to describe responses of dogs to uncontrollable shock (Overmier & Seligman, 1967; Seligman & Maier, 1967). Following investigations with animals to test the theory, Seligman (1975) described **helplessness** as a psychological state that frequently results when events are uncontrollable. Events are uncontrollable when they are independent of a person's voluntary responses. Voluntary responses can be modified by reinforcement or punishment. That is, certain consequences of voluntary behavior will increase the likelihood of the occurrence of the behavior (reward) or decrease the likelihood of the behavior (punishment). Those behaviors that are not voluntary are identified as reflexes or instincts.

As individuals are exposed to uncontrollable events they begin to learn that responding is futile. This learning of helplessness reduces the incentive to respond which decreases the motivation for instrumental behavior. Learned helplessness undermines a person's motivation to respond, reduces the ability to learn that responding works, and results in emotional disturbance (e.g., depression or anxiety).

Human Helplessness

The original theory of learned helplessness was criticized because of its inability to distinguish between cases in which outcomes are uncontrollable for all people and cases in which they are uncontrollable only for some people. This original theory did not explain when helplessness is general, specific, chronic, or acute. In response to these criticisms and many experiments conducted in the 1970s that substantiated the presence of learned helplessness in humans (Hiroto, 1974; Hiroto & Seligman, 1975; Klein & Seligman, 1976), Abramson, Seligman, and Teasdale (1978) proposed a reformulated theory based on attribution literature. The theory, further articulated by Garber and Seligman (1980), recognized that once people perceive noncontingency (the absence of a relationship between a person's actions and the desired consequence), they attribute their helplessness to a cause. In other words, the person believes that no matter what he or she does he or she will be unable to achieve his or her goal.

Human helplessness is perceived at a level related to oneself and related to other people. When people expect outcomes not to be contingent on their own responses yet expect the outcome to be contingent on other's actions, personal helplessness is experienced. This personal helplessness results from failures that erode self-determination. Some people also may expect outcomes not to be contingent on their own responses; however, they may expect that outcomes are not contingent on other people's actions either. This form of helplessness is identified as universal helplessness and produces feelings of hopelessness. When people expect outcomes to be contingent on their own responses, regardless of whether they expect outcomes to be contingent on other's actions, they will not perceive themselves to be helpless. In each of the aforementioned situations the outcome expectancies are not absolute; rather, they are on a continuum ranging from the expectation that outcomes are totally noncontingent on one's responses to expectations of limited controllability.

Consequences of Helplessness

Learned helplessness may be revealed in a person's cognition, emotional level, and motivation. In reference to cognition, people who learn to be helpless will experience difficulty understanding that their responses produce outcomes. Consequently, they will have problems learning to take control of their lives. Learned helplessness also can be manifested at an emotional level. People who expect that outcomes are independent of their responses will tend to have depressed affect. Depression is likely when people perceive that they cannot control an outcome that is possible. As individuals attribute their negative outcomes to internal, stable, and global factors, and their positive outcomes to external, unstable, specific behaviors, they experience a reduction in self-esteem. Individuals' level of motivation can be directly influenced by a perception of helplessness. As individuals expect that their responding is futile, they will experience a reduction in their initiation of voluntary responses.

Typically, people with disabilities have less knowledge and fewer skills than their same-age peers. Consequently, they are afforded fewer opportunities to make choices and demonstrate self-initiated leisure participation (Dattilo, 1991). At times, the environment does not respond to their attempts to initiate leisure participation. Repeated futile experiences result in the perception that one is helpless. With the perception of helplessness comes an elimination of attempts to explore the environment. As exploration decreases, opportunities to experience enjoyment also decline.

Interaction of Failure and Helplessness

People respond to **failure** in different ways at different times. For some people (on some occasions) failure can result in escalated effort, intensified concentration, increased persistence, heightened sophistication of problem-solving strategies, and enhanced performance. When people respond in this way they are identified as having a mastery orientation. Other people (on other occasions) may respond to failure with curtailed effort, reduced concentration, decreased persistence, a deterioration of problem-solving strategies, and a disruption in performance. These responses are indications that a person has learned to be helpless.

The manner in which people react to failure is dependent on their perspective. If they assume a **mastery** orientation they may: (a) perceive their mistakes to be rectifiable; (b) view their failure as a result of a lack of effort; (c) look forward to the future; (d) emphasize the positive aspects of their failures; and/or (e) engage in active problem-solving (Dweck & Light, 1980). However, Dweck and Light stated that if people expect that they cannot control outcomes, then they may: (a) perceive that their mistakes are inevitable; (b) view their failure as a result of a lack of ability; (c) dwell on the present;

(d) focus on negative aspects of a situation; and (e) stop attempts at solving the problem associated with failure.

As previously stated, individuals with disabilities have an increased chance of experiencing reactance and, with repeated failure to produce an effect, perceptions of helplessness. The presence of these conditions decreases the ability of the individual to experience the self-determination necessary for enjoyment. Therefore, interventions employed by TR specialists that try to enhance self-determination are needed. Further, systematic scientific inquiry about the effects of such interventions is a critical component in the advancement of therapeutic recreation.

Implications for Applied Research in Therapeutic Recreation

Following from the preceding theoretical review, future research in TR might well address the following questions:

1. Can successful participation in prescribed recreation activities during intensive therapeutic recreation treatment lead to increases in self-determination in spite of disabling conditions, as has been argued elsewhere (see Lee & Mobily, 1988)?

2. To encourage self-determination and enjoyment, is it necessary for interventions to include one or more of the following procedures: (a) encouraging individuals to increase their awareness by attending to motives and emotions that were previously denied or ignored; (b) helping people to evaluate thoughts that are based on irrational assumptions and then reorient those thoughts to neutral or positive evaluations that reduce anxiety and discomfort; or (c) eliciting the belief that motives, emotions, and the environment are manageable and selection of goals are realistic? In addressing a related question, Zoerink (1988) examined the effects of a short-term leisure education program using values clarification upon the leisure functioning of adolescents and young adults with physical disabilities. The mixed findings that resulted may be due, in part, to a failure to distinguish the impact of various procedures.

3. What are the effects of programs that teach people to discriminate between aspects of the environment that are changeable and those that are not? To what extent can a person learn to maximize experience when the environment is not changeable? What is the best way to teach people with disabilities to reduce: (a) the aversiveness of unavoidable outcomes, and (b) the desirability of unobtainable outcomes?

4. What are the effects on self-determination and enjoyment when: (a) perceptions of competence are enhanced; (b) optimal challenges are provided; and (c) external control and pressures are minimized? What are the effects of a recreation environment that is free from such extrinsic rewards as trophies and prizes? Francis (1991, pp. 43-44)[2] recommended that TRSs choose intrinsically motivated activities to increase flow by following these steps: minimize extrinsic rewards or make such rewards intrinsic by internalizing them through personal choice and values clarification, encourage trust in personal choices, minimize focus on outcomes, and explore individual levels of enjoyment from various activities.

5. How can TRSs promote communication of leisure preferences by people with communication disorders (Guess, Benson, & Siegel-Causey, 1985)? Dattilo (1986; 1988) has begun to address this question by using a computerized assessment procedure to determine leisure preferences of persons with severe mental and physical disabilities. More recently, Dattilo and colleagues (Dattilo & Camarata, 1991; Dattilo & O'Keefe, 1992) taught adults with mental retardation and language deficits to initiate communication concerning their interests and desires via augmentative and alternative communication systems. Although findings appear promising, many questions associated with each intervention have yet to be answered.

6. What strategies can be developed for people who perceive themselves to be helpless (believing that outcomes are not within their control) that redirect their expectations of *uncontrollability* to *controllability*? For example, in response to an observation by Moss and Halamandaris (1977)[3] that "nursing homes virtually abolish privacy, stifle individuality, defy the values of order and discipline and enforce arbitrary and discretionary rules" (p. 22), Shary and Iso-Ahola (1989) demonstrated the positive effects of enhanced personal control, choice, and responsibility in leisure contexts on perceived competence and self-esteem of people residing in nursing homes. Similar approaches could be tried with people with different disabling conditions.

---

2. Reprinted with permission of the National Recreation and Park Association, Arlington, VA, *Therapeutic Recreation Journal.*

3. Reprinted from *Too old, too sick, too bad: Nursing homes in America*, by F. E. Moss and V. J. Halamandaris, p. 22, with permission of Aspen Publishers, Inc., © 1977. Germantown, MD.

7. Based on the premise that individuals' attributions of failure should be altered from being unrealistic to realistic, what are the effects on enjoyment of providing therapeutic interventions that instill more realistic attributions for failure? What are the effects when helping individuals with disabilities to: (a) recognize that in many situations failure should be attributed to external factors (e.g., task difficulty) as opposed to internal ones (e.g., ability); (b) view failure as an unstable outcome (e.g., the result of effort) that is not expected to occur in each situation rather than expecting failure to be a stable outcome (e.g., ability); and (c) attribute failure to specific situations (e.g., failure with the expert ski slope attempted last week) as opposed to generalizing failure more globally to themselves on their leisure lifestyle (e.g., failure with all sports)?

8. What are the effects on enjoyment when changing individuals' attributions of success to those that are self-enhancing? What are the effects on enjoyment when the TRS helps individuals with disabilities: (a) attribute success in many situations to internal factors (e.g., effort) rather than to external ones (e.g., luck); (b) view success as a rather stable characteristic (e.g., ability) rather than unstable (e.g., chance); and (c) recognize that success is not specific to a given circumstance (e.g., swimming) but is often more globally attributed to the way they manage their entire lives?

It is unfortunate that enjoyment and the processes that produce enjoyment (challenge, competency and autonomy) have been virtually ignored by individuals responsible for the development of social policy (Murray, 1988). Nevertheless, attempts to answer the aforementioned research questions promise to improve our understanding of the dynamics of enjoyment and self-determination in the lives of people with disabilities. The ability to provide more effective therapeutic recreation will inevitably follow research examining external and internal conditions that facilitate and impede enjoyment. It is also important to note that the aforementioned questions may be answered through: (a) a normative paradigm using a variety of quantitative methods (e.g., experimental, single subject or survey); (b) an interpretative or naturalistic paradigm employing various qualitative research methods (e.g., participant observation or in-depth interviewing); or (c) a combination of both paradigms to allow TRSs to gain in-depth understanding (McCormick, Scott, & Dattilo, 1991). However, TRSs should select a research design based on the research question they are trying to answer and the hypothesized effects of the treatment.

Ethical Obligations for Research in Therapeutic Recreation

One way to respond to the leisure needs of individuals with disabilities is for TRSs to be concerned with encouraging enjoyment for their constituents. To respond adequately to this challenge, TRSs have a responsibility to respect the rights and dignity of every individual they serve and set the stage for enjoyment by providing opportunities for people to enhance their perceptions of self-determination. Professionals not only have an obligation to provide such opportunities for individuals, but they must be committed to systematically investigating the effects of such attempts. Therapeutic recreation services and research should be designed while keeping the rights of the individuals being served in the forefront of our thinking.

References

Abramson, L., Seligman, M., & Teasdale, J. (1978). Learned helplessness in human: Critique and resolution. *Journal of Abnormal Psychology, 87,* 49-74.

Brehm, J. (1977). *A theory of psychological reactance.* New York, NY: Academic Press.

Csikszentmihalyi, M. (1975). *Beyond boredom and anxiety: The experience of play in work and games.* San Francisco, CA: Jossey-Bass.

Csikszentmihalyi, M. (1982). Toward a psychology of optimal experience. *Review of Personality and Social Psychology, 3,* 13-36.

Csikszentmihalyi, M. (1985a). Emergent motivation. In D. Kleiber, & M. Maehr (Eds.). *Motivation and adulthood.* Greenwich, CT: JAI Press.

Csikszentmihalyi, M. (1985b). Reflections on enjoyment. *Perspectives on Biology and Medicine, 28,* 489-497.

Csikszentmihalyi, M., & Csikszentmihalyi, I. (Eds.). (1990). *Optimal experience.* Cambridge, England: Cambridge University Press.

Csikszentmihalyi, M. (1990). Flow: *The psychology of optimal experience.* New York, NY: Harper & Row.

Dattilo, J. (1991). Recreation and leisure: A review of the literature and recommendations for future directions. In L. M. Meyer, C. A. Peck, & L. Brown (Eds.), *Critical issues in the lives of people with severe disabilities* (pp. 171-193). Baltimore, MD: Paul H. Brookes.

Dattilo, J. (1988). Assessing music preferences of persons with severe handicaps. *Therapeutic Recreation Journal, 22*(1), 12-23.

Dattilo, J. (1986). Computerized assessment of preferences for persons with severe handicaps. *Journal of Applied Behavior Analysis, 19*(4), 445-448.

Dattilo, J., & Barnett, L. (1985). Therapeutic recreation for individuals with severe handicaps: Implications of chosen participation. *Therapeutic Recreation Journal, 19*(3), 79-91.

Dattilo, J., & Camarata, S. (1991). Facilitating leisure involvement through self-initiated augmentative communication training. *Journal of Applied Behavior Analysis, 24,* 369-378.

Dattilo, J., & O'Keefe, B. M. (1992). Setting the stage for leisure: Encouraging adults with mental retardation who use augmentative and alternative communication systems to share conversations. *Therapeutic Recreation Journal, 26*(1), 27-37.

Deci, E. (1975). *Intrinsic motivation.* New York, NY: Academic Press.

Deci, E. (1980). *The psychology of self-determination.* Lexington, MA: Lexington Books.

Deci, E., & Ryan, W. (1985). *Intrinsic motivation and self-determination in human behavior.* New York, NY: Plenum Press.

Dweck, C. S., & Light, B. A. (1980). In J. Garber, & Seligman, M. (Eds.). *Human helplessness* (pp. 197-221). New York, NY: Academic Press.

Ellis, G. D., Witt, P. A., & Aguilar, T. (1983). Facilitating "flow" through therapeutic recreation services. *Therapeutic Recreation Journal, 17*(2), 6-15.

Francis, T. (1991). Revising therapeutic recreation for substance misuse: Incorporating flow technology in alternatives treatment. *Therapeutic Recreation Journal, 25*(2), 41-48.

Garber, J., & Seligman, M. (1980). *Human helplessness.* New York, NY: Academic Press.

Goodstein, L. (1985). Inmate adjustment to prison and the transition to community life. In R. M. Carter, D. Glaser, & L. T. Wilkins, (Eds.), *Correctional institutions* (3rd ed) (pp. 285-305). New York, NY: Harper & Row.

Guess, D., Benson, H. A., & Siegel-Causey, E. (1985). Concepts and issues related to choice-making and autonomy among persons with severe disabilities. *Journal of the Association for Persons With Severe Handicaps, 10*(2), 79-86.

Gunter, B. G. (1987). The leisure experience: Selected properties. *Journal of Leisure Research, 19*(2), 115-130.

Hiroto, D. (1974). Locus of control and learned helplessness. *Journal of Experimental Psychology, 102,* 187-193.

Hiroto, D., & Seligman, M. (1975). Generality of learned helplessness in man. *Journal of Personality and Social Psychology, 31,* 311-327.

Iso-Ahola, S. E. (1979). Some social psychological determinants of perceptions of leisure. *Leisure Sciences, 2,* 305-314.

Kelly, J. R. (1987). *Freedom to be: A new sociology of leisure.* New York, NY: Macmillan.

Kleiber, D., & Dirkin, G. (1985). Intrapersonal constraints to leisure. In M. Wade (Ed.), *Constraints on leisure* (pp. 17-42). Springfield, IL: Charles C. Thomas.

Klein, D., & Seligman, M. (1976). Reversal of performance deficits in learned helplessness and depression. *Journal of Abnormal Psychology, 85,* 11-26.

Leary, M., & Miller, R. (1986). *Social psychology and dysfunctional behavior: Origins,diagnosis, and treatment.* New York, NY: Springer-Verlag.

Lee, L. L., & Mobily, K. E. (1988). The NTRS philosophical position statement and a concept of three freedoms. *Journal of Expanding Horizons in Therapeutic Recreation, 3,* 41-52.

Lepper, M., & Greene, D. (1978). *The hidden costs of rewards.* Hillsdale, NJ: Lawrence Erlbaum Associates.

Maughan, M., & Ellis, G. D. (1991). Effect of efficacy information during recreation participation on efficacy judgements of depressed adolescents. *Therapeutic Recreation Journal, 25*(1), 50-59.

McCormick, B., Scott, D., & Dattilo, J. (1991). Answering questions about therapeutic recreation part I: Formulating research questions. *Annual in Therapeutic Recreation, 2*(1), 78-84.

Mobily, K. (1989). Meaning of recreation and leisure among adolescents. *Leisure Studies, 8*(1), 11-23.

Moss, F. E., & Halamandaris, V. J. (1977). *Too old, too sick, too bad: Nursing homes in America.* Germantown, MD: Aspen Systems Corporation, Department TL.

Murray, C. (1988). *In pursuit of happiness and good government.* New York, NY: Simon & Schuster.

Neulinger, J. (1981). *The psychology of leisure.* Springfield, IL: Charles C. Thomas.

Overmier, B., & Seligman, M. (1967). Effects of inescapable shock upon subsequent escape and avoidance learning. *Journal of Comparative and Physiological Psychology, 63,* 28-33.

Roadburg, A. (1983). Freedom and enjoyment: Disentangling perceived leisure. *Journal of Leisure Research, 15*(1), 15-26.

Savell, K. S. (1991). Leisure, perceptions of control and well-being: Implications for the institutionalized elderly. *Therapeutic Recreation Journal, 25*(3), 44-59.

Seligman, M. (1975). *Helplessness: On depression, development and death.* San Francisco, CA: Miller Freeman.

Seligman, M., & Maier, S. (1967). Failure to escape traumatic shock. *Journal of Experimental Psychology, 74,* 1-9.

Shary, J. M., & Iso-Ahola, S. E. (1989). Effects of a control-relevant intervention on nursing home residents' perceived competence and self-esteem. *Therapeutic Recreation Journal, 23*(1), 7-16.

Shaw, S. (1985). The meaning of leisure in everyday life. *Leisure Sciences*, 7(1), 1-24.

Shivers, J. (1981). *Leisure and recreation concepts: A critical analysis*. Boston, MA: Allyn, & Bacon.

Voelkl, J. E., & Birkel, R. C. (1988). Application of the experience sampling method to assess clients' daily experiences. *Therapeutic Recreation Journal*, 22(3), 23-33.

Wortman, C., & Brehm, J. (1975). Responses to uncontrollable outcomes: An integration of reactance theory and the learned helplessness model. In L. Berkowitz (Ed.), *Advances in experimental social psychology*, (Vol. 8). New York, NY: Academic Press.

Zoerink, D. A. (1988). Effects of a short-term leisure education program upon the leisure functioning of young people with spina bifida. *Therapeutic Recreation Journal*, 22(3), 44-52.

Collaborative Research: Bridging the Gap Between Practitioners and Researchers/Educators

Keith S. Savell, Ann D. Huston, and Marjorie J. Malkin

Throughout the therapeutic recreation profession practitioners and researchers alike are often overheard discussing the lack of scientific evidence to support the efficacy of therapeutic recreation. As budgetary, staffing, third party reimbursement, and other professional issues become more critical, the cry for research supporting the need for the delivery of therapeutic recreation becomes even louder. Ellis (1989) suggests that as demands for professional accountability increase, pressures mount for answers to difficult questions concerning the benefits of TR. Ellis states that for the first time, the profession is being required to examine seriously its processes and outcomes.

> Clients, third party payers and the growing health care industry [become] acutely aware of the loosely defined benefits and random hodgepodge of therapeutic recreation interventions. What specifically, [is] being purchased by health care dollars spent on therapeutic recreation? What benefits [are] being obtained, and how efficient [is] therapeutic recreation as a process for obtaining those benefits? (1989, p. 110)

Knight and Johnson (1991) similarly suggest that the profession must examine closely its outcomes and the processes necessary to achieve these outcomes consistently and predictably. While these writers urge members of the profession to aggressively pursue the development of therapeutic recreation protocols, they also state that the development of such therapeutic or leisure education protocols must be based upon sound scientific research.

Indeed, Compton states that "determining the efficacy of our treatment has become the paramount issue facing our discipline" (1989, p. 490). Compton also notes the importance of a clinical focus in professional preparation and continuing education programs based upon treatment protocols. He indicates that TRSs need collective efforts in order to be recognized in the health care arena.

While the profession of therapeutic recreation has recognized the significance of research for professional growth and vitality (Aguilar, 1987; Austin, 1982; Austin & Kennedy, 1982; Bullock, McGuire, & Barch, 1984; Compton, 1984, 1989; Ellis, 1989; Iso-Ahola, 1988; Reynolds, 1982; Witt, 1988a, 1988b), many of its membership have avoided research for a variety of reasons. Indeed, despite the acknowledged centrality of research to the future of the profession, there has been remarkably little enthusiasm among practitioners to participate in or use research

In an effort to identify perceived barriers to practitioner initiated research, Bullock, McGuire, and Barch (1984) found that lack of time, adequate training, administrative support, and motivation, as well as cost of conducting research were the most restrictive factors. However, these practitioners did indicate that while conducting research and working cooperatively with researchers was important, it was less important than keeping up to date with research, and incorporating research findings into their jobs.

Witt purports that the primary barriers to therapeutic recreation research were related to a lack of professional awareness of the importance of research, as well as the implications of inadequate professional preparation at all levels of education:

> One of the major inhibitors to research involving special populations is the lack of a clear understanding on the part of both practitioners and academics of the value and necessity of undertaking research. Coupled with the failure to impress on students and practitioners the value of research is the failure of curricula to include adequate educational experiences in research methods and statistics (Aguilar, et al., 1987). As a result, both educators and practitioners end up perceiving that they lack the skills to successfully undertake or apply available research. Lack of perceived competence can lead to feelings of 'helplessness' with regard to research. This in turn leads to a lack of support for research undertakings and ultimately a lack of support for educational processes aimed at upgrading skills to both undertake and consume research. (1988a, pp. 132-133)

Researcher/Practitioner Gap

The very terms "researcher" and "practitioner" imply a dichotomy and have in the past contributed to the perception of a "researcher/practitioner gap." In order to narrow or eliminate this gap, this textbook uses the term "investigative TRS" or "investigator" to ensure that it is clear that professionals in all roles (educator, student, practitioner, administrator, consultant, or "researcher") can be empowered and taught to conduct scientific investigations in the field of therapeutic recreation. However, for clarity and differentiation of roles, the terms must be used in this chapter in their historical context. Researcher has generally meant academician, educator, or student. None the less, the profession is urged to adopt a less divisive term such as investigator to describe this role in the future.

Reynolds and O'Morrow (1985) asked readers of their text whether such a researcher/practitioner gap exists. Furthermore, they stated that university personnel appear to predominate in conducting TR research, as well as question whether this is appropriate and beneficial to the profession.

Many issues have been discussed in the literature regarding the causes of this perceived gap, and many solutions have been proposed. The literature is briefly reviewed below in the areas of the value and importance of research, theoretical basis for research, education/professional preparation, cooperation with field settings, publications, and funding.

Value and Importance of Research

Witt (1988b, p. 18), believes that the "failure to socialize educators and practitioners about needed research skills and (the) value of research" is a major inhibitor to research in TR. Earlier Witt (1984) indicated that there were differences in the perceptions of practitioners and researchers as to what to research, and the importance of various types of research questions. Mobley (1980) notes the common feeling that researchers' findings are of little value to practitioners. He states that research is most relevant when it "builds upon and involves the people directly affected" (p. 41). Related fields have similar concerns. In the field of physical education (PE) Rothstein (1990) indicates that the effect of research and theory upon PE practice has been minimal. The major problem in application is the "lack of vision in establishing a framework for application" (p. 39). Phillips (1980) analyzes research in education, and indicates that social science researchers are themselves somewhat skeptical about the discovery of long-lasting generalizations.

Theoretical Basis for Research

In terms of a theoretical basis for research, Tinsley (1984, cited in Kunstler, 1985) and Iso-Ahola (1986) stress the importance of establishing and clarifying a theoretical basis in the design and implementation of research projects. McCormick, Scott, and Dattilo (1991) state that anxiety about conducting research may be due to a lack of knowledge concerning the theoretical perspective underlying research and about research principles and methods.

Educational/Professional Preparation

Lack of sufficient educational preparation (or continuing education) in both research methods and statistical techniques is cited throughout the literature. Compton (1989, citing earlier works by himself, Witt and Iso-Ahola) indicates the need for training in research related subjects. He alerts the profession to the diminishing quality and number of doctoral programs and students. This will have crucial implications for the future of research in TR. Mobley (1978), Ewart (1986), and Iso-Ahola (1986) also emphasize the need to improve in the level of student research skills.

Kunstler and Kennedy stress that students can play a key role in cooperative research. Academic preparation must enable students to participate competently in the research process. These authors, echoing many voices in the field, note the crucial importance of the research process. "Ultimately, the survival of the therapeutic recreation profession may rest with each professional's motivation to join in demonstrating the efficacy of therapeutic recreation services" (1992, p. 51).

Cooperation With Field Settings

Mobley (1980) emphasizes the need to improve communication patterns between researchers and practitioners. The practitioners need to communicate about perceived research problems, while the researcher must clearly interpret and apply the results of research projects. Practitioners may be excessively concerned with immediate practical relevance and unaware that basic research may yield practical knowledge later on, according to Iso-Ahola (1986). He suggests however, as does Compton (1989), that agencies wanting practical knowledge team up with university researchers. Ewart (1986), referring to educational research, suggests that researchers and practitioners occasionally trade places, in order to understand better the problems faced by the other. He urges strengthening the information exchange between these groups to increase support for and understanding of research. Such suggestions are well taken in regard to TR. Readers are referred to Chapter 11 by Coyle, Kinney and Shank for a discussion of field trials in TR research and researcher/practitioner cooperation in field settings.

Publications

Research journals are frequently criticized as being difficult to understand, esoteric, and reporting results of little immediate practical import to the practitioner. Compton calls for "publications that link research findings to practice" (1989, p. 435). This focus upon dissemination and application of research results for practitioners is also indicated by the American Alliance for Health, Physical Education, Recreation and Dance (AAHPERD) Research Consortium's *Research for the Practitioner Committee* and related publications (Rothstein, 1990). Witt (1984) discusses such a publication in another recreation field, that of recreation administration. *The Journal of Park and Recreation Administration* was founded in 1983 to provide an outlet for research "aimed directly at practice or at least written in such a manner that the implications for practice are more discernible" (p. 60). Finally, Mobley (1980) called for new publications to bridge the researcher/practitioner gap. Within the field of TR, one such publication is aimed at explicating and applying results of research to the TR practitioner. This journal is *Research into Action*, published by the University of Illinois at Urbana-Champaign. The American Therapeutic Recreation Association also publishes a journal entitled the *Annual in Therapeutic Recreation*.

Funding

Difficulties in securing financial support for collaborative research may be a barrier. Compton (1989) states that professionals need actively to seek federal support for both research and training in TR, especially for efficacy research. Ewart (1986) suggests an innovative solution to the lack of funding. He proposes that agencies "adopt a researcher" (p. 49). In this way academicians/researchers can access research problems and participants, and practitioners can have more involvement/control over the research process. Ewart suggests that the costs involved in such collaborative projects can be minimal.

One Solution: Collaborative/Cooperative Research

Given the identified barriers to practitioner-initiated research, perhaps the most advantageous approach to research within the profession is a collaborative or cooperative approach which capitalizes upon the abilities and resources of both the therapeutic recreation practitioner and the therapeutic recreation researcher (Halberg, 1992; Kunstler & Kennedy, 1992; Savell & Huston, 1990). To facilitate this process, an increasing number of sessions are being offered at national and regional conferences to encourage practitioner/researcher collaboration, to increase knowledge about research design and methodology, and to assist investigators in writing up and reporting such research findings (Kunstler, 1985).

Such collaborative research approaches might combine the research ideas of the practitioner (who often has his or her finger on the pulse of changes both within the health care system and in terms of client needs), with the resources of the practitioner (the agency in which to conduct the study, and respondents within a "natural" setting). Such approaches would use the knowledge and abilities of the TR researcher in regard to research methodology, as well as provide access to computer based resources for the analysis of data, and support services for the development of research proposals for the procurement of research monies.

Models for researcher/practitioner collaboration may be viewed as being on a continuum, which ranges from the traditional researcher/educator dominated model, through the cooperative model explicated by Kennedy and Kunstler (1992), to the practitioner initiated model (Savell & Huston, 1991) which is an applied model described in detail below.

In contrast to the traditional model in which educators/researchers have predominated in both initiating and carrying out research studies, Kunstler and Kennedy (1992) have explicated a **cooperative research model** for conducting efficacy research. These authors stress cooperation between educators and practitioners, and the need for efficacy research to take place in real-world clinical or community settings.

The Kunstler model is theoretical, and as they indicate, such a model is two-dimensional and a simplification of a complex process. Their model involves the shared responsibility of both research partners in some aspects of the research, while each partner is solely responsible for other aspects. Within this process, the practitioner identifies the problem to be investigated, and the educator proceeds to conceptualize the problem and identify independent and dependent variables. The partners jointly select research methods and techniques. The practitioner implements the research project, the educator analyzes the data, and finally, both partners are responsible for disseminating results from the study.

The Collaborative Research Model developed by Savell and Huston (1990) is based upon and capitalizes on the unique contributions which both practitioners and researchers make to the research process. Through such a model, the abilities and resources of practitioners and researchers are optimized, and each group comes to perceive the centrality and interdependence of its own, as well as the other's role. It is a functional model in which the experience, enthusiasm, motivation, resources, expertise, and support of both the practitioner and researcher enable the initiation and successful completion of a scientific study. Moreover, by sharing the work of the investigation, the collaborative process greatly enhances the potential for a successful, satisfying, and (dare we say), fun research relationship!

The Collaborative Research Model

The **Collaborative Research Model** (Savell & Huston, 1990) is one in which the research study is initiated by the practitioner. This model involves a nine-stage process, and involvement of the educator or researcher may not begin until stage 5. Such a model involves progressive stages, which enable the systematic and comprehensive evolution of the research project from conception to completion. Specifically, the nine stages of the collaborative research model which guide the practitioner through the research process are detailed in Figure 5.1, page 84. Some of these nine stages, as discussed below, are *practitioner driven*. That is, the practitioner is responsible for the coordination and implementation of certain stages. In the parts that are "researcher driven," the researcher is responsible for the coordination and implementation of certain stages. When "practitioner/researcher driven," both the practitioner and the researcher are responsible for the implementation of certain stages.

Figure 5.1
The Collaborative Research Model

Stage 1. Problem Formulation —identify the topic/issue/concern/need

Stage 2. Review of existing, relevant literature

Stage 3. Hypotheses/Research Question Development-based upon your interest and the review of the literature

Stage 4. Variable Definition—define the variables you are interested in researching and operationalize the independent and dependent variables

Stage 5. Collaborative Relationship—with agency researcher and/or with university TR researcher

Stage 6. Research Design—identify the research design and the associated data collection and analysis procedures

Stage 7. Implementation—implement the study

Stage 8. Data Analysis & Interpretation—best conducted by agency or university researcher with access to computer resources

Stage 9. Dissemination of Results—involves both the dissemination of findings and implications for service delivery

Stage 1:
Problem Formulation

The first stage is one which is frequently already accomplished by the practitioner by the time that he or she decides to pursue a research project. Since the purpose of this stage is to identify the specific topic of interest, most practitioners have already begun by posing such questions as: How do I prioritize client/patient needs? How do I know what will work with this specific diagnosis or symptom? What outcome do I seek? How do I know that what I did helped to improve the client's/patient's condition . . . or was it another practitioner's intervention? How might I communicate more effectively with my clients/patients? How do I prove to my health care colleagues that what I am doing is of significant value within the treatment team?

It is important that the topic of interest be as clearly defined as possible in order to make the project manageable. The more specifically the topic is defined, and the more clearly the *parameters* of the topic of interest are presented, the better. This process may involve formal or informal discussions with other therapeutic recreation professionals or treatment team members concerning the area of interest. Moreover, if the research project involves several professional disciplines, it is very important to arrive at some level of consensus as to the specific topic of interest. At this point it is not essential to focus on the exact nature or mechanics of the study, since this will occur at a later stage of the collaborative process.

Throughout this stage, remember that the single most difficult aspect of research is not testing a significant hypothesis, but rather, finding a significant hypothesis worth testing.

Stage 2:
Review of the Literature

The second stage of the collaborative research process is also completed by the practitioner. This involves a review of available literature in order to further explore and identify specific elements of the topic of interest. The review of the literature will identify what is already known about the topic, theories or concepts that the practitioner is interested in, thereby providing further focus to his or her understanding of the issue. The review of the literature is also important since it will document the need for the study. Such substantiating documentation will be invaluable in obtaining administrative support for the study.

The review of the literature may be completed by the practitioner by using a variety of resources available in most agency or community settings. Within the literature review, the practitioner should attempt to obtain as thorough an understanding of the topic of interest as possible. This usually involves beginning with a broad conceptual understanding, and then progressively narrowing the focus of inquiry to more specific elements. A well designed research project will be based upon a sound conceptual or theoretical basis. Review of relevant concepts and theories is an essential initial component to any literature search. Such a theoretical basis must be determined and stated clearly before formulating any research questions or hypotheses. The review process typically involves the identification of "key words" related to the topic of interest and completion of a comprehensive review of the literature.

To illustrate, in a study of the relationship between leisure, perceived control, and well-being among the institutionalized elderly, the practitioner may identify the following "key words": leisure, life satisfaction, physiological well-being, psychological well-being, subjective well-being, perceived control, self-determination, and aging (Savell, 1991). A comprehensive review might include literature within the fields of therapeutic recreation, motivational psychology, behavioral psychology, and gerontology. Computer-based searches of the literature may then be conducted to locate available titles and abstracts within these professional fields. The practitioner would examine the obtained literature, typically beginning with the most recent work, and working backwards chronologically. Working backwards enables the reader to "glean out" the important older studies, those which are most frequently referenced within the more recent literature, without having to read all of the older literature. Having obtained a broad understanding of the topic of interest, the practitioner is now prepared to begin to *narrow* the field of review to the specific topic of interest.

Returning to the example above, the practitioner as investigative TRS would now focus on only the literature addressing the relationship between leisure, perceived control, well-being, and the institutionalized elderly. The practitioner should first explore resources within the agency by discussing the topic with the agency's library services. Should the agency library not have the required reference material or documentation, in-house library services are often able to conduct data-based searches and system-wide searches of other agency libraries. They are then able to obtain the material through inter-library loan.

The local community library provides a second source which may also have the capacity to complete a variety of computer and data-based searches. A medical school with available/accessible library services will prove to be a strong resource to the practitioner conducting a review of the literature.

Area community colleges and universities, as well as one's own *alma mater*, provide excellent resources for the review of the literature. Academic libraries may, in fact, prove to be the most revealing and important sources of information for the practitioner conducting a literature review.

It is important for the practitioner to recognize that each and every one of the resources is accessible whether or not one is a community resident or student at a college/university. These are public facilities, and access to them is open. The only restriction is that while resources may be read and/or photocopied by anyone, they may not necessarily be checked out by anyone.

There are, however, two potential barriers to a practitioner in completing a literature review. First, there may be an expense associated with some (but not all) computer-based literature reviews. The practitioner's agency should be able to provide the financial resources necessary to complete such projects. However, if the agency is unable/unwilling to provide the necessary funding, the local therapeutic recreation support network as well as state and/or national professional organizations may be able to complete (or fund) the review of the literature. Resources are available to assist with the review of the literature, providing one is willing to pursue them.

The second barrier concerns the support available from colleagues, supervisors, and administrators needed to complete the (sometimes) time-consuming process of research. Time spent away from direct therapeutic recreation practice must be justified in terms of the value of the study to the department, to patients/clients and to the practitioner's own professional development. The practitioner must ensure that these support systems are willing to commit to making available the time and resources necessary for the successful completion of such a project. It should be noted, given the need for research in therapeutic recreation, and the "support" inherent in the collaborative research process, that obtaining such support from peers, supervisors and administrators is often possible (see Chapter 11 for continued discussion of these issues).

Stage 3:
Hypotheses/Research Question Development

Through the completion of the review of the literature, the practitioner develops a thorough understanding of the topic of interest. At Stage 3, he or she should attempt to explicitly define the exact issue(s) or question(s) to be addressed through the study. It may be helpful to identify: (a) what the specific purpose of the study is, (b) what the sub-problems are, and (c) to complete the following statement: "The purpose of this investigation is to ...." It is also important that the practitioner states what the anticipated outcomes of the study are; that is, he or she offers an educated guess as to the findings the study. In short, the answers to these questions and statements represent the **hypotheses** and **research questions** to be addressed through the research project.

This third stage is crucial to the rest of the project. It requires that the practitioner formulate a clearly defined hypothesis or question that is based upon the interest or need (Stage 1), and the review of the literature (Stage 2). It cannot be emphasized strongly enough that the practitioner should attempt to define the hypotheses or research question in terms which are as specific as possible. This level of clarity will greatly enhance the communication between the practitioner and the researcher concerning exactly what the study is to accomplish.

Stage 4:
Define the Variables of Interest

Once a hypothesis or researchable question has been formulated, it is time to define the research variables. These variables explicitly identify the exact phenomenon to be studied (**independent** and **dependent variables**). In a classic experiment, all variables are controlled except the one being researched. This variable is manipulated (the independent variable) and the effect upon the variable under observation (the dependent variable) is examined (Minium, 1978). The other variables are the measures or outcomes to be observed or recorded which reflect changes in the phenomenon, and other unrelated factors (**exogenous variables**) which might occur during the study thus interfering with the eventual understanding of the phenomenon. These variables allow the practitioner to operationally define the phenomenon under investigation, the manner in which specific characteristics of the phenomenon will be measured, and those extraneous factors which might interfere with the understanding of the phenomenon. The practitioner will have gleaned this information from the preceding review of the literature as well as from informal initial collaborative discussions with the researcher.

To illustrate, consider an investigation of the efficacy of a specific TR protocol. In this example, the practitioner is interested in validating the therapeutic potential of a leisure-efficacy based intervention in the recovery of males who are chemically dependent (Robbins-Sisco & Savell, 1991). Here, the independent variable would be the leisure-efficacy intervention. The dependent variables would be measures of leisure-efficacy and recidivism. Exogenous variables in this particular study might include length of hospitalization, number of previous admissions, and access to community support services post discharge.

It is helpful at this point to introduce briefly the differences between **experimental** and **descriptive research designs**. Experimental designs are elaborated upon in Chapter 11. Within experimental investigations, the investigator typically observes the influence of one variable (independent variable) upon another (dependent variable). Within such studies both independent and dependent variables are required in order to effectively test and measure the prestated hypotheses (which states the nature of the relationship between the two variables).

This is not the case with descriptive investigations. Within these studies, no independent variable exists. Rather, the investigator develops a research question or series of research questions regarding the nature of a given phenomenon or the relationship between two or more phenomena. In these instances, the dependent variable(s) must be identified, but since there is no manipulation, there is no independent variable. In both experimental and descriptive research, extraneous or exogenous variables must still be identified.

Stage 5:
Develop the Collaborative Relationship

Having identified the variables, it is now time to formally develop the collaborative relationship. (If the practitioner experiences difficulty in successfully carrying out any of the previous stages (1-4), he or she is urged to consult with or involve an educator or researcher at an earlier stage). The most appropriate collaborators would be those researchers who have expertise in therapeutic recreation, research methodology, and who have access to research resources such as libraries, computers, statistical software, research assistants, and research monies. As discussed previously, collaborators with such resources may be found within the agency (research department, psychologists, research physicians, etc.). In the absence of "in house" resources, however, it would be necessary for the practitioner to approach an external researcher. Most likely, this would be someone within the academic environment. Specifically, the practitioner might contact: the therapeutic recreation educator at the nearest major university, a professor from his or her own *alma mater*, or a therapeutic recreation researcher with research interests similar to the practitioner's own (identified through the review of the literature).

Regardless of the source, most university-based researchers are quite receptive to collaborative research endeavors. Indeed, university-based researchers must be actively engaged in ongoing programs of research to meet the demanding requirements of promotion, tenure, and merit. It is strongly encouraged, however, that both the research and the practitioner clearly agree at the onset to a commitment of time, energy, and resources to the project. There is little else which is more frustrating—for either practitioners or researchers, than to be involved in a project which is begun with great enthusiasm, but which dies a slow death due to lack of time, energy, or commitment later on.

Stage 6:
Develop the Specific Research Design

The specific research design is developed at this stage. Here, the mechanics or "workings" of the study are clearly determined including: (a) the identification of the research participants; (b) the process for respondent selection; (c) the description of the intervention (if there is one); (d) the description of the psychometric measurement instrument, behavioral measures, etc., to be used to represent measures of the dependent variable; (e) data collection procedures; and (f) data analysis procedures.

The specific research design to be employed depends upon the nature of the questions to be answered or hypotheses to be tested. Depending on whether the practitioner is concerned with treatment efficacy, attitudinal measurement, or behavioral implications of a particular illness or disabling condition, the specific research design will vary. At this point it becomes the responsibility of the researcher to review the preliminary stages. In particular, the relevant literature must be reviewed in order to determine the appropriateness of the theoretical basis and research questions or hypotheses proposed by the practitioner. True collaboration and discussion are crucial at this juncture. The researcher's expertise in research design is of the utmost importance in order to ensure a valid, reliable, and meaningful research study. Furthermore, the researcher will specify the particular statistical processes to be used to interpret the obtained information.

Finalizing the research design itself is very much a collaborative endeavor, as noted above. Here, the practitioner and researcher must work closely in order to develop an investigation using the most appropriate methodology while taking into consideration the realities of resource availability and agency constraints. To facilitate this process, it is important that the practitioner is able to clearly and specifically define the hypotheses or research question(s) to be investigated. Second, the practitioner must be able to identify clearly and comprehensively the environment within which the investigation will take place. Third, the researcher must be able to identify (in consideration of these resources and constraints) those research designs most appropriate for testing the particular hypotheses or research question(s). Through collaborative dialogue, identification of the "best" methodological approach is eminently possible.

From this point on, Stage 6 involves: the development of the methodology for the investigation; the identification and/or development of appropriate assessment or measurement instruments for measuring changes in (or levels of) the dependent variable(s); and the specific statistical processes which will enable analysis of the data.

Stage 7:
Implementing the Collaborative Research Project

Implementing a collaborative research project is relatively painless once the methodology has been developed. From this point on, the procedure resembles completing a model airplane or assembling a child's swing set. That is, the actual process of research is very rule and procedure bound, requiring following clearly defined research processes and established procedural guidelines. These have been specified within Stage 6, the Research Design. However, a note of caution is in order. Ideally, all will proceed smoothly. Real life, however, is often far from *ideal*. It is simplistic to view the research process as tidy and formulaic. Researchers often have to respond to problems in the process of implementing a research study and make midstream adaptations. Of course all such modifications must be subsequently reported. (For further discussion of issues surrounding the implementation of field-studies in TR readers are referred to Chapter 11.)

As an applied collaborative process, implementation of the investigation will utilize the resources of both the practitioner and the researcher. For example, the practitioner might provide *on site* resources including staff, research participants and a laboratory or environment in which to conduct the investigation, while the researcher might provide research assistants for the implementation of the investigation and/or the collection of the data. In addition, the researcher would most likely provide training and monitoring of the procedural accuracy of the investigation for the agency staff and research assistants—those involved in actually conducting the study. This is very important, since the procedural guidelines developed by the researcher and the practitioner must be closely adhered to in order to protect the integrity of the investigation.

Stage 8:
Data Analysis and Interpretation

Data analysis is most typically conducted by the researcher since this involves specialized knowledge and costly computer-based resources. This is not to say, however, that the practitioner is not capable of conducting data analysis, or that she or he should/could not be involved in the process. Indeed, within the ideal collaborative relationship the practitioner would be closely involved in the data analysis process, thereby developing advanced abilities, as well as providing valuable assistance to the researcher.

While the data analysis procedure may at first appear to involve incomprehensible statistical manipulations, it is, in reality, neither mystical nor excessively complicated. Certainly, in today's time of computer applications, most of the difficulties in using and interpreting statistics are virtually removed from the process through "user friendly" statistical programs.

Stage 9:
Dissemination of Results

The dissemination of completed research results is a challenge. One of the most critical issues facing therapeutic recreation today is the absence of published research findings. This is not to say that quality research is not being conducted. Rather, in many instances this research, once completed, is not broadly disseminated through appropriate channels such as conference presentations and/or publication in refereed journals. The problem therefore, is not necessarily the lack of ongoing research, but that practitioners, researchers, and (in many cases) students, are not presenting or publishing the findings of their completed research projects.

Dissemination of information may be accomplished through several media. First, research findings may be presented at state, regional, and/or national research symposia held in conjunction with professional conferences. These symposia are attended by interested colleagues and often include publication of research abstracts. Second, results of investigations may be submitted for publication through one of several therapeutic recreation journals. The *Therapeutic Recreation Journal* and the *Annual in Therapeutic Recreation* are two such refereed journals which review submitted articles for quality and appropriateness. Review of the article by a panel of experts and subsequent revisions by the author (based on the suggestions of the panel) further enhance the quality of the publication. Regional publications are available in many parts of the country through state professional associations or regional TR symposia (cf. *Expanding Horizons in Therapeutic Recreation*, associated with the Midwest Symposium on TR).

A final comment on the dissemination of the results of research investigations is necessary. As is the case with clinical documentation— "unless it has been documented, it has not happened!" The importance of this cannot be overstated. Certainly, the results of research investigations are of little use to the profession of therapeutic recreation unless made available to colleagues. Once again, it is the responsibility of all investigators (practitioners and researchers) to ensure that their findings are shared with the broadest audience possible. Publication in the literature of related disciplines, such as allied health, special education, experiential education, counseling, rehabilitation, medicine, psychology, and health education, is strongly urged!

Conclusion

The collaborative research model presented in this chapter represents a working (and workable) approach to research within the profession of therapeutic recreation. Such an approach to research capitalizes upon the resources, knowledge, and abilities of both practitioners and researchers. Through the active employment of such a collaborative model, the process of research becomes less intimidating, more meaningful, manageable, and perhaps, even enjoyable!

Discussion Questions

1. What are the pros and cons of a Collaborative Research Model? Can both practitioners and researchers function within this model on a truly equal basis?
2. What are the greatest perceived barriers to practitioners in carrying out Stages 1-4 of the Collaborative Research Model? What are some solutions to these perceived problems?
3. As an exercise, plan a time line for a proposed specific research study. Which steps or stages do you plan to be initiated by the *practitioner*, which by the *researcher*, and which will be a joint responsibility?

References

Aguilar, T. (1988). Effects of leisure education programs: Expressed attitudes of delinquent adolescents. *Therapeutic Recreation Journal, 21*(4), 43-51.

Austin, D. R., & Kennedy, D. W. (1982). Sources of articles published in the Therapeutic Recreation Journal during the 1970's. *Therapeutic Recreation Journal, 16*(3), 35-41.

Bullock, C. C., McGuire, F. M., & Barch, E. M. (1984). Perceived research needs therapeutic recreators. *Therapeutic Recreation Journal, 18*(3), 17-24.

Compton, D. M. (1989). Epilogue: On shaping a future for therapeutic recreation. In D. M. Compton (Ed.) *Issues in therapeutic recreation: A profession in transition* (pp. 484-500). Champaign, IL: Sagamore.

Compton, D. M. (1984). Research procedures in recreation for special populations. *Therapeutic Recreation Journal, 18*(1), 9-17.

Ellis, G. D. (1989). The role of science in therapeutic recreation. In D. M. Compton (Ed.) *Issues in therapeutic recreation: A profession in transition* (pp. 109-123). Champaign, IL; Sagamore.

Ewart, A. (1986, March). What research doesn't tell the practitioner. *Parks & Recreation*, pp. 46-49.

Halberg, K. (1992). Research for the practitioner (Prove it—therapeutic recreation makes a difference). In R. Winslow and K. Halberg (Eds.) *The Management of therapeutic recreation services*. Arlington, VA: National Recreation and Parks Association (pp. 177-195).

Iso-Ahola, S. E. (1986) Editor's note; Concerns and thoughts about leisure research. *Journal of Leisure Research, 18*(3), iv-x.

Iso-Ahola, S. E. (1988). Research in therapeutic recreation. *Therapeutic Recreation Journal, 22*(1), 7-13.

Knight, L., & Johnson, D. (1991). Therapeutic recreation protocols: Client problem centered approach. In B. Riley (Ed.) *Quality Management Applications for therapeutic recreation* (pp. 137-47) State College, PA: Venture.

Kunstler, R. (Ed.). (1985, January). Research Update. *Parks & Recreation*, p. 24, 26-27.

Kunstler, R., & Kennedy, D. W. (1992). A cooperative model for conducting efficacy research in therapeutic recreation. *The Voice* (New York State. Recreation and Park Society Inc.), pp. 32-33, .51.

McCormick, B., Scott, D., & Dattilo, J. (1991). Answering questions about therapeutic recreation Part I: Formulating questions. *Annual in Therapeutic Recreation, 2*, 78-84.

Minium, E. W. (1978). *Statistical reasoning in psychology and education* (2nd ed.). New York, NY: Wiley.

Mobley, T. A. (1978, August). Research update: Research is practical. *Parks & Recreation*, p. 48.

Mobley, T. A. (1982, April). Practitioner/researcher: A team. *Parks & Recreation*, pp. 40-41, 72.

Phillips, D. C. (1980, December). What do the researcher and the practitioner have to offer each other? *Educational Researcher*, pp. 17-20, 24.

Reynolds, R. P. (1982, October). *Research in therapeutic recreation: Past, present and future trends.* Paper presented at the Leisure Research Symposium, National Congress for Recreation and Parks, Louisville, KY.

Reynolds, R. P., & O'Morrow, G. S. (1985). Scientific inquiry: The foundation for professional development. In R. P. Reynolds, & G. S. O'Morrow (Eds.) *Problems, Issues and Concepts in Therapeutic Recreation* (pp. 174-198). Englewood Cliffs, NJ: Prentice-Hall

Rothstein, A. L. (1990, February). Puzzling the role of research in practice. *Journal of Physical Education and Recreation* (JOPHER), pp. 39-40.

Robbins-Sisco, D., & Savell, K. S. (1991). *Sell-efficacy theory, addictive behaviors and therapeutic recreation: A proposed treatment intervention.* Unpublished manuscript.

Savell, K. S. (1991). Leisure, perceived control and well-being: Implications for the institutionalized older adult. *Therapeutic Recreation Journal, 25*(3), 44-59.

Savell, K., & Husdon, A. (1990). *Collaborative research; Bridging the gap between practitioners and researchers/educators.* Paper presented at the American Therapeutic Recreation Association Annual Conference, Kansas City, KS.

Witt, P. A. (1984, May). Research in transition: Prospects and Challenges. *Parks & Recreation*, pp. 60-63.

Witt, P. A. (1988a). Leisure programs and services for special populations; Past, present, and future research (pp. 127-139). In L. A. Barnett (Ed.) *Research about Leisure: Past, present, and future.* (pp. 127-139). Champaign, IL: Sagamore.

Witt, P. A. (1988b). Therapeutic recreation research: Past, present and future. *Therapeutic Recreation Journal, 22*(1), 14-23.

Ethical Considerations for Therapeutic Recreation Research: A Call For Guidelines
Norma J. Stumbo

In the recent past, there has been some information and discussion in the TR literature about ethical conduct (cf. Fain, 1989; Mobily, 1985; Patterson, 1985, Shank, 1985; Stumbo, 1985; Sylvester, 1982, 1985). Furthermore, ATRA and NTRS, both professional organizations, have ethical codes of conduct (cf. ATRA, 1990; NTRS, 1990). However, the bulk of this information, including the ethical codes, primarily focuses on the ethical conduct of professionals in practice settings. Ethical conduct in research endeavors is neglected.

Since no formal codes for research ethics exist within the therapeutic recreation profession, investigators interested in TR are left without sound and uniform guidelines to follow. The lack of uniform guidelines compounds the difficulty in making ethical as well as scientific decisions, often placing the researcher in problematic situations (Kimmel, 1991). For this reason, one frequently hears the words "ethical" and "dilemmas" in tandem (Grisso, Baldwin, Blanck, Rotheram-Borus, Schooler & Thompson, 1991). As Shank[1] stated:

> Ethical dilemmas occur when there appears to be a difficult problem with no apparent satisfactory solution, or when the choice is between two equally unsatisfactory alternatives . . . Both alternatives are compelling and defensible, but there is no one set of 'right' reasons. The choices can be desirable for some reasons and not desirable for others. (1985, p. 32)

---

1. All material from J. W. Shank, "Bioethical principles and the practice of therapeutic recreation in clinical settings," 1985, reprinted with permission of the National Recreation and Park Association, Arlington, VA, *Therapeutic Recreation Journal.*

In either event, decisions must be made so that the research can be implemented and the research participants can be protected. "In one sense, of course, all ethical obligations in research are obligations to research participants. Failure of ethical integrity at any stage of research demeans the participants' contributions" (Grisso et al., 1991, p. 760). Without specific guidelines to aid the research decision-making process, researchers are left with their own sets of moral values as the only bases for judgment. Problems arise as individual researchers' moral values differ, possibly causing harm to the research participants (Kimmel, 1991).

The major purpose of this chapter is to provide an arena where moral values and ethics in research can be discussed more fully by TR professionals. A main intent is to provide information concerning the differences in moral values that individuals hold. The remainder of the chapter illuminates common ethical concerns found in research settings. Borrowing heavily from the American Psychological Association's (APA) Ethical Principles (1990),[2] their Standards for Research (Grisso et al., 1991), and the ATRA Code of Ethics (1990), several ethical concerns in research are presented for discussion. Study questions at the end of the chapter urge the reader to further contemplate the ethical dilemmas presented within the research environment.

Difficulties in Codifying Research Ethics

Many factors affect the definition of research **ethics**, thereby presenting dilemmas to researchers and research participants alike. These factors can be viewed as *confounding* variables that affect the actions and decisions made in ethical situations, and cloud the strict interpretation of right and wrong. There are at least five factors that influence ethical decision-making: (a) distinctions between personal morality and ethics; (b) characteristics of the *offender*; (c) characteristics of the affected party(ies); (d) conditions surrounding the decision-making; and (e) lack of or imprecision of ethical codes. These five factors are explored in order to understand why ethical codes for research are difficult to construct, comply with, and enforce.

---

2.   The 1990 version of the ethical standards served as a major source for this chapter at the time this chapter was written. Since then, the American Psychological Association's Council of Representatives adopted their newest "Ethical Principles of Psychologists and Code of Conduct." The Code took effect on December 2, 1992. For a copy of this most recent update readers are encouraged to contact the: APA Order Department; 1992 Ethical Standards; American Psychological Assn.; 750 First St., NE; Washington, DC 20002-4242 or phone (202) 336-5510.

The first problem in defining ethical conduct is the potentially hazy distinction between personal morality and professional ethics. Heyman (1990, p. 48)[3] defines morality as "a personal sense of right and wrong," while professional ethical codes are created to protect clients and research participants from intentional and unintentional harm (Dickens, 1991; Grisso et al., 1991; Pettifor & Sinclair, 1991). Although the two concepts overlap, distinctions need to be made. For example, one might find topics such as racism, sexual harassment, or homelessness to be personally and morally wrong, but, research on racism, sexual harassment, or homelessness might be conducted in an ethical manner (Zuckerman, 1990).

Apparently, individuals are socialized by their research mentors to accept certain conduct as morally acceptable, while in fact, it may be unethical (Heyman, 1990; Stanley, Sieber & Melton, 1987). For example, for a researcher to piecemeal a study into several small articles may be seen as morally justifiable due to pressures for publication, while in fact, the practice is unethical (Grisso et al., 1991, p. 760-761). Where a behavior is judged to fall along the "ethical to unethical continuum" depends on the personal moral codes of the observer (Pope, Tabachnick & Keith-Speigel, 1987). Those moral codes may have been influenced greatly by the person's mentor, so that the researcher comes to accept largely unethical behavior as ethical.

A second problem is the specific factors relating to the individual allegedly committing the unethical act. "Whenever one observes or learns of a colleague's unethical behavior, a decision to intervene is unlikely to be made dispassionately. Several factors, in addition to the alleged misconduct itself, often intrude and thus may alter the course of action substantially" (Keith-Speigel & Koocher, 1985, p. 12).[4] When an unethical behavior is observed, the severity may be judged on criteria such as the offender's personality, degree of power over or relationship to the observer, or the *track record* of past conduct. Often, these elements play an important role in determining where the behavior is judged to fall along the ethical-unethical continuum as well as what actions should be taken to resolve the dilemma.

For example, say that a researcher neglected to fully disclose the potential risks of the study to the research participants. The judgment of the researcher's degree of "unethicalness" might depend on whether the researcher was a novice or experienced researcher, whether the lack of disclosure was intentional or unintentional, and whether full disclosure also had

---

3.   From Ethical issues with performance enhancement approaches with amateur boxers, by S. R. Heyman, 1990, *The Sport Psychologist*, 4(1), 48-54. Copyright 1990 by Human Kinetics Publishers, Inc. Champaign, IL. Reprinted by permission.

4.   All material from P. Keith-Speigel & G. P. Koocher, *Ethics in psychology: Professional standards and cases* (1985), reprinted with permission of McGraw-Hill, Inc., New York, NY.

been neglected in previous research. So while the ethical standard of full disclosure is expected, the severity of judgment about the person's behavior depends on several considerations.

A third concern addresses the personal and background characteristics of the observer or the affected party. Kimmel (1991) proposed that "variations in personal values, attitudes, temperament, and other individual characteristics might in some way influence scientists' resolutions of the ethical problems that beset their research" (p. 786). Keith-Speigel and Koocher (1985) noted that biases, attitudes, beliefs, personality traits, and commitments to professional obligations and responsibilities may all lead to differing evaluations of the seriousness of an act and what actions should be taken about it. Smith, McGuire, Abbott, and Blau (1991, p. 238) found that large discrepancies existed between "what clinicians know to be the ethically preferred course of action in dealing with professional-ethical dilemmas, and their stated willingness to implement this ideal." Pope (1991) and Pettifor and Sinclair (1991) reinforced that only a small percentage of unethical acts are reported due to the reticence of other professionals. In other words, for various reasons, people often fail to report unethical behavior, and this serves to further encourage acceptance of a wide range of behavior (Smith et al., 1991).

In a study of 259 psychologists, Kimmel (1991) found that those who interpreted ethical situations more liberally (i.e., held broad ethical interpretations) tended to be male, had held their degree for a longer period of time, had received their degree in a *basic* psychology area (e.g., developmental psychology), and were employed in research-oriented contexts. Those who were more conservative (i.e., had narrow parameters of ethical interpretations) tended to be female, had held their highest degree for the shortest amount of time, had received a degree in an applied area of psychology (e.g., community psychology), and were employed in service-oriented contexts. The results showed that there were personal factors of the *observer*, such as gender, job function, and education that influenced the interpretation of ethical or unethical behavior.

Fourth, the situation surrounding the behavior is also an important determinant. The intentionality, overtness, motives, artifacts, and consequences surrounding the act also become influencing factors. For example, if a person harms research participants during a study, confounding variables, such as whether the act was intentional (e.g., purposefully circumventing a human subject's review board evaluation) or simply misguided by poor judgment (e.g., not fully evaluating the consequences to the research participants), affect whether the act is viewed as unethical or inappropriate. Other situational factors that enter into such judgments include how severe the consequences were to the participants (e.g., physical harm versus inconvenience), whether the researcher tried to conceal the consequences either before, during or after the study was completed, the actions the researcher took to correct the consequences, and what mention these consequences receive in future research publications, reports, and presentations (Keith-Speigel & Koocher, 1985).

A fifth and key problem, especially for disciplines such as TR, is that ethical codes of conduct for research purposes are nonexistent. While ethical codes of conduct in practice are in place (ATRA, 1990; NTRS, 1990; Patterson, 1985; Shank, 1985; Sylvester, 1985), few guidelines have been created for research purposes. The lack of ethical codes for research may result in the dismissal of ethics as an unimportant topic, may increase the variability of *acceptable* practices (Kimmel, 1991), and may reduce the chance for adjudicating complaints of unethical conduct (Pettifor & Sinclair, 1991). In discussing the development of the APA's *Ethical Principles*, Kimmel (1991, p. 788) noted:

> If the relative importance of the many factors that influence judgments pertinent to ethical decision-making can be enumerated, clarified and weighed in subsequent research ... researchers may then be able to deal effectively with their ethical dilemmas and obtain a fuller understanding of their differences through reasoned and informed discussion.

When a research ethics code is totally absent, the potential for the "inconsistent application of ethical principles" (Kimmel, 1991, p. 788), is greatly increased. This lack of a standard, especially when coupled with individualized and situational interpretations, creates mayhem regarding ethical behavior. Without well-defined, comprehensive, and widely accepted codes, little coherence and adherence can be expected. While some regulation is available at the federal, university, or agency levels, through institutional review boards (APA Ethics Committee, 1988; Keith-Speigel & Koocher, 1985) or by federal regulatory codes (e.g., Health and Human Services, 45 Code of Federal Regulation Part 46), one mark of an advanced profession is self-regulation (Barber, 1965; Ben-David, 1963; Pavalko, 1971; Wilensky, 1964). Therapeutic recreation, as well as the broader recreation and leisure studies field, needs to begin discussion regarding self-regulation through a formal code of research ethics.

Until a formal code of research ethics is established, a short-term strategy is to borrow accepted codes from other professions that have been established and tested over a number of years (Shank, 1985). These, at least, are starting points for awareness, discussion, and consensus building.

Ethical Principles for Research

This section relies on concepts from two codes of ethics and splices these concepts into an organized set of parameters. The first code examined is the APA's (1990) *Ethical Principles of Psychologists.*[5] These principles were selected because of their: (a) focus on research; (b) long history of use; (c) applicability to TR; (d) level of specificity; (e) support by research and other references; and (f) close association with other APA publications (e.g., APA *Publication Manual* (1983a)) that are widely used by other fields, including TR. The second code is ATRA's (1990) Code of Ethics. It was chosen because: (a) most readers are familiar with its contents; (b) the principles relate to both practice and research (which have similar aims); and (c) their level of generality.

While structured by the headings of the general principles found in the ATRA Code (e.g., competence and confidentiality), specific information regarding research ethics found both within the APA *Principles* and other literature is contained within each section. The Appendix (page 122) contains two sections of the APA Principles regarding confidentiality and research with human participants. While section headings are given to provide clarity, readers should note that many ethical concepts overlap and information within each section is not necessarily exclusive to that particular ethical principle.

Competence

Keith-Speigel and Koocher (1985) assert that "competencies and personal characteristics and values of researchers have critical ethical implications" (p. 385). Beyond a firm comprehension of the field at hand, the researcher must have a solid understanding of a multitude of scientific concepts and methods.

> No meaningful information can result from poorly designed studies or improperly analyzed or interpreted data . . . . Using human beings or animals in a flawed project cannot be justified on any grounds. At best, the participants' efforts are wasted and, at worst, they could be harmed. In addition, the scientific enterprise has been failed as well. (Keith-Speigel & Koocher, 1985, p. 385).

A grave disservice is done to research participants, the general public, the profession, and the larger scientific community when studies are not properly designed, implemented, analyzed, and reported. While ethical codes do not specify exactly how research is to be conducted, codes such as the APA *Ethical Principles* do provide information and give direction concerning ethical considerations in the research process.

---

5.   All material from the American Psychological Association's (1990) Ethical principles of psychologists, (citations in text and appendix to Chapter 6) are copyright 1990 by the American Psychological Association. Reprinted by permission.

While any scientific inquiry of merit and ethical practices would seemingly be in harmony, there are times when these endeavors are not. In these cases, a compromise of some sort must be reached between the scientific value of the study and the ethical ideal. Keith-Speigel and Koocher (1985, p. 386) note and cite several examples of these compromises: (a) the ethical consideration of fully informed and voluntary consent which may weaken scientific validity; (b) intrusion into the privacy of vulnerable people in long-term studies designed to evaluate and improve treatment techniques; (c) withholding treatment in single-subject designs to obtain baseline data to make comparisons with later treatment effects; (d) balanced placebo designs requiring misinforming participants in order to reduce effects of expectancies; and (e) denial of effective treatment programs to control groups in true experimental designs.

In all of these cases and others, the ethical considerations must be weighed simultaneously with alternative designs as well as the potential value of the research results. APA Ethical Principles 9a and 9c discuss this fragile balancing act.

All researchers are encouraged to seek advice from experienced colleagues and ethicists to aid in the decision-making process. In most studies, the consequences to the participants should take precedence over the perceived value of the research.

Veracity

Veracity is the ethical principle that concerns truthfulness (Shank, 1985). In relation to research, at least three major areas are affected by this principle: (a) informed consent of research participants; (b) dual relationships between researcher and participant; and (c) dissemination of research results. The first area, informed consent, is expanded in the next section because of its crucial importance to TR research. The latter two are highlighted as follows.

Dual Relationships

One of the problems facing researchers in TR is the possibility of conflicting dual relationships between the researcher and the research participant. Examples include university faculty conducting research on students in their classes and clinical practitioners conducting research on clients while the clients are receiving services. This area is important because of potential exploitation of the research participants.

In most kinds of research, the researcher is in the *power position* or *position of authority* (APA, 1990, p. 395). Although ethical concepts such as voluntary participation, informed consent, and autonomy are of paramount importance, often there is some degree of subtle **coercion** involved in soliciting participants for research studies.

It has been argued that some element of coercion is involved in any investigator-participant transaction. Simply being approached with a request by a person perceived as having some prestige and authority may be persuasive, especially if the researcher is enthusiastic and likeable or if the potential participant is vulnerable, deferent, needy for attention, desperate for a solution, or is an inmate, student, or employee of the organization sponsoring the research. (Keith-Speigel & Koocher, 1985, p. 391)

The researcher, as the person who is responsible for designing, conducting, analyzing and reporting the study, knows the rationale and methods, and often, may have a preconceived notion of the intended findings or outcomes. In some cases, the researcher may be under pressure from funding agencies, or administrators to solicit large samples and produce *significant* results. In situations such as these, there are great pressures on the researcher to ensure that participants cooperate. Being in the power position, the investigator may, in turn, influence the subjects to participate beyond their wishes or may lead them to believe that the lack of cooperation will affect their treatment (or course of study). It may often be difficult for participants to delineate where treatment (versus the research) begins and ends, and whether their participation in the research will affect their treatment or relationship with the investigator. The ethical conflict comes to the forefront when the researcher begins to manipulate, even in subtle ways, the environment, the treatment, or the client, to influence the results. Investigators must take special cautions in soliciting participants with whom other types of relationships exist.

Dissemination of Research Results

A major mission of research is to expand the knowledge base of the field. However, this is not achieved if the results are not disseminated to deserving and interested publics. With the mandate for dissemination comes several ethical concerns, especially when the mandate becomes an overzealous and overriding factor at some agencies and institutions (such as higher education).

The latter part of this chapter contains a section on the ethics of publishing and presenting research results, specifically focusing on issues of acknowledging contributions toward the research efforts. These concerns, so rarely seen discussed in texts, seem to warrant additional coverage. However, in this section on veracity, other topics need to be noted, and although they are related, they become distinct considerations.

Investigators are frequently under pressure from a variety of external agents. Student researchers, often with limited knowledge, are expected to produce a quality study in a short amount of time. Faculty researchers, sometimes without adequate resources, are expected to produce volumes of research to retain their positions, earn promotions, and receive merit salary increases. Clinical researchers are expected to make important contributions to the understanding of quality client care. All of the categories of researchers are pressured to produce *significant* results in order for the manuscript or presentation proposal to be accepted by prestigious journals or research symposia. As this happens and the greater the pressures become, the greater the likelihood that ethical principles will be compromised.

Dissemination of research results brings its own set of possible dangers. First, researchers must be truthful. In the search for significant results, "going fishing" with a data set by running multiple statistical procedures to see which produce statistical significance is unfortunately all too common as well as being extremely unethical. Second, researchers are obliged to ensure that the results are not reported in such a way to be misleading. It is often said that "anybody can lie with statistics," but the fact remains that the responsibility of selecting and reporting the appropriate procedures and statistics that do not violate the assumptions on which they are based always rests with the researchers.

Third, researchers are presumed to report what they find, including disconfirming data or opposing results. Often the most illuminating studies are multivariate in nature, attempting to explain the complex nature of the phenomena under study by examining a variety of possible variables. The ethical compromise arises when only those which produce statistically significant results are reported. (Equally important are those variables that *do not* produce such results!)

Fourth, every good master's thesis or doctoral dissertation contains a section on the limitations (and/or delimitations) of the study. However, after this academic exercise, researchers often neglect this important consideration which allows the audience to more fully understand under which conditions the treatment was effective or ineffective. Without the inclusion of this information, the judgment of the worth or applicability of the study is at jeopardy.

The fifth consideration is made difficult by the fact that all research is value-ridden and biased in some way (Keith-Speigel & Koocher, 1985, p. 387). The fact that the researcher *chose* the topic includes the assumption that biases and values entered into the selection. Following accepted methodological and statistical procedures is one avenue to minimizing the effects of this bias. Further, the researcher should conscientiously seek out alternative hypotheses and explanations for the research results. Conclusions should be drawn based on the actual data, not the preconceptions of the investigator. Discussion with valued colleagues is encouraged to help alleviate misconstrued or value-laden reporting.

The sixth consideration is perhaps the most serious of all ethical violations: that of falsifying data. According to Keith-Speigel and Koocher (1985, p. 362).

> ... creating fraudulent data is considered among scientists and scholars to be one of the most dire ethical violations. However, the longer term impact of the reporting of fraudulent data is far more serious ... since the false information is absorbed into and then contaminates the knowledge stockpile. Application of the implications of fraudulent findings may ultimately harm the well-being of others.

Falsified or fraudulent data can be placed into three categories: (a) forged data that are invented without actual data collection; (b) tampered or fudged data that results from actual data being altered in some way; and (c) selective or *trimmed* data that are collected but edited to conform to the investigator's wishes (Keith-Speigel & Koocher, 1985, p. 362). Because this concern has gained recent publicity, the National Institutes of Health, the National Science Foundation and the U.S. Public Health Service (USPHS) have created regulations to monitor **scientific misconduct**. Scientific misconduct includes two key elements: (a) serious deviations from accepted practices in the implementation and reporting of research, such as fabrication, falsification, or plagiarism; and (b) failure to adhere to federal requirements affecting the research, such as protection of human and animal subjects (Grisso et al., 1991; Miers, 1985; USPHS, 1989). To reiterate, researchers and consumers of research must take a strong stand against any of these practices.

Informed Consent

Informed consent is closely related to veracity and autonomy. As discussed previously, veracity concerns truthfulness, and autonomy refers the participants' degree of independence and control over the situation or environment. In referring to clinical practice, Sylvester (1985, p. 15)[6] states: "Informed consent provides that the client has the right to know, in adequate detail and comprehensible terms, what is likely to occur during and as a result of professional intervention." The same statement is applicable to research settings. The interplay between informed consent, veracity, and autonomy is interesting because of their dependent nature; that is, when one element is taken away, the others are compromised.

---

6.   All materials by C. D. Sylvester, from An analysis of selected ethical issues in therapeutic recreation, 1985, reprinted with permission of the National Recreation and Parks Association, Arlington, VA, *Therapeutic Recreation Journal.*

Truthfulness in Informed Consent

Veracity in this context means that participants are fully informed about the potential risks, the conditions for participation, and, in the case of dual relationships, the relationship to participation in other clinical treatments. Citing the Nuremberg Code, first published in the *American Journal of Medicine* in 1946, Keith-Speigel and Koocher (1985, pp. 389-90) note that veracity:

> requires that before the acceptance of an affirmative decision by the experimental subject there should be made known to him the nature, duration, and purpose of the experiment; the method and means by which it is to be conducted; all inconveniences and hazards reasonably to be expected; and the effects upon his health or person which may possibly come from his participation in the experiment.

Autonomy in Relation to Research

Autonomy is when "[f]ull consideration is given to the person's freedom to form and act upon their own judgments. Individuals are free to determine their own destiny. The dignity of self-determination is preserved" (Shank, 1985, p. 33). In research terms, autonomy implies that research participants have the right to refuse to enter the study, to not participate in any intervention that is against their wishes, and to withdraw at any time (Keith-Speigel & Koocher, 1985). It is one factor that has influenced the shift in terminology from research *subject* to research *participant*, emphasizing the person's right to choice, decision-making, and empowerment.

Autonomy's Antithesis is Coercion

While most would agree that coercion is unethical, " 'voluntariness' is an attribute that can be manipulated in both subtle and blatant ways" (Keith-Speigel & Koocher, 1985, p. 391). For example, some studies use enticements or incentives to attract participants. Reasonable incentives (for example, reimbursement for travel expenses) seem justified, while excessive enticements, especially when used to attract low-income participants or to offset potential risk or harm, are not acceptable. In addition, emotional appeals to the person's altruism, deriding those who decline to participate as immature or irresponsible, or tying participation in the study to some other benefits (e.g., class grades) are also seen as unacceptable (Keith-Speigel & Koocher, 1985).

The ideals of veracity and autonomy are foundations for the concept of informed consent. Often, they are seen as being so closely interrelated that they are discussed simultaneously in the literature by suggesting that "research participation is entered into *voluntarily, knowingly,* and *intelligently*"

(Keith-Speigel & Koocher, 1985, p. 390). The APA Ethical Principle 9d addresses informed consent and suggests the creation of a "clear and fair agreement with research participants" that is finalized prior to the initiation of the study. (See the Appendix to this chapter.) Fowler (1988) suggests that this agreement include information on the: (a) organization; (b) sponsorship; (c) purpose; (d) right to confidentiality; (e) voluntary nature of participation; and (f) right to withdraw.

Three special notes need to be added to any discussion about informed consent. The first is that consideration must be given to individuals who may not have the capacity to give informed consent. Examples include children, individuals with severe or chronic mental health problems, individuals with mental impairments, and, in some cases, persons who are incarcerated (see Stanley, Sieber & Melton, 1987 for a more thorough discussion of ethical issues with these populations). While direct informed consent may not be entirely possible from members of these groups, it has been suggested that verbal assent be received from them, in addition to written permission from proxies, legal guardians, or responsible others (Grisso et al., 1991; Keith-Speigel & Koocher, 1985).

The second case is those in which the investigator (and, we hope, others, such as human subject review boards) can justify that the lack of informed consent is offset by the dire need for participation in the research treatment. Even in rare cases where the researcher has assumed that the benefits are greater than the participants' rights of autonomy, the consequences of participation must still be considered carefully.

The third case is when naturalistic research techniques are used. In these situations, quite often the researcher may become an *equal* participant in the situation and the fact that she or he is conducting research is unknown to the other participants. The purpose of this type of study is to be able to observe and describe the natural behaviors of the participants, and the assumption is that if the participants knew of the research, their behavior would be changed, and therefore, would not be natural. Depending on the nature of the study, this category of research often involves deception (giving misinformation) or concealment (omitting information) (Keith-Speigel & Koocher, 1985, p. 401).

In all three cases, additional safeguards should be executed by the researcher. The second part of the APA Principle 9d highlights the need for special consideration in these cases. (See the Appendix, page 122.)

Confidentiality

Any research involving human beings requires that those persons divulge, in some manner, some amount of information about themselves to the researcher. Whether it is a study that uses questionnaires, observations, or personal interviews, the research participant is revealing some kind of information to the researcher. After all, the intent of the researcher is to gather information about the research participants in order to make observations or draw conclusions about their behavior.

An interesting twist to confidentiality in research endeavors, as opposed to clinical practice, is noted by Keith-Speigel and Koocher, (1985, p. 409): "In general, then, the psychotherapist holds the interests and welfare of each individual as primary, whereas the researcher additionally contends with interests in gaining knowledge and the public's right to access to and use of it." However, the research participants, for the most part, always should maintain control of any information that is gained that is identifying, damaging or otherwise potentially harmful to the person as an individual. Two ethical considerations, privacy and confidentiality, are concerned with that control held by the research participant.

The ethical concerns of **privacy** and **confidentiality** center upon the amount and the availability of information that pertains to the research participants. The first privacy issue suggests that the researcher ask only the information that is needed to answer the research question(s). Questions about criminal records, religion, and socioeconomic status, for example, may be unethical if they do not pertain to the study. Some researchers use the unethical practice of a "shot gun" approach by asking many questions, hoping that eventually some data that is interesting or useful will be expressed.

The second privacy issue relates to disclosure of the study being conducted. In some limited cases, it may be necessary to conceal the purposes or execution of the research from the subjects, such as in some forms of naturalistic inquiry. In some situations, the research participants may not be aware of the research being conducted because the researcher's intent is to capture *natural* behavior occurring in *natural* environments. The justification or benefits for such research must outweigh the risks or costs of invasion of privacy.

Confidentiality concerns the access that other people have to the research data. The best possible practice is to not reveal the identities of or identifying information about the research participants to any one at any time. This includes not disclosing information to the participants' families, other participants, other professionals, other researchers not involved in the study at hand, and audiences of the research results.

Because it is such a primary ethical concept, the APA Principles contains a separate section on confidentiality issues (Principle 5) as well as additional clarifying statements within Principle 9j. (See the Appendix in this chapter, page 122.)

One of the very few instances in which confidentiality may be breached is when persons reveal information that they are in danger of harming themselves or others. These types of incidences pit several ethical concepts against one another (e.g., confidentiality versus veracity). Sylvester (1985) successfully highlights these dilemmas with regard to practice, and the applicability to research situations is evident. Although the legal precedent seems unclear at this time and the definition of harm is not definitive, such information should be revealed to authorities and to the individuals in danger. Additionally, the research participant should be informed of the decision to disclose the information to others (Keith-Speigel & Koocher, 1985, p. 412).

Fidelity

Fidelity refers to the obligation to act in good faith and follow through with commitments made to the research participant. Related to autonomy and informed consent, fidelity addresses the researcher's responsibility to act in a professional manner primarily to participants, but also to other researchers, audiences of the research, and the profession.

One avenue for ensuring fidelity is the development and use of a research participation agreement. In this agreement, the roles, functions, and requirements of both the researcher and the research participant should be outlined. This allows for a set of clear expectations and commitments from both parties, delineated from the onset. In this way, the research participant is assured of autonomy (control over decisions and choices) and the researcher abides by the related concepts of justice (fairness and equity to participants) and competence (ability to implement a well-designed study).

In this regard, the APA (1990) *Principles* emphasize that "The investigator has the obligation to honor all promises and commitments included in that agreement" (p. 394). Parallel with informed consent, the research participant should be given as much information as is feasible.

Justice

Justice refers to the fair treatment of all research participants. "Any denial of something that a person has a right to or is entitled to is considered an injustice" (Shank, 1985, p. 34). The concept of justice is closely tied to those of autonomy, veracity, and fidelity. Research participants have the right to expect choices when and where possible, truth, and follow-through from the investigator. These three related principles require that the researcher uphold ethical standards with regard to the fair and humane treatment of all research participants.

Three scenarios that explain the concept of fairness involve investigators and service recipients, faculty researchers and students, and multiple conditions of treatment. Investigators in health and human service settings often choose a traditional experimental design in which a treatment group receives some form of intervention and a control group does not. When the intervention is seen as beneficial, or *potentially* beneficial, to the condition of the clients, withholding this intervention may be seen as unethical (Shank, 1985). (Of course, if the intervention is not perceived to have some benefits or change some aspect of the clients, the research would not be conducted!) Fortunately, alternative research designs do exist to control for and eliminate this ethical conflict.

A second scenario involving faculty researchers and students is quite similar to the one above. For example, if the faculty member is researching whether focused study sessions improve the students' test grades, it would be considered unethical to provide such sessions only to a treatment group while withholding the same benefits to the control group of students. In both situations, the underlying principle is to treat all participants in the research study in a similar manner.

The third situation is different because in some research designs there are several treatment groups assigned to one of many treatment conditions. For example, in studying the effects of reinforcement, a researcher might have three treatment groups of positive reinforcement, negative reinforcement, and no reinforcement, while subjects are completing some task. While the overall purpose is to determine which of the three conditions has the most effect on them, care must be taken to treat all subjects fairly. In this example, it may be necessary to rotate participants through all three conditions, so that all are treated fairly and face the same benefits, risks, and consequences of the research.

For all three situations, alternative research designs exist that help eliminate or at least reduce the inequity of treatment and effects. Using alternative structures is likely to strengthen the total research design, thus yielding more confidence in the research results. All investigators are encouraged to explore research designs and methods that provide as much fairness as possible to all research participants (e.g., Campbell & Stanley, 1963; Glass & Stanley, 1970).

Beneficence/Nonmalfeasance

Beneficence is the concept that professionals "make a commitment to actively promoting good and being kind and charitable" (Shank, 1985, p. 33). In research, as in clinical services, the research or treatment should be beneficial to the research participants. The researcher must ask what real gains or benefits the research participants might obtain from being involved in this study. A related concept, **nonmalfeasance**, is the principle requiring the researcher to cause no harm. While it is easy to relate this concept to physical harm, it also relates to emotional and social health and well-being, as well as privacy and quality of life (Shank, 1985). Beneficence and nonmalfeasance enable the researcher to truthfully and completely identify the possible benefits and consequences of the research to the participants.

This part of the researcher's obligation can be met in several ways. First, during the design phase of the study, the researcher must assess the potential risks to the research participants. Levine (1975) suggests that the risk assessment review: (a) likelihood of risk occurrence; (b) severity of risk; (c) duration; (d) reversability of effects; and (e) potential for detection. Diener and Crandall (1978) additionally promote reviewing the probability of the same risk occurring in everyday life.

Second, also in the design stage, the researcher should actively seek out alternative designs that promote the best possible ethical practices. For example, perhaps the control group can receive treatment that is already proven effective while the treatment group receives only or additionally the new intervention. In this way, the control group is not in jeopardy regarding the total lack of an intervention.

Third, the researcher should consider alternative study groups. For example, instead of involving at-risk or vulnerable populations, the researcher should consider whether adequate information can be obtained from similar studies on "competent" adults.

Fourth, small-scale pilot studies are essential to pretest the procedures and methods to be used. While pilot studies should be used in almost all research to increase the validity and reliability of the study, an additional outcome is the determination of risks and benefits to the participants. Fifth, individuals who are known to be at risk (e.g., known to experience heightened discomfort in some situations) should be withdrawn from the study's sample.

Sixth, while the data are being collected, several safeguards should be in place. These may include accurate monitoring of equipment, scrutiny of participants for signs of adverse reactions, continued assurance of freedom to withdraw, back-up resources including skilled personnel, and post-session interviews or debriefing (Keith-Speigel & Koocher, 1985).

Seventh, and probably most important throughout the entire study, is the need to seek advice from informed colleagues. This may include co-workers, people similar to the research participants, thesis and dissertation committees, and institutional review boards (see Ceci, Peters, & Plotkin, 1985 for an enlightening discussion of review processes). These individuals may provide assistance in determining the total cost/benefit ratio.

The APA (1990) *Ethical Principles* devote three major paragraphs to covering the notions of beneficence and nonmalfeasance. See sections 9g, 9h, and 9i in the Appendix, which speak to the aforementioned issues.

Ethical Concerns in the Dissemination of Research Findings

Beyond the actual design and implementation of a study, the reporting and dissemination of results carry their own set of ethical problems. Some of these problems were discussed in the previous section on veracity. They include forging, fudging, and trimming data. Another area that is becoming increasingly problematic is that of establishing authorship credit.

It is common knowledge that pressures are continuing to mount on university and clinical researchers to publish the results of their research. Three types of ethical dilemmas are incurred in publishing practices: partial publication, dual publication, and coauthorship credit (APA, 1983a, 1983b; Grisso et al., 1991).

Partial publication "refers to the dissemination of research results in the least publishable unit, rather than publishing results as a coherent whole" (Grisso et al., 1991, pp. 760-761). The APA (1983a) publication manual admonishes that "piecemeal publication of several reports of the results from a single data base is undesirable and may be judged as duplicate publication" (p. 168). This practice is somewhat encouraged by journals with severe page limitations for articles reporting research as well as job promotion or tenure guidelines that refer to quantity rather than quality of articles (Grisso et al., 1991). However, the end result may be that reading audiences are misled by the lack of cohesiveness and integration in the literature.

Dual publication "is the practice of publishing the same data and results in more than one publishing source" (Grisso et al., 1991, p. 761). The APA manual also prohibits this behavior and requires that authors notify editors of simultaneous submissions or prior publication of any substantial portion of the article. The only justifiable reason for dual publication is to reach different audiences served by the journals or magazines in question. However, because of pressures to produce quantities of publications, many authors will continue this practice regardless of its unethical implications (Grisso et al., 1991).

In the instance of authorship credit, the unethical behavior often is committed against coresearchers, students, and/or front-line therapists. While the recipients of the unethical behavior change, the seriousness does not.

> Multiple-authored scientific works are increasing in frequency.
> ... Many might assume that decisions concerning who deserves authorship credit on joint projects, and in what order the names should be placed, is a reasonably straightforward procedure. The same forthright process would seem to operate when citing footnote acknowledgments for those who were helpful, though not in a major or critical way. Bitter disputes concerning

assignments of publication credit, however, are the most prevalent type of complaints to ethics committees from the academic-scientific sector of psychology. (Keith-Speigel & Koocher, 1985, p. 352)

Because of these problems, the APA is one of the few organizations that has attempted to establish guidelines with regard to coauthorship credit. Within Principle 7: Professional Relationships, the following general guidelines are given:

    f. Publication credit is assigned to those who have contributed to a publication in proportion to their professional contributions. Major contributions of a professional character made by several persons to a common project are recognized by joint authorship, with the individual who made the principal contribution listed first. Minor contributions of a professional character and extensive clerical or similar nonprofessional assistance may be acknowledged in footnotes or in an introductory statement. Acknowledgement through specific citations is made for unpublished as well as published material that has directly influenced the research or writing. Psychologists who compile and edit material of others for publication publish the material in the name of the originating group, if appropriate, with their own name appearing as chairperson or editor. All contributors are to be acknowledged and named (APA, 1983a, p. 20; APA, 1990, pp. 393-394).

While these general guidelines are helpful, they fall short in defining the extent of the "contribution" that may warrant a coauthorship or acknowledgment status. This definition becomes particularly vague and ambiguous when applied to the publication of graduate students' works, especially when faculty members demand that their names be included on every published version of the students' works. Students, on one hand, often argue that it is the faculty members' job to help them through the research process, including to the point of publication. On this side, it is argued that faculty members should only receive acknowledgement credit. On the faculty members' side, it may be argued that the research could not have been completed without significant assistance and this warrants coauthorship status (Keith-Speigel & Koocher, 1985, p. 353).

While not completely resolving this issue, the APA (1983b) published a policy statement in reaction to exploitation of graduate students by faculty members. These five statements are listed below:

    1. Only second authorship is acceptable for the dissertation supervisor.

    2. Second authorship may be considered obligatory if the supervisor designates the primary variables or makes major interpretative contributions or provides the data base.

3. Second authorship is a courtesy if the supervisor designates the general area of concern or is substantially involved in the development of the design and measurement procedures or substantially contributes to the write-up of the published report.
4. Second authorship is not acceptable if the supervisor provides only encouragement, physical facilities, financial support, critiques, or editorial contributions.
5. In all instances, agreements should be reviewed before the writing for publication is undertaken and at the time of submission. If disagreements arise, they should be resolved by a third party using these guidelines (Keith-Speigel and Koocher, 1985, p. 354).

Perhaps the most helpful directive of those above is the last paragraph. When and where possible, agreement on the listing of authorship and acknowledgement should be reached *prior* to the actual writing. In fact, to ward off future difficulties and possible ethics case hearings, the best alternative is to confirm these decisions prior to the onset of the research project.

Ethical Concerns in Research Using Animals

Although few research studies in TR involve the use of animals, their occasional use warrants some discussion. Most TR research involving animals involves some form of *pet therapy* or *animal facilitated therapy*, where animals may be used to study a variety of factors and reactions, such as social interaction, withdrawal, or depression.

In most situations, it would be difficult to imagine that animals could be harmed. However, the living conditions of the animal and the care given by the human research participants may be of concern. For example, the researcher is responsible for ensuring that the acquisition, maintenance, and handling (and disposal, if necessary) of the animals is done with consideration to their comfort, health, and humane treatment (APA, 1990; Speigel & Koocher, 1985). Thus, human research participants must be instructed and supervised regarding the care and handling of animals prior to interaction with the animals. In addition, consideration must be given to the selection of appropriate animals. Caution must be taken by the researcher to protect both the animal and human subjects during all phases of the study. Persons considering research involving animals are encouraged to explore further information regarding their care as well as alternatives to animal research (cf. Bowd, 1980a, 1980b; National Institutes of Health, 1984; Sperlinger, 1981; Zola, Sechzer, Sieber & Griffin, 1984).

Summary

Similar to other areas of professional behavior, ethics in research is an increasingly complex phenomenon that is interpreted differently by individuals. This chapter was presented as a forum for discussion within the therapeutic recreation profession about setting parameters for and regulating behavior of individuals conducting research. Until such a time that the relevant professional organizations create a code of ethics for research, investigators "must be particularly careful to avoid rationalizing the temptation to engage in unethical or illegal behavior by claiming that 'everyone does it' or by pointing to abuses by other professions, despite the apparently increased toleration of such behavior" (Pope, 1990, p. 1068). As Miers (1985, p. 831) noted, "[t]he temptation and opportunity to exploit the process have doubtless existed since the development of science as an organized activity, moderated by some combination of individual ethics, intellectual rigor, and the safeguards imposed by the processes of experimentation and publication." Individual researchers become responsible for the ethical decisions that they make, as well as journal editors and audiences, consumers and the profession as a whole. Each must be involved in the determination of risks and benefits of the research endeavor (Stanley, Sieber, & Melton, 1987). The following quote about psychology applies to therapeutic recreation:

> The integrity of psychology is contingent to a great degree on the extent to which we—both as a discipline or profession and as individuals—can regulate our own behavior. Our ability to engage in effective and ethical regulation, in turn, is contingent on our willingness to study our own behavior and our beliefs about that behavior. (Pope, Tabachnick, & Keith-Speigel, 1987, p. 1006)

Discussion Questions

1. Using the five scenarios below, write a short paragraph answering the questions as well as indicating what could have been done to avoid the conflict. Justify your statements with the ethical principles discussed in this chapter. Compare your answers with other colleagues for similarities and disagreements.

   (A) Claus Mate is a lab research assistant for Dr. X. R. Size. Dr. Size is conducting a six-month experiment on elderly men and their reactions to three weekly types of aerobic exercise, monitoring their heart rates and blood levels. After one research subject nearly dies during the fourth month, Claus Mate realizes the machines are uncalibrated and have been inaccurately recording data. Is it ethical to use the first four month's of data? What should Claus Mate do? What are his ethical responsibilities to the subject? The research results? Dr. Size? (See the Appendix: 9a, 9b, 9c, 9d, 9g, 9i)

   (B) Cloe Resterall was nearing completion of a year-long study involving a weight reduction program for low-income women. One of the subjects who had shown the greatest weight loss obtained a job before the posttest measures were taken and withdrew from the study. Ms. Resterall knew that without the subject's posttest measures, the results would be less likely to be significant. She called the subject several days in a row, pleading with her to complete the study. Was this ethical behavior on the part of Ms. Resterall? What are the individual responsibilities of the researcher and the subject? (See the Appendix: 9c, 9d, 9f)

   (C) Abbey Dee, a fourth year doctoral student, received a job offer in April from a prestigious university, even though she had not yet completed her dissertation research or degree. The major condition of employment was that her dissertation had to be completed by August of that year. Ms. Dee knew that the study could not be completed within that time frame, so she decided to "fake" the data and in June, submitted her "completed" dissertation to her committee and passed her final defense. Was this ethical behavior on Ms. Dee's part? What would you do as a committee member or the employing university if you later realized the data had been falsified? (See the Appendix: 9a, 9c)

   (D) Hap Hazard, a master's student, was conducting a study on the leisure behavior of undergraduate park and leisure studies majors. He inadvertently left his computer disk which had all the data and word processing files on it, in the departmental computer lab. An undergraduate major found the disk, which didn't have an identifying name on it, and put it in the computer to see if she could determine to whom it belonged. She was able to view the data and text files and see information on her student colleague's responses. Did either or both the master's and undergraduate student commit an unethical act? What could have been done to prevent the incident? What should be done after it happened? (See the Appendix: 5a, 5c, 9j)

(E) Meg Namimous and Connie Trite were conducting ethnographic research in a young adult female detention center. The study, which concerned the structure of gangs and the distribution of power within the center, was unknown to the inmates. The researchers led the inmates to believe that they also were incarcerated. When one inmate found out the truth three months later, she complained, but the researchers countered that deception was a necessity under these circumstances. Were the researchers ethical in concealing the purpose and extent of their research? Were the inmates' rights to privacy, confidentiality, and informed consent violated? Could this research be conducted without deception to the participants? Do the benefits or outcomes of the research outweigh the risks to the participants? (See the Appendix: 5a, 5b, 5d, 9a, 9c, 9d, 9e, 9j)

2. Create a research scenario in which two ethical concepts are at odds; for example, autonomy and beneficence, informed consent and fidelity, and veracity and competence. Determine the problematic areas and ask a group of colleagues for input on what their actions would be.

3. Explain the benefits and disadvantages of dual relationships, such as faculty/researcher and student/subject, and clinician/researcher and client/subject. When the roles are in conflict, which role should take precedence?

4. Outline the steps that the therapeutic recreation profession would need to take to establish an ethical code of conduct for research. Explain what mechanisms should be in place for ensuring compliance by investigators. What procedures should be in place to adjudicate complaints of unethical behavior?

5. Explain what role regulators, such as institutions or agencies, institutional review boards, governmental agencies or journal reviewers, now have or could have in ensuring ethical conduct in research. Locate the institutional review boards or committees at your institution or agency and obtain a copy of their policies and procedures.

References

American Psychological Association. (1983a). *Publication manual of the American Psychological Association.* (3rd. ed.). Washington, DC: Author.

American Psychological Association Ethics Committee. (1983b). *Authorship guidelines for dissertation supervision.* Washington, DC: Author.

American Psychological Association. (1990). Ethical principles of psychologists (amended June 2, 1989). *American Psychologist, 45*(3), 390-395.

American Therapeutic Recreation Association. (1990). *ATRA code of ethics.* Hattiesburg, MS: Author.

Barber, B. (1965). Some problems in the sociology of professions. In K. S. Lynn (Ed.), *The professions in America* (pp. 15-34). Boston, MA: Houghton Mifflin.

Ben-David, J. (1963). Professions in the class system of present-day societies: A trend report and bibliography. *Current Sociology, 12*(3), 246-330.

Bowd, A. D. (1980a). Ethical reservations about psychological research with animals. *Psychological Record, 30,* 201-210.

Bowd, A. D. (1980b). Ethics and animal experimentation. *American Psychologist, 35,* 224-225.

Campbell, D. T., & Stanley, J. C. (1963). *Experimental and quasi-experimental designs for research.* Chicago, IL: Rand McNally.

Ceci, S. J., Peters, D., & Plotkin, J. (1985). Human subjects review, personal values and the regulation of social science research. *American Psychologist, 40*(9), 994-1002.

Dickens, B. (1991). Unresolved issues concerning quasi-judicial proceedings. *Canadian Psychology, 32*(1), 79-81.

Diener, E., & Crandall, R. (1978). *Ethics in social and behavioral research.* Chicago, IL: University of Chicago Press.

Fain, G. S. (1989). Ethics in the therapeutic recreation profession. (pp. 187-203). In D. Compton (Ed.). *Issues in therapeutic recreation: A profession in transition.* Champaign, IL: Sagamore.

Fowler, F. J.,Jr. (1988). *Survey research methods.* (rev. ed.) Newbury Park, NJ: Sage.

Glass, G. V., & Stanley, J. C. (1970). *Statistical methods in education and psychology.* Englewood Cliffs, NJ: Prentice-Hall.

Grisso, T., Baldwin, E., Blanck, P. D., Rotheram-Borus, M. J., Schooler, N. R., & Thompson, T. (1991). Standards in research: APA's mechanism for monitoring the challenges. *American Psychologist, 46*(7), 758-766.

Heyman, S. R. (1990). Ethical issues with performance enhancement approaches with amateur boxers. Champaign, IL: *The Sport Psychologist, 4*(1), 48-54.

Keith-Speigel P., & Koocher, G. P. (1985). *Ethics in psychology: Professional standards and cases.* New York, NY: Random House.

Kimmel, A. J. (1991). Predictable biases in the ethical decision making of American psychologists. *American Psychologist, 46*(7), 786-788.

Levine, R. J. (1975). *The role of assessment of risk-benefit criteria in the determination of the appropriateness of research involving human subjects.* Paper presented at the National Commission for the Protection of Human Subjects of Biomedical and Behavioral Research. Washington, DC: Department of Health, Education and Welfare.

Miers, M. L. (1985). Current NIH perspective on misconduct in science. *American Psychologist, 40*(7), 831-835.

Mobily, K. E. (1985). The ethical dilemma of freedom in therapeutic recreation. *Therapeutic Recreation Journal, 19*(4), 22-30.

National Institutes of Health. (1984). Laboratory animal welfare. *NIH Guide, 13,* 1-27.

National Therapeutic Recreation Society. (1990). *NTRS code of ethics.* Alexandria, VA: Author.

Patterson, R. A. (1985). Interpretation and application of the NTRS code of ethics. *Therapeutic Recreation Journal, 19*(4), 51-56.

Pavalko, R. M. (1971). *Sociology of occupations and professions.* Itasca, IL: Peacock Publishers.

Pettifor, J., & Sinclair, C. (1991). Enhancing fairness and justice in the ethical complaint process. *Canadian Psychology, 32*(1), 63-71.

Pope, K. S. (1991). Discussion: Promoting ethical behaviour: The Canadian psychological association model. *Canadian Psychology, 32*(1), 74-76.

Pope, K. S., Tabachnick, B. G., & Keith-Speigel, P. (1987). Ethics of practice: The beliefs and behaviors of psychologists as therapists. *American Psychologist, 42*(11), 993-1006.

Shank, J. W. (1985). Bioethical principles and the practice of therapeutic recreation in clinical settings. *Therapeutic Recreation Journal, 19*(4), 31-40.

Smith, T. S., McGuire, J. M., Abbott, D. W., & Blau, B. I. (1991). Clinical ethical decision making: An investigation of the rationales used to justify doing less than one believes one should. *Professional Psychology: Research and Practice, 22*(3), 235-239.

Sperlinger, D. (1981). (Ed.). *Animals in research.* New York, NY: Wiley.

Stanley, B., Sieber, J. E., & Melton, G. B. (1987). Empirical studies of ethical issues in research: A research agenda. *American Psychologist, 42*(7), 735-741.

Stumbo, N. J. (1985). Knowledge of professional and ethical behavior in therapeutic recreation services. *Therapeutic Recreation Journal, 19*(4), 59-67.

Sylvester, C. D. (1982). Exploring confidentiality in therapeutic recreation practice: An ethical responsibility in need of response. *Therapeutic Recreation Journal, 16*(3), 25-34.

Sylvester, C. D. (1985). An analysis of selected ethical issues in therapeutic recreation. *Therapeutic Recreation Journal, 19*(4), 8-21.

U.S. Public Health Service. (1989, September). Responsibilities of awardee and applicant institutions for dealing with and reporting possible misconduct in science [special issue]. *NIH Guide for Grants and Contracts, 18*(30).

Wilensky, H. L. (1964). The professionalization of everyone? *The American Journal of Sociology, 58*(2), 137-158.

Zola, J. C., Sechzer, J. A., Sieber, J. E., & Griffin, A. (1984). Animal experimentation: Issues for the 1980's. *Science, Technology and Human Values, 9,* 40-50.

Zuckerman, M. (1990). Some dubious premises in research and theory on racial differences: Scientific, social and ethical issues. *American Psychologist, 45*(12), 1297-1303.

Appendix[7]

Selected Sections of the American Psychology Association's Ethical Principles (APA, 1990).

Principle 5: Confidentiality

Psychologists have a primary obligation to respect the confidentiality of information obtained from persons in the course of their work... They reveal such information to others only with the consent of the person or the person's legal representative, except in those unusual circumstances in which to not do so would result in clear danger to the person or to others. Where appropriate, psychologists inform their clients of the legal limits of confidentiality.

a. Information obtained in clinical or consulting relationships, or evaluative date concerning children, students, employees, and others, is discussed only for professional purposes and only with persons clearly concerned with the case. Written and oral reports present only data germane to the purposes of the evaluation, and every effort is made to avoid undue invasion of privacy.

b. Psychologists who present personal information obtained during the course of professional work in writing, lectures, or other public forums either obtain adequate prior consent to do so or adequately disguise all identifying information.

c. Psychologists make provisions for maintaining confidentiality in the storage and disposal of records.

d. When working with minors or other persons who are unable to give voluntary, informed consent, psychologists take special care to protect these persons' best interests. (APA, 1990, p. 392 - 393).

Principle 9: Research with Human Participants

The decision to undertake research rests upon a considered judgment by the individual psychologist about how best to contribute to psychological science and human welfare. Having made the decision to conduct research, the psychologist considers alternative directions in which research energies and resources might be invested. On the basis of this consideration, the psychologist carries out the investigation with respect and concern for the dignity and welfare of the people who participate and with cognizance of federal and state regulations and professional standards governing the conduct of research with human participants.

---

7. All material from the American Psychological Association's (1990) Ethical principles of psychologists are copyright 1990 by the American Psychological Association. Reprinted by permission.

a. In planning a research study, the investigator has the responsibility to make a careful evaluation of its ethical acceptability. To the extent that the weighing of scientific and human values suggests a compromise of any [ethical] principle, the investigator incurs a correspondingly serious obligation to seek ethical advice and to observe stringent safeguards to protect the rights of human participants.

b. Considering whether a participant in a planned study will be a subject at risk or a 'subject at minimal risk,' according to recognized standards, is of primary ethical concern to the investigator.

c. The investigator always retains the responsibility for ensuring ethical practice in research. The investigator is also responsible for the ethical treatment of research participants by collaborators, assistants, students, and employees, all of whom, however, incur similar obligations.

d. Except in minimal-risk research, the investigator establishes a clear and fair agreement with research participants, prior to their participation, that clarifies the obligations and responsibilities of each. The investigator has the obligation to honor all promises and commitments included in that agreement. The investigator informs the participants of all aspects of the research that might reasonably be expected to influence willingness to participate and explains all other aspects of the research about which the participants inquire. Failure to make full disclosure prior to obtaining informed consent requires additional safeguards to protect the welfare and dignity of the research participants. Research with children or with participants who have impairments that would limit understanding and/or communication requires special safeguarding procedures.

e. Methodological requirements of a study may make the use of concealment or deception necessary. Before conducting such a study, the investigator has a special responsibility to (i) determine whether use of such techniques is justified by the study's prospective scientific, educational, or applied value; (ii) determine whether alternative procedures are available that do not use concealment or deception; and (iii) ensure that the participants are provided with sufficient explanation as soon as possible

f. The investigator respects the individual's freedom to decline to participate in or to withdraw from the research at any time. The obligation to protect this freedom requires careful thought and consideration when the investigator is in a position of authority or influence over the participant. Such positions of authority include, but are not limited to, situations in which research participation is required as part of employment or in which the participant is a student, client, or employee of the investigator.

g. The investigator protects the participant from physical and mental discomfort, harm and danger that may arise from research procedures. If risks of such consequences exist, the investigator informs the participant of that fact.

Research procedures likely to cause serious or lasting harm to a participant are not used unless the failure to use these procedures might expose the participant to risk of greater harm, or unless the research has great potential benefit and fully informed and voluntary consent is obtained from each participant. The participant should be informed of procedures for contacting the investigator within a reasonable time period following participation should stress, potential harm, or related questions or concerns arise.

h. After the data are collected, the investigator provides the participant with information about the nature of the study and attempts to remove any misconceptions that may have arisen. Where scientific or humane values justify delaying or withholding information, the investigator incurs a special responsibility to monitor the research and to ensure that there are no damaging consequences for the participant.

i. Where research procedures result in undesirable consequences for the individual participant, the investigator has the responsibility to detect and remove or correct these consequences, including long-term effects.

j. Information obtained about a research participant during the course of an investigation is confidential unless otherwise agreed upon in advance. When the possibility exists that others may obtain access to such information, this possibility, together with the plans for protecting confidentiality, is explained to the participant as a part of the procedure obtaining informed consent. (APA. 1990, pp. 394-395)

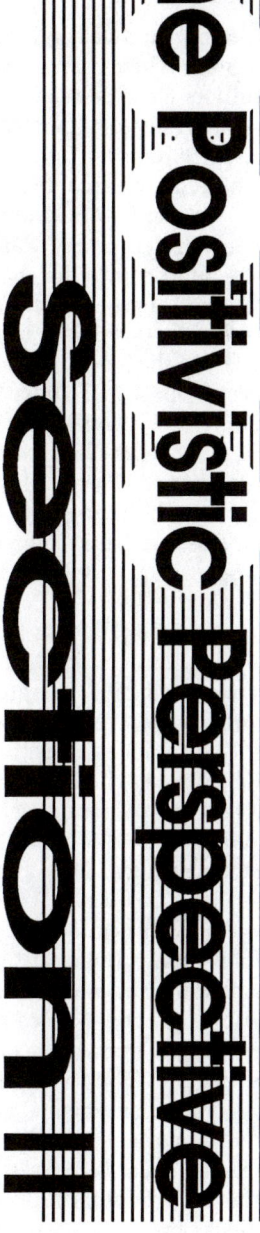

The Positivistic Perspective

section II

Section II—The Positivistic Perspective

Authors Caldwell and Weissinger in Chapter 7 provide the lead chapter in this section. Their chapter was one of the original inspirations for this text. The authors lead the readers through all of the parts of the research article, and explain how to understand, interpret, and use the information presented in the research report. This chapter sets the frame for the following two chapters and introduces much of the relevant terminology.

Chapter 8 is another contributed by Caldwell, who addresses survey research design and data collection issues. Relevant examples from actual research projects are included in this chapter. Caldwell focuses on survey research employing closed-ended items and structured interview questions within the positivistic research paradigm so that the results yielded are appropriate to the kinds of quantitative analyses offered in the chapter that follows.

Dunn, in Chapter 9, tackles a difficult issue, that of interpreting positivistic research, and issues of validity and reliability. By describing and explaining these concepts, Dunn clarifies the meaning of such terms. Readers are aided by reference to TR examples. Dunn emphasizes the necessity to judge the quality of research findings and to evaluate the circumstances related to the research process which might threaten the quality of these results. This must be done in order to draw reasoned conclusions and to interpret the meaning of the results.

Within Chapter 10, authors Dattilo, Gast, and Schleien provide a comprehensive introduction to design considerations (internal validity, external validity, and reliability) in single-subject research. This chapter also describes what single-subject research is and how it may be used when investigating persons with disabilities. There is a series of examples of situations in which single-subject research has been used in TR settings. A major premise of this chapter is that this form of quasi-experimental research is intuitively appealing and quite compatible with the day-to-day responsibilities of the TRS , thereby representing a viable avenue for better understanding of the TR consumer of services.

To conclude this section, authors Coyle, Kinney, and Shank analyze "trials and tribulations" in conducting field-based research in TR, as well as practical realities and concerns. The intent of Chapter 11 is to encourage readers to engage in field-based research trials in order to assist in the advancement of the body of knowledge in TR and the development of empirical evidence of the efficacy of TR interventions. Positivist research design is explained (experimental, quasi-experimental and preexperimental) and examples are presented of studies implemented in TR settings. Practical realities of implementing research in field-based settings are discussed, such as determining institutional and departmental support, staff training, pilot testing, etc. Impact on routine client care is discussed.

A Model for Research Utilization in Therapeutic Recreation
Linda L. Caldwell and Ellen Weissinger

We frequently hear therapeutic recreation specialists say "We recognize the need and value of research. We believe it is important for the future of therapeutic recreation. We are competent people and can understand it if we are taught— BUT—we are also busy people and have many competing important things to accomplish, as well as research. What can we do? How do we develop at least minimal research skills? How do we begin to incorporate a research orientation in our work?" These questions probably sound only too familiar to the busy TRS.

First, we applaud the TRSs who ask these questions and have these concerns. Busy TRSs are on the right track in acknowledging the need for research. We hope the TR research community, as represented by us, is also on the right track by attempting within this chapter to provide readers with some tools and strategies for reading, interpreting, and utilizing research. We also hope that this chapter will help to demystify TR research, and that it will provide an inspiration to begin to consider the ways in which research or researchers can be used in practice.

There are three main goals to this chapter. First, we want to provide a conceptual model of how research and program evaluation fit together. Second, we wish to offer specific strategies so that the investigative TRS may pick up a typical, positivistic research article and read, understand, and use this information on the job. Finally, to echo Chapter 5, we want to encourage TRSs to find local/regional TR researchers with whom to establish collaborative efforts. TR researchers at universities and colleges, and their students, are continually looking for programs and populations with whom to work. They want to do something beneficial for the field in general as well as for specific programs and/or organizations.

CHAPTER 7

Collaboration in Research

Before presenting our ideas and strategies, it will be helpful to discuss some issues that arise in collaborative efforts and acknowledge some potential problems areas. We have had the fortunate experience of conducting several research workshops in the U.S. and Canada for TRSs. The researchers who present and/or discuss various issues related to research usually encourage the TRSs who attend to contact them or any other researcher and set up research projects. The trap that everyone has fallen into is the "Rosy Picture Syndrome"; it's too easy to paint a rosy picture about how easy it is and great it will be to collaborate. To ignore or fail to recognize potential problem areas will cause frustrations and possible failure. By recognizing potential problem areas and addressing them promptly, collaborators can avoid frustration and the loss of valuable time and energy.

Most professionals can identify and recognize general differences between TRSs, TR managers, TR administrators, and TR researchers. These differences, while they don't always exist (as is the problem with any generalization), do need to be recognized so they do not cause undue frustration and lead to thwarted collaborative efforts. In fact, in a 1986 workshop sponsored by the Ontario Therapeutic Recreation Council, Central West Branch, one of the authors conducted a session designed to initiate such collaborative research efforts among TRSs, researchers, and students. A large portion of the workshop was devoted to each group helping the other group "walk/wheel a mile in my shoes." TRSs related the difficulties they encountered by having research (by faculty or students) conducted in their facility, while nonresearch students and faculty related similar problems and frustrations from their perspective. For example, in one institution, the institutional review board in the TRS's facility was on a different time table than what was most expedient for the student and faculty researchers. The beginning of the research study had to be delayed due to this difference in time schedules.

So, did the audience give up and walk out after hearing all these negative aspects of research? No. All agreed that the dialogue was extremely productive and beneficial strategies were an outcome of this endeavor. *Realistic* enthusiasm was generated. Researchers and students realized they couldn't just walk into a facility/agency and be met with open arms when they said they wanted to do research. TRSs realized that if they had something they wanted to find out about their program or population, they couldn't just call up any researcher and ask to have research conducted in their facility. They must first give some real thought regarding types of research questions to be addressed (even though they may be nonspecific), protocols, and resources needed. Participants were reminded that most individual research projects are specific and limited to one problem or question whereas the TRSs are open to information from all sources and mix and employ a variety of protocols. It surely seems that TRSs have a broader perspective than researchers.

The most important outcome of the workshop was that each group realized how important the other group was, and that collaborative efforts could lead to positive and productive results for TR and its clients.

With this introduction in mind, we believe that to begin to learn how to be an informed consumer of research—reading, conducting, contracting for, and utilizing research—a basic knowledge base or research literacy is necessary. We all know what it's like to sit in a class (e.g., physics) where we are bombarded with new information and then asked if we have any questions. Formulating any type of question, let alone an intelligent question, is almost impossible because we have no knowledge base, experiential base, or context from which to draw. Therefore, the intent of this next section is to acquaint the curious and interested TRS with the entire research process from a holistic perspective. Hopefully this will assist the reader in developing or enhancing his or her knowledge base about research.

The Research Process and Program Evaluation

The relationship between research and program evaluation (also called evaluation research) is often unclear. The model provided in Figure 7.1, page 130, is an attempt to clarify this relationship. The first thing to note about the model is that both program evaluation and research are processes; in fact, they are similar processes.

Each process is briefly examined. First, look at the upper portion of the model which represents the **evaluation** process. The development of *goals* is critical to this process. Moreover, these goals must be *measurable* and *observable*. From these goals the program is developed and evaluated. During and after implementation of the program, many observations are made. In the evaluation process, *observations* are utilized in determining to what extent program goals have been met. In other words, did the program work? Did it have an effect? The findings of the evaluation lead back into refinement and modification of the program. In addition, evaluation findings can be a direct source of evidence in the justification of services and of quality assurance. Program evaluation is concerned with evaluating the effectiveness of *specific interventions or programs*.

Next we examine the research process which is depicted in the bottom half of the model. Note that observations can be used not only to evaluate a specific program but to stimulate more *generalized thinking*. This can lead to the development of research questions. Just as goals guide the evaluation

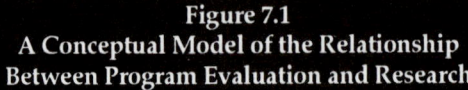

Figure 7.1
A Conceptual Model of the Relationship
Between Program Evaluation and Research

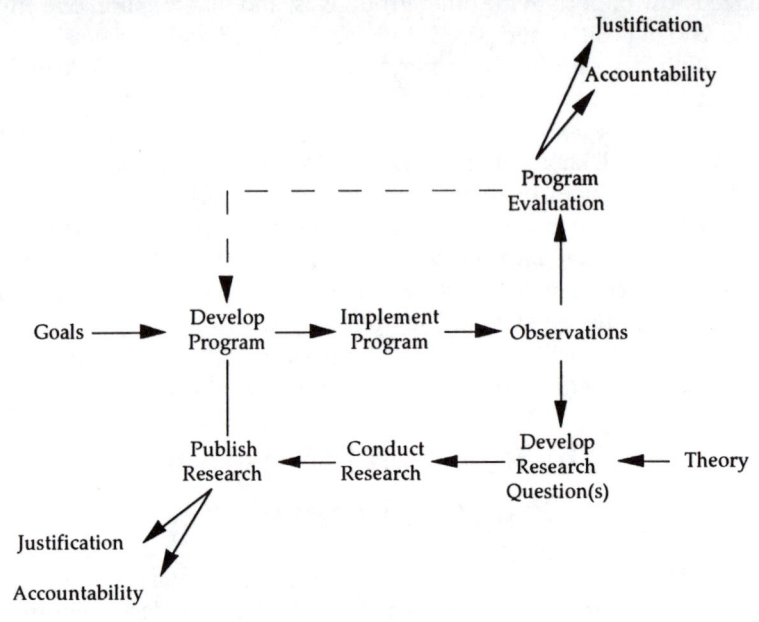

process, **research questions**, which are based on *theory* and/or observations, guide the research process. The research process is concerned with relationships—not as they are unique to a specific program, but as they are generalizable to other programs, settings, and populations. The outcome of the research process, published research reports, can generate ideas and rationale for program development. This knowledge is also important for further theory building. Published research, too, is useful as documentation in the justification for and accountability of services.

As one can see, then, research and program evaluation follow similar processes. Both are geared toward answering questions in a systematic, logical progression of steps and ideas. The principles involved in the program evaluation process can be fairly easily transferred to the research process. The major difference is that in research, there are some additional scientific principles (such as probability theory) that are employed to help ensure generalizability and the broader application of results.

An illustration of the relationship depicted in the model can be found in a *Therapeutic Recreation Journal* article entitled "The Effect of Refreshments on Attendance at Recreation Activities for Nursing Home Residents"

(Gillespie, McLellan, & McGuire, 1984). The researchers were interested in finding out whether or not there were differences in attendance between recreation activities where refreshments were served and activities where refreshments were not served. In this study "refreshments" is the independent variable (presumed cause) and "amount of attendance" is the dependent variable (presumed effect).

The type of question that this study examined could have been addressed either through research or program evaluation. The authors were primarily concerned with evaluating their program. At the same time, however, in the interest of making their findings generalizable to other nursing home settings, they employed the research process. The researchers employed a **quasi-experimental** design using techniques such as random assignment, comparison (treatment and control) groups, and tests of statistical significance. (See Chapter 11 by Coyle, Shank, and Kinney for a further discussion of this design.) In addition, the researchers also relied on theory to provide them with a solid foundation for their research. If the authors had been interested primarily in determining whether goals *specific* to their program and setting had been met, then an evaluation process would have been used that just focused on their particular setting. As predicted, they found that refreshments did positively influence attendance.

Note that, as suggested in the model, this published research has direct implications for program development. Also, this report could be a useful way to justify program services and expenditures. It is an interesting note that the senior author of this particular study is a TR practitioner. We feel this is exciting because it represents an important example of positive and successful collaborative efforts between researchers and TRSs.

Strategies for Reading Research

Now that we've examined how research fits into the scheme of things, we will suggest some strategies that will enable readers to decipher positivistic research language and reports. There is no doubt that a different language is used in these reports. Just as physicians, nurses, PTs, and community organizers have their own language, so do researchers. This language exists for precisely the same reason as other professional languages exist: for efficient communication of ideas and information. Researchers, even those in the social and behavioral sciences, consider themselves scientists. In order that a researcher in a TR journal can communicate with a developmental psychologist, or vice versa, a common and precise research language must be shared.

Generally, each research article has a similar format. We will address each section of a research article separately and indicate what types of information one should be trying to gather from each section. It may help to think of reading a research report as similar to reading a good mystery novel.

The readers want to find out who the characters are, what they did, why they did what they did, how they did it, and what implications follow from their actions.

There is one qualifier to keep in mind before continuing. The following discussion relates to reading research articles based on positivistic and rationalistic research studies. These types of studies are reported similarly, based on well-accepted, standard and traditional protocol. Studies conducted using a phenomenological framework are reported much differently (see Chapter 14 by Stumbo & Little).

The Introduction Section to an Article

Typically, the positivistic research article begins with an introductory section. In this section, the author acquaints the readers with some background information about the topic under study. Included is a review of relevant literature that lends support to the significance of the problem and demonstrates the *theory(ies)* behind the research effort. In addition, the researcher should provide a clear *statement of the specific problem* under study, the *variables* involved, and the *hypothesized relationship(s)* between the variables. Often, a researcher will specify the *research questions* that were the focus of the study, or specify the exact **hypotheses** of concern. Taking the example of the study on refreshments mentioned earlier, the major variables were refreshments and attendance. The hypothesized relationship was that refreshments influenced attendance. The research question could be formulated as "Does the provision of refreshments increase attendance at activity functions?" This question was the basis for the entire study.

When reading the introduction, the investigative TRS should gain an understanding of what is being studied. It is important to clearly understand the research questions the author(s) is investigating. The TRS will want to keep this research problem in mind when reading the rest of the article because the methods and results will stem from the research question. The rest of the article will make more sense if the question(s) under study are understood.

Another valuable contribution of the introduction to an article is that it provides the reader with *sources for additional references*. If the article addresses a topic of specific concern, one can use the literature review as a starting point to collect materials for follow-up reading.

The Methods Section

Now that *what* is being studied is known, the researcher describes *how* the problem was studied. The methods section contains this information. While each author presents information in a unique fashion, there are some fairly standard pieces of information, such as:

1. **Research participants** (subjects or respondents). The author should state who was studied. Characteristics of the participants/subjects/respondents such as age, sex, disability, race, region, and group membership may be included. This is important because it indicates to which groups the study findings apply most directly.
2. **Sampling**. The sampling method used should be indicated. It should be clear how the respondents in the study were chosen. What was the group from which the sample was drawn? Did every member of the group have an equal chance of being chosen to become a part of the sample (that is, were participants *randomly selected*)? Was the sample a good representation of the overall population of concern? Were respondents assigned randomly to experimental conditions? These are important questions that the researcher should answer. The research texts identified at the end of this chapter all provide information on sampling methodology.

   Knowing the sampling method will enable the evaluation of how much confidence one may have in the results. This enables readers to better judge the degree to which the sample represents a larger population that wasn't *directly* studied. In general, random sampling methods are superior because they increase the representativeness of the sample, and therefore reduce the likelihood that the sample is greatly different from the larger population it was intended to represent. There are, however, times when other types of sampling strategies are acceptable or desirable.
3. **Variables**. The specific variables under study should be introduced. In the introduction section, the researcher explained conceptually what the variables were. Now the researcher needs to state exactly what variables were used to represent each concept, and how each variable was measured. For example, what specific refreshments were used? It makes a big difference if liverwurst sandwiches or ice cream sandwiches were served. Further, specifically how was attendance measured—by the number of people who came initially or by the number of people who remained at the end of the activity?

For any given variable in any given study, many types of measurements are possible. As was mentioned, **conceptual variables** (e.g., satisfaction or attendance) can be defined (**operationalized**) in various ways. Some variables (e.g., satisfaction) are more difficult to measure than others (e.g., attendance). Researchers decide how to measure a variable based on the intent of the study and the nature of the research question. Often, the goal is to maximize the degree to which the variable in the study reflects the way that variable happens in the real world.

Once the variable has been operationalized (defined), the researcher has several options about how to collect information about the operationalized variable. For example, in positivistic research variables are often measured via self-reports from the participants, observations of behavior, or perhaps structured interviews with the individuals under study. The way in which the variable is operationalized, and the way in which the data are collected, affect how valid (measuring what you think you are measuring) and reliable (obtaining the same results repeatedly, and under different circumstances) the information gathered is. All researchers are concerned with the *validity and reliability* of the measurement of the variables in the study.

If the author is describing relationships between variables and is concerned about one or more variables *influencing* one or more other variables, the author should clearly specify which variables are assumed to influence which others. That is, the author should identify the **independent** *and* **dependent variables.** In the refreshment study, refreshments (the independent variable) were thought to influence attendance (the dependent variable). One should take care to note which variable is presumed to influence the other.

Often, there are a number of independent variables thought to influence one dependent variable. For example, if a TRS wanted to understand leisure satisfaction with the programs that are offered (the dependent variable, the one that is being influenced), he or she would think about all the things that may influence one's satisfaction. Things like the time of day the program is offered, the leader of the program, the motivation of the participant, and the prior expectations of the participant may all influence satisfaction and would all be considered independent variables if they were included in the study. Remember, based on the model presented earlier, the inclusion of these variables should be based on some conceptual or theoretical premise.

The author may not have been interested in the influence of one or more variables on another, but rather may have been interested in *describing* the variables. This is common when no prior theory exists to suggest a relationship among/between variables. Nevertheless, the variables should be identified, but no distinction is made between independent and dependent variables. This type of research is called exploratory research.

The Procedures Section

A thorough outline of the steps involved in the study should be presented in the procedures section. This enables the reader to understand exactly how the data were collected. One should consider how logical these procedures were, and what relevance they have to "real world" settings.

Several general types of research procedures are utilized in positivistically-oriented therapeutic recreation research. Three common methods are illustrated here. **Survey** studies use questionnaires, interviews, or observations to gather information from many people or groups. It is best when the respondents in the survey have been randomly selected to participate. The resulting data can then be analyzed to discover relationships between the variables included in the survey. For example, Caldwell, Adolph, and Gilbert (1989) conducted a survey of individuals who had been discharged from a rehabilitation facility. In this study, the authors were interested in examining the relationship of having participated in a leisure counselling program while in the facility, and leisure satisfaction, boredom in leisure, and postdischarge constraints to leisure.

Experimental studies are those in which the researcher randomly assigns study participants to various groups (conditions), then does something (the treatment) different to each group. Often, researchers will employ a control group where nothing is done to the group. Groups are then compared to find out if different treatments result in different outcomes or responses. As an example, Backman and Mannell (1986) conducted a quasi-experiment to examine the efficacy of a leisure counselling program (study group 1) by comparing it with an activity exposure program (study group 2), a control group (group 3) who received neither program, and a group who got both the leisure education and activity exposure programs (group 4).

Single-subject studies are research projects in which *one* person, or one group of persons, is studied for a period of time in order to determine outcomes resulting from some treatment. The data from one individual or group are assessed for a baseline level and then analyzed for changes that occur after the treatment is introduced. Dattilo and Barnett (1985) conducted a multiple baseline, single-subject study with four school-aged children with severe handicaps. In this study a strategy was designed to teach subjects to activate a television program by manipulating an electronic switch. (Single-subject experimental designs are elaborated upon in Chapter 10, while quasi-experimental designs are covered in more detail in Chapter 11.)

The Results Section

Many people tend to skip this section because it is often difficult to understand! We hope the following suggestions will provide the tools to decipher this section of a research article.

After the researcher has collected the data, they are analyzed. Before one reads the results section he or she should think again about the question(s) under study and what the variables are. After reading through the methods section, it is often easy to forget what the overall purpose of the research was. The researcher should reveal what *statistical procedures* were used, and why. The results section is where the researcher tells what was discovered about the variables, and ultimately, what *conclusions* were drawn about the research question.

The findings are often summarized in tables or graphs representing the frequency of occurrence of a given variable. Useful statistics such as mean (average) scores on variables are provided. Also, it is in this section that the researcher will present the results of analyzing the relationships among variables. While these results are often confusing to the novice research reader, it is important to determine which relationships were **statistically significant**. It is those relationships that are generally most important. One should also ask if what the researcher reports as statistically significant has any *practical significance*.

Statistics are used instead of intuitive methods because statistics allow the researcher to reduce and/or control *error*. In addition, certain types of statistics, such as the ones described below, allow the researcher to make generalizations from a smaller sample to a larger population.

Almost always in positivistic research, significance is represented through a "shorthand" notation such as $p < 0.05$ or $p < 0.001$. The first example indicates that 95 times out of 100 the researcher is sure he or she found a "true" relationship and that the results didn't happen by chance (error). The latter example follows the same logic, but in this case the researcher is sure 99.9 times out of 100.

Following is a brief description of several statistics commonly used in therapeutic recreation research. These are presented NOT to create a statistics whiz, but to make it easier to decipher what is in a research report. The **Chi-square** or X^2 is used when two variables are compared to each other to see if knowing something about one variable will tell anything about the other variable. (If they don't, they are independent of each other.) Each variable usually has one or more levels or categories. For example, a researcher could examine the relationship between *type of disability* (e.g., mental, physical, and sensory) and *age* (under 20 years, between 21 and 50 years, and over 51 years). If the researcher indicates a significant result, then, in this case, type of disability is related to age. That is, knowing something about one variable (type of disability) will give you information about the other variable (age). If the researcher presents a table of these results, you may see, for example, that there are more people in the over 51 category that have sensory disorders.

The **t-test** is used to compare means (averages) between two levels of one variable (e.g., type of disability). For example, one could compare means of perceived self-confidence between people who are physically disabled and people who are mentally disabled. If the researcher indicates a significant result, then there is a statistically significant difference between the means, and one can determine which group has a higher level of perceived self-confidence.

ANOVA, or analysis of variance, is basically the same as a t-test. The difference is that instead of comparing variable means on two categories or levels, a variable has more than two categories. In the above example, if we also wanted to compare mean self-confidence scores for people who are sensorially disabled, we would use an ANOVA. This test is also used to compare *two* variables with two or more categories for each variable (a 2x2 design). If the researcher indicates a significant result, then there is a difference among the means.

Regression analysis allows the researcher to determine whether a group of variables (independent variables) influence another variable (dependent variable). Many independent variables can be tested simultaneously to see whether they influence the dependent variable. Those variables that are significant *do* influence the dependent variable.

A **correlation** is a measure of how related one variable is to another. In other words, it is a measure of how much the two variables share in common. The following scale may help in understanding a correlation. Correlations range from -1 to +1 (see Figure 7.2).

Figure 7.2		
-1	0	+1
Strong negative relationship	No relationship	Strong positive relationship

If a researcher reports a correlation of 0.63, one would conclude that the two variables being correlated have a fairly strong, positive relationship with each other. If the correlation was -0.63, one would also conclude that there was a strong relationship, but this time the relationship is inverse. That is, as scores on one variable go up, the scores on the other variable go down. A correlation does not have to be significant to be meaningful.

The Discussion Section

The final section of the research report should do several things. First, the researcher should summarize in a general way the findings of the study. This summary is intended to *interpret* the results in light of the research question. Did the results support the researcher's expectations (hypotheses), or were there unintended or unanticipated results? Second, the discussion section should address *competing explanations* for the findings. That is, what are some plausible explanations for what occurred in the study besides the original hypothesis offered by the researcher? This is particularly helpful if there were unintended or unanticipated results. The researcher should note any unplanned changes in the procedures, or any unusual occurrences that might have affected the results.

Finally, a discussion of the *implications* of the research findings is offered. One set of implications regard future research needs related to the question at hand. Research usually generates many more questions than it answers; consequently, this section is a fertile one for determining future research efforts. Perhaps most important to the practitioner, the researcher should attempt to describe possible implications of the research findings to other appropriate settings. The researcher, however, will only be able to discuss the generalizability and possible utilization of the results in a broad manner. Therefore, readers need to think about how to extract information for their own purposes.

Utilizing the Research

We offer the following list of questions as a suggested guideline for utilizing information from a research report. Again, these are broad questions to be tailored to the TRS's own situation. Remember to keep in mind that, although the research study may not apply to all situations at all levels, it is very possible that there is useful information that can be derived from the study for reader's personal situations.

1. Are the variables under study in some way of interest to me? Is the research question at all like the questions I have asked in my setting? Is the researcher interested in examining relationships among/between variables that may occur in my setting?
2. Do the behaviors, attitudes, treatments, etc. under study occur in my setting?
3. Does the population under study exhibit relevant commonalities to the population I serve? If not, does it matter? Or, are the ideas or concepts (variables) more important to me?
4. Is the sequence of events in the research study somehow relevant to procedures that I follow?
5. What can the findings of the study tell me about my situation? What modifications to my existing procedures are suggested by the findings? How do the findings inform me about the impact of treatments or interventions? What innovations or new procedures are suggested for my setting, based on the findings?

6. How can I use the results of this study to justify my program? Does the study demonstrate the efficacy of a treatment program similar to my own? Do the results indicate the important or significant outcomes of a relevant treatment? Do the results suggest effective benefits for acceptable costs?

7. What new questions does this study raise for me? How can my thinking about my situation be stimulated by the results?

In short, the key to utilizing published research is to determine how the results of the study may be informative to you in understanding or improving the services provided. Investigative TRSs must keep in mind that research must be conducted on very specific populations and by very specific methods, but that should not block their ability to visualize that the concepts or ideas from the findings may be relevant, even though the TRS's specific population or situation is not identical to that of the original study.

Summary and Conclusion

The authors of this chapter have attempted to enable readers to better understand and utilize research reports. It should be obvious that the task of interpreting research is not always easy, but neither is it unknowable or incomprehensible. We hope that the information provided will provide a foundation from which to work, thereby in some way motivating TRSs to think about collaboratively conducting research in their facilities or departments.

There is another motivation for reading, conducting, and utilizing research. A secondary, generally unintended outcome of research as well as program evaluation is the reduction of burnout. While this has not been empirically shown to be true, it is at least intuitively obvious that if professionals can demonstrate through rigorous research that therapeutic recreation is indeed a viable process, they are bound to be more satisfied with their jobs. In TR, it is well-known that the changes that professionals are trying to effect often come slowly or appear invisible. If research can show that the processes and techniques of TR do contribute to clients' well-being, TRSs are bound to believe in themselves and what they do all the more.

As previously mentioned, reading research is like being involved in a good mystery novel. One has to figure out the plot by sifting through lots of details. But in the same way that figuring out "who done it" can be challenging and satisfying, determining the applicability of a research study to a given setting can be satisfying as well. In the final judgment, utilizing research findings to enhance the quality of client services, to strengthen the justification of services, or to improve professional efficacy in any way is a goal worthy of one's time and attention.

Discussion Questions

1. What is the relationship between research and program evaluation? While both use the research process, what is the major difference between the two?
2. What information will one usually find in the introduction section of a research article?   Be specific, and state what function each type of information serves for the reader of the article.
3. Generally, what kind of information should the reader glean from the methods section? Identify some concerns related to the participant characteristics and sampling procedure portions of the methods section.
4   What do variables represent?   What is the relationship between a dependent variable and an independent variable?
5. Identify three specific research procedures often used in positivistic TR research.
6. If something is statistically significant at a level of $p < .05$, what does this mean?
7. What is the primary function of the discussion section? How should the reader go about determining the generalizability of the results of the research article?

References

Backman, S. J., & Mannell, R. C. (1986). Removing attitudinal barriers to leisure behavior and satisfaction: A field experiment among the institutionalized elderly. *Therapeutic Recreation Journal, 20*(3), 46-53.

Caldwell, L. L., Adolph, S. A., & Gilbert, A. (1989). Caution! leisure counselors at work: Long term effects of leisure counseling. *Therapeutic Recreation Journal 23*(3), 41-49.

Dattilo, J., & Barnett, L. A. (1985). Therapeutic recreation for individuals with severe handicaps: An analysis of the relationship between choice and pleasure. *Therapeutic Recreation Journal, 19*(3), 79-91.

Gillespie, K., McLellan, R. W., & McGuire, F. M. (1984). The effect of refreshments on attendance at recreation activities for nursing home residents. *Therapeutic Recreation Journal, 8*(3), 25-29.

Suggested Sources for Further Information

Babbie, E. (1992). *The practice of social research.* (6th ed.).   Belmont, CA: Wadsworth. This is a highly readable, comprehensive text that covers both methodological and statistical issues. Dr. Babbie writes with great clarity and uses examples throughout the presentation. The book is written (believe it or not) with humor and warmth. We recommend it as the place to begin your search for further information about research and its implications.

Borg, W., & Gall, M. (1990). *Educational research: An introduction.* (5th ed.). White Plains, NY: Longman. We recommend this because of the similarities between educational research and some aspects of TR research. Since educators must deal with "applied" research questions and evaluation issues, many of the examples in Borg and Gall may have parallels in TR settings. The book provides a complete overview of the research process and has a useful chapter about critically evaluating published research.

Carlsmith, J. M., Ellsworth, P., & Aronson, E. (1990). *Methods of research in social psychology.* (2nd ed.). Reading, MA: Addison-Wesley. This is the most readable text about experimental methodology we've seen.

Cook, T., & Campbell, D. (1979). *Quasi-experimentation: Design and analysis issues in field settings.* Boston, MA: Houghton Mifflin. This is a somewhat technical, but very comprehensive, text concerned with "treatment" type studies. It is based on educational interventions but can be easily generalized to TR setting. Quasi-experimental designs are often very useful in evaluation research.

Katzer, F., Cook, K., & Crouch, W. (1991). *Evaluating information: A guide for users of social science research*. (3rd ed.). New York: McGraw-Hill. This is a very well-written book that provides in-depth information about reading and using research studies.

Kerlinger, F. (1986). *Foundations of behavioral research*. (3rd ed.). New York: Holt, Reinhart and Winston, Inc. This is a more technical and more statistical than Babbie's text, but may be a good source of information on higher-level concerns and questions about research design and analysis.

Williams, F. (1992). *Reasoning with statistics: How to read quantitative research*. (4th ed.). Orlando, FL: Harcourt, Brace, Jovanovich. This is the best reference book for understanding more about statistical analysis. It is written in plain, common sense language and can be a very useful tool for comprehending the results section of any positivistically based article.

Survey Research in Therapeutic Recreation Settings: Design and Data Collection Issues
Linda L. Caldwell

CHAPTER 8

Survey research is a process with which most TRSs are familiar. Most readers have probably taken part in numerous surveys, from telephone surveys, to mail surveys, to those person-on-the-street surveys. The popularity of surveys suggests that there are reasons that surveys are good ways to collect data. This is true, but there are also drawbacks to the use of surveys, as well as poorly constructed surveys. This chapter explores these and other issues surrounding the use of surveys in TR settings. Specifically, this chapter covers the purpose of surveys; kinds of information derived from surveys; types of surveys; considerations in using surveys; and research and practical issues surrounding the use of surveys. At the end of the chapter two case studies involving the use of survey research are presented.

Purpose of Surveys

Essentially, **surveys** are a relatively inexpensive way to collect information from a large group of people. Surveys are most often used when it is imprudent or impossible to question everyone of interest. For example, if a TRS wants information about people who live in extended care facilities in his or her state, it would be inefficient to query everyone who lived in such facilities. Rather, the TRS would sample a select group of residents to be in the study group with the idea that this group would be representative of everyone in a similar situation.

There are a number of issues to consider when using a survey. In the above example readers may already see that who is selected to complete the survey and how he or she is selected are important considerations. Before these and other issues are addressed, what are the kinds of questions surveys can answer and what types of surveys exist?

Information Derived from Surveys

Surveys allow TRSs on the research team to collect data to; (a) *describe* people and situations; (b) *predict* future behavior and events; and (c) *explain* phenomena. The way the survey is conducted and the types of questions asked will determine the ability to describe, predict, or explain. Surveys may be used to describe, predict, or explain the following things about individuals with disabilities: opinions, attitudes, interests, knowledge, and behaviors.

A word of caution seems appropriate here. Just because TRSs have data doesn't mean they have information. This is true in all forms of research (both positivistic and phenomenological), but is especially important to keep in mind with survey research. It is easy to become seduced into collecting large amounts of data. A research team can think of many questions that would be interesting to examine. Beware of the "wouldn't it be interesting" trap, though. Pragmatically, the more questions that are asked the more fatigued the individual responding will become. Also, more time and money will have to be spent putting the data into useful form. Many competent researchers have piles of data languishing because of the "wouldn't it be interesting" trap.

To solve this problem, it is crucial to pose clearly defined, unambiguous **research questions**. These global questions will spawn the items actually used on the survey instrument. These specific survey questions should be kept to a reasonable minimum. Each survey item should have a purpose and should be directly linked to a research question. Before the survey is administered, the TRS should have thought through how the data are going to be used and the specific information each item will yield. Often it helps to actually construct mock tables of the results. Not only does this assist the TRS in understanding how the variables are expected to relate to each other, but also it helps to understand the purpose of each item on the survey instrument. The key is to turn data into information for use in practice, theory, and research—ultimately for the benefit of the clientele served.

Types of Surveys

Some surveys require the respondent to complete a questionnaire. These **self-administered questionnaires** are quite popular and versatile; they can be mailed to respondents or they can be distributed in a TR program or during a particular activity. A survey can also be conducted using an **interview** format where the interviewer asks the interviewee a number of questions, often from a preconstructed interview schedule/form. Interviews can be face-to-face or they may be done over the telephone; in fact, interviews are similar to having a structured (or semistructured) conversation with someone. Interviews that are conducted with groups of individuals are commonly called **focus groups**.

A number of factors determine which is the most appropriate method of data collection. While self-administered questionnaires and structured interviews are widely used as the sole means of data collection in survey research, both questionnaires and interviews can be used with other forms of data gathering efforts such as experiments or observations. Questionnaires and interviews can also be combined and used together in one study, as the rehabilitation hospital case study, which follows later in the chapter, illustrates.

Considerations in Using
Self-Administered Questionnaires

When self-administered surveys are used, research teams are making a number of important assumptions. First, teams assume that the respondent will understand the questions and be able to complete the questionnaire. Research teams also assume that the respondent will answer honestly and accurately. In some TR settings, the first assumption may be especially problematic. Many individuals with whom TRSs work may have difficulty understanding and interpreting items on a questionnaire in the way the researcher meant for the question to be interpreted. This situation would compromise the validity of the information gathered. One way to address this issue is to pretest the survey instrument. Chapters 9 by Dunn and 11 by Coyle, Kinney, and Shank provide detailed discussions on validity in TR research.

Even if a person can understand the items, it is possible that the individual may be unable to physically complete the questionnaire. Having someone such as a family member complete the questionnaire with the respondent may be a solution. It is important to keep in mind, however, that this situation would mean that the respondent would have to succinctly communicate his or her answer to the family member who is filling out the questionnaire. Then, the family member would have to accurately reflect the respondent's answer on the questionnaire. If the questionnaire is comprised of closed-ended items this may not be a problem. But, if there are a number of open-ended items, the validity of the information may be compromised due to inadvertent bias from the family member misinterpreting the respondent's answer.

Furthermore, if a questionnaire is mailed to a respondent, the research team has no control over who actually completes the questionnaire. When questionnaires are mailed out, there is almost always a specific person for whom the questionnaire is intended. This is done because the research team has specific items they would like addressed by a specific individual. But it is quite possible that the intended respondent's family member or care provider may actually complete the questionnaire.

Another consideration in using a self-administered questionnaire is that the research team must be able to ask its questions in very direct and simple ways. Clear, unambiguous language is essential. The questionnaire must also be as easy to complete as possible. The more complex the items or the questionnaire format, the more the research team will face problems regarding who fills out the questionnaire, the response rate, and the reliability of the responses.

Well-conceptualized and developed questionnaires do have a number of advantages over other methods of data collection. As mentioned earlier, the research team can collect a large amount of data. This is advantageous because it allows the team to make a determination about *generalizability* of the sample to the population it is intended to represent. The research team can compute how much error exists in the sample statistics. This is both a design and statistical issue which is beyond the scope of this chapter. Any good research text, however, will describe the notion of *standard error* and sample selection. (See the list of references and suggested readings at the end of this chapter.) A related issue is that a large sample will help the research team to determine the *reliability* of the items or measures on the questionnaire. (See Chapter 9 for a thorough discussion of reliability in TR research.)

From a practical perspective, surveys (particularly self-administered questionnaires) are relatively inexpensive and fast as compared to other methods of data collection. Efficiency is an important consideration to many managers and TRSs, especially when time is of the essence.

Considerations in Using Interviews

As previously noted, gathering information through the use of interviews is another common way to collect data about people's attitudes, opinions, behaviors, knowledge, and interests. Chapter 12 by Howe discusses interviews from a phenomenological perspective; the discussion in this chapter centers on structured and semistructured interviews used positivistically in a survey research approach.

One advantage of interviews that is particularly relevant to TR settings, is that interviewees need not physically complete a questionnaire. Rather, interviewees can verbally communicate their answers. Therefore, as long as the interviewee can understand the question and is able to communicate his or her answer, an interview is a viable means of gathering data. Of course, the same cautions are extended here as with the self-administered questionnaires. The interviewer must be able to accurately interpret the interviewee's answer and reflect that answer on the interview schedule. Usually the interviewer is trained to write down the interviewee's answer *verbatim*. The term "interpret" was just used, however, to indicate that in TR settings, if the interviewee has difficulty communicating, the interviewer sometimes must interpret the interviewee's answers for the purposes of filling out the interview form. If the interviewer is not able to do this, the problem of **bias** or error occurs. As with self-administered questionnaires, this situation would compromise the validity of the information obtained.

Interviews also allow the interviewer to clarify the interview items if they are not understood by the interviewee and to clarify the response if the interviewer does not fully understand what is being communicated. There are a number of ways bias could be introduced in this process; therefore, it is essential that the research team does everything possible to control and/or eliminate possibilities for bias to occur.

Interviews are not as efficient as self-administered questionnaires, although they are still relatively cost- and time-efficient for the depth of data gathered. If a large amount or more in-depth data are collected, usually more than one interviewer or interview session is necessary. Thus, it is important that all the interviewers are well-trained in the research protocol so that bias is not introduced. (Readers are quickly catching onto the fact that "bias" is a four-letter word in research, aren't they?) Interviewers are required to go through extensive role-playing situations which simulate the interview so that they all handle questions and situations consistently. This is very much like the concern with many observers of behavior in experimental research (see Chapter 11 for a further discussion of this topic) and raises the issue of *interrater* or *interobserver reliability*.

These days everybody is becoming increasingly sensitive to over use of the telephone as a means to collect data. This is primarily due to the backlash against telemarketing. Nevertheless, quality telephone surveys (interviews) can be very useful. While they do not provide the opportunity for the interviewer to pick up the visual clues that are possible when face-to-face interviews are used, they still allow for clarification of questions and answers and provide a more personal touch to the survey process. The upcoming rehabilitation hospital case study effectively used telephone interviews.

Surveys as Change Agents

It is important to think of any type of survey as a form of intervention or a change agent in itself. Surveys are intrusive methods of data collection that require the respondent to think and react to the material. As soon as someone does this, latent attitudes or interests are brought into consciousness. Respondents are made to think about the subject material. If TRSs reflect on their own experiences with surveys, they may recall that unless the question elicited an automatic response they probably sat and considered the question for a moment. After they finished the questionnaires, they probably still thought about the questions and the answers given.

Depending on the overall purpose of the questionnaire, this introspection is not necessarily a problem. If the questionnaire is designed to take a snapshot of what respondents feel or think at one particular moment in time, then all is well. This situation occurs in a *cross-sectional* design. It is important to realize, however, that respondents may actually learn something about themselves from completing the questionnaire. If a TRS gives a questionnaire which inquires about how much an individual with a disability values leisure, the person may come to realize that he or she does not have enough free time and may decide to do something about it. This often unanticipated, secondary consequence of administering a questionnaire is something that all research teams should keep in mind.

If the questionnaire will be used to measure changes in behavior or attitude across time, this consciousness-raising or learning from completing the questionnaire could be problematic. When used in program evaluation efforts a questionnaire is often given before a program begins and again after the program is completed. When using questionnaires in a *longitudinal* design as just described, it is important to determine the influence of the first administration of the questionnaire. Chapter 11, which discusses quasi-experiments, explores this issue further. The teen program case study at the end of this chapter discusses other issues related to this section.

Practical and Research Issues in Survey Research

Practical Issues

Rarely are research studies carried out by one individual. Research teams are usually more efficient and productive ways of conceptualizing and carrying out a research project; they also offer camaraderie. Putting together the right mix of people to collaborate on the study is important. Some of the most rewarding research we have done has been with research teams which consisted of TRSs, students, and fellow educators. This sentiment is also shared by many colleagues based in universities and TR settings and is the primary topic of Chapter 5. Everyone in these teams learns something, has unique perspectives to offer, and valuable roles to play regarding the many decisions to be made during a study.

The research team is responsible for conceptualizing the problem to be researched, designing the research method, deciding how the data are to be treated, and deciding what the information means and how to use it. It is beneficial to the management and operation of collaborative studies to develop a realistic time line of events and to decide who is responsible for accomplishing the different tasks.

From an agency or institutional perspective, the **research team** should consist of individuals who are responsible for conceptualizing the questions under investigation as well as individuals who are responsible for gathering the data. These individuals should be included in all phases of the research study, from beginning to end. Often, those people who are responsible for collecting the data are not included in the entire process. Not only does it make their jobs more difficult, but the level of commitment to the project in general, as well as the level of commitment and understanding needed to conform to the research protocol, is jeopardized. If data collectors do not understand the reasons behind the numerous decisions made about the research protocol, they are not as likely to abide by these decisions. If the protocol is not adhered to, unintentional bias during data collection is likely to compromise the results. So, information sharing, open communication, and ownership or investment among all involved in conducting the study are of paramount importance to an unbiased research effort.

Agency and institutional commitment is essential in carrying out the research project. Tangible resources, such as money for supplies and time for staff to devote to the project are necessities. Time is especially important, but difficult to come by. Time to think is not often considered a priority in agencies and institutions which are more action oriented. Many agencies and institutions have their own research committees. These committees, as noted in Chapter 6, have to approve the project and often have ideas for strengthening the proposed research.

A team comprised of practitioners, students, and educators often must make compromises. Compromises generally juxtapose the need to be "practical" with the need to follow a rigorous research process. Students and practitioners have deadlines and time constraints within which they must work. Academic researchers need to make sure that the study is as rigorous as possible so that the results are not compromised. In addition, everyone also has other legitimate, competing, and sometimes conflicting responsibilities as Chapters 5 and 6 point out. However, these conflicts can be anticipated and remedied in order to produce the needed information. The teen program case study presents the need for compromise.

The previous discussion is pertinent to all research efforts, but is also quite salient to survey research in TR settings. Practical considerations may seem to border on common sense, and as a result, often get overlooked. When seemingly trivial things are overlooked, however, problems often arise. The following comments pertain to research issues that specifically relate to conducting survey research in TR settings.

Research Issues

Research Questions

One of the hardest parts of any study is to identify and define exactly what the research questions are. Yet, this is one of the most crucial steps in ensuring that the collected data will yield meaningful information. Although one person may have the initial ideas, only through focused discussion by the entire research team will a productive set of research questions emerge. The person with the original ideas may be a practitioner, a student, or an educator. The ideas may emerge one day through conversation or team meetings, or they may emerge from reading and thinking about other research. Past experience is one of the best sources of research questions. TRSs should always be on the lookout for ideas and keep a file of them. At first, it doesn't matter if the idea is well-formulated—the most important thing is to get it down on paper. Then work on refining the idea. This is an iterative process, but important so that the final questionnaire is focused and doesn't turn out to be a fishing expedition.

Research questions are important because they set the foundation for the rest of the study. These research questions dictate the type of study that will be conducted as well as the type of items that will be asked of the respondent. For this chapter it is assumed that the research questions lend themselves to a survey approach. The research questions also often determine who will be included as participants in the study.

Research questions are *not* the questions or items that are included on the questionnaire or in the interview. The **research questions** are the purposive, "guiding light" questions. There may be three to five of these for any given study. A set of specific hypotheses or experience outcomes often accompany these questions. It is from these broader questions that the specific items are developed for the questionnaire or interview. This is called *operationalization* and is discussed later.

Sampling

After the research questions are solidified, and the type of survey is determined, the question of who will be included in the study needs to be addressed. This is a *sampling* issue. A detailed description would not be appropriate here as sample selection can get very complicated. A few issues, however, are worthwhile to discuss.

The rationale behind selecting a sample is that since the research team cannot ask questions of everyone of interest, a sample of people who will likely be representative of everyone (the population) must be selected. The driving question in choosing a sample is: To whom does the research team want to generalize its findings? There are a number of strategies that allow the research team to select an appropriate sample. Usually the "best" samples are those which are based on probability theory. These employ some form of *random sampling*. Nonprobabilistic samples are also used in survey research, and often in TR research. In these cases, however, the research team cannot generalize its findings beyond the sample. Both case studies described at the end of this chapter used nonprobabilistic samples.

There are many other sampling issues to consider, but two other important, related ones have to do with **response rate** and **nonresponse bias**: both of these can yield error in the sample. The response rate is usually given as a percentage and indicates how many people actually complete the questionnaire or interview out of the total number possible. If this response rate is judged to be low, e.g., 50%, then the research team may have to question the results of the study. A logical question to ask is what happened to the other 50%? Were they in some way different from those who agreed to participate in the survey? If they are different, then the research team runs the risk of having a strong nonresponse bias in the data.

To mitigate a low response rate, there are a number of strategies available. For example, appropriate incentives can be offered. Coupons to eateries or attractions, the ability to participate in a lottery for a prize, and tangible products such as key chains, literature, or T-shirts have all been used successfully to motivate people to agree to participate in surveys. Another successful method of increasing response rates with mail questionnaires is to follow the mailing of the questionnaire with a reminder postcard, and possibly even a letter, thanking the individual if he or she has participated, or reminding him or her to participate in case of forgetfulness. Finally, if the intended research participants can see the value of the survey and are motivated by an introductory letter or preface to an interview, they are more likely to agree to participate. As Chapter 6 confirms, all surveys must ensure the respondent of anonymity and confidential treatment of the information provided. The letter of introduction or preface to the interview will explain how this is to be accomplished. If the intended respondents trust that the information they provide will be treated in a confidential manner, they are also more likely to participate in the survey.

Sampling is a very complicated and critically important issue in survey research. If TRSs decide to conduct a survey, they must ensure that someone on the research team is well-versed in this process.

Questionnaire Design and Format

The overall organization of the survey instrument must follow a logical sequence. The order of sections of items as well as the order of items in each section should facilitate ease of completion and should be designed to maintain the respondent's or interviewee's interest. The research team should also be aware of sensitive areas of inquiry. Many people are uncomfortable when queried about their ages or income, for example. These types of items are often reserved for the end of the questionnaire.

A related concern is the placement of any other sensitive or more personal questions. Design the instrument such that the easy and nonthreatening items come first. This builds a rapport with the respondent or interviewee. After this rapport is established, individuals are more likely to provide answers to sensitive items.

Items that are intended to measure the same concept should be grouped together. If the TRS is interested in understanding attitudes about leisure and satisfaction with leisure pursuits, it would be preferable to group all items measuring attitudes together, and then group all items measuring satisfaction together. This assists the respondent or interviewee in thinking about the responses in a coherent manner. Another consideration is that if the questionnaire is somewhat lengthy, sections of questions that are more important than others should come near the beginning of the questionnaire. Respondent fatigue can cause missed answers or skipped sections of a long questionnaire.

The format of a self-administered questionnaire is very important. The initial impression of the questionnaire should be inviting. Effective use of colored paper (not going overboard like shocking pink!), pictures or graphics, the print as well as font sizes, and spacing of items must be deliberately addressed. While again much of this may seem to be common sense, often these details are overlooked, resulting in a poor instrument.

The last issue to be addressed with regard to instrument design and layout has to do with what will be done with the data after the survey is administered. Some foresight at this stage will prevent a lot of needless effort later. The data (in this case usually numbers) from the instrument must be put into a format that can be read by a statistical software program. Taking items from an instrument, deciding the code (number) to give each response for each item, and entering it into a data file (a file consisting of numbers to be used with the statistical software package) is called *coding* the data. As the instrument is developed, assign someone on the research team to address the issues of how the data are to be coded.

Measurement

Issues of survey instrument design and format are technical issues. Obviously these issues are important, but even more important are measurement issues. A TRS can take part in the most elegantly designed survey with a carefully selected sample, but if the survey items do not measure the intended variables in a reliable or valid fashion, the whole research study will have been in vain. As Chapter 9 goes into detail about reliability and validity issues; this chapter addresses some other concerns related to measurement.

Measurement of variables is a complex topic and can only be touched on here. When the investigative TRS turns the concepts and variables identified in the research questions into specific items on the questionnaire, this conceptual process is called **operationalization.**

Using published scales and measures with established reliability and validity is probably the best way to measure variables. In therapeutic recreation, however, there are not many published instruments that measure variables and concepts in which we are interested. The *Leisure Diagnostic Battery* (LDB) is an excellent example of a published instrument with established reliability and validity that is useful in TR settings (see Ellis & Witt, 1986). If the research team does not find a suitable published instrument, then the team will have to construct the survey items itself. This process takes much time, energy, and thought. Thoroughly reviewing the literature, pretesting the instrument for face validity, and measuring the reliability and validity of the instrument's scales are important in the instrument development process.

Survey items can be **open-ended** so that respondents or interviewees supply their own answers. Conversely, items can be **closed-ended** such that the research team supplies the response categories. For example, if the research team wanted to find out which activities persons with disabilities participated in, the team could state: "Please list the three activities you participate in on a regular basis." This open-ended question would allow the respondent to generate his or her own answers. On the other hand, the research team could have supplied a list of activities and instructed the respondent to "check all that apply." What is the difference between these two approaches? Several studies have indicated that closed-ended items produce a higher frequency of responses while open-ended items produce many answer categories which would not have appeared on a researcher-generated list of options (Shimizu, 1988). As a rule, use open-ended items when inquiring about complex issues or when all possible answer categories are not known. Keep in mind, however, coding open-ended items is a time consuming and often difficult process. Closed-ended items are best used when answer categories are mutually exclusive and exhaustive. These closed-ended items are often easier for a respondent to answer than are open-ended items. In TR settings, if communication with a respondent is difficult, closed-ended items may be more appropriate.

Writing clear, unambiguous items is both a skill and an art. Take a closer look at the item used to illustrate an open-ended question: "Please list the three activities you participate in on a regular basis." This is a poor item. Why? Because one might ask, what is a "regular basis"? Is it once a month, once a week, once a day, or some other time referent? Also, the reader may be thinking that the answer depends on what the activity is. Going kayaking, playing golf, and needlepoint may be regular activities in a person's repertoire, but the term "regular" has a different meaning for each activity.

Another confusing aspect of this question has to do with how long ago a respondent should begin thinking about being "regular"—in the past 6 months, in the past year, since age 18? A related issue here is that the further back in time a respondent is asked to search his or her memory, the less accurate the answer will be. When constructing items with a time referent, make very sure the amount of time to be recalled is reasonable for the question asked. The survey item being critiqued has other flaws as well: What are they?

So far this chapter has provided readers with a general discussion of many important issues in survey research. Since many of the concerns touched on in this chapter are complex and can not be adequately covered in this chapter, we encourage the reader to turn to the references provided at the end of the chapter for more in-depth coverage of survey research issues.

Two Case Studies[1]

This next section presents two case studies where survey research was used.[1] The case studies are not meant to fully describe the research protocols and all the issues in each study, but rather to illustrate some of the points raised earlier in this chapter. These case studies can be used to provide a basis for individual analysis or group discussion of key chapter concepts.

---

1. Both of these case studies are based on real studies in the experience of the author. The names of the agencies have been changed for the purposes of this chapter.

Case Study One: Rehab Hospital

Agency

Rehab Hospital is a rehabilitation hospital for adults who have sustained spinal cord injuries. The Recreation Therapy and Leisure Services (RTLS) Department provides a general recreation program and a leisure counselling program which is prescribed by a physician.

Research Team

The research team was comprised of a Recreation Therapist, an undergraduate student, and two professors from a neighboring university. The study was funded through a grant from a governmental agency and was written by the TRS and one of the professors. The student was the primary data collector; she used a portion of this study to write her senior honors thesis which was required of all undergraduate students.

Purpose of the Study

The purpose of this study was to determine the leisure and social lifestyles of individuals discharged from Rehab Hospital and to evaluate their ability to pursue their leisure interests independently. The focus was on identifying benefits gained from participation in the general recreation programs and leisure counselling program offered by the RTLS Department. In addition, the RTLS Department wanted information to understand constraints faced by individuals post-discharge in their pursuit of recreation and leisure. The study was primarily descriptive in nature and inquired about behavior, attitudes, and opinions of the respondents.

General Procedures

A telephone survey was used for data collection. This was the most appropriate method because many of the individuals in the sample would have been unable to physically complete a self-administered questionnaire. Rather than to telephone interviewees from "out of the blue" the research team decided to prepare them. Each person in the survey was mailed a letter from his or her physician endorsing the study and asking for cooperation. This type of institutional support was very important for legitimizing the study in the eyes of the interviewees and for encouraging participation. This endorsement may have helped the response rate for the study.

Enclosed with this letter was the actual structured interview schedule that was to be used. This instrument was provided so that the interviewee could think about the answers beforehand. The research team felt that this increased the validity of responses. Also, it allowed the interviewee to follow along during the telephone interview. This helped the interviewee to better understand the questions themselves as well as the response categories (the possible answers) on the instrument. As described in Chapter 6, the letter sent to the research participants outlined the procedures that would be followed if they agreed to participate, what to do if they did not wish to participate, and explained how confidentiality would be maintained.

Sample and Sample Selection

This study used what is called a **census sample.** With a census sample, everyone possible is used in the survey instead of selecting certain individuals to be representative of the whole population of interest. In this study, the RTLS staff were interested in the behavior and attitudes of clients discharged only after the RTLS began its leisure counselling program. This left a five year time period that was appropriate to study. In the five years of interest, 202 individuals had been discharged. The research team judged that this many people were needed in the sample, and the there were enough resources to collect data on all of these people. The final group of respondents included 155 people, which was 77% of the possible 202.

Important Points

This study allowed the RTLS staff to understand what happened to their clients after discharge. In a way, the study served as an evaluation. A number of surprising results were found in this study which were contrary to the research team's expectations. For example, individuals who had been through the leisure counselling program were actually more bored and less satisfied with their leisure than individuals who were not part of the leisure counselling program (Caldwell, Adolph & Gilbert, 1989). This type of finding allowed the RTLS staff to reconsider and restructure their programming.

Case Study Two: Teen Program

Agency

Teen Program (TP) is a multifaceted program that runs in-school and after-school groups. It is run by a County Department of Social Services located in a rural county. For this study, the in-school TP group was of concern. The program consists of weekly meetings with 8th grade students who have been identified as high-risk adolescents. Information sharing and discussions about teen pregnancy, drug and alcohol use, use of leisure, violence, and job training are the focus of these groups.

Research Team

The research team was primarily comprised of the social worker in charge of TP, another social worker who works with TP, a faculty member from a Department of Public Health, and a faculty member from a Department of Leisure Studies. A master's degree student was also added to the research team.

The research team represented a true interdisciplinary, collaborative effort to understand high-risk adolescents from a number of perspectives. It is this type of research team that may hold the most promise for developing a holistic understanding of the individuals served by therapeutic recreation and other types health and social service agencies.

General Purpose

The overall purpose of this research effort was to evaluate the effectiveness of the TP in-school group. Another purpose was to describe and understand the leisure behavior and attitudes of these high-risk adolescents. These are really two distinct purposes having two distinct implications for the procedures of the study. This is pointed out because when TRSs are involved in inter- or multi-disciplinary studies, this type of plurality of purpose occurs.

Procedures

Because the major research purpose was to evaluate the program's effectiveness, this research study was similar to a quasi-experiment. Data were collected through the use of a questionnaire before the program began and after it was finished. But, it was not a very good quasi-experiment because it lacked a control group. (Read more about important considerations for this type of design in Chapter 11.) It should be noted that the design flaw identified was not because the research team made a huge error and forgot to include a control group. Rather, as in many research endeavors in practical settings, compromises had to be made due to lack of resources. The research team knew that a control group should have been used. Yet, there were no funds for personnel to administer the questionnaires to a control group or do something with the data once they were collected. So, the research team did what they thought was propitious and realized that there were certain conclusions they could not make about their study based on the design flaw. Although this comment relates more to experimental design, it is a good illustration of practical glitches that occur in real versus ideal research studies.

For this chapter the questionnaire administration is viewed as a cross-sectional, one-shot survey. That is, because of the overall design flaw, we could not validly evaluate change in behavior due to the TP (this would be an explanatory type of study). This is particularly true with regard to the questions addressing leisure behavior and attitude. Because little was known about the leisure behavior and attitudes of these high-risk youth, the primary purpose of including questions about these variables was to explore and describe these things. Therefore, the leisure information used in the study came from the first time the questionnaires were distributed (the pretest), thus making it cross-sectional in nature.

For all administrations of the questionnaires, the social workers who ran the TP groups distributed the questionnaires. The questionnaires were self-administered. The social workers found, however, that often the teens could not comprehend some of the questions. Therefore, the social workers needed to read many of the questions aloud to the teens so that they could fill out their responses.

Sample and Sample Selection

Once again, a random sample was not used for this study. This is partially because a very select group of students were targeted to be in this study. This group of students had been identified by school personnel and other individuals as being "high-risk." A sample of this nature is often termed *purposive*. This sampling situation is faced in many TR studies.

Important Points

Because of the lack of random sampling, the results from this study could not be generalized to a larger group or population. That is, readers could not take the results of this study and apply it to high-risk youth in other cities or states. In order to do this, a larger study that used random sampling techniques would have to be conducted. Despite these limitations, however, valuable insight was gained by the program providers about various components of these high-risk adolescents' lives from a comprehensive perspective. Moreover, these findings, while not generalizable in a statistical sense, also may provide insight to other program providers of similar programs.

References

Caldwell, L. L., Adolph, S., & Gilbert, A. (1989). Caution! Leisure counselors at work: Long term effects of leisure counseling. *Therapeutic Recreation Journal*, 23(3), 41-49.

Ellis, G. D., & Witt, P. A. (1986). The leisure diagnostic battery: Past, present, and future. *Therapeutic Recreation Journal*, 20(4), 31-47.

Shimizu, J. (1988). A comparison of open-ended and closed-ended questioning systems. *Recreation Research Review*, 13, 18-22.

Suggestions for Further Reading

Babbie, E. (1986). *Observing ourselves: Essays in social research.* Belmont, CA: Wadsworth.

Babbie, E. (1992). *The practice of social research,* (6th ed.). Belmont, CA: Wadsworth.

Becker, R. H., & Iliff, T. J. (1983). Nonrespondents in homogeneous groups: Implications for mailed surveys. *Leisure Sciences*, 5, 257-267.

Belson, W. A. (1981). *The design and understanding of survey questions.* Aldershot, Hants, England: Gower.

Belson, W., & Duncan, J. A. (1962). A comparison of the check-list and the open response questions systems. *Applied Statistics*, 11, 412-416.

Borg, W., & Gall, M. (1990). *Educational research: An introduction* (5th ed.). White Plains, NY: Longman.

Brown, T. L., & Wilkins, B. T. (1978). Clues to reasons for nonresponse, and its effect upon variable estimates. *Journal of Leisure Research*, 10, 226-231.

Dillman, D. A. (1978). *Mail and telephone surveys: The total design method.* New York: Wiley.

Heberlein, T. A., & Baumgartner, R. (1978). Factors affecting response rates to mailed questionnaires: A qualitative analysis of the published literature. *American Sociological Review*, 43, 447-462.

Field, D. R. (1973). The telephone interview in leisure research. *Journal of Leisure Research*, 5, 51-59.

Fink, A., & Kosecoff, J. (1985). *How to conduct surveys: A step by step guide.* Newbury Park, CA: Sage.

Frey, J. H. (1989). *Survey research by telephone* (2nd ed.). Newbury Park, CA: Sage.

Kerlinger, F. (1986). *Foundations of behavioral research*. (3rd ed.). New York: Holt, Reinhart & Winston.

Kraemer, H. C., & Thiemann, S. (1987). *How many subjects? Statistical power analysis in research*. Newbury Park, CA: Sage.

Johnson, R. (Ed.). (1988). *Research on research: Understanding the implications of research design decisions*, [Special issue]. *Recreation Research Review, 13*(10).

Laurent, A. (1971). Effects of question length on reporting behavior in the survey interview. *Journal of the American Statistical Association, 67*, 298-305.

Miller, D. C. (1991). *Handbook of research design and social measurement* (5th ed.). Newbury Park, CA: Sage.

Noelle-Neumann, E. (1965). Wanted: Rules for wording structured questionnaires. *Public Opinion Quarterly, 34*, 191-201.

Interpretation of Positivistic Research: Issues of Validity and Reliability
Julia K. Dunn

As stated in Chapters 1 and 7, the profession of therapeutic recreation is faced with a continual need to justify the efficacy of recreational therapy services, to demonstrate accountability through quality assurance activities, and to conduct research in areas such as the recreational and leisure behavior of persons with disabilities. These evaluation and research efforts are designed to accomplish goals such as to: describe or explain phenomena; identify causal relationships; understand and predict behavior; demonstrate the worth of programs and interventions; and validate assessment procedures. In positivistic TR research and evaluation (as a form of applied research), data are used for theory development, programmatic decisions, client and program descriptions, explanation of phenomena, and prediction of behavior. The results must be viable for professionals to use them. It is essential, then, that TRSs are confident that the findings of their investigations accurately reflect reality.

To draw reasoned conclusions and interpret the meaning of research findings, it is necessary to judge the quality of the findings and evaluate the circumstances under which they were produced. More specifically, an investigative TRS must understand the circumstances related to the research process which would threaten the quality of the results. In addition, in planning an investigation, it is necessary to understand the appropriate procedures to employ during the design and implementation of research in order to reduce or eliminate these threats to quality. The use of these procedures will help TRSs gauge the amount of confidence they can place in their conclusions.

CHAPTER 9

The "quality" of data generated through a scientific study is indicated by the demonstration of *reliability* and *validity* in research design and procedures. Unless active steps are taken to estimate, improve, and report reliability and validity, no foundation will exist on which to judge the "quality" of research findings. Thus, little confidence can be placed in decisions, conclusions, judgments, or generalizations based on such results. It is, therefore, a necessity to examine validity and reliability as they apply to both the research design and procedures. Reliability and validity are affected by every phase of the research process. In turn, they influence research design, procedures, and the conclusions that can be drawn from the results.

In this chapter, both research design and procedures are examined in light of their contribution to the "believability" of findings, the interpretations made, and the conclusions drawn. In conducting research, the investigator is attempting to answer questions. All phases of the research process impact the ability of the researcher to identify the real or truthful answer to those questions. In quantitatively-oriented research, numbers are used as ways to help answer questions.

Concepts of Measurement

Numbers and how they are used is the essence of measurement in positivistic research. As stated in Chapter 8, numbers are used to represent and describe **variables**. That is, numbers are assigned to concepts. Then, it is those numbers that are analyzed (typically using statistics) and interpreted to generate results, which answer research questions. Fitz-Gibbon and Morris summarize the use of **statistics** to analyze numbers stating that, "quantitative data provide answers to such questions as 'how much?' 'to what extent?' and 'how many?' In addition the analysis of quantitative data involves looking at relationships between quantities" (1987, p. 10).

Levels of Measurement

The first step in understanding numerical results is to understand how numbers are used in research. When research questions are asked, they are composed of **variables**, or those concepts which compose the questions. In the research process, those variables must be carefully defined so that they can be measured. **Measurement** of variables implies the assignment of numbers according to an established plan, based on the nature of the variables and the level of sophistication or precision desired in the study. This plan for assigning numbers is called **"levels of measurement."** The levels of measurement selected for the variables of a specific study govern the way that variables are addressed on a questionnaire or other measurement instrument and the type of statistics which can be used in the study to answer the research question. (See Appendix A, page 178, for information regarding statistical tests which are permissible for each level of measurement.) There are four levels of measurement: nominal, ordinal, interval, and ratio.

In **nominal measurement**, numbers are assigned to variables as if they were names. Thus, if TRSs at a hospital were interested in the variable of "unit," numbers might be assigned in the following way:

1 = adolescent unit;

2 = adult unit; and

3 = substance abuse unit.

Ordinal measurement implies that a variable can be rank-ordered. Examples are found in many rating scales. This means a relationship exists between numbers, reflecting the concepts "greater than" or "less than." For example, a list of activities is presented and the research participant is asked to rank them in order of preference with 1 being the most preferred, producing the following results:

[1] weaving;

[2] tennis; and

[3] gardening.

These data say that weaving is the most preferred activity. An important characteristic of the ordinal scale is that there is not an "equal distance" between numbers. Thus, this same result would be produced by both of the following scenarios: (a) the person preferred both weaving and tennis and was forced to choose between them, but intensely disliked gardening or (b) the person preferred weaving far more than either gardening or tennis.

Interval measures imply that there is equal distance between the numerical units which measure a variable. According to Siegel (1956) the measures are "characterized by a common and constant unit of measurement" (p. 26).[1] In the interval scale it is not important to identify a "0" point or the complete absence of the variable. Interval measurement is the first truly quantitative level and allows many statistical procedures to be used in analysis. Through certain scaling theories, some intensity scales assume interval level for the purpose of analysis. However, scale construction must be carefully addressed in order to allow it to fulfill the needed characteristics of the interval scale. In other words, not every Likert-type scale can be averaged (obtain a mean). When there is a question, it is safer to treat the data as ordinal.

---

1. All material from S. Siegel, (1956), *Nonparametric statistics for the behavioral sciences*. reprinted with permission of McGraw-Hill Publishing Co., New York, NY.

In the **ratio level of measurement,** the "0" point is an essential characteristic. In order for a variable to be measured at this level, the absence of that variable must exist in the physical world. Ratio level measurement is common in the physical sciences; however it is not often used in the social sciences or in TR research.

Two points are important in understanding levels of measurement. First, each level of measurement has all of the properties of the less rigorous levels below it. Second, though a variable can be measured at a higher level, a researcher may choose to use a lower level. Regarding this second point, for example, the variable of "age" can be measured at the interval level, in years. However, it could also be measured at the ordinal level by assigning numbers to the following definitions:

1 = child;
2 = adolescent; and
3 = adult.

Using Numbers

An important issue in using numbers is to realize that they are not absolute, but indicative of probabilities (Patton, 1982). Thus, numbers can be applied to variables to allow them to be studied. When numbers are used "as indicators and estimates subject to interpretation, statistics contain varying degrees of error" (Patton, 1982, p. 244).

Numbers can be used in descriptive and explanatory types of research. The research approach used is determined by the nature of the research problem. Descriptive research serves to describe variables whereas explanatory research attempts to explain events or phenomena. Explanatory research frequently uses **hypothesis testing** to organize the research design. A **hypothesis** is a statement of what is expected from a specified set of variables in relation to each other, based on a theoretical foundation (Babbie, 1992). Hypotheses are usually based on a theory and are stated in such a way as to predict either the relationship between variables or the difference of units of measurement of variables. Both the level of measurement and the nature of the hypothesis will dictate the type of statistics which can be used in a study.

Statistical tests can be divided into two types, descriptive and inferential. **Descriptive statistics** serve to describe a sample or population on one variable, such as the age of clients in a rehabilitation unit who receive TR services. **Inferential statistics** are used to generalize phenomena from a sample to a population. The appropriate selection of a statistical test will contribute to the validity of the findings of a research study. Quantitative research implies the assignment of numbers to describe variables and the application of statistical analyses to those numbers to answer research questions.

The Positivistic Research Process

To ensure the validity of the findings from research, it is essential that the project be well-planned and follow the accepted conventions of positivist social science. Babbie (1992) has outlined that process which is often referred to as **"the scientific method."** It begins with an idea, interest, or theory which generates a research problem or hypothesis. Then, three processes occur somewhat simultaneously: the conceptualization and definition of the variables; the selection of the research technique (e.g., experiment, survey); and the identification and selection of the sample. This is followed by the specification of procedures for data collection and analysis. The study is then carried out and data are collected. These data are analyzed and interpreted. Based on the interpretation, conclusions are drawn which answer the research problem.

Many decisions are made during the design of a research project. Each of these decisions and subsequent actions can create **error** in the findings, thereby reducing their validity. In other words, problems in the design or implementation of a study can reduce the investigator's ability to describe or explain the variables or relationships between variables under study. The need to follow the conventions of the research design process carefully and precisely is paramount. Doing so helps the investigative TRS to minimize error. Thus, when final interpretations are made, each phase of the research process must be considered to determine if there were any sources of error which need to be taken into consideration. Within the research design itself, sources of error are considered "threats to validity" or "sources of invalidity." These threats can be viewed as both internal and external in nature.

Sources of Error in the Research Design

As stated earlier, in all research efforts the investigator is trying to answer the questions that have been posed. The investigator hopes that the answers to those questions which are obtained through a research design will closely approximate what is real. In fact, understanding that research efforts are limited by the definitions used, procedures employed, and statistics applied to the data, leads to the need to understand error. A perfect picture cannot be produced in any research study. In any project there is some degree of error. One role of the researcher is to identify possible sources of that error. Through the research design and procedures, he or she tries to control those sources and to take into account the effect of uncontrolled error on the findings. Then, the investigator interprets the findings accordingly.

Positivist Research Design

Internal Validity

The concept of internal validity traditionally has been applied to experimental research design. However, internal validity can also be used as an evaluation or judgment of worth of the research design in general. **Internal validity** implies that adequate steps have been taken to control variables and situations which would affect the clear understanding of the nature of the problem under investigation (error). In research, the design of a particular investigation is the point at which the concepts that will be studied are defined or specified. Also, hypotheses are generated based on these variables. Therefore, to ensure that internal validity is addressed in positivist research design, variables need to be specified to the point that they can be measured, and hypotheses can be generated. If the relationships in hypotheses are causal in nature, then the criteria for causality must be considered. These criteria include: an empirical relationship between the independent and dependent variables, the independent variables occurrence in time prior to the dependent variable, and the existence of a relationship which cannot be explained as a by-product of another variable (Babbie, 1989).

Thus, an experimental design is selected based on several considerations. One of these is its ability to control for the threats to internal validity. Such procedures attempt, through the design, to ensure that the results of a study can be attributed to the relationships hypothesized. Internal validity implies that the findings of a study are attributed to the hypotheses under investigation rather than other extraneous influences. Campbell and Stanley (1963), Cook and Campbell (1979), and Babbie (1989) have identified twelve **threats to internal validity** which can be controlled by the rigor of the selected research design. These threats to validity include: (1) history (events which occur between two testings); (2) maturation (changes within the respondents as a result of time passage); (3) testing (the effect that the process of initial testing may have on a second testing); (4) instrumentation (lack of reliability and validity in the measurement instruments); (5) statistical regression (applicable in studies which use subjects with extreme scores, it implies that there is only one direction for change, therefore changes in scores may not be the result of the experimental intervention); (6) selection bias (lack of compatibility of groups of subjects because of the group selection procedures used); (7) experimental mortality (the loss of subjects from the experiment); (8) causal time-order (questions regarding the inference of causal relationship between variables because of an inability to determine the time relationship between variables); (9) diffusion or imitation of treatments (contamination of the control group by interaction with subjects from the experimental group); (10) compensation (provision of "something extra" to a control group in compensation for their lack of benefit from an experimental intervention which causes the control group to lose its purpose as a control in the study); (11) compensatory rivalry (the control group exerts extra effort in competition with the experimental group); and (12) demoralization (the control group "gives up" as a result of feelings of deprivation).

Internal validity is one of the major considerations in the selection of an appropriate experimental or quasi-experimental design (Campbell & Stanley, 1963). **Sampling methods** (Cook & Campbell, 1979) also affect internal validity in experimental research. By far the most highly recommended procedure in the selection of a sample or assignment of the sample to groups is **randomization**. When randomization is not possible other sampling methods can be employed. Examples in which randomization may not be possible may occur in survey, field, or evaluation research. In these situations acceptable sampling techniques include systematic sampling, cluster sampling, and stratified sampling (Babbie, 1989).

External Validity

External validity is an additional concern in the design of investigations. This concept refers to the generalizability of research findings to the real world. Factors which would alter the sample or experimental group in a way which would not enable them to adequately represent a population for which the results are intended to be generalized would threaten external validity (Campbell & Stanley, 1963). Sampling also affects the external validity of a research study. The importance of representative sampling procedures has been historically emphasized. However, modern sampling theorists are stressing lack of bias in samples (Chen & Rossi, 1987) rather than representativeness.

Sample selection designed to reduce bias will depend on the degree to which knowledge of the population and program or intervention is available to the researcher. This level of knowledge will influence the form of external validity; implicit or explicit. **Explicit generalization** in evaluation research implies that the researcher can build further expectations into the research design. For example, a sample from the total group whose specific program or intervention is being investigated would be selected as subjects for the experiment (Chen & Rossi, 1987), not some "other" subjects. On the other hand, if the specific target population was able to be specified, or multiple target groups were identified, a similar "other" group might be selected. This would constitute **implicit generalization** (Chen & Rossi, 1987).

Chen and Rossi (1987, pp. 101-102) provide the following guidelines to designing an evaluation when considering external validity:

1. Specify the conditioning variables, interaction variables, and intervening variables which realize the causal relationship between the **treatment variables** and **outcome variables,** both in the researched system and in the prospective system in which the program is installed;

2. Develop an understanding of the ways in which the program in question would operate when enacted, including the population elements to be served, the agencies to be given administration responsibilities, and the potential distribution of contingencies and interactions involved; [and]

3. Develop a sampling strategy and an administrative apparatus for the evaluation which mimics as closely as possible the images of the future of the program developed under (2) above.

Thus, it is essential that researchers consider the importance of the design and procedures, particularly sampling, to ensure that the data produced are both internally and externally valid.

Construct validity, though generally thought of in relation to measurement, is also related to research design through the rigorous operationalization of the variables to be studied. The more thoroughly constructs are understood, the better the definition of variables will be within a study. In studies related to the further investigation of constructs, specific designs may be indicated such as multi-trait multi-method, correlational, and factorial analyses.

Validity is improved by the ability of the researcher to adequately specify the area of focus of the study and link research observations to theory. At issue in research design is improvement of the validity of findings by selection of the most appropriate design, specification of variables, and the ability to link observation to theory.

Error in the Measurement of Variables

Reliability and validity are considered essential elements in measurement (Allen & Yen, 1979; Gronlund, 1981; Thorndike & Hagen, 1977). **Validity** is concerned with the ability of the instrument to measure what it intends to measure. **Reliability** is concerned with the ability of the instrument to measure accurately, with precision and consistency. Without efforts to address these issues in the development and selection of measures, little confidence can be placed in the results of such measures. This challenges each investigator to use accepted development procedures in the design of measures and to conduct validation studies on existing measures. Validation studies serve to demonstrate the appropriateness of the measure for a particular sample and generate estimates of reliability and validity to be considered in drawing conclusions and making generalizations. An important consideration in the use of a particular measure over time is possible change of characteristics of the population due to a variety of social, economic, or cultural factors (Tatsuoka, 1976). This would mandate continual monitoring of the estimates of reliability and validity of the measurement instruments employed.

At issue in the development and validation of measures are construct, criterion-related and content validity, and reliability estimates of both stability and internal consistency. The determination of the most appropriate forms of reliability and validity is of primary importance and is defined by the nature of the construct, the intended use of the measure, the design of the study, and the characteristics of the measure itself.

Construct Validity

Construct validity can be viewed as the "extent to which a measure performs in accordance with theoretical expectations" (Carmines & Zeller, 1979, p. 27). It is concerned with the description and understanding of theoretical concepts. For example, an investigative TRS might examine the construct of perceived competence in regard to the self-perceptions of adolescents participating in an outdoor adventure program. When concerned with measuring constructs, studies designed to contribute to construct validity become necessary. Of particular concern in this case is measurement development and validation when the construct being measured needs validation. According to Carmines and Zeller (1979), the demonstration of construct validity "involves three distinct steps. First, the theoretical relationship between the concepts themselves must be simplified. Second, the empirical relationship between the measures of the concepts must be examined. Finally, the empirical evidence must be interpreted in terms of how it clarifies the construct validity of a particular measure" (p. 23).

Criterion-Related Validity

Criterion-related validity implies that there is a known measure of a specified concept, referred to as the criterion. The measure under review is statistically compared to this existing criterion measure. If found to be strongly related, then it can be said that the target measure does measure the same thing as the criterion measure. In establishing criterion-related validity, both the criterion as well as the target measure must be evaluated. According to Thorndike and Hagen (1977), the criterion must have evidence of relevance, freedom from bias, reliability, and availability. Relevance refers to the ability of the criterion measure to reflect the construct measured. Freedom from bias is a quality which reflects the ability of the criterion not to discriminate based on irrelevant variables. Reliability indicates the criterion measure's stability, and availability refers to the researcher's ability to obtain and use the criterion measure. A major concern in TR research is the lack of available criterion measures. Therefore, this form of validity is not addressed often in the literature. However, as more measures are developed, they may serve as criteria for other measures. For example, a researcher may compare a global (single) measurement of life satisfaction with an existing, valid and reliable set of scale scores.

Criterion-related validity is established by administering both the criterion measure and the target measure to the same sample and comparing the results of both using a correlation coefficient or other measure of association. The stronger the statistical relationship between the two measures, the higher the validity estimate.

Content Validity

Content validity is of concern when an existing domain of content is at issue. Such areas of content can be illustrated by program content (Morris & Fitz-Gibbon, 1978); achievement of objectives (Thorndike & Hagen, 1977; Gronlund, 1976); and personnel evaluations (Allen & Yen, 1979). In any of these cases, **content validity** is a judgment regarding the extent to which the measure reflects the specified content. The first step in establishing content validity is defining the content. Frequently sources such as professional literature and expert opinion are used for content definition. So, before evaluating a program, it must first be described. In the second step, the content is structured in such a way as to allow the researcher to identify the key elements of the content and their relative importance. From this then the measurement instrument can be developed. Establishing content validity involves the review of the measurement instrument based on its degree of representation of the nature of the content and its elements. Following established measurement procedures in the development and selection of items is critical in ensuring a content valid measure. A researcher might, for example, use these procedures to evaluate the appropriateness of the content of a stress management program by reviewing the literature, other established programs and measurement instruments, and consulting "experts."

Reliability

Reliability can be thought of as consistency or precision of measurement. Absolute accuracy cannot be expected in measurement instruments. Accuracy is eroded by the existence of error. Reliability estimates give the researcher indications of the amount of error that can be explained by the measurement instrument itself. The instrument with a high reliability estimate will have less measurement error.

Stability reliability focuses on the ability of a measure to produce similar results on repeated usages. Establishing this form of reliability involves administering the measure twice to the same sample and comparing the results. Thus, the same individual should achieve a similar result on both testings if the instrument is accurate. This method is called test-retest, and is one of the most frequently used methods to estimate reliability.

Internal consistency reliability is more concerned with the relation of the instrument's elements to each other and to the instrument as a whole. The process of generating the internal consistency reliability estimate is a single administration and the application of one of several formulae. The most common of these formulae is Coefficient Alpha.

In both stability and internal consistency, reliability estimates are indicated by a statistic between 0 and 1 with estimates closer to 1 indicating a higher reliability (see Chapter 7). Thus, a reliability estimate of .95 would be more acceptable than one of .65.

Improving the reliability and validity of measurement instruments largely consists of steps designed to eliminate sources of error from the measurement instrument itself. Thus, as described in Chapter 8, the quality of items, directions, and format of the instrument are of concern. Additionally, the representativeness of the items and the relation of the items to the theoretical foundation also need to be examined and improved to reduce sources of error which would cause the instrument to be ineffective in measuring what it intended to measure.

Sources of Error in Analysis and Interpretation

To ensure confidence in the results of an investigation it is important to examine both the decisions regarding the selection of an appropriate statistic for analysis and the interpretation of the results of the findings as they relate to the hypotheses.

The first criterion that needs to be met in the selection of a statistical procedure is related to the research problem; that is, whether the problem is related to describing variables or to explaining relationships between variables. In the first case, **descriptive statistics** are used to describe the distributions of a sample or population on a single variable. These statistics include **measures of central tendency** such as mean, median, and mode (selected based on the level of measurement of the variable) and measures of variability which indicate the dispersion or spread of scores within the sample or population. These statistics include the range of scores, the variance, and the standard deviation. In the case of **inferential statistics**, the primary concern is testing a hypothesis on a sample in order to draw conclusions about the population from which that sample was drawn. Using inferential statistics implies that a hypothesis exists as the research question, the hypothesis will be examined using the established research methods, and specific statistics will be used to generate results.

Inferential statistics can be seen in two categories; *parametric* and *nonparametric*. Each of these classes of statistics is designed to address different situations in the research project. **Parametric statistics** are more precise and thus more powerful. However, in order to use parametric procedures, the variables must be measured at least at the interval level and the variables must be assumed to be distributed normally. **Nonparametric statistics** can be used when variables are measured at the nominal or ordinal level and there is not evidence of normalcy, or the sample size is too small to assume that the variables will have a normal distribution.

Inferential statistics are selected based on several factors: the level of measurement of the variables, the assumption of the normal distribution, and the nature of the hypothesis (Siegel, 1956). Level of measurement and assumptions about the distribution of the variables will determine the selection of either a parametric or nonparametric procedure. Basically, **hypotheses** can be seen as hunches relating to the association of variables or the difference between variables. Thus, different statistics provide evidence of association or relationship (e.g., correlations) and others relate to the question of differences in variables (e.g., ANOVA).

Selection of the most appropriate statistic is important in ensuring the validity of the results of the statistical analysis. Appendix B, page 179, illustrates some of the more common statistics as they can be applied to types of hypotheses and the parametric-nonparametric criterion.

Not only are the findings important, but it is also necessary to identify the meaning of those findings. The results of a single statistical analysis will give an indication of a relationship between two or more variables. However, if a decision is to be made regarding the meaning and importance of that relationship in responding to the hypothesis, additional information is needed. That additional information involves statistical significance.

Statistical Significance

Significance involves the probability that an error has occurred in the decision made about the hypothesis based on the results of the statistical analysis. "Using significance testing simply allows us to rule out, more or less, one source of anxiety about our sample of data: the anxiety that a relationship in our sample might not have been there had we happened to look at other samples ... Statistics provides a way of quantifying confidence, of saying how much confidence we place on certain statements" (Fitz-Gibbon & Morris, 1987, p. 9).

The concept of **statistical significance** shows how confident the researcher is that his or her findings represent reality. To understand significance it is necessary to return to the concept of hypothesis testing. Early in the research process, hypotheses are written in two ways. First, as a **null hypothesis** which basically states that there is no relationship between variables or second, as an alternative hypothesis which says that there are relationships. The **alternative hypothesis** may also further specify the nature of those relationships. In understanding significance, it is specifically to the null hypothesis that thinking is directed.

Based on the findings of a research study, several **interpretive decisions** are made. The first of those is whether the null hypothesis be accepted or rejected. In research it is assumed that the null hypothesis is true unless evidence can prove otherwise. So this first decision is based on whether there is enough evidence of a relationship between variables that the null hypothesis can be rejected. The second step in this logic is that if the null hypothesis is rejected then the alternative hypothesis must be accepted.

In addition to this are the elements of significance, which basically provide evidence of confidence in the correctness of the first decision. In other words, it is the probability that the researcher would make a mistake and reject the null hypothesis when it is, in reality, true. This is called **Type I error** and is referred to as statistical significance. It means that the researcher concludes that there are differences between groups when there are none. For example, following a leisure education intervention, the researcher concludes that the differences noted were due to the intervention, when in fact they were merely due to sampling error, inappropriate use of statistical techniques, or inadequate measurement instruments. In generating a numerical value which represents significance, the researcher is actually ascertaining the probability of making a mistake in the decision to reject the null hypothesis. As a rule of thumb, the minimum level of significance usually accepted is .05 (there are 5 chances in 100 that an interpretation error has been made). However, other levels of significance can be set, depending on the researcher's expectations. One way that a Type I error can be reduced is to increase the expectation of significance to a more rigorous level such as .01 (one chance in 100 that the investigator would make a mistake).

If a significant relationship is found it is important to determine the significance level to understand the probability that an error in judgment has occurred. If a significant result is not found, several possible explanations occur, and need to be considered in explaining the results. First, the variables may not have been defined specifically enough to allow them to be measured accurately. Second, the sample size may have been too small or not representative of the population. Third, a Type II error may have occurred. A **Type II error** occurs when the null hypothesis is accepted when it is actually false. This is another error in judgment. The researcher concludes that there is no difference between groups, when in fact there is a difference. For example, a program of choice is presented to residents of a long term care facility. Measures of perceived control or self-efficacy indicate no difference between groups. This may occur when the statistic used is not precise or "powerful" enough to detect the relationship or because the level of significance was set too rigorously (e.g., .001 instead of .01).

Careful balance should be considered when selecting the level of expected significance. If it is set too low (.25) then the chance of making a Type I error is increased, if it is set too high (.001) the chance of making a Type II error is increased.

Significance is viewed as the probability of making an error in judgment regarding the hypotheses. It is assumed that when using inferential statistics, where a sample is used, some sampling error will exist. However, the nature of significance looks at the possible existence of error other than that which may be there as a result of sampling.

Reducing Error

Error can be caused by the decisions of the researcher at every phase of the research process. Therefore, in reducing "unexplained" error, the first step is to carefully design the study to address sources of possible error. Each phase of the research process needs to be examined, including the theoretical foundation for the hypotheses that are being tested, the degree to which variables are well-defined and exclusive from each other, the belief that the research method is appropriate for the hypotheses that have been specified, the contention that the most rigorous form of the given research method is used within the limitations of the study, and that the sample size is sufficient and representative of the population. The procedures for gathering data need to be addressed to control external variables which may effect the results. The measurement instruments need to be both reliable and valid and the analysis strategy needs to be appropriate to the level of measurement of the variables and the nature of the hypothesis. Finally, the judgment in interpreting the results based on the hypotheses needs to be examined using significance testing to increase the understanding of the "correctness" of that judgment.

Drawing Conclusions

It is essential to discuss the conclusions which can be drawn from the findings. Once hypotheses have been accepted or rejected, conclusions are drawn and results are generalized. In order to ensure validity at this phase of the research process the following considerations should guide these decisions:

1. Any conclusions should be based on the hypotheses and only the hypotheses that were used to guide the study.
2. Conclusions can only be discussed within the limitations of the study. For example, the population from which the sample was drawn is the only population to whom the conclusions can be applied. The conditions of the research are the only conditions under which the conclusions would apply to the population.
3. The conclusions offered must be tempered by the amount of error possible in the study. Thus, if other possible conclusions or explanations of the findings can be considered, those must be discussed. This is particularly important in discussing results that are not "acceptably" significant. This is not to say that these results are not important, just that caution should be exercised in their acceptance.

Summary

Studies using quantitative methods are an important and valuable part of the research conducted in TR. When research is conducted it is essential to do it correctly. As Patton states, "The integrity of the evaluation rests ultimately on the integrity of the information that emerges from the evaluation" (1982, p. 241). Thus, investigative TRSs must strive for integrity in their research, if they want confidence in the results of their efforts. This chapter and the following exercises provide an overview of the means by which investigative TRSs aim for integrity in positivistic inquiry. Readers are urged to closely review the references listed for a more in-depth examination of the elements of the research process introduced here.

Discussion Questions

1. In a small group, select a variable that could be used in therapeutic recreation research. Have each group member write a measurable definition for the variable. Discuss the various definitions and come to a group definition which can be measured in a research study. How could the validity of this definition be demonstrated?
2. For the variable defined in the first exercise, operationalize it at each level of measurement which can be permitted based on the nature of the variable.
3. A research study is planned to evaluate the effectiveness of a therapeutic recreation program on the social skill level of participants. The design for the study includes evaluating the social skills of each of the participants prior to the program and again after the program, then comparing the results of the two evaluations. Which of the sources of invalidity are a threat to the results of this design? How could the design be improved?
4. In your own words define the concept of reliability of measurement and why it is important in demonstrating validity.
5. Identify a case in which the three types of validity would be used in research.
6. Review the research published in the therapeutic recreation literature and identify a study which used only descriptive statistics, and one in which inferential statistics have been used. Compare the intent of these two studies and the conclusions that were drawn from the findings.
7. Review a research article which reports statistical significance. What was the significance of the findings and how was significance discussed in the interpretation of findings? Relate this discussion to the concepts of Type I and Type II error.

References

Allen, M. J., & Yen, W. M. (1979). *Introduction to measurement theory.* Monterey, CA: Brooks/Cole.

Babbie, E. (1992). *The practice of social research* (6th ed.). Belmont, CA: Wadsworth.

Babbie, E. (1989). *The practice of social research* (5th ed.). Belmont, CA: Wadsworth.

Campbell, D. T., & Stanley, J. C. (1963). *Experimental and quasi-experimental designs for research.* Chicago, Il: Rand McNally.

Carmines, E. G., & Zeller, R. A. (1979). *Reliability and validity assessment.* Beverly Hills, CA: Sage.

Chen, H., & Rossi, P. H. (1987). A theory driven approach to validity. *Evaluation and Program Planning, 10,* 95-103.

Cook, T. D., & Campbell, D. T. (1979). *Quasi-experimentation: Design and analysis issues for field settings.* Chicago, Il: Rand McNally.

Fitz-Gibbon, C. T., & Morris, L. L. (1987). *How to analyze data.* Newbury Park, CA: Sage.

Gronlund, N. E. (1976). *Measurement and evaluation in teaching.* New York: Macmillan.

Morris, L. L., & Fitz-Gibbon, C. T. (1978). *How to measure program implementation.* Beverly Hills, CA: Sage.

Patton, M. Q. (1982). *Practical evaluation.* Beverly Hills, CA: Sage.

Priest, S., & Davis, L. (1987). *Conceptually speaking: Students workbook on statistics for HPER.* Eugene, OR: University of Oregon.

Siegel, S. (1956). *Nonparametric statistics for the behavioral sciences.* New York, NY: McGraw-Hill.

Tatsuoka, M. M. (1976). *Validation studies: The use of multiple regression equations.* Champaign, IL: Institute for Personality and Ability Testing.

Thorndike, R. L., & Hagen, E. P. (1977). *Measurement and evaluation in psychology and education.* New York, NY: Wiley.

Appendix A

Examples of Statistics Appropriate for Each Level of Measurements[2,3]

Nominal: Mode
     Frequency
     Contingency Coefficient
     Chi Square

Ordinal: Median
     Percentile
     Spearman rs
     Central t
     Central W

Interval: Mean
     Standard Deviation
     Pearson Product Moment Correlation
     Canonical Correlation
     Regression
     Path Analysis
     Factor Analysis

Ratio: Geometric Mean
     Coefficient of variation

---

2. Adapted from S. Priest and L. Davis (1987), and S. Siegel (1956). This is not a complete listing of all statistical tests which can be used. Additional tests can be employed when comparing variables of different levels of measurement.

3. All material from S. Siegel, *Nonparametric statistics for the behavioral sciences*, 1956, reprinted with permission of McGraw-Hill.

Appendix B

Selection of Statistics[4]

	Nature of the hypothesis	
	Association	Difference
	Pearson Product Moment	t-test
	Regression Analysis	ANOVA
	Canonical Correlation	ANCOVA
Parametric	Discriminant Analysis	MANOVA
	Factor Analysis	
	Path Analysis	
	Spearman r_s	Sign Test
	Kendall t	Man Whitney U
		Wilcoxon Rank Sum
Nonparametric		Wilcoxon Signed-Ranks
		Kruskal Wallis
		Chi Square

---

4. Adapted from S. Priest and L. Davis (1987).

Implementation of Single-Subject Designs in Therapeutic Recreation Research
John Dattilo, David L. Gast, and Stuart J. Schleien

To answer questions important to the practice of therapeutic recreation, professionals increasingly recognize the need for conducting systematic research. Many TRSs may find this prospect overwhelming given their inexperience at pursuing research and the many options of research methods available in the social sciences (McCormick, Scott, & Dattilo, 1991). Anxiety among TRSs in these matters, can result from a lack of knowledge of research principles, and unfamiliarity with the linkage between the creation of research questions and the choice of appropriate research methods.

To reiterate what has been stated throughout this text, investigators should select an experimental design based on the experimental question they are trying to answer and the expected effects of the treatment. Often investigators bypass these determinants of design selection because of an unquestioning reliance on tradition as a guide (Kazdin, 1980). An understanding of the various design characteristics will prepare TRSs to become better producers and consumers of research.

The purpose of this chapter, as has been the authors' purpose in previous writings (e.g., Dattilo, 1985; 1986a; 1987a; 1989; Tawney & Gast, 1984; Gast & Wolery, 1988), is to introduce readers to single-subject research design, one of the many research methods, in an attempt to increase understanding and appreciation for this methodology. Single-subject research is suited to answer various questions about the implications of TR services on the lives of persons with disabilities (Dattilo, McCormick, & Scott, 1991).

Characteristics of Single-Subject Research

Many characteristics associated with the single-subject research methodology minimize the separation between practitioners and researchers (McReynolds & Thompson, 1986). Because of these characteristics, there is increasing use of these research designs in the behavioral sciences (Kratochwill, 1978). Single-subject research lets practitioners understand research findings and apply this information to practice, to empirically evaluate interventions to increase accountability, and to conduct and disseminate research in a therapeutic environment (Kent, 1985).

Single-subject research methodology evaluates the effects of interventions on the individual. The essential feature of single-subject designs is that all conditions are applied to the same subject, and results of any change in behavior are analyzed about that individual (Repp, 1981). Typically, single-subject research experiments examine a few cases extensively, via repeated measurement, to determine if functional relationships exist between an individual's behavior and environmental changes (Dattilo & Nelson, 1986). Inferences made in these experiments should not be confused with those drawn from groups of individuals. Single-subject research requires careful identification and measurement of dependent variables (behaviors in need of treatment) that are influenced by the systematic application of independent variables (treatments). The goal of single-subject research methodology is to permit the design of studies that allow investigators to determine an individual's performance and infer with confidence that a functional relationship between planned interventions and behavior changes exists.

Since investigators use single-subject research in applied (practical or real world) settings, this methodology provides a feasible procedure for investigative TRSs. Single-subject designs do not require elaborate recording and scoring procedures and can occur without disrupting therapeutic services. The implementation of these procedures frequently increases the effectiveness of such services by encouraging practitioners to develop and use systematic programming procedures. Single-subject research allows practitioners to meet the needs of people with limitations and also contribute to the collective knowledge of the profession (Kent, 1985).

Many practitioners who want to conduct research find it difficult to locate a large homogeneous sample needed to conduct between-group comparison research. When a treatment is presented consistently across a sample of individuals, the researcher can infer with confidence that similar results will occur with others. However, this conclusion assumes treatment and subject stability often present in a laboratory, yet typically absent in a therapeutic environment. Because single-subject research requires repeated measurement of a behavior or behaviors of a person or a small sample of people, this approach is well-suited for TR investigations.

Siegel and Spradlin (1985) observed that the provision of services for people with limitations is most useful when practitioners organize and integrate research-based knowledge. This knowledge should be drawn from various sources into comprehensive services that result in a positive behavior change. Frequently, practitioners can interpret single-subject research investigations more easily than traditional group designs (Smith, 1983). This methodology enhances an understanding of the individual and facilitates the evaluation of interventions on the individual's behavior. The ability of TRSs to interpret and implement single-subject research will result in improved and innovative leisure programming for persons with disabilities.

The most central idea in research, basic to all experimental designs, is **experimental control** (Drew, 1976). Once investigators conduct a study they should be able to attribute results of the study to the treatment. To accomplish this with any confidence, other possible explanations of the results must be reduced. Single-subject research methodology provides a means to evaluate effects of interventions on individuals by allowing each to receive the identified treatment, serving as his or her own control. Investigators observe the individual when they withhold treatment **(baseline period)** and when they administer the intervention **(experimental period)**.

Investigators examine effects of interventions through observation of treatment performance of the same person. Repeated measurement of performance must occur in single-subject research because of the need to examine intervention effects over an extended period. Ongoing observations help investigators avoid attribution of change to historical accidents. These procedures let investigators examine trend, level, variability, and stability of an individual's performance. Investigators establish **experimental control** by accounting for changes in level and trend through introduction of the treatment (Kazdin, 1982). They examine the effects of interventions through observation of treatment on performance of the same person. As a result, these designs aid in prediction of effects for individuals and promote individualized instruction.

Research Requirements Applied to Single-Subject Designs

The three primary requirements for empirical research, as indicated in Chapters 7, 8 and 9 of the text, are internal validity, external validity, and reliability of measurement (Isaac & Michael, 1981). As stated earlier, internal validity relates to the extent to which an intervention brings about the same effect with the same individual or group of individuals. It is the cornerstone to all experimental research, including single-subject research methodology. While internal validity addresses intrasubject (within the subject) replication, external validity addresses intersubject (between subjects) replication, or the extent to which the effects of an intervention generalize across other people, behaviors, and conditions. Internal and external validity are both dependent upon the reliability of measurement attained during an investigation. Reliability of measurement refers to the consistency of measurement or the extent to which two independent observers record the same behavior using the same measurement system (e.g., response definition, observation recording procedure, data collection sheet). Only with a high percentage of interobserver agreement can there be confidence that a behavior change is a function of an intervention (internal validity) and that the results will generalize beyond the original subjects and conditions (external validity).

Internal Validity

Investigators try to examine the influence of an intervention so that extraneous variables or outside factors will not interfere with reported conclusions. After examining the threats to internal validity, Kazdin (1982) and Kratochwill (1978) concluded that single-subject investigations can readily reduce or eliminate these threats.

Threats to internal validity involve the presence of extraneous and difficult to evaluate variables influencing the individual. These threats introduce reasons that could account for change that is not attributable to the therapeutic intervention (Cook & Campbell, 1979). Investigators can reduce or eliminate threats to internal validity in single-subject research through systematic application of experimental designs. These designs are based on objective, repeated, and reliable data collection. As a result of using individual subjects as their own controls, investigators can lessen the problem of differences among individuals before the experiment and encourage examination of individual differences.

Single-subject designs evaluate whether the introduction of a treatment (*independent variable*) is responsible for a change in behavior (*dependent variable*). These designs can show that a functional relationship exists between variables (Tawney & Gast, 1984). The purpose of using any positivistic research design is to increase experimental control while decreasing extraneous variables. According to McReynolds and Kearns (1983), experimental control prevents extraneous variables from confounding the effect of the independent variable. **Extraneous variables** are those environmental conditions that are not controlled but may affect behaviors. Experimental control promotes the belief that changes in dependent variables relate to manipulation of the independent variable.

Requirements of single-subject designs include: (a) operational specificity, (b) repeated measurement, (c) baseline performance levels, and (d) implementation of an intervention. **Operational specificity** relates to precise and complete descriptions of behaviors (dependent variables) and the treatment (independent variables) to permit replication. **Repeated measurement** entails regular, ideally continuous, observations of the same behavior over time for one or a few subjects to determine behavior pattern before and after the introduction of intervention (Birnbauer, Peterson & Solnick, 1974).

To measure the effects of an intervention, investigators must examine the behavior without influence from the intervention. The observation period of measuring the target behavior prior to the intervention is the **baseline phase**. Baseline data show the level and trend of behavior (dependent variable) before an intervention is introduced. The function of baseline involves description and prediction (Kazdin, 1982). The descriptive function of baseline delineates the existing level and trend of behavior over several sessions or days while the predictive function projects future behaviors if there are no changes in conditions.

To describe accurately and predict future occurrences of existing behavior, investigators must measure behavior often enough for a clear picture of the behavior to emerge. To accomplish this, investigators obtain a representative sample of the target behavior under intervention conditions. This is typically three to five consecutive observation days, or until the level and trend of the behavior stabilize. **Level** refers to the magnitude of the behavior (frequency, percentage correct, duration), while **trend** refers to the direction of the data over consecutive observation periods (accelerating or decelerating). Both level and trend are characterized as being stable or variable. **Stability** and variability refer to the amount of fluctuation or "bounce" there is across consecutive measures of the target behavior. The less fluctuation the greater the stability and the better the data will predict the future level and trend of the target behavior, if the conditions are not changed. With few exceptions, investigators wait for the level and trend of the target behavior to stabilize prior to changing conditions (i.e., introducing an intervention). This practice increases the predictive validity of the data and enhances the internal validity of the investigation. Common within condition (as opposed to comparison between conditions) data patterns are presented in Figure 10.1, page 186. After investigators collect three or more days of baseline data, and when data are stable, they employ an intervention. Single-subject designs include several baseline and intervention phases in the design across time, behaviors, people, or settings. The purpose of changing from one phase to another is to show how behavioral change is a result of the independent variable. There are a variety of single-subject experimental designs available to answer TR research questions. According to Barlow, Hayes, and Nelson (1984), the choice of which design to use depends on factors such as the: (a) nature of target behaviors, (b) setting in which the study is conducted, (c) availability of additional subjects, and (d) other practical concerns. The four most common designs in single-subject research are the withdrawal or reversal design, multiple baseline design, multiple probe design, and multielement or alternating treatments design. Each of these designs is described later in this chapter.

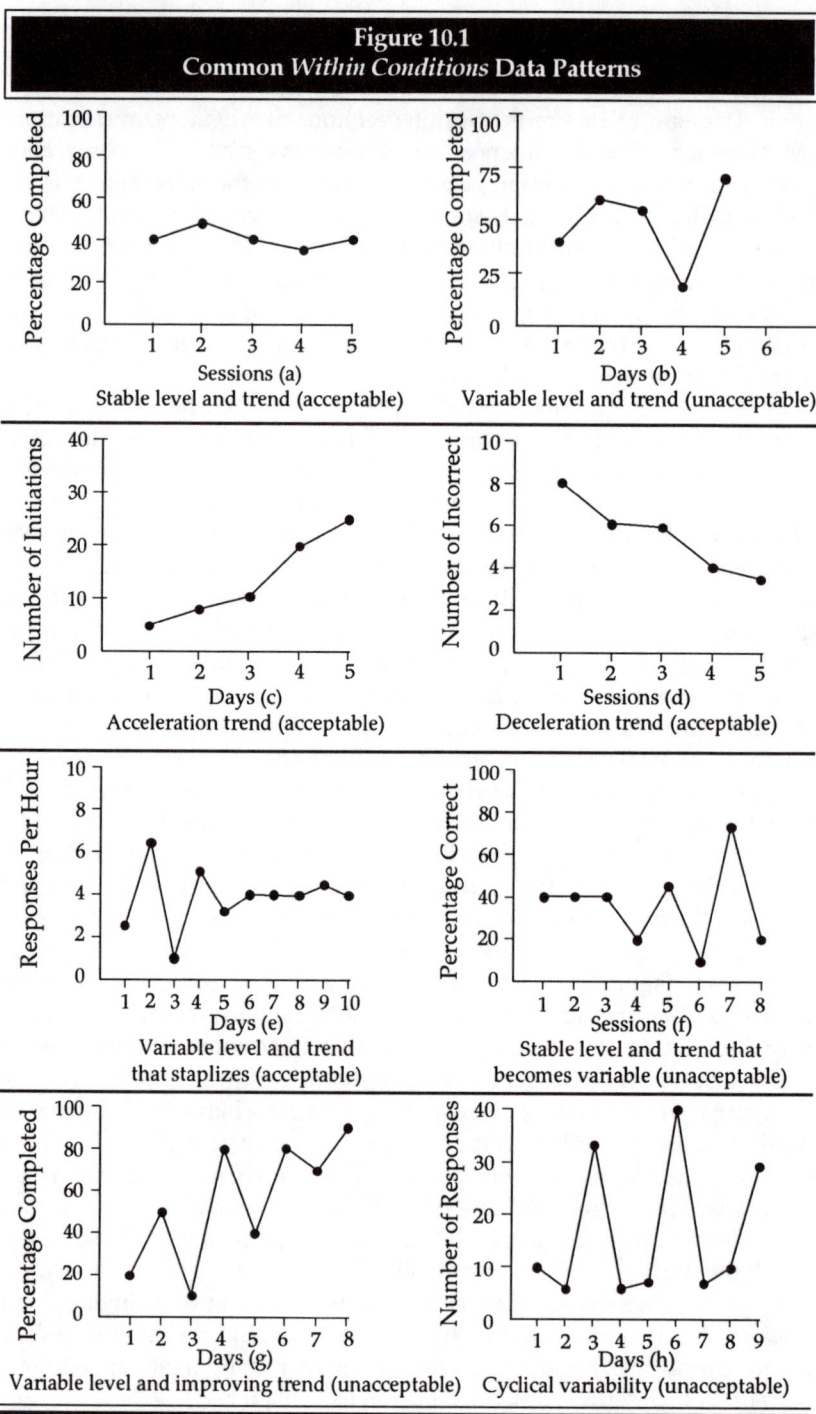

Figure 10.1
Common *Within Conditions* Data Patterns

Sessions (a)
Stable level and trend (acceptable)

Days (b)
Variable level and trend (unacceptable)

Days (c)
Acceleration trend (acceptable)

Sessions (d)
Deceleration trend (acceptable)

Days (e)
Variable level and trend
that staplizes (acceptable)

Sessions (f)
Stable level and trend that
becomes variable (unacceptable)

Days (g)
Variable level and improving trend (unacceptable)

Days (h)
Cyclical variability (unacceptable)

Single-subject designs help investigators evaluate experimental control (Siegel & Spradlin, 1985). These designs: (a) incorporate objective measures, (b) schedule assessments on several occasions over time, (c) provide information regarding performance stability, and (d) note marked changes in behavior with an intervention. In addition, they arrange administration of the intervention to reduce further threats to internal validity (Kazdin, 1982).

Specifically, six of the major threats to internal validity that an investigator must either control or account for include history, maturation, testing, instrumentation, multiple treatment interference, and instability.

1. History refers to those extraneous variables (any events other than the treatment) that occur over time that may influence the outcome of the study. Such variables may provide alternative explanations if they are not properly controlled or isolated. Failure to do so threatens the internal validity of findings.

2. Maturation refers to changes that occur in subjects during an investigation simply due to the passage of time. Changes associated with the aging process are the most common variables that need to be accounted for when attempting to attribute behavior change to the independent variable.

3. Testing refers to the effect repeated observation and measurement has on the dependent variable, independent of the intervention.

4. A threat to internal validity resulting from instrumentation is brought about by a change in some aspect of the measurement system (e.g., modified response definition, altered recording procedure, malfunction of an automated recording device).

5. A prominent threat to the believability of findings when two or more interventions are being studied is multiple treatment interference. Multiple treatment interference refers to the interactive effect interventions (e.g., leisure education, relaxation training, vocational instruction) may have, thus masking the effect one intervention (e.g., leisure education) would have without the person having been exposed to the others.

6. Finally, the most damaging threat to internal validity is when there is a failure to replicate the effect an intervention has on the target behavior or when the change in behavior is only temporary. This inconsistent effect is referred to as instability.

As with all research designs, group or single-subject, there is no perfect experiment. Rather, it is the investigator's task to describe what happened during the study and to account for planned and unplanned outcomes—those which may have influenced the findings (Tawney & Gast, 1984).

External Validity

A goal of research is to show that the relationship between intervention and behavior change can generalize to different people, settings, and situations. External validity is the extent to which the results of an investigation generalize beyond the experimental condition (Kratochwill, 1978). Various threats to external validity diminish through replication of intervention effects (McReynolds & Thompson, 1986). Through replication, investigators can examine generalization of results across behaviors, settings, people, and measures (Tawney & Gast, 1984). Two different methods for replication of experimental findings (direct and systematic) are available.

Direct replication refers to the repetition of the same investigation, using the same procedures by the same investigator (Sidman, 1960). There are two types of direct replication: intrasubject and intersubject. **Intrasubject direct replication** addresses the internal rather than external validity of the findings of an experiment. Specifically, in an intrasubject replication everything remains the same including the subject. Two questions that may be addressed by this type of *direct replication* are, "Will the intervention have the same effect on the behavior of the same person if it is withdrawn or reintroduced?" or "Will the intervention have the same effect on the behavior of the same person if it is systematically introduced to other similar behaviors of that person in a time lagged fashion?" Answers to these two questions address consistency of effect rather than generalizability of findings. **Intersubject** (between subject) *replications* address generalizability to the extent that people in a single investigation differ. In an intersubject replication everything remains the same except for the individual, as more than one research participant is involved. In most single subject research design investigations at least three research participants are included in order to evaluate the generalizability of the findings (effectiveness of the intervention) across similar subjects. In addition, one or more intrasubject (within subject) direct replications will be attempted with each research participant to increase confidence in the findings. Intersubject direct replications address the following question: "Will the intervention have the same effect on similar behaviors of other participants in the investigation?"

The generalizability of findings of an experiment are primarily demonstrated through systematic replications. **Systematic replication** entails changing two or more of the conditions of the original investigation, but not the independent variable in any significant way. When investigators attempt to duplicate a study they have read in a professional journal, they are undertaking a systematic replication in which the investigator, participants, settings, and target behaviors change. The greater the differences from the original investigation, while obtaining the same results, the greater the generalizability or external validity of the intervention. In single-subject research, a series of systematic replications must be conducted before TRSs gain confidence in the generalizability of the intervention across people, conditions, and behaviors.

Reliability of Measurement

The requirement of **reliability**, which means the degree to which a measurement system (i.e., definitions, observers, instruments) yields similar results for the same person under different conditions, is addressed through data collection procedures. Investigators must design measurement systems to accurately record behavior change (dependent variable) for them to be reliable. When conducting single-subject research, investigators must define participant behavior (dependent variable) with observable and measurable terms (Dattilo & Murphy, 1987). This requirement is compatible with systematic programming guidelines that encourage practitioners to use behavioral terminology when developing objectives (cf. Dattilo & Murphy, 1991; Peterson & Gunn, 1984).

Since observational methods are the primary method to obtain information on what is actually happening in a situation (Pelegrino, 1979), data collection procedures must ensure observer accuracy and interobserver agreement. Observer accuracy requires that observations reflect the actual behavior. To achieve observer accuracy, investigators establish a standard or criterion (Kazdin, 1982). Videotaping may aid investigators in developing a criterion. Investigators might videotape the participant and review the tape many times using an observational checklist. The final results would then become the standard for the actual observers. Observers would then learn to reach this criterion.

When direct observation yields evaluative data, it is possible that observers will not record behavior consistently. Therefore, determination of agreement among observers is necessary when applying single-subject research methodology. **Interobserver agreement** refers to the correspondence of data obtained by two or more individuals independently watching a behavior at the same time (Kratochwill, 1978). Investigators calculate a comparison to determine correspondence between their observations. Using more than one observer and analyzing the extent to which the observers agree or disagree provides a method to detect inconsistencies in observer analysis of participant response. Confidence in the data escalates with increased agreement between observers.

Although interobserver agreement checks on each recording session would be valuable, it is unlikely that TRSs have adequate staff and time to make this practice possible. Therefore, Kazdin (1982) suggested investigators use interobserver agreement probes. **Interobserver probes** require appointing one trained observer as the primary observer to examine a particular situation. Another trained observer must then be systematically involved in periodic examination of some sessions. Tawney and Gast (1984) reported that observation by the secondary observer during 20% of the sessions is an acceptable number of reliability checks. Investigators can then calculate interobserver agreement between the corresponding data of the two observers.

Data Analysis Through Visual Inspection of Graphic Displays

Single-subject research controls for variances by experimental design rather than by relying on statistical procedures (Kratochwill, 1978). The strength of the conclusions lies in the degree of experimental control established during the investigation. This is done through continual decisions about manipulating the independent variable. Although investigators can use statistical analysis, visual inspection of graphic displays is often the most effective means to determine effects of an intervention (Parsonson & Baer, 1978). Visual inspection of graphed data provides the basis for judgment about reliability or consistency of intervention effects and permits determination of dramatic effects (Kazdin, 1982; Tawney & Gast, 1984).

Visual inspection requires the graphic depiction of data to enable investigators to evaluate data patterns. **Graphic presentation** is the depiction of numerical data in visual form. Investigators should graphically display each target behavior across baseline and the intervention phases, thereby providing a detailed and compact summary of the data. Pelegrino (1979) suggested that investigators make a line graph with a grid upon which to plot the relationship of two variables. To promote accurate and efficient data display, Jones, Vaught, and Weinrott (1977) recommended the use of: (a) concise titles describing the purpose of the study, (b) explicit captions describing the meaning of variables, and (c) appropriate scale units on the ordinate and abscissa scales. Guidelines for selecting and constructing graphic displays have been presented by Tawney and Gast (1984).

Visually depicted data should reflect systematic interventions and result in consistency of judgment about the impact of the intervention. Investigators use visual inspection because significant effects ought to be obvious when examining graphed data. Therefore, investigators will be more likely to accept only those interventions that have major effects, while dismissing weak results.

Visual analysis of graphic data has several advantages over statistical analysis. First, it is a dynamic process which permits continuous analysis as data are collected. This allows TRSs to make data-based treatment decisions throughout the program, potentially saving valuable therapy time. Second, the visual analysis method can be used with individuals as well as small groups. Third, other concerned people may independently analyze graphically displayed data permitting them to draw their own conclusions regarding the relationship between the independent and dependent variables. Fourth, by analyzing each individual's performance, investigators neither overestimate nor underestimate the effectiveness of an intervention with a subject. Fifth, the plotting of all *primary* data permits discovery of *serendipitous findings* that may coincide with extraneous events. Visual analysis of graphic data is certainly compatible with current best clinical and research practices.

There are no concrete rules for analyzing graphed data; however, properties of data that demand attention and general guidelines for determining adequacy of an experimental demonstration have been developed (Tawney & Gast, 1984). Properties identified as important in visual analysis of graphed data include the: (a) number of data points plotted within a phase, (b) number of variables that are changed between adjacent conditions, (c) level stability and changes in level within and between conditions, and (d) trend direction, trend stability, and changes in trend within and between phases (Tawney & Gast, 1984, p. 159). More specifically, there should be a minimum of three consecutive data points in each phase (baseline and intervention) of an investigation. Additional data will be necessary if data are variable. When moving from one experimental condition to another (baseline to intervention, intervention to baseline, or one intervention to another) only one variable should change between adjacent conditions—the independent variable. Only when one variable changes is it possible to identify the cause of change in the target behavior.

As discussed earlier, the stability of level and trend of data during each phase of the investigation is important in predicting the future path of the data under similar conditions. To determine level stability, investigators calculate the median level of the data points of a phase and determine whether 80% of the data points fall within 20% of the median value. Although different investigators may use different criteria for defining stability, seldom will the criteria be less stringent than the 80-20 percentages. Whatever criteria are used, it is important that investigators specify them when describing data as variable. Similar to measuring level stability, investigators may want to calculate trend stability when the direction of the data path is not readily apparent. When the data are variable (level and trend) investigators may estimate the trend direction by using a simple statistical procedure known as the **split-middle method** (White & Haring, 1980). This method relies on the median value of a condition and the percentage of data points that fall around the trend line. Interested readers are referred to White and Haring (1980) or Barlow and Herson (1984).

After visually analyzing data within each phase, investigators then compare data between phases. Specifically, they look for consistent differences in level, trend, and stability of the data between adjacent baseline and intervention phases or between two adjacent intervention phases. If there are consistent differences between phases (e.g., mean and median levels, range, trend) and if these differences are replicated at least twice in the investigation, then there is support for attributing these differences to the independent variable. Comparison between condition data patterns are illustrated in Figure 10.2.

Examples of Therapeutic Recreation Single-Subject Research

Withdrawal Designs

As previously mentioned, the single-subject designs most commonly used to evaluate the effectiveness of interventions are the withdrawal or reversal, multiple baseline, multiple probe, and multielement or alternating treatments. **Withdrawal designs**, also known as **reversal designs** and **ABAB designs**, are the most basic experimental designs in single-subject research. These designs examine effects of an intervention by altering the baseline condition (A phase) with the intervention condition (B phase). Investigators repeat the A and B phases to complete the four phases. Effects of an intervention have internal validity if performance improves during the first intervention phase, reverts to or approaches original baseline levels of performance when treatment is withdrawn, and improves when investigators reinstate treatment in the second intervention phase (Kazdin, 1982). External validity is enhanced when the effects are replicated with other people in the same study (intersubject direct replication) and across studies (systematic replication).

Although few investigators report use of withdrawal designs to examine leisure issues related to people with disabilities, there are some examples. Wehman and Marchant (1978) used a withdrawal design to examine effects of an intervention strategy on the play behavior of children with severe disabilities. Kelly, Jarvie, Middlebrook, McNeer, and Drabman (1984) employed a withdrawal design to explore effects of leisure participation on reduction of pain behavior experienced during hydrotherapy by children with severe burns. The effects of a leisure skills package (counseling, social reinforcement, and availability of materials) on the leisure behavior of six adults with mental retardation residing in a group home within the community were examined by Schleien, Kiernan, and Wehman (1981) who used a withdrawal design.

Figure 10.2
Common *Between Conditions* Data Patterns

Summary of data patterns across two conditions

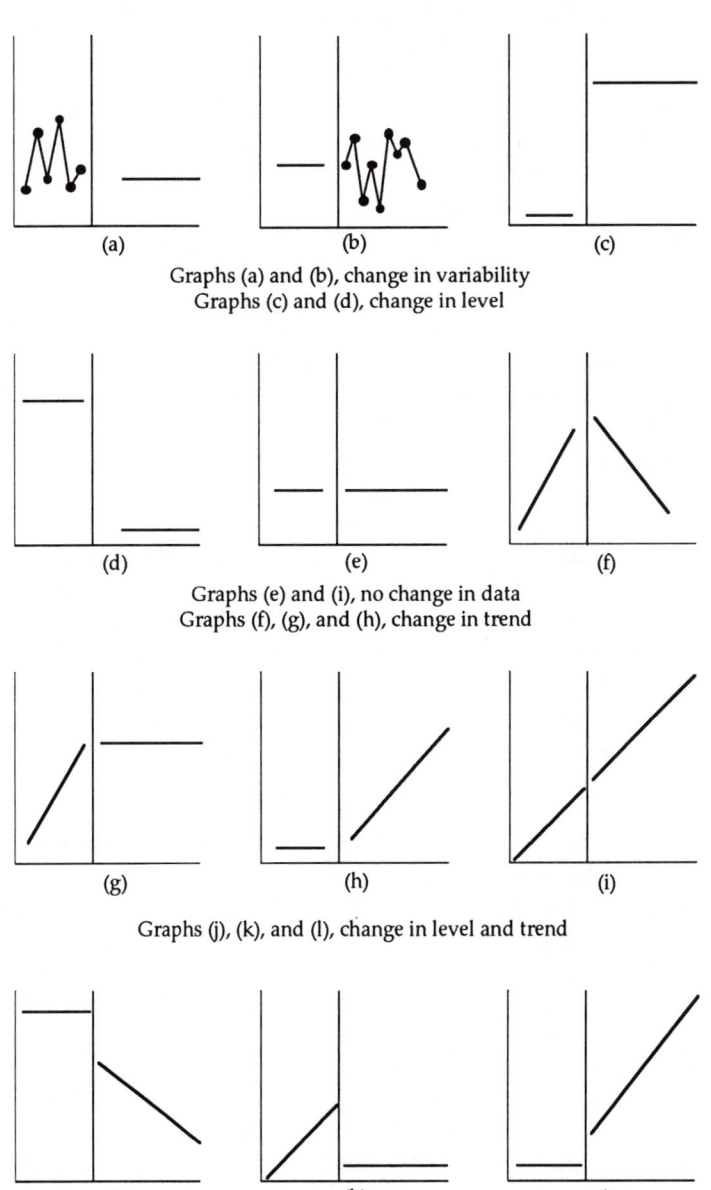

Graphs (a) and (b), change in variability
Graphs (c) and (d), change in level

Graphs (e) and (i), no change in data
Graphs (f), (g), and (h), change in trend

Graphs (j), (k), and (l), change in level and trend

Multiple Baseline Designs

The **multiple baseline design** evaluates experimental control by introducing the intervention across three or more data series (behaviors, phases, or people) in a time lagged fashion. Figure 10.3 presents a prototype of a multiple baseline design across behaviors. With all three types of multiple baseline designs, continuous data are collected across all data series (baseline phase). After a stable level and trend are evident, the intervention is introduced to the first behavior, while maintaining the baseline condition with the other behaviors. When criterion level performance is reached with the first behavior, the intervention is introduced to the second behavior. This staggered introduction of the intervention across behaviors continues until all target behaviors have been exposed to the intervention. If all behaviors maintain baseline phase performance levels prior to the introduction of the intervention, and there is an abrupt change in level and trend in a therapeutic direction, then the TRS's confidence that the intervention was responsible for the behavior change is high. As with the withdrawal design, the generality of findings increases through a series of intersubject and systematic replications.

Some studies have used multiple baseline designs to examine leisure issues related to persons with disabilities. Hill, Wehman, and Horst (1982) employed a multiple baseline design across participants to evaluate effects of an instructional program on acquisition and generalization of age-appropriate leisure skills with adolescents with severe disabilities. In another investigation, Dyer, Schwartz, and Luce (1984) used a multiple baseline design across conditions (settings) to determine effects of a training program on the amount of time youth with severe disabilities engaged in age-appropriate leisure activities. The ability to teach an adolescent with severe disabilities to use a bowling facility was examined using a multiple baseline design across skills by Schleien, Certo, and Muccino (1984). Lagomarcino, Redi, Ivancic, and Faw (1984) applied this technique across participants to evaluate an approach for teaching leisure skills to persons with severe mental retardation. A leisure education training program designed to teach two adults with severe mental retardation how to use a community recreation center was examined by Schleien and Larson (1986) via a multiple baseline design across skills. More recently, Schleien, Cameron, Rynders, and Slick (1988) used a multiple baseline design across behaviors (different activities) replicated across two children with multiple disabilities. Schleien et al., examined the effects of a multifaceted training program on the acquisition and generalization of three recreation skills, social interaction skills, and play behaviors. Using a series of multiple baseline designs, Dattilo and colleagues (Dattilo, 1986b, 1987b, 1988; Dattilo & Mirenda, 1987, Mirenda & Dattilo, 1987) examined a computerized assessment procedure that determined

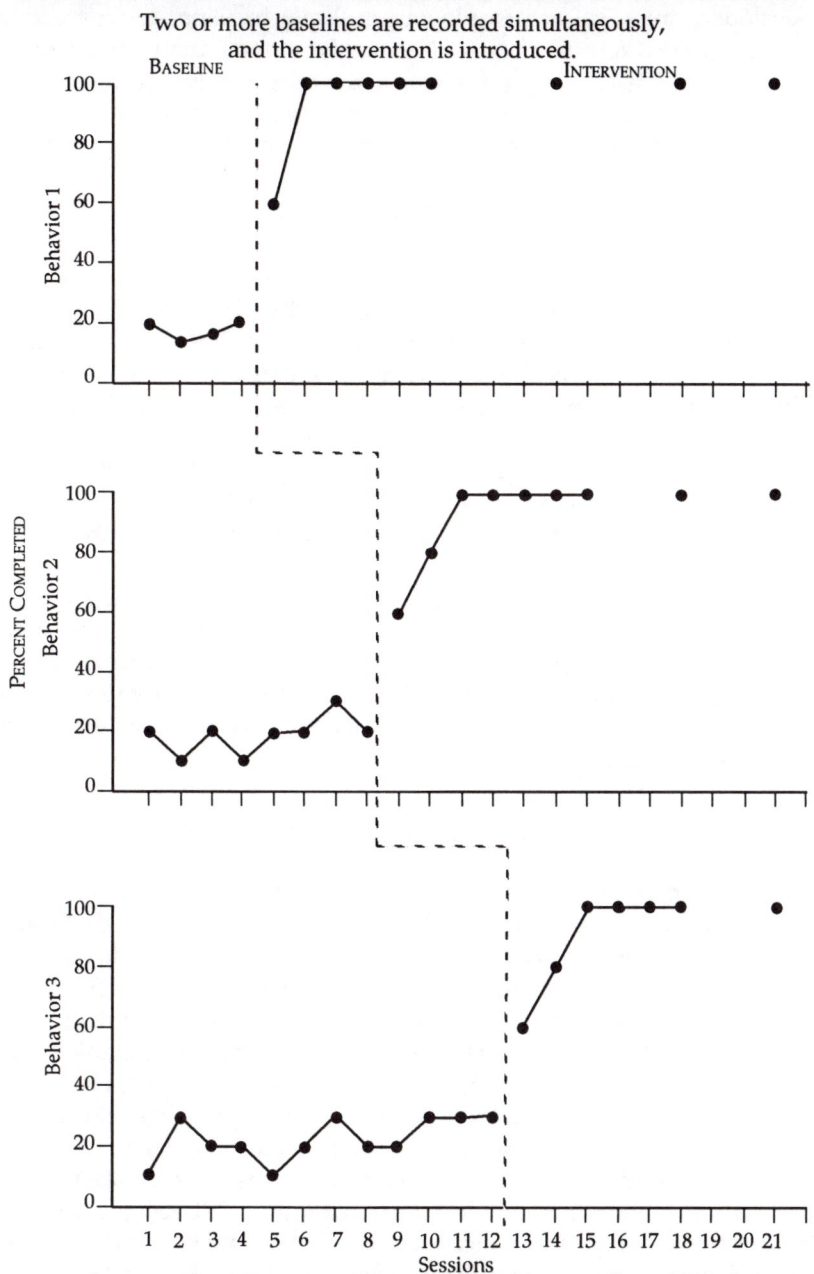

Figure 10.3
Hypothetical Data Using the Multiple Baseline Design Across Behavior

leisure preferences of persons with severe mental and physical disabilities. In other related studies, Dattilo and associates (Dattilo & Camarata, 1991; Dattilo & O'Keefe, 1992; Light, Dattilo, English, Guttierez, & Hartz, in press) developed investigations employing multiple baseline designs across participants to determine the effectiveness of communication interventions. The investigators taught practitioners and adults with mental retardation who had language deficits to engage in conversations that promoted leisure involvement via augmentative and alternative communication systems.

Multiple Probe Designs

A variation of the multiple baseline design, which has practical advantages, is the **multiple probe design** (Horner & Baer, 1978; Murphy & Bryan, 1980). This design is identical to the multiple baseline design except that data collection during baseline is intermittent rather than continuous. There are several variations of the multiple probe design, one of which is depicted in Figure 10.4. In one of the few studies to use this technique in TR, Schleien, McAvoy, and Feller (in progress) evaluated the participation of youth with mental retardation in an 8-week integrated resource interpretation/outdoor education program with peers without disabilities. A multiple probe design across behaviors revealed that three skill levels for snowshoeing (snowshoe preparation, basic snowshoe, and advanced snowshoe skills) were acquired by all four youth. In addition, a positive change in attitudes of peers without disabilities toward the youth with mental retardation was noted from pre- to postprogram. The multiple probe design is likely to be used more frequently by TRSs due to the time savings during baseline and the maintenance of experimental rigor.

Multielement Designs

The fourth single-subject research design that warrants attention of TRS is the **multielement design** (Sidman, 1960), also known as the **alternating treatments design** (Barlow & Hersen, 1984). This design can be used to evaluate the effectiveness of two or more interventions on the same target behavior. This is accomplished by the rapid alternation of interventions within the same therapy session, across time of day or across days. An example of the basic and most commonly used multielement design is presented in Figure 10.5 (see p. 198). It depicts the assessment of the target behavior under baseline, followed by a comparison of the target behavior under two different intervention conditions. In this example, conditions are alternated across days. As can be seen, there is a clear difference in the effectiveness of the two interventions. To further enhance internal validity, a *final phase* is introduced in which the superior intervention is implemented with the target behavior

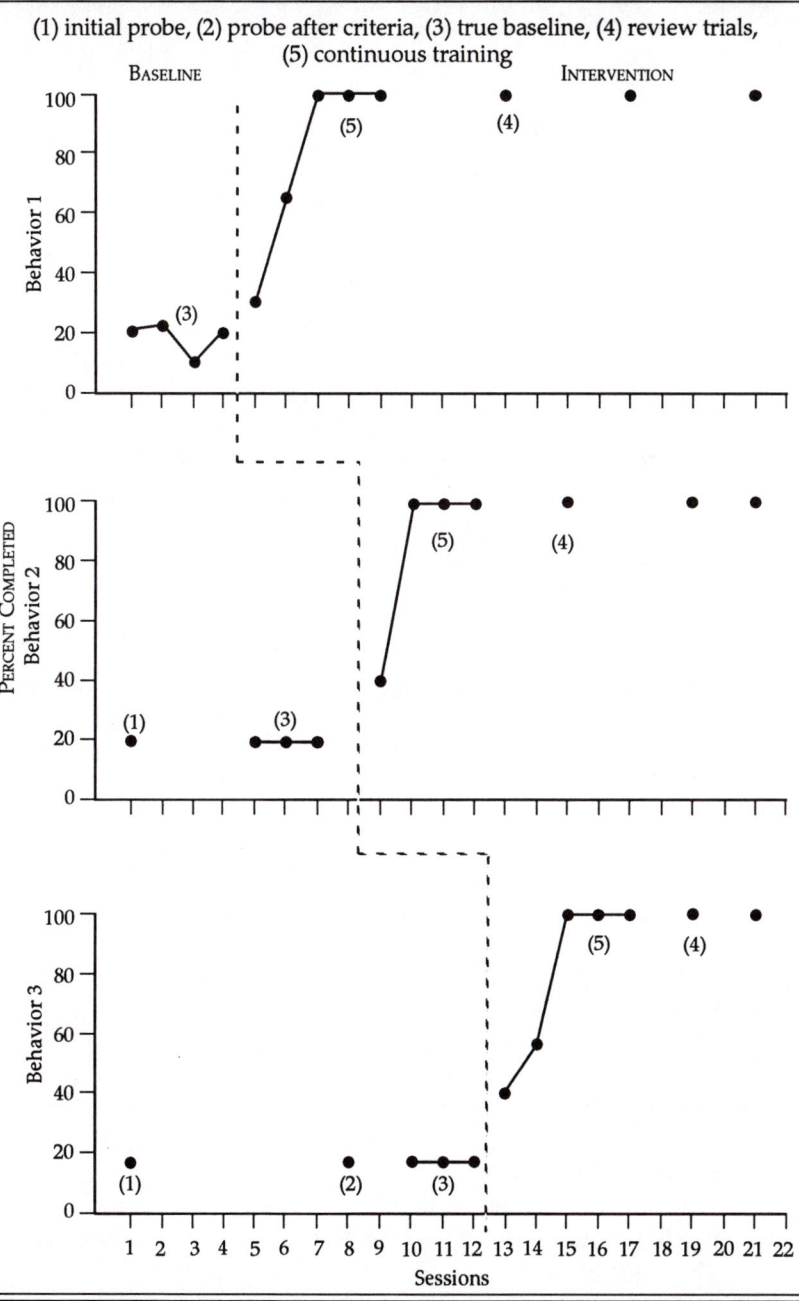

Figure 10.4
Multiple Probe Design Across Behaviors

(1) initial probe, (2) probe after criteria, (3) true baseline, (4) review trials, (5) continuous training

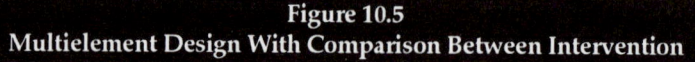

Figure 10.5
Multielement Design With Comparison Between Intervention

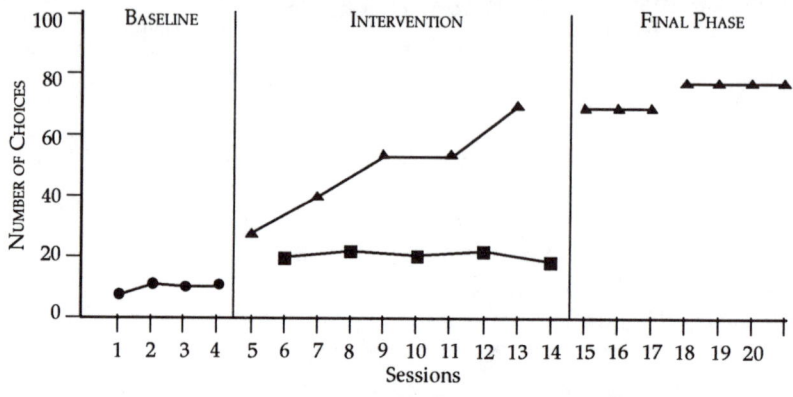

on several consecutive days without alternation with the other condition. The addition of this final phase is optional, but desirable. In one of the few studies to employ a multielement design in TR, Schleien, Rynders, Mustonen, and Fox (1990) explored the effects of using four social levels of play (isolate, dyadic, group, and team) on the play behavior of children with autism who were in an integrated leisure education/physical education program. Recreation activities representing the four social levels of play were implemented during 10-minute periods on a randomized basis within a multielement design. Results indicated that not only did the type of play activity influence the frequency of play, but that participants consistently played more appropriately in the more advanced (i.e., team, group, dyadic) play activities as compared with their play in isolate play activities.

Combination of Designs

The four single-subject research designs discussed are the most common single-subject designs used by investigators. There are, however, many other designs such as changing criterion, multiple treatment, and parallel treatments designs (Gast & Wolery, 1988) that may be very effective in answering leisure-related questions. In addition, investigators may use various single-subject designs in combination to increase confidence in results. For example, Dattilo and Barnett (1985) applied a combined design to compare the behaviors of children with severe disabilities during participation in a chosen recreation activity to their behaviors during participation in the same activity without the opportunity for choice. The design incorporated alternating intervention and baseline conditions in separate phases over time (reversal) and presenting the intervention to each person at different points in time (multiple baseline). In another example, Schleien, Wehman, and Kiernan (1981) showed acquisition and generalization of dart skills by adults with multiple disabilities by combining a multiple baseline across subjects design with a changing-criterion design.

Not only can investigators use different single-subject designs together, they can use various other research methods with single-subject designs. For example, Halle, Gabler-Halle, and Bemben (1989) combined an experimental control group design with a multiple baseline design across groups of children with moderate and severe disabilities. Halle et al. found that an aerobic conditioning program enhanced fitness levels. In another investigation, Lanagan and Dattilo (1989) used a combination design employing an experimental between group design with a withdrawal design. Lanagan and Dattilo determined that adults with mental retardation participated more actively during leisure education than when they attended general recreation sessions.

Ethical Implications of Single-Subject Research

Therapeutic recreation has been defined in the past as the development of a meaningful leisure lifestyle for people with limitations that would otherwise create barriers to leisure involvement (Peterson & Gunn, 1984). More recently, TR has been defined as having as a primary purpose the improved functioning and independence of persons with illnesses or disabling conditions through the provision of treatment and recreation services. A second purpose is to reduce or eliminate the effects of illness or disability (ATRA, 1990). Regardless of which definition of TR is accepted, single-subject research methods are appropriate to use, and address some ethical concerns. Individuals with limitations vary greatly in cognitive, emotional, physical, and social skills. Because of the heterogeneity of persons with limitations, practitioners develop specialized interventions (McReynolds & Thompson, 1986) and predict the effects of these interventions on the individual. As a result, this methodology allows investigators to make inferences about the individual. When investigators can make inferences about the individual, they can contribute to the development of more effective interventions.

Single-subject research is a procedure that allows practitioners to avoid withholding helpful treatment from clients participating in a TR program. Frequently, intervention research requires administering a treatment to one group while not allowing another group (the control group) to receive the treatment. The action of withholding useful services from people in need of treatment may create an ethical dilemma for practitioners trying to conduct systematic research. One of the virtues of single-subject designs is that they require each person to act as his or her own control (Walker, 1983), thus every person in the investigation receives the intervention.

There has been an increasing demand by consumers, administrators, accrediting bodies, and third-party funding agencies that TRSs show the effectiveness of their interventions. One potential benefit of single-subject research is an increase in accountability related to the provision of effective therapeutic recreation services for people with limitations. Results of single-subject investigations provide practitioners with data that can result in development of more effective treatment.

Conclusion

To respond to the diversity of people served and the myriad of service delivery environments, TRSs can employ a variety of intervention strategies (McCormick, Scott, & Dattilo, 1991). Since therapeutic recreation is an eclectic profession (Austin, 1982), practitioners must be open to different perspectives and recognize that certain interventions may be more effective than others. Acceptance of an eclectic position for TR is not only valuable but appears necessary for survival of the profession (McCormick, Scott, & Dattilo, 1991). Professionals can continue to use the eclectic perspective when trying to answer empirically questions related to TR.

Investigators can carefully examine individuals participating in TR programs by repeatedly measuring their performance during baseline and intervention phases. Single-subject research represents one viable method for making informed decisions about the quality of TR programs. This methodology provides a context for understanding the behavioral dynamics of individuals with limitations or disabilities. Single-subject designs, used alone or with other research designs, can be responsive to various practical dilemmas in TR.

Discussion Questions

1. What are the advantages of employing single-subject research designs?
2. How can investigators address internal validity concerns when conducting an investigation using single-subject research designs?
3. What can be done to increase the external validity when initiating an investigation incorporating single-subject research methods?
4. How can investigators increase their confidence that they are using reliable single-subject research methods?
5. What are some practical and ethical aspects of single-subject research methods which are relevant to TR?
6. What is the difference between "within condition" and "between condition" data pattern analysis (see Figure 10.1 and 10.2)?
7. What are the differences between "multiple baseline," "multiple probe," and "multielement" research designs (see chapter text and Figures 10.3, 10.4 and 10.5?
8. What are some of the advantages of visual inspection?

References

American Therapeutic Recreation Association. (1990, March). *ATRA Code of Ethics*, p.1. Hattiesburg, MS: Author.

Barlow, D. H., Hayes, S. C., & Nelson, R. O. (1984). *The scientist practitioner: Research and accountability in clinical and educational settings.* New York, NY: Pergamon.

Barlow, D. H., & Hersen, M. (1984). *Single case experimental designs: Strategies for studying behavior change.* New York, NY: Pergamon.

Birnbauer, J. S., Peterson, C. R., & Solnick, J. V. (1974). Design and interpretation of studies of single-subjects. *American Journal of Mental Deficiency, 79*, 191-203.

Campbell, D. T., & Stanley, J. C. (1966). *Experimental and quasi-experimental designs for research.* Chicago, Il: Rand McNally.

Cook, T. D., & Campbell, D. T. (1979). *Quasi-experimentation, design and analysis issues for field settings.* Chicago, Il: Rand McNally.

Dattilo, J. (1985). An alternative to studying individuals with disabilities: Single-subject research. *Leisure Information Quarterly, 17*, 11.

Dattilo, J. (1986a). Single-subject research in therapeutic recreation: Implications to individuals with limitations. *Therapeutic Recreation Journal, 20*(1), 76-87.

Dattilo, J. (1986b). Computerized assessment of preferences for persons with severe handicaps. *Journal of Applied Behavior Analysis, 19*(4), 445-448.

Dattilo, J. (1987a). Encouraging the emergence of therapeutic recreation research-practitioners through single-subject research. *Journal of Expanding Horizons in Therapeutic Recreation, 2*, 1-5.

Dattilo, J. (1987b). Computerized assessment of leisure preferences: A replication. *Education and Training in Mental Retardation, 22*(2), 128-133.

Dattilo, J. (1988). Assessing music preferences of persons with severe handicaps. *Therapeutic Recreation Journal, 22*(1), 12-23.

Dattilo, J. (1989). Unique horizons in research: Single-subject designs. In D. M. Compton (Ed.), *Issues in therapeutic recreation: A profession in transition* (pp. 445-462). Champaign, IL: Sagamore.

Dattilo, J., & Barnett, L. (1985). Therapeutic recreation for individuals with severe handicaps: Implications of chosen participation. *Therapeutic Recreation Journal, 19*(3), 79-91.

Dattilo, J., & Camarata, S. (1991). Facilitating conversation through self-initiated augmentative communication treatment. *Journal of Applied Behavior Analysis, 24*(2), 369-378.

Dattilo, J., McCormick, B., & Scott, D. (1991). Answering Questions About Therapeutic Recreation Part II: Choosing Research Methods. Submitted to: *Annual in Therapeutic Recreation, 2*, 85-95.

Dattilo, J., & Mirenda, P. (1987). The application of a leisure preference assessment protocol for persons with severe handicaps. *Journal of the Association for Persons with Severe Handicaps, 12*(4), 306-311.

Dattilo, J., & Murphy, W. P. (1987). *Behavior modification in therapeutic recreation: An introductory learning manual.* State College, PA: Venture.

Dattilo, J., & Murphy, W. D. (1991). *Leisure education program planning: A systematic approach.* State College, PA: Venture.

Dattilo, J., & Nelson, G. (1986). Single-subject evaluation in health education. *Health Education Quarterly, 13*(3), 249-259.

Dattilo, J., & O'Keefe, B. M. (1992). Setting the stage for leisure: Encouraging adults with mental retardation who use augmentative and alternative communication systems to share conversations. *Therapeutic Recreation Journal, 26*(1).

Drew, C. F. (1976). Introduction to designing research and evaluation. St. Louis, MO: The C. V. Mosby Company.

Gast, D., & Wolery, M. (1988). Parallel treatment designs: A nested single-subject design for comparing instructional procedures. *Education and Treatment of Children, 11*(3), 270-285.

Halle, J. W., Gabler-Halle, D., & Bemben, D. A. (1989). Effects of peer-mediated aerobic conditioning program on fitness measures with children who have moderate and severe disabilities. *Journal of the Association for Persons with Severe Handicaps, 14*(1), 33-47.

Hersen, M., & Barlow, D. (1976). *Single-case experimental designs: Strategies for studying behavior change.* New York, NY: Pergamon.

Horner, R. D., & Baer, D. M. (1978). Multiple-probe technique: A variation of the multiple baseline design. *Journal of Applied Behavior Analysis, 11*, 189-196.

Isaac, S., & Michael, W. B. (1981). *Handbook in research and evaluation: For education and the behavioral sciences.* San Diego, CA: EDITS.

Jones, R. R., Vaught, R. S., & Weinrott, M. (1977). Time-series analysis in operant research. *Journal of Applied Behavior Analysis, 10*, 151-166.

Kazdin, A. (1982). *Single-case research designs: Methods for clinical and applied settings*. New York, NY: Oxford University Press.

Kazdin, A. (1980). *Research design in clinical psychology*. New York, NY: Harper & Row.

Kearns, K. P. (1986). Flexibility of single-subject experimental designs Part II: Design selection and arrangement of experimental phases. *Journal of Speech and Hearing Disorders, 51*, 204-214.

Kelly, M. L., Jarvie, G. J., Middlebrook, J. L., McNeer, M. F., & Drabman, R. S. (1984). Decreasing burned children's pain behavior: Impacting the trauma of hydrotherapy. *Journal of Applied Behavior Analysis, 17*, 147-158.

Kent, R. D. (1985). Science and the clinician: The practice of science and the science of practice. *Seminars in Speech and Language, 6*, 152-163.

Kratochwill, T. R. (1978). *Single-subject research: Strategies for evaluating change*. New York, NY: Academic Press.

Lanagan, D., & Dattilo, J. (1989). The effects of a leisure education program on individuals with mental retardation. *Therapeutic Recreation Journal, 23*(4), 62-72.

Light, J., Dattilo, J., English, J., Guttierez, L., & Hartz, J. (in press). Instructing facilitators to support the communication of persons using augmentative communication systems. *Journal of Speech and Hearing Research*.

McCormick, B., Scott, D., & Dattilo, J. (1991). Answering questions about therapeutic recreation part I: Formulating research questions. *Annual in Therapeutic Recreation, 2*, 78-84.

McReynolds, L. V., & Kearns, K. P. (1982). *Single-subject research: Strategies for evaluating change*. New York, NY: Academic Press.

McReynolds, L. V., & Thompson, K. (1986). Flexibility of single-subject experimental designs Part I: Review of the basics of single-subject designs. *Journal of Speech and Hearing Disorders, 51*, 194-203.

Mirenda, P., & Dattilo, J. (1987). Instructional techniques in communication for students with severe intellectual handicaps. *Augmentative and Alternative Communications, 3*(3), 143-152.

Murphy, R. J., & Bryan, A. J. (1980). Multiple-baseline and multiple-probe designs: Practical alternatives for special education assessment and evaluation. *Journal of Special Education, 14*, 325-335.

Parsonson, B. S., & Baer, D. M. (1978). The analysis and presentation of graphic data. In T. R. Kratochwill (Ed.), *Single-subject research: Strategies for evaluating change* (pp. 101-166). New York, NY: Academic Press.

Pelegrino, D. A. (1979). *Research methods for recreation and leisure: A theoretical and practical guide.* Dubuque, IA: Brown.

Peterson, C. A., & Gunn, S. L. (1984). *Therapeutic recreation program design: Principles and procedures.* Englewood Cliffs, NJ: Prentice-Hall.

Repp, A. C. (1981). *Teaching the mentally retarded.* Englewood Cliffs, NJ: Prentice-Hall.

Schleien, S., Cameron, J., Rynders, J., & Slick, C. (1988). Acquisition and generalization of leisure skills from school to the home and community by learners with severe multihandicaps. *Therapeutic Recreation Journal, 22*(3), 53-71.

Schleien, S., Certo, J., & Muccino, A. (1984). Acquisition of leisure skills by a severely handicapped adolescent: A data based instruction program. *Education and Training of the Mentally Retarded, 19*(4), 297-305.

Schleien, S., Kiernan, J., & Wehman, P. (1981). Evaluation of an age-appropriate leisure skills program for moderately retarded adolescents. *Education and Training of the Mentally Retarded, 16*(10), 13-19.

Schleien, S., & Larson, A. (1986). Adult leisure education for the independent use of a community recreation center. *Journal for Persons with Severe Handicaps, 11*(1), 39-44.

Schleien, S., McAvoy, L., & Feller, J. (in progress). "Integrating youth with Down syndrome into winter ecology on snowshoes program." Unpublished manuscript.

Schleien, S., Rynders, J., Mustonen, T., & Fox, A. (1990). Effects of social play activities on the play behavior of children with autism. *Journal of Leisure Research, 22,* 317-328.

Schleien, S., Wehman, P., & Kiernan, J. (1981). Teaching leisure skills to severely handicapped adults: An age-appropriate darts game. *Journal of Applied Behavior Analysis, 14,* 513-519.

Sidman, M. (1960). *Tactics of scientific research: Evaluating experimental data in psychology.* New York, NY: Basic Books.

Siegel, G. M., & Spradlin, J. E. (1985). Therapy and research. *Journal of Speech and Hearing Disorders, 50,* 226-230.

Smith, H. (1983). Single-subject research: Application in leisure services. *Impact, 10,* 7-8.

Tawney, J., & Gast, D. (1984). *Single-subject research in special education.* Columbus, OH: Merrill.

Walker, C. E. (1983). *The handbook of clinical psychology: Theory, research, and practice*. Homewood, IL: Dow, Jones-Irwin.

Wehman, P., & Marchant, J. (1978). Improving free play skills of severely retarded children. *The American Journal of Occupational Therapy, 32*, 100-104.

White, O., & Haring, N. (1980). *Exceptional Teaching* (2nd ed). Columbus, OH: Merrill.

Trials and Tribulations in Field-Based Research in Therapeutic Recreation

Catherine P. Coyle, W. B. (Terry) Kinney, and John W. Shank

At this point in the profession of therapeutic recreation it would be unusual to find a practitioner in the discipline who would claim that research is unimportant. Yet, appreciating the importance of research and actually engaging in it require two different mind-sets. Indeed, there are several constraints to the conduct of field-based research in this discipline. The two most typically mentioned barriers are "limited or no knowledge and skills" and "too little time" (see Chapters 1 and 5). In an effort to address these issues, this chapter acquaints readers with a variety of research designs that can be implemented in clinical trials and, it is hoped, increase readers' research knowledge and skills. It also includes comments on some of the practical realities and concerns of field-based research, such as the lack of sufficient time to engage in it. The information and discussions found here are intended to encourage the reader to engage in field-based research trials, developing empirical evidence of the efficacy of TR interventions and the advancement of its body of knowledge.

Purpose of Positivistic Research Design

The term **"research design"** in experimental and quasi-experimental research refers to the plan by which the research will be conducted. It is the "game plan" for selecting subjects, providing an intervention, and collecting data. In essence, design considers when, where, and under what conditions the research will be conducted. The primary purpose of the research design is to answer the research questions while controlling for sources of error that could invalidate the results of the research.

There are a number of possible sources of error to be considered when selecting a research design. These error sources are threats to the *internal validity* of the research and will, if not controlled, become **plausible rival hypotheses**. Plausible rival hypotheses are alternative explanations that could account for the research results obtained. As such, they threaten the ability of the investigative therapeutic recreation specialist to determine whether the TR treatments caused the change observed in the participants. The research design that the investigative TRS develops should limit the number of alternate explanations for the results obtained in the study.

Controlling Error in Positivistic Research

The following discussion extends some of the ideas that were introduced in Chapter 9. There are several methods used to reduce possible error sources in positivistic research. According to Wiersma (1986), they include: *randomization of subjects, holding conditions or factors constant, building conditions or factors into the design, and making statistical adjustments.*

Participants in a study could be randomly assigned or randomly selected for involvement in a study. **Random assignment** of subjects means that any individual who is eligible for the research study has an equal chance of being assigned to the group receiving the experimental condition (the treatment that one wants to examine) or to the control group (those not receiving the treatment). With random assignment, the researcher controls for any error that could arise because of the individual differences of clients in either the treatment or control groups.

In contrast, **random selection** refers to the process by which individuals are randomly chosen to be in a research study, *prior to* randomly assigning them to either a treatment or control group. With random selection, the investigative TRS is able to make generalizations beyond his or her sample to a larger population (external validity). Both random selection and random assignment are necessary to have a classically valid research study. In reality, random assignment from a randomly selected sample rarely occurs.

For instance, suppose a TRS works on an inpatient psychiatric unit which is composed of two treatment teams directed by different psychiatrists. This practitioner wants to examine the effectiveness of a leisure education program for clients on the unit. In one research scenario, only individuals from one treatment team receive the leisure education program (the treatment) while individuals from the other treatment team are used as controls (do not receive the treatment). The investigative TRS finds that the leisure education program was extremely effective in improving the self-image and time management skills of the involved clients; therefore, he or she concludes that leisure education is an effective TR treatment modality. However, the psychiatrist of the individuals in the treatment group met with the participants on a daily basis for individual psychotherapy; whereas, those individuals in the control group were only seen by their psychiatrist for individual therapy once a week. This represents a plausible rival hypothesis (i.e., the improvement in self-image and time management observed in the treatment group could be the result of the more intense psychotherapy received rather than the leisure education intervention). If clients had been randomly assigned to either the treatment or control group in a manner in which individuals receiving therapy from either psychiatrist had an equal chance of being in either group, this particular threat to the validity of the results would have been controlled.

Besides using random assignment to control for threats to internal validity, researchers occasionally **hold a condition constant**. Using the previously presented research scenario, if the investigative TRS had chosen a research design in which only subjects from one treatment team were randomly assigned to the treatment and control groups, the practitioner would have held one condition constant (e.g., the psychiatric care) and randomly distributed other important client characteristics (e.g., gender, age, medications) among the treatment and control groups. This design would control for more sources of error than the research design in the first scenario.

Another technique used to control for sources of error or threats to validity is to deliberately include in the research design a variable that cannot otherwise be controlled. The researcher, therefore, is able to analyze the effect of this variable. In this approach, the investigative TRS would include enough (at least five) clients from each treatment team in the experimental and control groups and document which clients were from which treatment team. Thus, the investigative TRS would have a treatment and control group for *each* treatment team (i.e., leisure education and daily psychotherapy, leisure education and weekly psychotherapy, *no* leisure education and daily psychotherapy, and *no* leisure education and weekly psychotherapy). In the statistical analysis, the investigative TRS would be able to determine if leisure education in conjunction with weekly psychotherapy is less or more effective than leisure education in conjunction with daily psychotherapy. In this research scenario, the investigative TRS has included or factored into the research design a variable which could be considered a validity threat (sometimes called a confounding variable), thus controlling this factor.

The investigative TRS who decides to use a positivistic (quantitative) perspective can choose from single-subject designs (discussed in Chapter 10) or group (treatment and control) designs. This chapter discusses a variety of group-oriented quantitative research designs. Before proceeding, however, a quick review of other possible sources of error or threats to internal validity is needed. For a more detailed discussion of this topic, the reader is referred to Chapter 9.

Threats to the Validity of Research Designs

As Chapter 9 stated, the literature identifies several threats to the internal validity of research designs. For field-based research, among the most important threats are: history, selection, mortality, maturation, testing, instrumentation, experimenter bias, and diffusion of treatment (Campbell & Stanley, 1963; Cook & Campbell, 1979). Differing research designs control to varying degrees for each of these error sources. The following sections review these threats from the point of view of an investigator working in a clinical context.

History is a validity threat that refers to incidents or events that occur during the research process that could affect the outcomes of the research. These events could occur within the groups (e.g., a member of either the treatment or control group commits suicide) or occur outside the context of the study (e.g., a clinical administrator decides that all clients with schizophrenia on a given unit should receive a new medication during a research study examining the effects of a reality orientation program on their delusional behaviors). Either of these events could seriously threaten the validity of the research project. History is one of the most difficult validity threats to control in research.

A **selection** threat exists whenever individuals cannot be randomly assigned to each of the treatment and control groups. Failure to randomly assign clients to the groups and the varying conditions raises the possibility that one or more of the groups are systematically different from the other. In the first research scenario, the systematic difference between the two groups in the leisure education experiment was the psychiatric care. A selection threat exists whenever intact (pre-existing) groups are used to form the treatment and control groups. For example, the use of one unit of a facility as the experimental groups and another unit as the control group represents intact groups unless unit assignment is done randomly.

Mortality refers to the loss of subjects from either the treatment or control group. Quite often in research studies, especially in longitudinal studies, individuals who initially agree to participate later withdraw or drop out of the research project. This loss of subjects or the **attrition rate** creates a possible threat to the validity of the research findings. For instance, suppose individuals in a rehabilitation hospital for spinal cord injuries were randomly assigned to treatment and control groups for a research project examining the effectiveness of the TR department's community reintegration program. This particular program may require that clients actively participate in a number of community outings over a four week period. Over the course of the study, approximately 30% of the individuals assigned to the treatment group may withdraw after the first community outing stating that the program was too strenuous for them at this time. Any findings of difference between the treatment and control group can be seriously challenged because of the self-selected dropouts. It may be that individuals who remained in the treatment group and complete the community reintegration program may be systematically different (e.g., had a higher level of initial work capacity or fitness level) than those who withdrew. The "new" treatment group (because of the attrition rate) may be systematically different from the control group that (due to the original random assignment) contained individuals who had both **low** and **high** fitness levels. Therefore, if differences were observed in the work capacities between the treatment and control groups, it is quite possible that the differences had existed prior to the treatment program and were not a result of the TR intervention. Mortality threats are very similar to selection threats; however, mortality occurs after the research has begun.

In longitudinal research, a serious threat to the validity of any research findings is **maturation**. Maturation, as the name implies, refers to normal changes that occur over time to individuals involved in a research study. For instance, suppose an investigative TRS in a rehabilitation facility notices that at discharge, individuals who were in a social support recreation group during their two month hospital stay had higher mean scores on the Adjustment to Disability Scale than did individuals who were in the same program during their one month hospital stay. From this information, the TRS concludes that involvement in the TR social support program is needed for at least two months to assist the individual with the adjustment process. One alternate explanation for the differences observed in adjustment to disability, however, may be maturation. Individuals involved in the TR program for two months may be showing a normal adjustment process that would have occurred over time without any TR treatment.

Maturation can also be a threat to validity in research projects of shorter duration. Maturation can manifest itself in terms of fatigue, hunger, or boredom. This threat is especially important when considering the sequence of questions in long (more than 30 minutes) interviews. Clients may not provide accurate data at the end of a lengthy interview because they are bored or fatigued. Likewise, collecting research data at varying points in a client's day may introduce a maturation threat as clients may be more fatigued or annoyed at the end of an intense clinical day than they are in the morning or afternoon. For this reason, efforts should be made to collect research data at similar points in the client's daily routine.

Testing and **instrumentation** are two additional threats to the validity of a research study that need to be considered in the design phase. A testing threat can occur whenever the investigative TRS decides to use a pretest. It refers to changes that the pretest itself causes in the individuals involved in the research project. For instance, suppose an investigative TRS decides to collect data on the depression level of individuals in his or her research project. It is conceivable that some clients may be actively denying any affective responses to their disability and the mere act of asking them questions related to their feelings may create in them an awareness of loss and sadness. This new found awareness emerges as a result of the pretest, not any TR treatment.

Instrumentation, in contrast, refers to errors/changes that occur in the instrumentation itself. For instance, suppose an investigative TRS was collecting functional performance data through the Level of Rehabilitation Scale (LORS) (Carey & Posavac, 1977) which is routinely completed on each client by the treatment teams in his or her hospital. However, midway through the research project the hospital switches to the Functional Independence Measure (FIM) (Granger, Hamilton, & Sherwin, 1986). The investigative TRS is now faced with an instrumentation threat. The two instruments, although designed to measured functional ability, are quite different in terms of the type of data assessed. Moreover, they differ in terms of their sensitivity and variability as the FIM uses a 7-point Likert scale while the LORS uses a 4-point Likert scale.

Instrumentation threats typically occur in observational research in which observers record clients' behaviors. As the research progresses, observers can become more careless, and less stringent, or tolerant and therefore, evaluate subjects differently. Instrumentation threats are most easily controlled in observational research by using multiple observers and providing extensive training to the observers prior to initiating the research.

Experimenter bias refers to deliberate and/or unintentional behaviors displayed by the researcher that influence the outcomes of the research. Sometimes called the ROSENTHAL effect, it occurs whenever the researcher/practitioner's behavior creates differential treatment of individuals in the treatment and control groups. Examples include using different tones of voice, being more assuring or friendly to one group over another, or selectively observing different behaviors in one group.

A final validity threat is **diffusion of treatment**. This occurs whenever members of one group come in contact with members of another group in the research study. In such a scenario, it is possible that knowing about the treatment of the other group could affect members from either group and thereby invalidate the results. Diffusion of treatment occurs whenever one of the groups in a research study is aware of differences in the treatment they are getting. It may result in rivalry or resentment among the groups which affects their feelings and behaviors and, consequently, the results of the research study.

Besides these internal validity threats, there are a number of threats or sources of error that influence the generalizability or external validity of the research. Briefly, they include: (a) interactional effects of testing; (b) interactional effects of selection biases; (c) reactive effects of experimental arrangements; and (d) multiple treatment interference. Readers interested in learning more about these external validity threats are referred to Chapters 9 and 10 and to works by Campbell and Stanley (1963), Kerlinger (1986) and Cook and Campbell (1979).

Types of Research Designs

Research designs used in the positivist paradigm can be classified as true experimental, quasi-experimental, or pre-experimental designs (McMillan & Schumacher, 1989). The distinguishing characteristic of these research designs is the intent to examine cause and effect relationships. The investigative TRS who chooses one of these designs is attempting to examine the outcomes associated with the delivery of some type of TR intervention. There are six distinguishing characteristics typically associated with experimental research (McMillan & Schumacher, 1989). They are: (1) comparison of two or more groups; (2) statistical equivalence of groups (usually achieved through random assignment to the treatment and control group); (3) direct manipulation of an independent variable (the treatment); (4) quantification (measurement) of dependent or outcome variables hypothesized to change as a result of the treatment; (5) use of inferential statistics; and (6) maximum control of extraneous variables which could create sources of error or plausible rival hypotheses.

True Experimental Designs

True experimental designs have all six of the above mentioned characteristics. Most notably, true experimental designs have random assignment of clients into the treatment and control groups. The most familiar design of this type is the **pretest-posttest control group** design. In this design, two groups are formed. One group receives the treatment to be examined (the independent variable) and the other group is the control group as those in it do not receive the treatment. Subjects are randomly assigned to either of the groups. The purpose of randomization is to control for any differences that might otherwise exist between the two groups. The more individuals involved in the research, the more likely that this control will actually occur. However, in experiments which involve only a small number of people (e.g., fewer than 40), the investigative TRS should first match them on the basis of any key variables that might influence the results *and then randomly assign* one member from each matched pair to the treatment and control condition. The use of matched pairs increases the likelihood that the groups will be really statistically equivalent despite the relatively small number of participants in the study.

The second step in this design is to pretest all members from both groups on the dependent variable(s). Next, the treatment is administered only to members of the treatment group. Finally, all subjects are posttested. It is important both that pre- and posttesting take place at the same point in time for members of both groups. Excerpt 11-1, page 214, is an example of a pre-posttest control group design.

Excerpt 11-1. Pretest-Posttest Design[1]

Purpose

The purpose of this study was to determine if challenge/initiative games could be an effective treatment to enhance the self-concept of abused children living in a residential care facility.

Method

Thirty-eight children, between the ages of 8 and 17 were participants in the study. All participants in the study completed the Piers-Harris Children's Self-Concept Scale (PHSCS) (Piers, 1977) and a confidential demographic data form designed by the researcher to collect basic demographic information. After completion of the PHSCS, children were randomly assigned to either the treatment (experimental) group (N = 18) or the control group (N = 20). Children in the experimental condition received a challenge/initiative program for one hour for 28 consecutive days. The control group received an hour of traditional playground-type recreation program for the same time span. The challenge/initiative activity involved 40 minutes of game play and 20 minutes of debriefing. During the debriefing, the researcher led a discussion of the game, emphasizing the group dynamics that transpired and soliciting feelings from the participants about how they felt about themselves and others during the game. The control group was not exposed to the debriefing component; rather members of this group participated in the activity for the entire hour. When the four week treatment period ended, the PHSCS was readministered to the 38 participants.

A number of variations can be made from this design. Often additional treatment conditions are added. This increases the number of groups needed (and hence the number of subjects) for the research. In most TR research, it is best to include at least three groups: a group receiving the TR treatment, a control group, and a comparison group who receives additional attention but not the TR intervention. The addition of the comparison group allows the investigative TRS to determine whether it is the TR intervention alone that causes the change in the dependent variable (outcome measure) rather than the additional human contact that members in both the TR intervention and the attention-only comparison group receive.

---

1. Adapted from McDonald, R. G., & Howe, C. Z. (1989). Challenge/initiative recreation programs as a treatment for low self-concept children. Reprinted with permission from the *Journal of Leisure Research, 21*(3), 242-253.

Another common true experimental design is the **posttest-only control group design**. In contrast with the previous research design, this design does not include any pretesting, but, it does include random assignment and posttesting. It is assumed that since subjects are randomly assigned to the treatment and control groups, a pretest is unneeded, as the random assignment controls for systematic differences. This design is typically used when the investigative TRS believes that the pretest may affect the treatment or when it is infeasible or impractical to give a pretest.

By not using a pretest, the investigative TRS cannot determine statistically that the treatment and control groups were truly equivalent. The ability to do this is especially important when there are fewer than 15 individuals in each group. Furthermore, the investigative TRS will be unable to form subgroups on the basis of pretest scores and therefore will be unable to examine if there were any differential effects of the treatment. For instance, a posttest-only control group design will not allow the investigative TRS to determine if the TR intervention was more effective for certain individuals (e.g., low scoring individuals on the pretest measure) than other individuals (e.g., high scoring individuals on the pretest measure). In addition, not having pretest scores will make the statistical analysis less precise and the investigative TRS will be unable to learn whether there were differences in the dependent variable(s) among those individuals who dropped out of the research and those who remained.

Quasi-experimental Designs

Randomization of clients into treatment and control conditions is often difficult in field settings. Because of this, a number of research designs have been developed that attempt to provide reasonable control over sources of error, yet are not true experimental designs.

A **quasi-experimental design**, which is often seen in the literature and is a variation of the pre-posttest control group design discussed previously, is entitled **pre-posttest with nonequivalent groups**. In this design, instead of randomly assigning subjects into the treatment and control groups, the investigative TRS uses intact groups (e.g., wings of a nursing home or patients from two different treatment teams). The most serious validity threat to this type of research design is selection. Hence, the investigative TRS who wants to use this type of design should try to use groups that are as similar as possible. Likewise, statistical adjustments on the pretest measures or other variables that might influence the results should be made during the analyses. For instance, suppose an investigative TRS in a rehabilitation facility wanted to examine the effect of a training program on cooking for persons with diabetes on the health maintenance behaviors of clients who had experienced a lower extremity amputation. In this particular facility, there are two units to which clients with lower extremity amputations are assigned. The clients on both units are quite similar in age, race, religious affiliation, and marital status, with one notable exception—type of insurance coverage. The health care costs of clients on one unit are reimbursed by private pay insurance companies. Such a difference suggests that household income may be an important demographic difference between the clients on the two units. Differences in ability to afford/cook heathy foods could dramatically affect a client's health maintenance postdischarge behavior. The investigative TRS would therefore be well-advised to control for this initial difference (type of insurance) between the two groups by making statistical adjustments in the analyses conducted (e.g., utilizing analysis of covariance with insurance/ income level as a covariant). Then the investigator could make a better judgment about the effect of the training program *per se*. Excerpt 11-2 is an example of this type of research design.

Another series of quasi-experimental design are called **time-series designs** and in many ways these designs are similar to the A-B design in single-subject research (see Chapter 10). In time series designs, repeated observations are made of members in the groups prior to and after the treatment intervention. Time series methodologies allow for patterns of stability and change to emerge. As in the other research designs, discussed in this chapter, time series designs are best when they include a control comparison group. These designs are most effective when it is not difficult to make repeated observations of individuals involved in the research and the intervention is something easily identifiable as "new"; that is, something distinctly different from operations/ programs which typically are provided.

For example, suppose a TRS who was interested in determining whether an aquatic program for persons with chronic pain was beneficial in decreasing the amount of pain verbalization of clients, decided to use a time series methodology. This investigative TRS leads two daily stretch programs for clients with chronic pain and routinely documents the number of pain verbalizations made during the programs. Individuals participate in the groups for five weeks. The TRS leads the groups in a stretch routine for the first two weeks in the gym. At the beginning of the third week, one of the groups is asked to perform their stretch routine in the pool and they continue to exercise there for the remainder of their meetings. The investigative TRS documents the average number of pain complaints for each group resulting in the graph found in Figure 11.1, page 218.

Excerpt 11-2. Pre-Posttest With Nonequivalent Groups[2]

Purpose

This purpose of this quasi-experimental study was to evaluate the effect of a leisure counseling program on the self-esteem and leisure attitudes of adult outpatient psychiatric patients.

Method

Sixteen subjects were selected for this study. Clients were selected from the outpatient population of a private, long-term care psychiatric hospital. Those selected met the following criteria: (a) they were involved in the hospital's outpatient program; (b) they were capable of verbal interaction and maintaining regular attendance at the counseling program; (c) they were 18 years of age or older; (d) they were not previously involved in a leisure counseling program offered at the facility and (e) they voluntarily consented to participate in the study. The treatment condition was composed of eight individuals who had been meeting on a weekly basis, as a discussion group, for the three months prior to this study. Members of the control groups   received the typical outpatient program which consisted of individual psychoanalysis four to six times a week and individually or group adjunctive therapies (TR, occupational therapy, art therapy, music therapy, etc.) once or twice a week. Members of the treatment group received a modified version of Pellett's Leisure Counseling Program (1974). Prior to the implementation of the leisure counseling program, self-report instruments were administered to members of the treatment and control groups. They were the Leisure Attitude Scale (Ragheb and Beard, 1982) and Rosenberg's (1965) Self-Esteem Scale. These scales were again readministered after completion of the ten week leisure counseling program.

---

2.   Adapted from Wolfe, R. A., & Riddick Cutler, C. (1984). Effects of leisure counseling on adult psychiatric outpatients. Reprinted with permission from the *Therapeutic Recreation Journal*, *18*(3), 30-37.

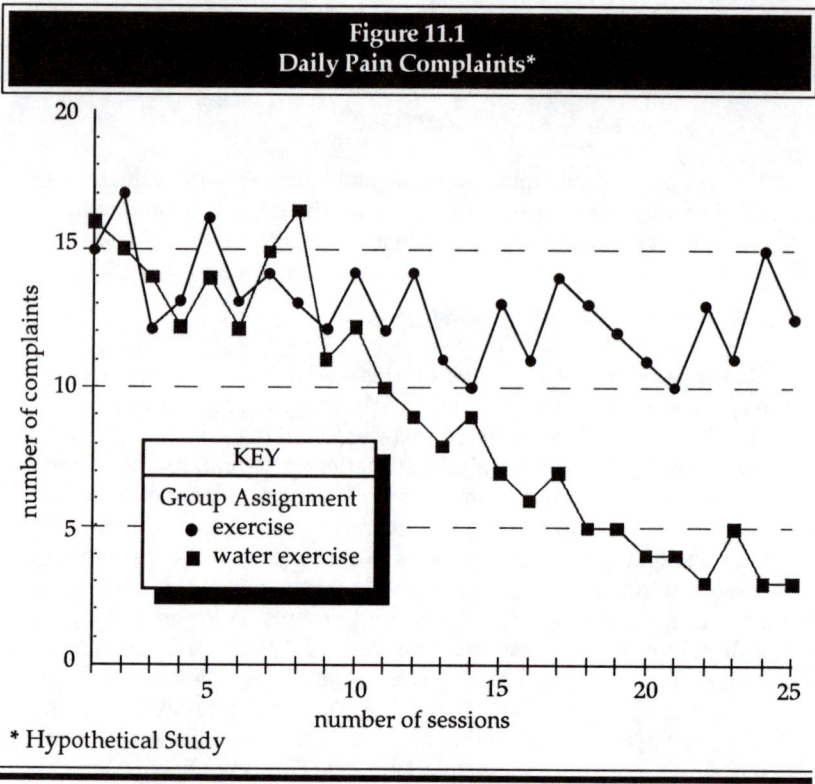

Figure 11.1
Daily Pain Complaints*

* Hypothetical Study

As can be seen from Figure 11.1, the group of individuals who exercised in the pool showed a significant decline in the number of pain complaints verbalized. The investigative TRS could calculate the mean change in the number of pain verbalizations between each group and compare them to determine if the illustrated change was statistically significant. Excerpt 11-3 is another example of a time-series design.

Pre-experimental Designs

There are a number of pre-experimental designs which can be used to conduct research; however, all of these designs fail to control for a variety of plausible rival hypotheses and therefore are not recommended for any positivistic research other than a preliminary pilot study. Types of research designs which fall into this category include one-group designs (i.e., one group pre- and posttest or one group posttest only) and posttest only with nonequivalent treatment and control groups (e.g., no randomization). One-group designs fail to control for history, mortality, maturation, and experimenter bias threats to validity. In addition, each of the designs has a number of other weaknesses. The interested reader is referred to Kidder and Judd (1986) and McMillan and Schumacher (1989) for a more detailed discussion of these designs.

Excerpt 11-3. Time Series Design[3]

Purpose

This study was designed to evaluate the success of a facility-wide recreation program regarding increasing staff and clients' engagement in daily leisure activities.

Method

This study was implemented on two units at an intermediate care facility for adults with severe and profound mental retardation. Data were collected by trained observers every 15 minutes during a hour-long recreation time. Observers were trained to record the total number of clients and staff in the designated recreation area, as well as the number of staff involved in engaging clients in recreational activities and the number of clients engaged in recreational activities. During the baseline condition, which extended over four days, staff were instructed to engage clients in recreation activities. A variety of craft and sports materials were available but staff were not specifically directed to use any of the recreational material. All staff had received prior training in the use of the recreational material available. During the treatment phase of the study, a packaged recreation program was implemented. It involved: assigning staff to specific roles, pre-planning materials, monitoring staff at random times, and publicly posting the data. The treatment condition extended over 45 days. Observations were made over the entire length of the study. Percentages of staff and clients engaged in recreation activities were calculated and charted.

---

3. Burch, M. R., Reiss, M. R., & Bailey, J. S. (1985). Facility-wide approach to recreation programming for adults who are severely and profoundly retarded. Reprinted with permission from the *Therapeutic Recreation Journal, 19*(3), 71-78.

Implementing Positivistic Research Designs in Field Settings[4]

Discussion of positivistic research designs from a purely scientific viewpoint is useless if investigative TRSs are unable to use this information to create research designs that can be implemented in their agencies and that control for as much error or plausible rival hypotheses as possible. With this thought in mind, this section presents two sample research designs which can be implemented in field settings. The first example involves two units in a facility and represents the application of a quasi-experimental design in a field setting. The second example involves one unit and exemplifies a true experimental research design.

Two-Unit Design

Where two units exist that are very similar in nature (same type of clients, staff, scheduling, and environment), it is possible to simulate a quasi-experimental design. The quasi-experimental design gathers data regarding a unique intervention that is currently occurring or in the planning stages rather than after the intervention has occurred, as in the *ex post facto* design. This makes the quasi-experimental design somewhat stronger since the unique intervention can be isolated and controlled and, thus, studied in a more rigorous manner.

In the two-unit design, the experimental unit would be given some type of unique intervention that is, in fact, the focus of the **efficacy research.** This unique intervention might be a specifically designed leisure education program or some other service that is thought to be effective. The control unit does not receive the experimental treatment but does receive the standard services that otherwise would be provided (diversional programming). The differences between the experimental subjects and control subjects on outcome indicators testifies to the effect of the particular experimental variable. While this design, too, lacks certain "scientific" strengths, it blends well with the realities and demands of field settings. The results will be strengthened by the extent to which the researcher ensures that the clients, staff, scheduling, and environment are similar. Figure 11.2 depicts this research design. It should be noted that practitioners do not have to include every person on each unit as part of the efficacy study. Individuals can be screened to meet certain criteria, and only those who meet the criteria are included in the data gathering. An example of screening criteria for an efficacy study on community reintegration techniques might be: (a) right sphere CVA;

---

4.   Material and Figures 11-2 & 11-3 presented in this section are adapted from Shank, J. W., and Kinney, W. B. (1991). Monitoring and Measuring Outcomes in Therapeutic Recreation. In B. Riley (Ed.), *Quality management: Applications for therapeutic recreation.* State College, PA: Venture.

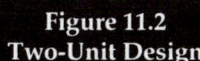

Figure 11.2
Two-Unit Design

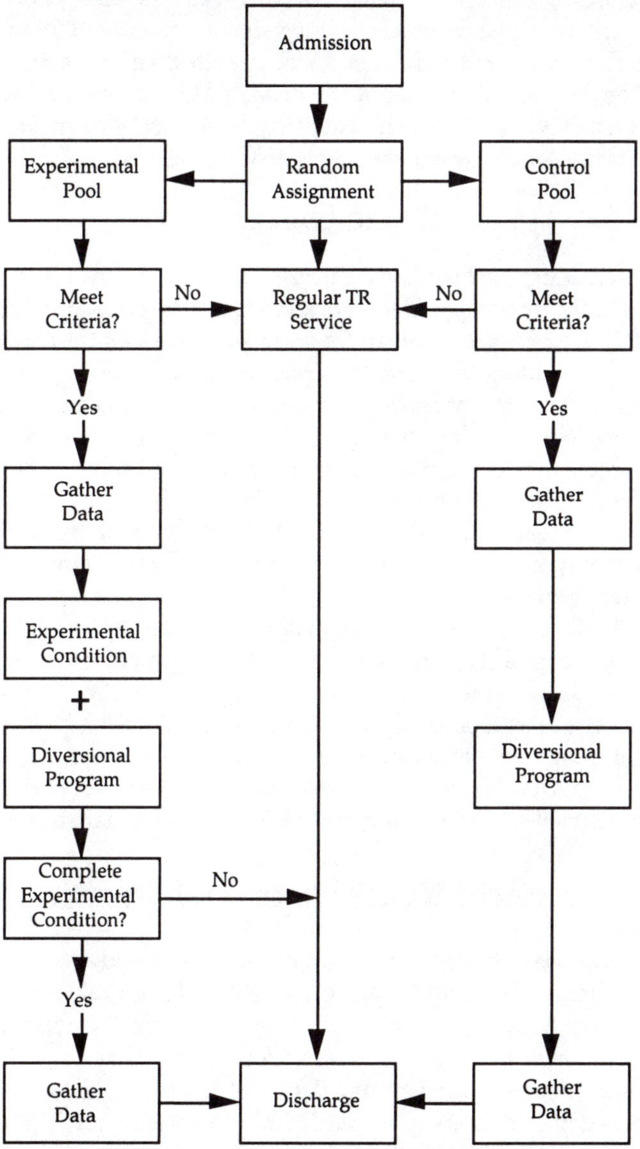

Admission → Random Assignment

Random Assignment → Experimental Pool (left)
Random Assignment → Control Pool (right)
Random Assignment → Regular TR Service (down)

Experimental Pool → Meet Criteria?
Meet Criteria? — No → Regular TR Service
Meet Criteria? — Yes → Gather Data
Gather Data → Experimental Condition
Experimental Condition + Diversional Program
Diversional Program → Complete Experimental Condition?
Complete Experimental Condition? — No → Regular TR Service / Discharge
Complete Experimental Condition? — Yes → Gather Data
Gather Data → Discharge

Control Pool → Meet Criteria?
Meet Criteria? — No → Regular TR Service
Meet Criteria? — Yes → Gather Data
Gather Data → Diversional Program
Diversional Program → Gather Data
Gather Data → Discharge

Regular TR Service → Discharge

(b) below the age of 70; (c) evidence of family support; and (d) likelihood of discharge to home. Only those clients who meet the established criteria become experimental or control subjects. This would save time and energy as the choice of outcome indicators is narrowed to a select population.

Also, this type of research allows the investigative TRS to determine whether a particular treatment protocol was effective with a certain population. The intervention is specifically designed to achieve specific outcomes with a certain type of client. The extent to which those outcomes are achieved in an effective and efficient manner is **efficacy research**.

Single-Unit Design

A research design that is more rigorous and more demanding is depicted in Figure 11.3. In this design clients are admitted to the same unit. Like the two-unit design, clients are screened for appropriateness for the study and then placed on a waiting list. The therapist responsible for implementing the experimental treatment carries a limited case load of clients who are randomly selected from the waiting list. This ensures an equal chance for any eligible client to become either a treatment or control subject. When a client is discharged, the TRS randomly selects another client from the waiting list to fill the case load. The TRS conducts the treatment with his or her selected case load only, and those who are not selected from the waiting list serve as the control subjects.

While it is best if outcome data are gathered twice, as indicated in Figure 11.2, page 221, the actual data gathering process may be extremely lengthy or inconvenient for the clients or agency. An alternative is to eliminate the first instance of data gathering and simply rely on the second set of data. The fact that subjects are randomly selected from the waiting list allows for this modification. Since eliminating the first set of data scientifically weakens the results, this modification should remain a last resort.

Practical Realities of Field Settings

Before considering the implementation of a research endeavor in an agency, the investigative TRS should review a number of practical issues which can greatly effect the success of this effort. They include: (a) ascertaining the level of institutional support for research and determining the agency's guidelines regarding informed consent and denial of treatment; (b) evaluating the amount of departmental support and commitment to research; (c) evaluating and determining a feasible time frame in which to conduct the research project; (d) evaluating the impact that the research may have on routine departmental and agency operations; and (e) evaluating the impact that the research will have on routine client care.

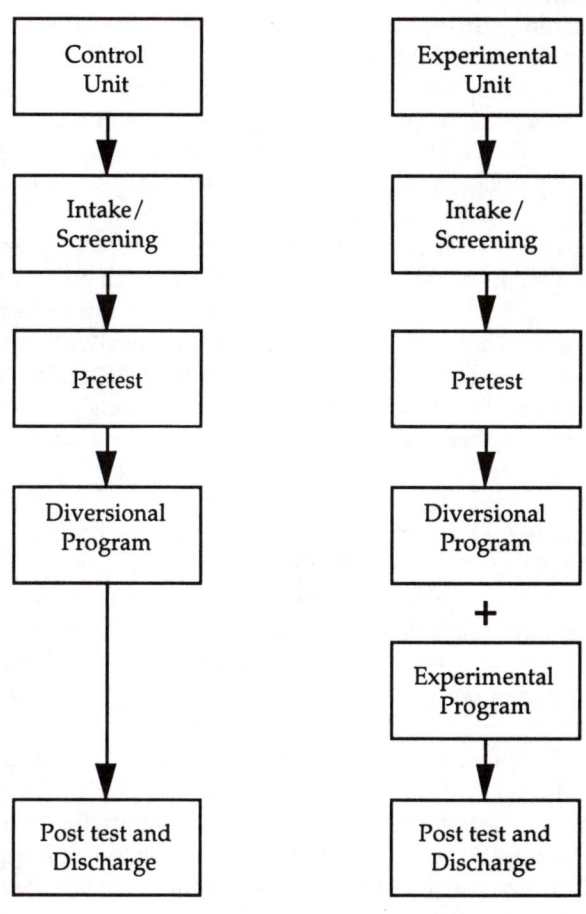

Figure 11.3
Single-Unit Design

Determining Institutional Support

It is important for investigative TRSs to examine the degree of institutional support for research that exists at their agency. Each institution will vary in how much actual and implied support is given to research endeavors. Usually, if the agency is committed to research, and active research endeavors are an ongoing part of the institution, investigative TRSs should find support for their research study. However, occasionally, there may be concerns as to whether the research will conflict or somehow compromise (remember the validity threats) the ongoing research agenda of physicians.

The investigative TRS who wants to know how much support for research activities exists at his or her agency should discuss the research proposal with the physicians involved, with the personnel in the agency's Institutional Review Board (IRB), the department which reviews and approves all research proposals; and with other allied health professionals and department heads. The commitment of each of these groups to the proposed research endeavor is crucial for its success. Discussions should focus on the ways in which the research may affect and improve the treatments which clients receive from TR. Any additional support or considerations which may be needed to enhance the viability of the research project should be discussed at this time (e.g., resolving scheduling conflicts).

To obtain approval to conduct a research study at an agency, as Chapter 6 indicated, a research proposal must be sent to the agency's IRB. A representative of the TR department must be prepared to spend the necessary time to advocate and educate the personnel who comprise the IRB. Engaging in research may not be what others think the TR department ought to be doing, and the agency may not view the research problems and proposed study as important as other kinds of research at the agency. The level of initial support and understanding will likely require extra time and energy by the TR representative to promote the research proposal and ensure its full consideration by those involved with IRB.

A common concern usually raised at this point in the research (provided the study employs a control group design) is whether it is appropriate to deny treatment to clients. When presenting the research designs to the various groups mentioned above, the investigative TRS should be prepared to present justification for the withholding of treatment from clients. A logical rationale for using this procedure is that no research evidence presently exists that confirms the TR treatment is effective in the particular setting or circumstances in which it will be researched. A second appropriate rationale can be built into the design itself if the TR department uses waiting lists. In this instance, it is standard procedure for some clients to get the TR intervention, while others do not, because there is a waiting list. The clients who remain on the waiting list serve as the control group. It is also useful to point out that all clients receive some form of TR services although not necessarily the same type. Regardless of the rationale used, the investigative TRS must be ready and able to explain and defend the design chosen for the research study to physicians, administrators, colleagues, and clients.

Determining TR Department Support

It is important that the TR department and *all* staff within it support the research effort if it is to be successful. Rushing into a hastily designed research study without consensus among all involved will doom the efforts and result in disappointment and frustration. Such an experience can serve as a disincentive to conducting future research and confirm many skeptics' worse fears about the research process. To echo Chapter 5, in order for field-based research to be successful, it needs to be developed with all of the TR staff collaborating in the planning process.

Planning should include a thorough examination of the theoretical perspective which guides the research, thus giving everyone a clearer understanding of why certain variables are being examined and measured. This is particularly important when TR staff are questioned by colleagues about the reasons for doing the research and the methodology used. Collaboration also is needed to address issues of treatment (the interventions) and data collection techniques. Ensuring that all staff have a reasonable sense of what will be involved with the research process can avoid surprises and perhaps disagreements after the study is under way. If anyone has an objection or a reason for concern, the planning stage is the time for these questions and concerns to be aired, and a mutually agreeable course of action can be decided on.

All staff must be thoroughly committed to the research study and understand that its purpose is *not* to evaluate their skills as therapists, but to determine the efficacy of a particular treatment. It is not uncommon for staff to be concerned that *they* are being evaluated during a study. Working under conditions of constant observation and evaluation (even if they are imagined) can be stressful. Staff, therefore, must be supported and supervised in a nonthreatening manner during the investigation so that feelings of intimidation and mistrust are verbalized and addressed and an atmosphere of cooperation and commitment to the research endeavor is maintained.

Determining a Time Frame

Another important consideration which needs to be made at the TR department level is the time frame for the study. Research is a long and arduous process. Staff need to be made aware of the lengthy process which is involved in collecting data. Furthermore, they need to be made aware of the time it takes to input and analyze data, and to write research reports. Rarely is any of this accomplished in a few weeks. When developing a time frame for the study, the investigative TRS should ascertain the time required for staff training, pilot testing, and reaching an acceptable sample size.

Staff Training

Research that directly involves TRSs in data collection necessitates thorough training. If the TRS is expected to obtain informed consent from potential study participants and is expected to administer tests or scales or any other data collection techniques, he or she must be trained in these procedures. Although staff normally use interviews to conduct assessments, the conduct of a research interview is technically different. Positivistic structured interviews typically require consistency and precision and do not permit as much discretion by the interviewer. Likewise, when administering a psychometric test the TRS cannot deviate from the administrative directions even if the client exhibits feelings or shares thoughts to which the TRS ordinarily would respond. Training staff in data collection procedures, reviewing validity and reliability threats (so that staff have a clearer understanding of the distinction between positivistic research interviews and clinical assessments), and training staff in the appropriate delivery of the treatment being researched lengthens the anticipated time frame of the study. Nonetheless, these training components must be considered and incorporated into the development of a research time frame if the study is to be successful.

Pilot Testing

Even when the research design has been developed collaboratively, time should be allotted for pilot testing. The appropriate amount of time depends on the complexities of the research design and the degree to which it involves and/or impacts on staff from other disciplines. For instance, if the investigator is asking that nursing staff complete and forward weekly evaluations of clients, then a pilot test should include the amount of time needed to ascertain that the nursing data are being accurately collected and forwarded. Pilot testing ensures that the research project can be implemented as designed without any serious validity threats and that all the mechanisms for data collection are operating appropriately.

Reaching an Acceptable Sample Size

The final consideration which needs to be made in terms of a time frame involves estimating the amount of time it will take for the research to be completed on an appropriate sample of clients. The investigative TRS should allow for more time than it is thought may actually be needed to reach an adequate sample size. It is important to remember that if there are numerous restrictions which limit the type of clients who are appropriate for a research study, the restrictions will generally increase the length of time needed for data collection. Typically, a minimum of 20 clients in each of the conditions (treatment and control(s)) is needed for any statistical analyses.

Impact on Routine Operations

Members of TR departments should recognize the need for flexibility when conducting a study. Efficacy research often requires alterations in the normal routines of service delivery. Staff will be required to perform functions that they might not do otherwise, such as seeing some clients more often and reducing contact with others. This may change the number of "billable hours" of service provided. Paperwork, administering interviews, or using other data collection methods will require consistent attention, time, and effort above and beyond what is normally given by staff.

All who are involved in the research must know exactly what will occur and the impact that the research process will have on routine operations. When the project requires certain tasks that alter the normal service delivery, or when the staff is expected to comply with certain data collection procedures, it is vital that the TR staff understand the integral role they play in the success of the research.

Staff who are not directly involved will also be impacted by the study's very existence. They may be asked questions, or may even need to substitute for those who were originally involved. So, they must completely understand the study's purpose, design, and procedures. For this to occur the TR staff must be able to devote time at staff meetings (or add on additional meeting times) to discuss issues related to the research study. This is the only way that clear communication and a successful research endeavor can be nurtured and accomplished.

Impact on Routine Care

The final area that the investigative TRS should consider when determining the feasibility of conducting a research study at his or her agency involves the degree to which the research will impact on the routine care provided to clients. As mentioned earlier, the research design may require that less time is spent with some clients in order to provide time for the intervention to others or to allow for the completion of paperwork. Other subjects will not be allowed to receive particular TR services because they are members of the control condition. These limitations impact on the routine care that clients receive. The investigative TRS needs to anticipate where such changes will occur and how they can be least disruptive to client care. Staff will need to remember that, ultimately, the research should improve the care of all clients entering the facility.

Finally, the research project may change the way clients view TRSs and TR services. Clients who are asked to comply with research interviews may be puzzled, hostile, or surprised that the TRS is involved in research and that the services which he or she has been receiving are being studied. Clients may be concerned about confidentiality issues and about any potential effect their participation or responses may have on their overall treatment. Such concerns must be openly discussed during the process of obtaining participants' informed consent and throughout the course of the research study. Often clients resent the intrusion of standardized instruments into a personal relationship and are concerned about being evaluated. Therapists should be aware that such changes may occur and be prepared to handle clients' concerns without jeopardizing the investigation.

Summary

In spite of the rigidity which is required for truly valid positivistic research designs, conducting field-based research demands an attitude and a demeanor that are flexible and adaptable. The one reality of field-based research is Murphy's Law: "If something can go wrong, it will." As much as TRSs can prepare for disruptions and unintended occurrences, field-based researchers must accept the reality that there can never be total control. This is *not* laboratory research. Field-based research occurs in relatively natural environments with predictably unpredictable human beings.

Despite the unpredictability of humans and the tribulations of research, there are numerous benefits which the investigative TRS will accrue through his or her research efforts. Research involvement increases the credibility of therapeutic recreation. Other allied health professionals are forced to really examine TR services in light of the research that is being conducted. Furthermore, research activities increase the stature of the TR department in the eyes of administration. TR practitioners are viewed as "emerging professionals" who are willing to engage in the scholarly activity of documenting that their services do make a difference in the rehabilitation and habilitation of their clients. Finally, research involvement increases the understanding of all those involved with the research process. It encourages staff to read research "critically" and to think "critically" about what it is they are doing with clients.

The present health care environment is focused on outcome measurement. According to Seibert (1991), outcome measurement is designed to manage health care costs and document treatment efficacy in order to determine which protocols and services are the most effective with respect to given illness, conditions, and/or disabilities. Those allied health disciplines that can document that their service outcomes are effective and efficient will survive the financial downsizing in the health care industry. Experimental research is one mechanism by which TR can produce empirical data to withstand this financial crunch. Research, despite its tribulations, will determine the future of TR. The discipline stands a better chance at flourishing in the 21st Century with clinical research trials (with all their headaches and anxieties) than it does without them.

Discussion Questions

1. Describe the purpose of a research design and the validity threats which need to be considered when designing research.
2. Distinguish between random selection and random assignment. Explain the purpose of each in experimental research.
3. Define "plausible rival hypotheses." Discuss the methods available to the investigative TRS to minimize the number of rival hypotheses.
4. List the six characteristics of experimental research. Distinguish among true experimental, quasi-experimental, and pre-experimental research designs, listing the strengths and weaknesses of each.
5. Describe the randomized pre-post control group research design. What are some of the difficulties with implementing this design in field-based research? List ways in which these difficulties can be overcome without jeopardizing the research design.
6. List and discuss three of the practical realities of conducting field-based research and provide suggestions as to how they can be circumvented.

References

Burch, M. R., Reiss, M. R., & Bailey, J. S. (1985). Facility-wide approach to recreation programming for adults who are severely and profoundly retarded. *Therapeutic Recreation Journal, 19*(3), 71-78.

Campbell, D. T., & Stanley, J. C. (1963). Experimental and quasi-experimental designs for research on teaching. In N. L. Gage (Ed.), *Handbook of research on teaching* (pp.171-246). Chicago, IL: Rand McNally.

Carey, R., & Posavac, E. (1977). *Manual for the level of rehabilitation scale* (LORS). Park Ridge, IL: Parkside Associates.

Cook, T. D., & Campbell, D. T. (1979). *Quasi-experimentation: Design and analysis issues for field settings.* Chicago, IL: Rand, McNally.

Granger, C., Hamilton, B., & Sherwin, F. (1986). *Guide for use of the uniform data set for medical rehabilitation.* Buffalo, NY: Uniform Data System for Medical Rehabilitation.

Kerlinger, F. N. (1986). *Foundations of behavioral research* (3rd ed.). New York, NY: Holt, Rinehart and Winston.

Kidder, L. H., & Judd, C. M. (1986). *Research methods in social relations* (5th ed.). New York, NY: Holt, Rinehart and Winston.

McDonald, R. G., & Howe, C. Z. (1989). Challenge/initiative recreation programs as a treatment for low self-concept children. *Journal of Leisure Research, 21*(3), 242-253.

McMillan, J. S., & Schumacher, S. (1989). *Research in education: A conceptual introduction.* Glenview,Il: Scott, Foresman.

Pellet, L. (1974). *The development and implementation of a leisure counseling program with female psychiatric patients based upon value clarification techniques.* Unpublished Master's thesis, Clemson University, Clemson, South Carolina.

Piers, E. V. (1977). *The Piers-Harris children's self-concept scale: Research Monograph #1.* Nashville, TN: Counselor Recordings and Tests.

Ragheb. M., & Beard, J. (1982). Measuring leisure attitudes. *Journal of Leisure Research, 2,* 155-167.

Rosenberg, M. (1965). *Society and the adolescent self-image.* Englewood Cliffs, NJ: Prentice-Hall.

Seibert M. L. (1991). Chapter 2: Keynote. In C. Coyle, W. Kinney, B. Riley, & J. Shank (Eds.), *Benefits of therapeutic recreation: A consensus view,* (pp. 5-15). Philadelphia, PA: Temple University.

Shank, J. W., & Kinney, W. B. (1991). Monitoring and measuring outcomes in therapeutic recreation. In B. Riley (Ed.), *Quality management: Applications for therapeutic recreation*. State College, PA: Venture.

Wiersma, W. (1991). *Research methods in education: An introduction* (5th ed.). Boston, MA: Allyn and Bacon.

Wolfe, R. A., & Riddick Cutler, C. (1984). Effects of leisure counseling on adult psychiatric outpatients. *Therapeutic Recreation Journal, 18*(3), 30-37.

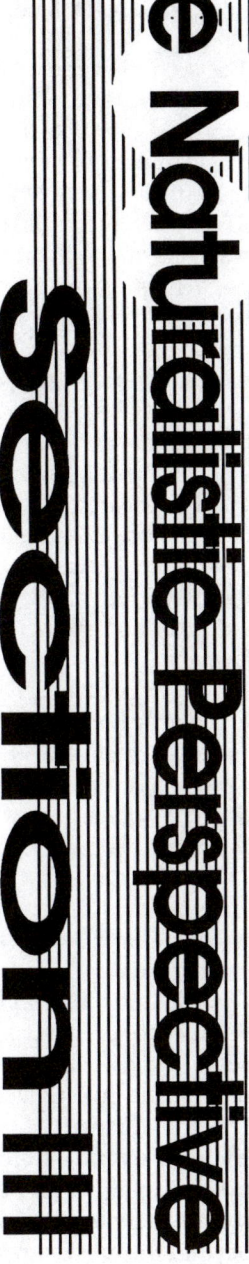

The Naturalistic Perspective

section III

Section III—The Naturalistic Perspective

The section is rooted in the phenomenological philosophy of science or naturalistic/interpretive paradigm which views the world and "truths" about the world as being: "within the eye of the beholder," dynamic, and contextual. Subjectivity in the good sense of the term, not the biased sense of the term, is a major tenet of naturalistic inquiry. The three chapters in Section III collectively combine to illustrate the applicability of naturalistic inquiry to research in therapeutic recreation. Such applicability occurs when the research questions are conceptualized to focus on TR as a process that yields socio-psychological outcomes. These outcomes are believed to be best understood through the "lived lives" or the observed behaviors and spoken words of the research participants themselves. The research participants are believed to be best understood through spending time with them in their own habitat and honoring the reality that "they" are "us."

Habitats change, as do people's perceptions of them. We, as researchers and research participants change, as do our perceptions of ourselves in each of those roles. Each change or perceived change influences the other. To document (typically through qualitative research methods) and comprehend (typically through inductive analyses) those actual changes, perceived changes, and influences is the apogee of the naturalistic investigator's journey.

The process of naturalistic research can be closely coupled, but it is not necessarily linear or distinctly sequential as in the classical steps or stages to "scientific method." Naturalistic research may not be tidy, but it is neat. It is rigorous, but its indicators of rigor come from its meaningfulness, or the degree to which the findings ring true to what the research participants know or knew to be true at the time of the study.

Chapter 12 by Howe picks up where Chapter 2 left off. The author leads readers into naturalistic research design as a recursive process of information collection and analysis that is done in the habitat of the research participants.

Glancy, in Chapter 13, continues with this highly interrelated process but focuses on analysis. She demonstrates how naturalistic investigators come to know what they know and how people can have confidence in what naturalistic investigators have done.

In Chapter 14, Stumbo and Little address three difficult tasks that confront naturalistic investigators; confirming and disconfirming ideas, making interpretations that are not mistaken, and reporting findings in a concise manner, but not at the expense of losing their significance or meaning beyond the most expedient or economical expression to text.

Naturalistic Research Design: An Interrelated Approach to Data Collection and Analysis
Christine Z. Howe

Phenomenologists suggest that human beings, whether alone, with their families, among their reference group, or with care providers, are constantly involved with constructing meaning from their experiences (cf. Howe, 1991; Howe & Rancourt, 1990; Scott & Godbey, 1990). This process may include: recollecting experiences from the past, reflecting on current experiences, and pondering the possibilities in store for the future.

Unless limited by severe cognitive impairments, people are aware of their conscious thoughts about experience. They may idly pursue their thoughts out of curiosity, or more intently pursue them for some needed answer. Thoughts form mental impressions that appear to first enter peoples' minds through the senses as percepts, the basic building blocks of perceptions. The act of organizing these bits into perceptive frames of reference appears to occur at the speed of light, without conscious awareness. The human mind is capable of absorbing great amounts of impressionistic information. Some perceptions and thoughts formed through experience are useful data or information to the investigative TRS. Perceptions and thoughts are links to the layers of meaning that underlie the outward, most "apparent," or readily observable behavior of people (M. Glancy, personal communication, December 2, 1991), including the responses to interventions by consumers of TR—persons who are differently abled.

In naturalistic inquiry, as Chapters 13 by Glancy and 14 by Stumbo and Little illustrate, the collection, analysis, and interpretation of information are interwoven like the threads of a tapestry. Together, they make up the product—the piece of tapestry. The weaver probably begins with an inspiration about creating some thing of beauty. Just as the weaver decides to weave a beautiful tapestry, selects the colors and threads, plans the dimensions of the piece, and establishes a pattern that may range from structured and predetermined to free flowing and evolving, the naturalistic investigator is intrigued by a puzzling research question, and determines to search for an answer through a research design which may fall on a continuum from **preordinate** (predetermined) to responsive.

As Kirk and Miller (1986) put it:

> Qualitative research, like other science, is a four-phase affair. Accordingly, the full qualitative effort depends upon the ordered sequence of invention, discovery, interpretation, and explanation . . . *Invention* denotes a phase of preparation, or research design; . . . *Discovery* denotes a phase of data collection; *Interpretation* denotes a phase of evaluation, or analysis; . . . this phase produces understanding. *Explanation* denotes a phase of communication . . . (p. 60)

This chapter presents some issues about research paradigms, naturalistic research design, and research participants as the sources of subjective, contextual information. It also introduces ways of obtaining data or information in the habitat of the research participants. In this sense, **naturalistic inquiry** is about describing, documenting, and understanding the lived lives of people, including people with disabilities, and the changes that occur when something extraordinary (e.g., a TR intervention) happens to them in the course of their lives/life experiences.

The Human Aspect of the Research Act

In collecting subjective data in a participant-observation study for example, the naturalistic researcher is the instrument. He or she looks, asks, listens, and to some degree participates. He or she plays a role in the unfolding of things, typically trying to be as unobtrusive and nonreactive as possible (Scott & Godbey, 1990, p. 198). However, recognizing that all research using human beings is intrusive to some degree and that some amount of contrivance is inherent in every research act (see Chapter 6 for a discussion of this issue), the naturalistic researcher records, describes, and interprets the influence of his or her intrusion on the experience being investigated.

The human aspect of the research act is an important consideration in the design of *any* study, positivistic or naturalistic, preordinate or responsive, because investigators are sources of **bias** (as falsehood and prejudice) as well as stewards of the inquiry process. Paradigmatic and procedural differences occur regarding how to handle **intrusion** (either the psychological or the physical presence of the investigator) when it leads to bias/nonfactual information (Hultsman & Anderson, 1991, p. 65). The possibility of reconciling procedural differences remains undetermined at this time. However, the maturing body of knowledge in recreation, leisure, and TR is a reflection of the ways in which investigators implicitly or explicitly direct their thoughts, their values, their feelings, and their energy. It is the investigative TRS's responsibility and privilege to protect and further develop the character and intellectual health and well-being of the body of knowledge (Howe, 1990).

Naturalistic Research Design: The Question of Rigor

Poor conceptualization and inadequate or inappropriate development of investigations are common reasons for even the most open-minded positivists' skepticism to studies described as "phenomenological" (E. Ruddell, personal communication, February 13, 1992). Hultsman and Anderson (1991, p. 63) purport that when the variables of interest are perceptual in nature, the scope of research protocols in leisure studies needs to expand beyond the traditional "scientific method" of the positivists. For example, they question the fit between the positivist paradigm and how people perceive leisure. Germane to this chapter, as pointed out by Hultsman and Anderson (1991), is one of several concerns: the lack of faith that positivists have regarding the rigor of naturalistic inquiries that employ qualitative research methods. Their question might become: How does the naturalistic investigator design and present a study in a way that demonstrates rigor to the positivist, if in fact this can be done?

Paradigms at Odds?

It may be impossible to answer this question satisfactorily because of the different paradigms involved. According to Guba and Lincoln (1983, p. 311), paradigms are axiomatic systems characterized by their differing assumptions about the phenomena under study. **Axioms** are propositions accepted by convention or established by practice as the building blocks of theoretical structures (p. 313). Weissinger (1990) offers some relevant insights. Coming from the point of view of positivist social science, in her commentary on the intellectual and personal tensions that occur during paradigm shifts (or conversations about them), Weissinger states:

> The revolutionary metaphor that Kuhn provides is instructive because it illustrates the intellectual and emotional dynamics that exist between two groups. By definition, revolutionaries seek to change paradigms in the ways that the paradigms themselves prohibit. And so the dialogue is complex in that it is not just about ideas, but also about conventional wisdom, existing power structures and cherished assumptions. (1990, pp. 310-311)

Weissinger (1990, p. 311) continues that " . . . it is often difficult for proponents of competing paradigms to communicate effectively because each uses their [sic] own paradigm for judging the other." Another one of Weissinger's observations concerns the " . . . corollary responsibility for interpretive researchers to produce concrete evidence of the usefulness of their paradigm" (1990, p. 314).

That observation directly relates to the issues of poor conceptualization and inadequate or inappropriate development. What may be believed to be concrete evidence, well-reasoned conceptualization, and informed development by the naturalistic investigator, may be believed to be some assemblage of blocks of information so porous that when rained on by a few drops, they crumble and fade away, by the positivistic scientist. So much for the durability of concrete.

Although this dilemma, too, remains to be resolved, the work of Guba and Lincoln (1981, 1983), as it has been applied by recreation, leisure, and TR researchers, is convincing regarding the existence of rigor in naturalistic inquiry. The "evidence" is there for those, as Weissinger graciously writes, who in the spirit of collegiality and open-mindedness, are willing to "suspend their disbelief" (1991, p. 311). Transformation in social-psychological inquiry about TR is discussed in Chapter 3 of this text and further supports the advent of a paradigmatic shift and paradigmatic pluralism. See also Scott and Godbey (1990).

Guba and Lincoln's Standards for Rigor in Naturalistic Research Design

As a brief aside, Guba and Lincoln (1981) provide four primary criteria for rigor in the positivist paradigm, for which naturalistic researchers have a different vocabulary. The positivistic criteria include: internal validity, external validity, reliability, and objectivity which were discussed in detail in Chapters 8 and 9. To very simply introduce the criteria in the phenomenological paradigm, Guba and Lincoln's respective terms are: *truth value, applicability, consistency,* and *neutrality*. On the surface, there appears to be some degree of shared meaning, but Guba and Lincoln (1981) caution that the criteria are only somewhat comparable. Hultsman and Anderson (1991) present an overview of these criteria as they are specifically related to leisure research and discuss the unique aspects of truth value, applicability, consistency, and neutrality. Chapter 14 illustrates the consideration of naturalistic criteria for rigor as used in a **triangulated** (Denzin, 1978) or multiple method study of the camping experience of women who are imprisoned.

Preordinate and Responsive Designs

Perhaps one of the best ways to demonstrate selected elements of **"rigor"** in naturalistic inquiry is by showing clarity, order, coherence, and cumulation in its design (Miles & Huberman, 1984a). This means that the TRS must provide contextual information, narrative coherence (a sequenced portrayal of what has occured), and a compelling logic (Howe, 1991).

When developing a naturalistic research design, the investigative TRS may select one that is on the *preordinate* or the *responsive* end of the design continuum. The more **responsive** the design is, the more flexibility there is within the entire conceptualization-collection-analysis-interpretation-schema or the invention, discovery, interpretation, and explanation phases as Kirk and Miller (1986) call it. For example, using an unstructured, open-ended interview data collection format, the forces shaping an investigation would be the responses of the research participants and the ensuing dialog. Their emerging data direct the subsequent lines of questioning (Howe, 1991). In a preordinate design, the issues, questions, or stimuli are standardized to items such as behavioral objectives, goals, and structured (and typically close-ended) interview items (Stake, 1983, pp. 295-298). There is more predetermination because the pathway through the investigation is more certain.

The Investigative TRSs' Values and Beliefs

A research method is not only a set of techniques or procedures for obtaining convergent, homogeneous, and repeatable (Glaser & Strauss, 1967) information about a phenomenon. It is of part of investigators' decision-making processes. Mobily (1985, p. 8), over half a decade ago, urged leisure researchers to discuss the rigor found in various methods. This has occurred in Chapter 2 by comparing the major elements of positivist and naturalistic inquiry based on their assumptions and as they are operationalized in quantitative and qualitative research methods. Such comparisons are even more useful when framed by an explicit consideration of investigators' values and beliefs about such items as: What is their view of the world, what can be known, and how can they best come to know it?

Miles and Huberman (1984b) and Stones (1985) prefer stated beliefs over unstated beliefs because stated beliefs may be illuminated, questioned, and argued. Researchers' values filter investigations via their substantive decisions, methodological decisions, and their interpretation of findings (Hultsman & Anderson, 1991; Tuthill & Ashton, 1984). Dawson (1984, p. 18) declares that "disciplined" scientists are self-critical and should be willing to put themselves and their methods out for public scrutiny. Then, the public can make informed decisions regarding scientific merit. Values, as filters, likely influence what is acceptable to investigators as ways of knowing (Howe, 1991). It could be, however, that enough variability in the behavior of real people in the real world exists, that a range of paradigms that evolves into a continuum of research methods could be of value (cf. Howe & Keller, 1988; Scott & Godbey, 1990). This could hold true particularly for deeper understandings of TR as a dynamic, subjective, and contextual experience (Howe, 1991).

The Muddied Waters of "Objectivity"

Guba (1978, p. 17) writes, "the naturalistic inquirer ... places little store in [the positivist's] form of objectivity and strives instead for confirmability, i.e., agreement among a variety of information sources." Positivists' objectivity is presumed to yield unbiased, reliable, and rational data and results, whereas subjectivity denotes biased, unreliable, and irrational data and results. The positivists' means for ensuring objectivity is to separate or remove the researcher from the setting and to use quantitative measures which are manipulated through statistical applications.

In contrast, naturalistic investigators hold that it is through close, intensive interaction with research participants that the most revealing (and potentially confirmable or **objective**) data are collected (Scott & Godbey, 1990). It is true that investigative TRSs cannot be observers without some degree of "filtering" in as much as they are human and are affected by their values, previous and current beliefs, knowledge, and experience. In naturalistic inquiry, investigative TRSs must participate in some fashion in the experience and action of those observed if they are to understand research participants *subjectively or from their own frames of reference* (Bruyn, 1966). This means that objectivity is of concern to the naturalistic inquirer if bias, prejudice, or falsehood has unknowingly or unaccountably crept into his or her study. So, in naturalistic inquiry, intensive interaction is biasing only if it leads to falsehood. Otherwise, being human with histories and hopes gives *all* investigators filters.

The Investigator's Tacit Knowing of the Experience of the Research Participants

Within the phenomenological paradigm, the naturalistic investigator "apprehends" knowledge. He or she is empathic, taking the role of the other and studying his or her experience by identifying with the life of the research participant (Bruyn, 1966). The details of this are elaborated in the next chapter, but again, as an introduction, the key acts are to recognize, acknowledge, and as appropriate, take advantage of the filtering influences (values and the empathic understanding that universal human experiences provide) in a given study. See also Guba (1978, pp. 73-78) on neutrality; Hultsman and Anderson (1991, p. 65) on truth; and Scott and Godbey (1990, pp. 192-194) on empathy and the interactionist perspective.

In the **interactionist perspective** (which values field-based research), the experience of the other is deemed to be knowable. Scott and Godbey (1990, p. 199) discuss this in terms of *knowing*, not merely *knowing about* an area of study. Knowing facilitates rapport and enables naturalistic researchers to be close at hand to the research participants. Empathy and positioning often result in an extensive narrative description that captures the perceptions of the research participants themselves, using their own forms of expression. The goal is to synthesize human meaning within a given context (Guba & Lincoln, 1983).

Douglas (1976, p. 111-117) calls intensive interaction "**depth probing**," which allows trained investigative TRSs to apprehend the recreation participation and leisure experience of clinical, transitional, or community life similarly to the research participants' perceptions. He says that interaction/ depth probing enables the naturalistic investigator to access the latent information or TR-related phenomena of people's lives, absorb the information, and process it through his or her relevant universal human experience. Then the naturalistic inquirer can construct his or her own understanding of the experience to communicate to others (e.g., readers).

Thus, the naturalistic inquirer as a field-based researcher strives to be close to the research participants and the research setting. This is done in order to maximize understanding while maintaining an analytical distance. If the trained researcher senses that he or she is "going native," getting sidetracked, or becoming co-opted in some way, then that in and of itself must be documented. So, when using qualitative data collection techniques (a coherent participant-observation, a conversationally-oriented interview, or the review of artifacts), the naturalistic inquirer must describe and record his or her beliefs, feelings, and behaviors that may be leading to bias as falsehood and includes them as additional data for analysis (Howe, 1991; Stones, 1985). In doing so, the self-aware naturalistic investigator reflects on beliefs, decisions, and behaviors and how each may affect the trustworthiness of the conclusions he or she has drawn (Miles & Huberman, 1984a).

Subjective, Qualitative Data

Chapter 13 in the text also provides extensive coverage of data, indicating that for investigative TRSs, **data** are usually field notes: observations of behavior described in words, words themselves from informants or interviewees, or descriptions of artifacts, all of which have meaning to the individuals under study. Floden (1983, p. 271) calls on investigators to determine the meanings people attach to their actions. Meanings include individuals' values, assumptions, and language (Bruyn, 1966). These notions are not necessarily best expressed or understood as numbers (Howe, 1991). In a striking passage that is quoted here as well as in other writings, Stones (1985, p. 65) offers:

> Similarly, it is more meaningful to ask what it means to feel anxious, or to be in love, than to investigate the number of times that a given person feels anxious, or in love, in a given situation over a given period of time, and so on.

Ambiguity, subtlety, and nuance, as they are found in the interchange of symbols and gestures in the discourse of meaning, are "data" that may be deeply revealing to the TRS (Howe, 1991).

The following passage is from a triangulated naturalistic inquiry to evaluate selected social-psychological outcomes of involvement in a transitional program called the Community Reintegration Program (cf., Bullock & Howe, 1991). The data illustrate the idea of deep meaning via subtlety, nuance, and intersubjective knowing through the universal human experience of wanting social acceptance, comfort, and intimacy.

A young adult, under conditions of informed consent, was a research participant in the Community Reintegration Program (CRP). He was a wheelchair user who had an adventitious injury. Upon discharge into the community, he responded to structured, open-ended interview questions at preset intervals over one year. One of the recreation activities that he had fun doing that was a carry-over from before his injury was 'going to clubs.' As a co-investigator from the Midwest, I first inferred that this interviewee from eastern North Carolina meant that he participated in some special interest group (e.g., the chess club, the rock hounding club, or the stamp collecting club). Well, he clarified that his phrase was synonymous with my phrase from undergraduate school days in central Illinois, 'going to the bars.'

Even on the most superficial level, the meaning of his club experience definitely had a different connotation than that of (at least in terms of my filters)—the chess club. Through continued interviewing, which allowed for depth probing, clarification, and refinement of meaning, the ambivalence he felt when going to the clubs in his wheelchair, as a wheelchair user, emerged. He also spoke of no longer being 'able bodied,' but being independent in his 'own mind' given reasonable architectural accessibility. He talked about wanting to, but not asking [nonwheelchair using] girls to dance and how he felt *shy* about that.

Because our interview contacts were limited to monthly intervals, as the co-investigator, I never felt to my own satisfaction that I *fully* apprehended all that 'shy' meant to this young man as he continued to engage in this form of recreation. But, more than a one shot questionnaire or a one time observation, I did feel that the series of structured open-ended interviews gave me, a 38 year old nonwheelchair user, a much fuller understanding of this young man's *ambivalence* about going to clubs in terms of the social-psychological constructs of independence, identity, social comfort and acceptance, and intimacy. I recollected and drew from my filters of twenty years ago the certain desperation that I felt wanting to ask someone to dance, and, even more so, hoping against hope that someone would ask me to dance. Those memories of my own *shyness* about going to dances, as a universal human experience, enabled me to better understand the young man's ambivalence. More intensive contact would have yielded an even deeper empathy.

Drawing Subjective Meaning from Research Participants

Stake (1983) encourages capitalizing on the natural abilities of people to experience, understand, and ascribe meaning to their own lives/life events. By drawing meaning from research participants, through extended observation, in-depth interviewing, and the review of artifacts, Stake (1983, p. 280-282) says that this enables naturalistic generalization. **Naturalistic generalization** means that people recognize similarities in and out of context and sense the "natural covariance" in things that happen. People are intuitive and empirical in their ways of knowing, deriving from tacit knowledge how things are, why they are, how they feel about things, and how things may probably be later on or in other places.

A intuitive and tacit (implied) analytical and interpretive process as shown in Chapters 13 and 14 is not undisciplined. Rather, as with all inquiry, it requires discipline and introspection. Naturalistic discipline, beyond vigorous self-reflection, has its protocol of which **recursive** (cyclical or reiterative) schema and inductive analysis through intersubjective knowing are just two parts (Glancy, in press; Scott & Godbey, 1990; Stones, 1985). **Recursivity** means non-linearity; an unrolling inquiry or an unfolding of design and method as the study proceeds (Guba & Lincoln, 1983, p. 324). Recursive design is a dynamic, yet orderly and cumulative process.

Bruyn (1966, p. 177) informs readers that social science knowledge has three sources: reason, sense, and intuition. Each yields a different type of understanding, but all three function complementarily in any single act of knowing and conveying meaning. To the naturalistic inquirer, leisure, therapeutic, and re-creative experience are multifaceted personal and social constructions. Surely TR is a phenomenon that is well-served by investigations that offer each type of understanding.

Data Collection in Naturalistic Inquiry

As stated earlier, naturalistic researchers believe that the investigator is a part of the human experience he or she is studying (Scott & Godbey, 1990; Stones, 1985). Naturalistic investigators seek words, actions, and artifacts, and record them most often as language to build theory (Goetz & LeCompte, 1984) or to compare with existing theory. Hunches as "working hypotheses" may emerge within the interrelated data collection, analysis, and interpretation process (Guba & Lincoln, 1983) or may precede it.

Collecting data through participant-observations, in-depth interviews, or the systematic review of artifacts, uses investigatory skills and practices that are already part of the TRS's repertoire. **Artifacts** include both the familiar and conventional documents and records, and the things produced by consumers: drawings, paintings, sculptures, letters, stories, poems, game playing sequences, dances, musical scores, etc. Think about writing progress notes at the end of a session or the end of the day, or reviewing case records, histories, or other documentation. Those tasks are tiring, but necessary. Likewise, when transcribing hours of interview tapes or field notes from observations, the investigative TRS may feel overwhelmed by the sheer volume of words! But, he or she can find a little comfort in knowing that findings contain meaning insofar as they appear in the research participants' own language. When writing an article or research report, as Chapter 14 of this text indicates, the next challenge becomes reporting these verbatim or paraphrased expressions with both brevity and credibility (Scott & Godbey, 1990; Howe, 1991).

Observation in Naturalistic Inquiry

Owing to page constraints, comments about the review of artifacts as defined in this chapter are subsumed under the following discussion of observation. Looking at actions (observing) and writing field notes about them is similar to reviewing artifacts and writing notes about them. Both actions and artifacts are viewable data.

The list of classic and contemporary articles and texts from the traditional disciplines of the social and behavioral sciences and education about "qualitative" observation is vast, and sometimes contradictory in content. However, it is very compelling reading. It is impossible to do much more than introduce some ideas about observation in naturalistic inquiry within the confines of this chapter. Fortunately, Chilcott (1987) details a set of recommendations for reporting ethnographic research that provides some order to this overview. McCormick (1991) offers an exemplary, recently reported participant-observation (with in-depth interviews) of members of Alcoholics Anonymous.

First, the continuum of roles which the naturalistic **observer** may take ranges from passive (overt or covert) observer to active **participant-observer** as an overt, full participant. In other words, one extreme would be the observer sitting behind a one-way mirror and watching and recording the interplay in a one-to-one leisure education session between a TRS and a client. The other extreme would be the observer as an integral part of the paddling/steering of a raft on an extended whitewater rafting expedition, while at the same time collecting and later recording auditory and visual perceptions from consumers/data sources about the meaning of aspects of the expedition. Other roles of observer-as-participant and participant-as-observer vary by degree of participation and fall in between the extremes (see Denzin, 1978).

Because of the value naturalistic inquirers place on intersubjective knowing, and the author's personal filters about informed consent, the active, full participant role, with disclosure about the investigation is emphasized here. Again, recognizing that all research acts have elements of contrivance, the participant-observer strives to watch, listen, and ask over some length of time. The goal is to come to know the perspectives of the persons under study as much as tangible and psychological resources permit. This means, in a way, to cohabit with the lived lives of the other(s) without losing one's own life.

The written report of the participant-observation may begin with a rationale which may include a review of the relevant empirical and theoretical literature. Then, the initial guiding research question may be stated.

This is followed by *process* concerns which include procedural and contextual information. The setting/duration of the study is described as well as how the participant-observer gained access to it. The research participants and the role of the participant-observer are characterized. The ways in which data are collected (from whom and/or what) are delineated. The system of sampling [see Glaser & Strauss (1967) on theoretical sampling and the search for negative cases; Howe (1991) and McCormick (1991) for examples in leisure inquiry] and resampling with the same or different questions is reported. Strategies to enhance rigor, such as methodological triangulation are often specified under data collection.

As stated earlier, this process is recursive. In Phase 1 of McCormick's (1991) study, he simultaneously collected and analyzed his data. So, he accounted for his analysis under his discussion of data collection. Howe (1991) explicated her analysis following the data collection section, continuously emphasizing the cyclical nature of the sampling-data collection-data analysis relation, as did McCormick (1991) in his report of Phase 2 of his study.

Finally, **outcomes** are given in the form of findings. Findings are presented according to the conventions of the particular journal in which the study appears. Then, the findings may be discussed by comparing them to the literature or they may suggest new explanations. Convention often urges that substantive, methodological, or practical implications are offered to the readers.

Interviewing in Naturalistic Inquiry

By now, having read the words continuum and context so many times, the investigative TRS is probably wondering if there is anything that is not on a continuum or in need of being studied within context? Well, there may be, but the interview process in naturalistic inquiry is not one of them. The interview process may be thought of in terms of three components: (a) the nature of the items asked on the **interview schedule** (or form) itself; (b) the predominant structure of the interview schedule as a whole; and the (c) dynamics between the interviewer and interviewee.

The Nature of the Items Asked

The items or questions that can be asked on an interview schedule range from **closed-ended** to **open-ended**. Closed-ended questions are also known as forced choice or scaled items in which the interviewee is presumed to be able to respond to items that are preset by the interviewer (Malik, Ashton-Shaeffer, & Kleiber, 1991). Closed-ended questions are typically thought to be very matter of fact, requiring little or no contextual elaboration in order to understand the meaning of the answer.

Open-ended questions may also be initially preset by the interviewer. But these types of items are presumed to elicit more elaborate responses from the interviewee in his or her own form of language. The interviewee's answers are sometimes called **emergent responses**. Further, if the interviewee or interviewer is unclear about the question or emergent response in an open-ended item, the interviewer may offer a "prompt" to explain the question in other words or to probe the response to ensure clarity. The interviewer may also follow-up on a particular part of a response to an open-ended question for further elaboration. For some examples of closed-ended and open-ended questions used in the CRP study (Bullock & Howe, 1991) see the following page.

A Special Circumstance

It should be briefly mentioned that interviewing within a participant-observation study offers some special data collection opportunities. When interviewing under this circumstance, the naturalistic inquirer may select purposively, seeking the "gate keeper" research participant or "case" that is most typical of the whole; a "key informant" who has special access to information or a way of communicating that is representative or captures the essence of what the others say (fluency); and any "negative" or discrepant case(s). The investigative TRS intensively collects information from the key

Sample closed-ended interview items

From: [CRP] Structured Interview Schedule for Clients, Coversheet

1. What is client's disability/disabilities? Please check __X__ all that apply.
    Amputation   _____
    Head Injury   _____
    Neurological Disorder   _____
    Spinal Cord Injury   _____
    Stroke (CVA)   _____
    Other   _____
                                        (specify)

2. How old is client?
    Age in years   _____

· · · ·

4. What is client's living situation? Please check __X__ all that apply.
    Live Alone   _____
    Live With Spouse   _____
    Live w/Other Relative _____
    Live With Friend(s)   _____

Sample open-ended interview items
Questions

1. How has your involvement in the Community Reintegration (CRP) program affected you? *Prompt*: How has it benefited you?

2. Has the program affected/benefited you in other ways? *Prompt*: How has your attitude toward recreational activities/pursuits or your free time changed? How have your recreation skills changed? What have you learned about the role of recreation in your life?

· · · ·

5. How have your community recreation providers worked with you to adapt their offerings to your disability? Please tell me some examples. **Note**: *Could prompt with an example of an activity that the interviewer is already aware of.*

6. Based on what we've gone through in the program, is there any activity or special thing(s) that you are looking *forward* to doing? *Prompt*: Tell me about what you are already doing that you plan to continue to do . . . or about something new that you intend to do.

7. How do you *feel about* your disability? How do you feel about the role this program has played related to your disability?

· · · ·

10. What do you suggest to improve this program for others?

11. Is there anything else that you would like to say? Any other comments?

informant. The TRS is free to enlarge or shrink the sample size depending on when the answers (or the research participant) reach the point of exhaustion. (This is not literal, physical exhaustion, although sometimes this happens to everybody in participant-observations; it is, information exhaustion, when there is nothing new being said/seen). So, data collection may have a timed or a natural end called "saturation" (Howe, 1990).

The Structure of the Interview Schedule/Form

The **interview schedule** (form) itself has varying degrees of structure or standardization (Denzin, 1978; Howe, 1988; Lofland, 1971). On one hand is the "pure structured" or "scheduled standardized" interview. On the other hand is the "unstructured" or "nonstandardized" interview. A hybrid is the "semistructured" or "nonscheduled standardized" interview. The structured interview is helpful when the interviewer is confident in his or her knowledge of what the "important" questions are, desires to put some boundaries on the responses, and already has some familiarity with the interviewees' lives.

The unstructured interview is helpful when there is a need to explore many facets of the interviewees' concerns, when the fullest expression of the interviewees is desired, and the interviewees' perceptions assume precedence over the interviewer's preconceptions. The semistructured interview is helpful when there is a foundation of predetermined questions from which the interviewer may freely come and go to inquire about emergent topics in greater depth. There is a bit more direction given than in the pure unstructured interview schedule. On the whole, the interview process *per se* enables the interviewer to pursue intensively complex questions and elusive answers somewhat more effectively than the typical closed-ended questionnaire in a mail-out/mail-back survey (Howe, 1988).

Selected Interview Dynamics

This discussion of interview dynamics is limited to presenting the idea of "guided conversation" and some brief comments about reliability and validity in interviewing. The sources cited in this section elaborate on these concerns. The advantages and disadvantages of interviewing in leisure research are highlighted in Howe (1988, pp. 307-308), Malik, Ashton-Shaeffer, and Kleiber (1991, pp. 60-64), and elsewhere. Howe advocates the use of a variation of the face-to-face interview as a guided conversation. The interviewer's role is an attentive listener who uses a relatively natural way of obtaining data in a familiar and comfortable form of social engagement—a conversation. Schatzman and Strauss (1973, p. 73) refer to the interviewer's guiding of the conversation as "implicit coaching" which sets the stage/tone for the interview. Howe (1988) contends:

... at some point depending on the degree of structure, purpose, and form of an interview, all interviews lose their egalitarian quality. Even if it is only in the act of opening and closing an interview, the interviewer 'governs' the event. That may be one of the lightest forms of implicit coaching ... [Ultimately] someone must be in charge and have an agenda, even if those items to be investigated and/or accomplished are acknowledged only in the most general sense. Thus, at some point, the interviewer is in a position of greater power ... However, *the outcome of the [interview] process must remain the interviewee's* [italics added]. (pp. 307-308)

Reliability and Validity Concerns.

Further, in their description of a case study on interviewing young adults with mental retardation, Malik, Ashton-Shaeffer, and Kleiber (1991, pp. 65-69) document the diverse methods that they used to address interview reliability and validity issues. To determine the reliability of their interview techniques, they used interview-reinterview and inter-rater reliability. To determine validity, they triangulated data sources among the consumers, their parents or care providers, and artifacts (recreation agency participation records).

Contemporary Technology in Naturalistic Data Collection

There are volumes that are written about the skills, techniques, and ethics of covert and overt use of automation and technology in data collection (cf., Isaac & Michael, 1983; Webb, Campbell, Schwartz, Sechrest & Grove, 1981). However, a few notes to consider are offered as follows.

Should resources and the comfort and consent of the consumer permit, the investigative TRS as research instrument can augment his or her senses by using today's technology. That is, anything that can be seen with the eyes can be filmed, videotaped, photographed, or sketched. Anything that can be heard by the ears may be audiotaped via cassette or reel-to-reel tape recorders. Anything that can be said face-to-face may be stated over a telephone or dictated into a dictating machine. Finally, anything that can be written by hand can be entered directly into a portable microcomputer, presuming that one has typing skills beyond the "hunt and peck" level.

Among the most apparent advantages of the use of technology are: the total record of the actions or words, the permanence of the record, and the capacity for rewinding and seeing or hearing repeatedly. Entering text directly into a portable microcomputer also eliminates one step in the transcription process. Among the clearest disadvantages of the use of technology are: the possibility of equipment failure and the added elements of artificiality introduced into the interaction between the investigative TRS and the consumer. The obvious presence of technology reinforces that the interaction is in fact a research act and may serve initially to inhibit disclosure.

Concluding Comments

Douglas (1976, pp. 124-125) notes that the naturalistic investigator wants to develop an empathic understanding of the intimate and the particular that uses the perceptions and methods of expression of the research participants as much as possible. The investigative TRS tries to portray what the research participant/consumer has felt, evoking in the reader a *knowing* of the experience of the research participant/consumer.

The increasing attention to subjectively and contextually defined experience as an outcome of TR interventions for consumers may evolve into a growing line of inquiry. Research designs and data collection techniques that enable the data to be heard from the voices of the research participants themselves are encouraged. Others' calls for continuing conversations about philosophies of science; research paradigms; assumptions; the theoretical/conceptual underpinnings of recreation, leisure, and TR; values; ethics; investigators' personal stakes in research; disclosure; privacy and protection of research participants; and methods of investigation are echoed (Howe, 1990).

Fain (1990) concurs with Mobily's (1990) emphasis on values and valuation in the conceptualization of research problems. Fain (1990) concludes by urging investigators to consider the relevance of their research questions to the important issues of the 21st Century: cultural diversity, global interdependence, environmental responsibility, economic inequity, and so on. These are the concerns of humankind and they are complex, long-term, and huge! But their enormity should not be cause to shy away. Investigative TRSs have a role to play in addressing these concerns, both as professionals in a human service occupation, and as part of the human species. The first step does not have to be a leap into the forefront of determining methods for ensuring world peace. The first step can be the design of a small investigation about an individual's peace of mind.

A Covert, Nonparticipant Observational Exercise

The content of this chapter suggests that an observational exercise might be a good way to practice some of the decision-making, processes, and actions that have been presented.

Mini-Naturalistic Observation of Recreation Participation
Purposes of Exercise

This simple learning experience has three purposes:
- observing
- recording what you observe
- note taking, drafting, revising, and re-revising your writing

Process

Whom to observe:
- one consumer of TR Services per short observation period (may be a different person at each different observation period)

Where to observe:
- public area/day room/cafeteria/recreation room of your facility (as unobtrusively as possible, seat yourself so that you may view the room)

When to observe:
- on one Saturday (assuming an "open" or self-directed time for self-initiated recreation participation)
- four 15-minute observation periods starting at (examples, depending on the hours of operation of such areas at your facility):

> 2:00 p.m.
> 4:30 p.m.
> 7:00 p.m.
> 8:30 p.m.

What to observe and record:
- the behavior of the consumer whom you are watching as it occurs in the public area/day room/cafeteria/recreation room of your facility
- the characteristics that describe the consumer whose behavior you are watching in public area/day room/cafeteria/recreation room of your facility

How to observe and record:
- **Look,** but don't stare. Situate yourself to be unobtrusive, but with a clear line of sight
- **Act Subtly and Casually**

On-site Follow-up Directions
As soon as your observation period is done:
- go quickly to another part of the facility
- fill in details that you remember to make your jotted notes more complete
- refresh yourself between sessions, as it will be a long day

At Home Follow-up Directions
On Sunday (assuming a Saturday observation):
- review your notes
- draft them into complete sentences
- have a competent, trusted peer read and critique your draft for content, or how well you describe what you saw, and grammar, or mechanics and style
- revise your report
- consider your feelings about not disclosing yourself as an observer in relation to informed consent, harm, "natural" behavior vs. the likelihood of "changed" behavior if your consumer knew he or she was being watched. (Review Chapter 6.)
- think about how your report would be different if you had also interviewed the consumers you observed
- turn to Chapter 13 and read about examining and reexamining your data and Chapter 14 about interpreting and reporting findings

Self-Evaluation Criteria
The written report should show your ability to:
- observe in detail
- record your observations
- expand or elaborate on your observations without making judgments
- write a report of your observations using a logical and meaningful organizing system
- consider the ethical and legal implications of a covert observation
- apprehend meaning/make inferences that are grounded in the observations
- link the meanings/inferences to theoretical explanations of recreation activity participation or generate new explanations

Audience for Report
- Yourself or your supervisor in the role of an investigative TRS interested in the self-directed/initiated recreation participation of a consumer of TR Services

The value of this small observational exercise is that it gives you practice at looking, listening, and recording so that you may progress from superficially watching people through (and perhaps being unconscious of) your own interpretive filters to apprehending meaning/making inferences that are grounded in less biased/nonfactual observations. You may also practice pondering ethical and legal choices, linking inferences to theoretical explanations of recreation participation, or generating new explanations.

References

Bruyn, S. T. (1966). *The human perspective in sociology: The methodology of participant observation.* Englewood Cliffs, NJ: Prentice-Hall

Bullock, C. C., & Howe, C. Z. (1991). A model therapeutic recreation program for the reintegration of persons with disabilities into the community. *Therapeutic Recreation Journal, 25*(1), 7-17.

Chilcott, J. H. (1987). Where are you coming from and where are you going? The reporting of ethnographic research. *American Educational Research Journal, 24,* 199-218.

Denzin, N. K. (1978). The research act: A theoretical introduction to sociological methods (2nd ed.). New York, NY: McGraw-Hill.

Douglas, J. D. (1976). *Investigative social research: Individual and team field research.* Beverly Hills, CA: Sage.

Fain, G. S. (1990, October). *Moral life of the leisure scientist.* Invited paper presented at the Opening General Session of the Leisure Research Symposium of the annual meeting of the National Recreation and Park Association, Phoenix, AZ.

Floden, R. E. (1983). Flexner, accreditation and evaluation. In G. F. Madaus, M. Scriven, & D. L. Stufflebeam (Eds.), *Evaluation models: Viewpoints on educational and human services evaluation* (pp. 261-268). Norwell, MA: Kluwer.

Geertz, C. (1973). *The interpretation of cultures.* New York, NY: Basic Books.

Glancy, M. (in press). Achieving intersubjectivity: The process of becoming the subject in leisure research. *Leisure Studies.*

Glaser, B. G., & Strauss, A. L. (1967). *The discovery of grounded theory: Strategies for qualitative research.* Chicago, IL: Aldine.

Goetz, J. P., & LeCompte, M. D. (1984). *Ethnography and qualitative design in educational research.* Orlando, FL: Academic Press.

Guba, E. G. (1983). *Toward a methodology of naturalistic inquiry in educational evaluation.* (CSE Monograph Series in Evaluation, No. 8). Los Angeles, CA: UCLA, Center for the Study of Evaluation.

Guba, E. G., & Lincoln, Y. S. (1981). *Effective evaluation.* San Fransisco, CA: Jossey-Bass.

Guba, E. G., & Lincoln, Y. S. (1983). Epistemological and methodological bases of naturalistic inquiry. In G. F. Madaus, M. Scriven, & D. L. Stufflebeam (Eds.), *Evaluation models: Viewpoints on educational and human services evaluation* (pp. 311-334). Norwell, MA: Kluwer.

Howe, C. Z. (1988). Using qualitative structured interviews in leisure research: Illustrations from one case study. *Journal of Leisure Research, 20*(4), 305-324.

Howe, C. Z. (1990, October). *Research on the psychological and the social psychological aspects of leisure: Continuing questions of meaning.* Paper presented as the featured speech at the Psychological and Social Psychological Aspects of Leisure Session of the Leisure Research Symposium of the annual meeting of the National Recreation and Park Association, Phoenix, AZ.

Howe, C. Z. (1991). Considerations when using phenomenology in leisure inquiry: Beliefs, methods, and analysis in naturalistic research. *Leisure Studies, 10*(1), 49-62.

Howe, C. Z., & Keller, M. J. (1988). The use of triangulation as an evaluation technique: Illustrations from regional symposia in therapeutic recreation. *Therapeutic Recreation Journal, 22*(1), 36-45.

Howe, C. Z., & Rancourt, A. M. (1990). The importance of definitions of selected concepts for leisure inquiry. *Leisure Sciences, 12*(4), 395-406.

Hultsman, J. T., & Anderson, S. C. (1991). Studying leisure perceptions: A need for methodological expansion. *Leisure Studies, 10*(1), 63-67.

Isaac, S., & Michael, W. B. (1983). *Handbook in research and evaluation* (2nd ed.). San Diego, CA: EDITS.

Kirk, J., & Miller, M. L. (1986). *Reliability and validity in qualitative research.* Sage University Paper Series on Qualitative Research Methods Series, Volume 1. Beverly Hills, CA: Sage.

Lofland, J. (1971). *Analyzing social settings: A guide to qualitative observation and analysis.* Belmont, CA: Wadsworth.

Malik, P. B., Ashton-Shaeffer, C., & Kleiber, D. A. (1991). Interviewing young adults with mental retardation: A seldom used research method. *Therapeutic Recreation Journal, 25*(1), 60-73.

Marshall, C. (1984). The wrong time for mechanistics in qualitative research. *Educational Researcher, 13*(9), 26-28.

McCormick, B. (1991). Self-experience as leisure constraint: The case of Alcoholics Anonymous. *Journal of Leisure Research, 23*(4), 345-362.

Miles, M. B., & Huberman, A. M. (1984a). Rejoinder to Marshall. *Educational Researcher, 13*(9), 28-29.

Miles, M. B., & Huberman, A. M. (1984b). *Qualitative data analysis: A sourcebook of new methods.* Beverly Hills, CA: Sage.

Mobily, K. E. (1985, October). *Thoughts on a reconstruction of leisure research.* Paper presented as the featured speech at the Methodology and Statistical Issues Session of the Leisure Research Symposium of the annual meeting of the National Recreation and Park Association, Dallas, TX.

Mobily, K. E. (1990, October). *The problem of leisure valuation in American intellectual tradition.* Invited paper presented at the Opening General Session of the Leisure Research Symposium of the annual meeting of the National Recreation and Park Association, Phoenix, AZ.

Schatzman, L., & Strauss, A. L. (1973). *Field research.* Englewood Cliffs, NJ: Prentice-Hall.

Scott, D., & Godbey, G. C. (1990). Reorienting leisure research—the case for qualitative methods. *Society and Leisure, 13*(1), 189-205.

Scriven, M. (1983). Evaluation ideologies. In G. F. Madaus, M. Scriven, and D. L. Stufflebeam (Eds.), *Evaluation models: Viewpoints on educational and human services evaluation* (pp. 229-260). Norwell, MA: Kluwer.

Stake, R. E. (1983). Program evaluation, particularly responsive evaluation. In G. F. Madaus, M. Scriven, & D. L. Stufflebeam (Eds.), *Evaluation models: Viewpoints on educational and human services evaluation* (pp. 287-310). Norwell, MA: Kluwer .

Stones, C. R. (1985). Qualitative research: A viable psychological alternative. *The Psychological Record, 35,* 63-75.

Tuthill, D., & Ashton, P. T. (1984). Response to Miles and Huberman. *Educational Researcher, 13*(9), 25-26.

Webb, E. J., Campbell, D. T., Schwartz, R. D., Sechrest, L., & Grove, J. B. (1981). *Nonreactive measures in the social sciences* (2nd ed.). Boston, MA: Houghton Mifflin.

Weissinger, E. (1990). Of revolutions and resistance: A response to philosophical criticisms of social scientific leisure research. *Journal of Leisure Research, 22*(4), 309-316.

The Analysis of Subjective Information: A Process for Perspective-Taking
Maureen Glancy

The focus of subjective data analysis is the symbolic system which human beings create as they interact with people, objects, and other elements of the environment. What leads investigative TRSs to knowledge of this system is the process of taking the perspective of one who is experiencing the symbolic system under study; in this case, that of the individual(s) with disabilities.

The symbolic system is a social construction; thus, the unit of analysis is a social entity of some sort. Often, the subject of study and **unit of analysis** is a small informally organized group, or a larger organization of like-minded or contractually related persons, with a similar interest or concern. In TR settings, examples of units of analysis could include a single client engaged in an intervention program, a group of clients or others who are together regularly for a similar purpose such as treatment, recreation, or dining; or a more formal association of clients. A resident planning committee, wheelchair sports team, or a milieu therapy team illustrate the formal association concept.

People's symbolic systems are influenced by social experiences through their mental thought processes; thus, analysis occurs at the social-psychological level. The individual is in interaction with self, objects, people, and situations all of which have the potential to be endowed with symbolic meaning which, through the process of interaction, create and alter meaning in people's minds. Meaning construction is the process which Mead (1934) wrote about, where the "I" (ego) interacts with the "ME" (society) through mental dialogue and memory recall. This inner interactive drama shapes one's sense of identity in reference to persons, places, and things and provides the individual with a rich lore of meaning taken from

CHAPTER 13

these experiences with self and others. This means that the individual is never really isolated from a socially meaningful environment because she or he carries memories and perceptions of social meaning in the mind. Therefore, whether studying one individual with disabilities, a small interest group, or an association of members, the investigative TRS is studying the person(s) in interaction with a social environment, even when the research participant may be one client engaged in a game of solitaire.

Varied sources of data were discussed in Chapter 12. These sources of data provide the means by which the symbolic system can be accessed and studied systematically in order to take the research participant's perspective. Analysis of those data is directed toward discovering, interpreting, and understanding the symbolic system employed by an individual or group when interacting in the situation(s) of interest. The intent is to learn how to see a particular aspect of the world from the research participant's perspective.

Learning the **meaning** a client perceives when engaging in recreation can advance the TR planning and treatment process because it is a way of expanding the information base which frames intervention decisions. Learning meaning is a way of coming to know *why* a client does something, not merely *what* that individual does. The investigative TRS who focuses on discovering perceptions and thoughts about the everyday recreation experience is an investigator involved in revealing hidden layers of meaning which lead to understanding the intrinsic motives important to the individual involved.

Meaning is not inherent in recreational objects or actions, however; it grows out of cultural contexts—the associations that people create and feel with others who share the same situation. The meaning a person attaches to things she or he does is always associated with values that have been created in a specific social context: the family; groups of personal, school, or special-interest friends; or more abstract communities of regional, business, or religious contacts. Developing and changing behavior really depends on socially constructed meanings and values. Thus, to understand what is valued by someone else and why it is meaningful, TRSs, as investigators, attempt to *share* their clients' experiences mentally and emotionally, and physically if possible. As investigative TRSs, the purpose is to gain access to the percepts and frames of reference used by the client, to learn to follow that individual's process of thinking about whatever it is he or she does that is of interest.

To illustrate the concept of valued meaning, the TRS may be working with a client with depression, one who is unable to show enthusiasm and effort for doing anything. Yet, the TRS may have observed the client leaping to his or her feet to look out the window when a plane flies overhead. To the TRS, this means nothing in particular and offers a variety of explanations in general. It may just as easily be the behavior of someone who is startled by loud noise, recalls air raid drills from wartime, or feels violation of territory. This could also be the behavior of someone who participated faithfully in the Civil Air Defense, was an ardent member of a remote control airplane club, or cannot forget being a passenger on a plane that experienced mechanical failure in an emergency landing.

These examples serve to demonstrate that people learn and act according to valued insights gained from their experiences in life. To become informed about the **subjective perspective**, the inner way of knowing that frames the thinking and behavior of a client or group must be learned as it is known by them. In Chapter 12, the sources of subjective information and ways to obtain them were discussed. This chapter examines how the investigative TRS can analyze qualitative data which express the perspective of the client-as-research participant. In actual practice, naturalistic inquiry using qualitative methods is performed so data collection, analysis, and interpretation are interwoven much of the time. However, here the focus is on *how to find* the meaning, themes, cultural configurations, and theories in the qualitative data collected. So, the analysis process is singled out.

A Metaphor for Subjective Data Analysis

Analyzing subjective data is reminiscent of the experience of finding a large pebble washed up on the beach as the tide turns. Imagine the following analogy to illustrate the process of qualitative data analysis:

> We hold the pebble in our hands and turn it around every which way, feeling it, fondling it, sensing it with our imaginations. In examining the pebble, we detach ourselves from the water, sand, sun, and others we may have been with and whatever had transpired up to this point. It seems like the pebble weighs on our hands and our minds at the same time. We attempt to understand it from the inside out as if it could speak to us. Our minds are consumed, being totally engaged in the process of discovery. We read a language of colors, patterns, striations, embedments, cavities, texture, weight, shape, and fit in our hand. The pebble may tell a story of birth, of journey, of travail, or of alchemical power. Whatever its tale, we are spellbound by the mystery it reveals to us when we interact with its information to understand its essence.

Briefly, then, the process of **analyzing qualitative data** from a recreational experience can be described as an interactive process by which the investigator becomes knowledgeable about the research participant's perspective. It is as if the investigator holds chunks of information in her or his hands, examines them carefully, over and over again by interacting mentally with the data in a variety of ways. Using all the clues provided, the investigator learns the research participant's way of thinking as a frame of reference that gives meaning to the experience of interest.

Since the origin of meaning is in the individual's experience, investigative TRSs who engage in naturalistic inquiry seek to reconstruct the original meanings using qualitative data. To reconstruct the theories grounded in experience, a mentally involving analysis process is used. Instead of a computer-driven statistical analysis, all analysis is thinking performed by the researcher. *Analysis* begins with recall of experience and includes categorization; comparison; insight; analytical breakdown; discovery of hidden meanings in language, actions, objects, and relationships between people or activities. It ends with synthetic rebuilding or reconstruction of the social systems that give meaning and substance to the experience being studied.

In using personal mental capabilities to analyze data, the investigative TRS seeks to *become of one mind* with the research participants. The investigative TRS thinks of the persons under study as "we" instead of "they" (Glancy, in press). From the data emerge thoughts, themes, and eventually theories grounded in the reality of human experience.

Ways of Being Informed by Qualitative Data

Qualitative data may come to the investigative TRS as words spoken or unspoken, gestures, actions performed, or **artifacts** of experience—the painting, letter, poem, sculpture, game play sequence, or dance memory. There are many forms of human expression and interaction that occur with recreational engagements and each is a source of information. Since qualitative analysis is developing in the recreation and leisure field mainly with data recorded as words, this chapter concentrates on understanding the meaning represented by the words. The objective is to learn what is meant by words, gestures, actions, or artifacts to the people who use them. What follows are primarily principles or examples useful in developing ways of analyzing verbal and nonverbal expression of recreation interactions. Investigative TRSs should feel free to adapt and create methods more appropriate to understanding their clientele's view of the re-creative experience, given the particulars of their setting and/or research participants.

Knowledge can be pictured as occurring to people in a variety of ways. The possibilities range from **quantitative** in character, or numerically transformed observations, to **qualitative**, or expressions of personal meaning. As noted in Chapters 2, 8, and 9, at one end of the continuum, researchers literally apply rules of logic to operationalize the transformation of sensed data into numerical codes. These numbers lead to *statistical analysis* and inferred or indirect knowledge as tests of existing theory (see Figure 13.1).

Figure 13.1
Ways of Being Informed From a Data Analysis Perspective

STATISTICAL	RATIONAL	INTUITIVE
ANALYSIS	ANALYSIS	SYNTHESIS

Knowledge also includes inducing substantive meaning from human experience data. Knowledge provides a means for generating new theory. In naturalistic inquiries, most often data are recorded as spoken words or thoughts by the research participant. In word form, data communicate information about actual qualities associated with the human experience. Rather than implement logical rules of correspondence, the naturalistic investigator intuits meaning from written transcriptions, imaging the phenomenon and receiving a synthesis or impression of meaning intended; meaning that is uniquely understood by the particular people involved. Holism, sensitivity toward the research participant, personal regard for the research participant's lifestyle, thinking from an inner perspective, and stylizing one's thoughts and writing to take the research participant's perspective in reporting outcomes would describe this region of the continuum: *intuitive synthesis.*

Somewhere in between the two poles of thought is a gray area that is represented in Figure 13.1 as **rational analysis** of subjective phenomena. Rational thought processes are useful to complement the analysis of qualitative data and bring a balance to the investigation. Breaking down data-events into smaller bits of data means creating categories that are analytically factual but not necessarily in the research participants' terms. Viewing the research participant from an outer perspective suggest that rational analysis is a way of seeing him or her in more general or objective ways.

Just as quantitative analysis is better understood when presented in light of rational explanations, so, too, is qualitative analysis better understood. Thus, the qualitative data analysis process can be thought of as one that runs the gamut back and forth between intuitive to rational or between mental acts of synthesis and analysis.

Analysis approaches and tools can be viewed as falling somewhere along this continuum. Using a recursive process, flowing between the two points in thinking style, is the objective in selecting strategies for analysis. Keeping a balance between using the more rational approaches with the more intuitive approaches is likely to add depth and scope to final understandings of the other's perspective gained from the research project.

Interacting with Qualitative Data: Finding the Other Perspective

The analysis process will seem natural to most TRSs because so much of their job involves planning and organizing TR interventions and recording, studying, and tracking information about clients. Performing data analysis or perspective-taking will call upon familiar skills and practices, too. Thinking, writing, and reading are the main skills needed to analyze qualitative data. Since the investigative TRS is seeking to learn from the data, a variety of learning possibilities can be created by choosing among different analysis methods. Depending on what one needs to learn or how one best learns, methods of interacting with the data can vary from more or less cognitive in character, to more or less participative or psychomotor, or more or less affective in nature. One general rule applies to analysis: **perspective-taking** is an ongoing process involved with data collection. Start analyzing the data right from the beginning of the study (otherwise the investigator can feel inundated by information).

In this section, general skills and processes are reviewed first. Further on, information about several data handling techniques is explained. Understanding the general concepts about perspective analysis allows the investigative TRS to adapt existing methods and invent new ones in order to better understand the problem or situation at hand.

Organizing the Data

The act of **organizing data** should be part of the process of data collection if at all possible, but don't let "should" prevent the use of perfectly good information available from the past. A great deal can be learned just by organizing the information found in previous documentation. Developing an **organized filing system** requires both a review of the question to be studied and consideration of the potential or existing data. Most important is that the investigative TRS creates a useful framework for filing and retrieving specific information elements.

Synthesis Files

Whether retained in file cabinets or in computer memory, the organization scheme must relate to the research question and one's personal style of order. Thus, for investigators who are normally intuitive in their *thinking* process, a more holistic system may be in order. Files might be organized by data collection method, date of occurrence, experience type, or a combined method.

Examples:
1. By data collection method:
    - Field Records
    - Interview Summaries
    - Media Records
    - Secondary Data

2. By date of occurrence:
    - Week of March 13 to 19
    - Week of March 20 to 25

3. By experience type:
    - Weekly Meetings
    - Group-Planned Events
    - TRS/Hospital-Planned Events
    - Independent Events/Informal Meetings

Analysis Files

If the framework is a logical breakdown which relates to *specifics* in the study questions, the way people are organized, or certain therapeutic and/or recreational functions, then the system is nearer the rational analysis part of the continuum. **Cross files** may be needed for information useful in more than one section of the organizational system. Miles and Huberman (1984) provide useful details for organizing data in this fashion.

Examples:
1. By study question:
    - What brings people back?
    - Why do some groups last longer than others?
    - How does information get around?

2. By participants' organizational structure:
    - Success Principles
    - Norms
    - Beliefs

3. By therapeutic/recreational functions:
    - Independence
    - Skill-Building
    - Ego-Development

Mental Modes for Investigating

Reading, rereading, and rereading as well as writing, rewriting, and rerewriting are the fundamental processes for analyzing qualitative data. Analysis is not difficult, but it must be given a great deal of time so the resultant findings will offer more depth of meaning than the averaged responses on a quantitative survey. The point is to discover what the clients find meaningful in the routine of everyday recreation or therapeutic recreation. Investigative TRSs are generally not concerned with isolating momentous occasions or unusual outcomes in their qualitative research.

As often as possible, the investigative TRS should review each document in the file. Some documents will be rich in information; these should be read more often. Others may provide scant information, but offer the potential to direct or deepen the study of some element of the broader findings. Reviewing these data can be done less frequently.

Reading and writing can be approached with reference to the scope of possibility for ways of becoming informed as suggested in Figure 13.1. Therefore, reading and writing activities can be approached mentally anywhere along the data analysis continuum from more analytic in process to more synthetic in process. The investigative TRS must knowingly engage in these tasks, that is, being aware of the thinking styles used.

Synthesis Approach

The approach often needed in performing qualitative data analysis is reading or writing with a *clear* mind. This reflects the **intuitive-synthesis** position, and no expectations, assumptions, or ulterior motives are included. The idea is to read or write as if it is a new experience with these data. Thinking with a freshness is the objective, implying an emotional openness to new discoveries and findings that might occur as insightful thoughts. Ideas may emerge from the data as whole concepts; thus, advancing analysis dramatically.

Analysis Approach

Another approach to reading or writing is to go in search for particular evidence in order to support (verify) or disqualify an emergent finding. This is elaborated in Chapter 14. Rational-analytic thought processes allow the investigator to analyze smaller units of data or focus on limited data to study possible links between meanings, people, or actions. Overall, it suggests a purposeful approach to interacting with the data.

Data as Units for Study

The essence of a **phenomenological research approach** is to keep whole the experience being studied. The reason is that the experience does not have the same meaning from start to finish. Meaning is created and adjusted in a client's mind as she or he interacts with the changing situation brought about by others, the things they are doing, or other situational effects. Selecting only part of the experience unit has the potential to produce erroneous interpretations.

Natural Experience Units

Typically, the journalistic diary developed from field notes contains a complete sequence of data for the given date and is written within a matter of hours following the experience. The act of writing one's field notes into a journal or record should be an intuitive flow process where notes and memories come together to produce a detailed record. In this first writing, perceptions often become clearer and ideas spring to mind, all of which can be jotted down as an identifiable part of the record. Keeping the data together in natural experience units creates opportunity for intuition to work. The idea is to create records of clients' TR interventions that permit review of experiences from natural start to a natural end. Allowing the meanings and intents of research participants to remain intact, even if hidden, increases the possibility of the investigative TRS tuning in to underlying information.

Rational Data Units

Large chunks of data often need to be subdivided into smaller chunks for rational analysis. Furthermore, when rewriting or rethinking later in the investigation, small data units may be regrouped and broken down in new ways to see if other information has been overlooked. The investigative TRS is challenged to arrive at a compromise whereby the integrity of the experience is not violated, yet the data-unit being reviewed is of a size that the investigator can think about in detail (see unitizing, Lincoln and Guba, 1985). For this reason, the investigative TRS may want to break the research participant's experience down into smaller chunks which have an integrity of their own.

Examples of rational data chunks (small chunks) useful in studying an art room program could include the start-up or warm-up part of the program, the working part, reintegration phase, and departure from the program area. In this way, separate elements are formed which permit independent analysis and comparison across time, as well as comparison to other elements within the same meeting time/date. Some naturalistic researchers break data down into very small independent units like conversations or lines of related activity. The danger in this is that original meaning is not necessarily inherent in rational views of the data. If the TRS is to understand what the research participant understands, then the TRS needs to view the experience in its related situational context. Rarely does the start and end of a conversation mark the start and end of an interactive experience.

In the study of auctions (Glancy, 1988), initial analysis chunks related to the auction as a process event: previewing of goods, early arrival, warm-up phase and sale of goods, contested goods, and clean-up sales. Another analysis (Glancy, 1990) uses units that involve roles (novice, regular attender, and audience). Studying a softball group (Glancy, 1986) grew from studying each evening or day's events as a whole to studying the pre-game interactions, on-field warm-up, game, postgame departure, and postgame social. Unexplored chunks relate to the developmental time as another way of understanding significance, such as the stage in the softball season: early season stage, mid-season tourney stage, and final competition stage. It is important to remember that *data units will only be useful to research if the research participants themselves think about their experience in this same framework*. In the TR environment, evolution of the therapeutic process provides a natural timing mechanism, though it may or may not affect the cultural meanings subjectively experienced by clientele. Trying out various rational data unit concepts is part of the data manipulation process engaged in by naturalistic investigators. The purpose is to see which, if any, may reveal or affirm information about meanings and themes.

Writing Tools

A number of common forms have emerged to record and analyze data. These range from recording a mental train of thought to information assessment inventories. Keeping in mind the objective of balancing the data analysis process by selecting methods which range from analytical to synthetic will help in making decisions about how to document and write about the research participant's experience.

Intuitive Tools

Naturalistic researchers use a number of intuitive writing techniques to analyze qualitative data. Bruyn (1966) says record the experience, being sure to include the time, place, social circumstances, language, intimacy, psychological barriers and openings, as well as, consensus experienced.

Journal narration, notations, and weekly summaries are the main activities with which to begin the analysis process. Most important is the point that writing is used as a way of mentally reflecting about events and recording intuited meaning. The investigative TRS is not thinking in a logically rational frame of mind, rather one that is emotionally in tune with the experiences being reviewed, mentally experiencing the data as if he or she were the individual with disability. The following journal record provides an example of the investigator-as-experiencing research participant.

> ... It was a Tuesday morning and, as usual, student interns had arrived to provide a recreation program for residents in the geriatric unit. I was observing two of the students who had been particularly smug about their preparations. They had worked long hours to prepare and had let it be known that this would be a really special event ... Two students, Barb and Rick, finished their explanations about the Italian luncheon party which everyone was going to be able to help construct and enjoy this morning. Today, the women would be able to do the food preparation, and the men would be needed to do the room setup and decoration. The 22 women and 15 men had been assembled together in the women's day room for the meeting. I watched for their reactions to surface and waited, feeling a knot of programmer anxiety tighten in my stomach. It was as if nothing had been said. The effervescent student interns glanced at each other, showing their fractured poise by the facial expressions they shared with each other. Each may have hoped the other was prepared to save the situation, but it was obvious that neither had a quick answer. It was their program; their problem; their opportunity to learn, I kept telling myself, but I still couldn't separate myself from the building feeling of dread that was hypnotizing me.
>
> When Barb and Rick looked back at their audience, nothing had changed. Most stood or sat where they had been placed with customary placid looks on their faces. A few, mostly men, shifted their weight back and forth and seemed to be occupying the silence by scratching their heads or looking around in unfocused ways as if to get a clue about how to react. Two nurses and four aides were lined up on the sidelines, arms folded across their chests, smiling. No one spoke; maybe no one was able to react.
>
> Without warning, Barb just started giving orders loudly and to everyone. The trance-like atmosphere began to melt. It was a slow motion study in silence at first. Women and men began looking into each other's eyes, then moving in directionless fashions. The staff burst to life; they had ideas about what to do. They began ushering the withdrawn people. Barb and Rick grabbed at the most able residents and helped them start on things that could be done without much supervision. Gradually, the hall filled—with motion first, then with noise: words, conversation, banging of chairs and bowls, and finally laughter, real laughter. I

even heard Evo, one of the male residents, giving directions loudly to some of the men who were not arranging things the way he decided they should be. An aide stared in wonder at what he was doing . . .

If an idea occurs while writing, follow the mental track it opened—write it down. This is the *discovery possibility* that reflective writing, especially summaries, is intended to offer. Weekly summaries and summaries about individuals, process elements, and experience elements suggest a wide variety of options. Even when involved in other operations, an idea may pop into the investigator's mind; this should immediately be noted on a piece of paper and filed so it can be further developed. Next are examples of experience topics that retain the holistic concept.

Examples:

Summary for Week of April 10-16
Summary of Potter's Wheel Building Project
Summary of L. Johnson as Radio Club Member
Summary of Winter, 1992, for Residents in Unit 4-A

Analytical Tools

Other types of writing are seeming more objective. They are logical, analytical, less personalized, and brief in nature. This approach may use existing narrative data in a rational way, or original data recording can be carried out in a more objective format.

Recording where people sit and with whom they interact can prove interesting over time. Forms can be developed to assess different situations objectively and uniformly or to synthesize information from meetings for quick study and comparison (Miles & Huberman, 1984). Analytic memos (Miles & Huberman, 1984) and abbreviated topical summaries are useful ways to focus on limited pieces of data. Standardized questions may be used in a number of ways: informal interviews; recording information about the site(s); reviewing progress or change; or comparing objects, situations, or personalities. For example, when interviewing members of a puppeteer club diagnosed as emotionally disturbed, the standard question regarding which puppet a client felt like working with that day, was not just a therapeutic technique; it was a way of collecting information to study and compare individuals over time. When interviewing softball group members in other social situations, care was taken to repeat several questions. (I didn't expect to see you here, why are you here today? Do others from the group come here? How do you think things are going with the team?)

Marginal Organization

Miles and Huberman (1984) have written about ways to organize and present data. They suggest using the left margins for coding key elements, a rational way of simplifying analysis. This habit is common for many people. The concerns in this work are: to be systematic and thorough; keep master lists of exactly what the code labels mean; and be able to delete the unproductive codes and add new codes as the analysis takes shape. The right margins can be used for recording key themes or patterns as they occur in the mind during reading or writing; this is space and opportunity for the intuitive thought to be jotted down before it is lost.

Turning Thoughts into Displays

The analysis process is interactive; that is, the investigative TRS mentally interacts with the data to understand the meaning or culture being studied, and being able to manipulate the data is important to expose different facets of information. Much like the way people may handle the pebble found on a beach, investigative TRSs need to find ways to rotate this data around in their minds to see what other information it has to offer. Generally, one way to accomplish this is to create some kind of **data display**. Displays may look like matrix figures, tabled arrays, pictures, rambling diagrams, or graphic representations like maps and relational charts. There is no standard format; the purpose is to assist the researcher in learning more about the data. The display communicates information in another way.

In searching for the appropriate display format, the naturalistic researcher interacts with the data, trying to understand its potential significance and meaning. At later stages in the study, the intent may be to work findings together with other concepts from the study or from comparative studies or theory. The process of constructing a display and formatting data to correspond to its structure is a mental exercise which takes place on two or more visual dimensions. Building the display has the effect of physically experiencing the data for some researchers, like a sculptor letting the clay express itself in his or her hands. Constructing relational concepts visually is a way to learn more about what is going on in the research participants' experience. Examination of the display can continue to add insights to the interpretive process.

What drives an investigative TRS to create a display may be anything from having a hunch about something, to finding similar fragments of data for a number of participants or situations, or simply feeling at a dead end. Whatever the motive, data need to be viewed in a new light. Sometimes the format can be constructed from the outside in; that is, the structure and concept labels of a matrix are the first to be drawn. This is a rational approach to analysis. Data are filled into the open spaces in the matrix. Wherever possible, refinement of the structure continues as application of data suggests. Other times, the investigative TRS will start toying with data, perhaps as puzzling pieces, or perhaps just things that stand out. From these bits and visual review, a useful structure may emerge allowing additional data to be added. These intuitive displays often begin as clusters of meaning and take the form of pictures (flowers, stick figures, etc.) or free-form diagrams which grow as if with a life of their own to subsume ideas that need to be expressed.

Inducing Meanings and Themes from the Data

Discovering the meaning in the subjective experience is at the heart of analysis process. To find the meaning carries with it the idea that the investigative TRS will have a firsthand experience, repeatedly, with the data. In other words, without directly interacting with the data in a number of ways there is little chance that the TRS will learn anything about the client's perspective. Several specific procedures for interacting with subjective data are described to show the range of mental approaches possible in data analysis.

Intuitive Approaches

Examples of analysis procedures presented in this section follow the precept that the more the analysis process retains the whole form, enlists the language of the research participant, and reflects the research participant's experiential context, the more the data conform to intuitive mental process. These approaches are overlooked by many investigators because they appear simplistic or simply natural. This is precisely why they are so effective. Naturalistic researchers use ways of thinking and writing that are common, but they do so with the intent of digging as deeply into the real world of the research participant as possible by accurately illuminating the detail and importance of the experience.

Concrete Description

Making an idea, or understanding concrete turns it into convincing fact. Bruyn (1966, p. 29) explains **concretizing** as a combination of two descriptive goals. One goal is to carefully explain the experiences which lead to the investigator's understanding. The second goal is to provide details on how the meaning is shared by the subjects being studied. Investigative TRSs use a variety of techniques to communicate accurately. Analogy is probably the most popular way to illustrate the intended meaning. Another technique is negation, to write about what is not meant. Comparison to rituals such as washing, eating, or reading the newspaper; or the trauma of the first day of school; or any other experience that may strike a similar chord for readers, helps communicate. It is this process of concretizing that earns qualitative research the reputation for providing **thick** or **rich description**. Without it, findings are not substantial and not trustworthy.

Constant Comment

Listening and looking for repetitious words, phrases, or physical actions is one technique for isolating symbolic language. It seems that people speak the phrase or question, using words as a form of shorthand language, to convey an idea that has a deeper meaning to them. To the uninformed, the deeper meaning is not apparent, and their ignorance communicates their outsider status to those who are in the know. To the insiders, the constant comment can imply more than its universal meaning offers. Finding a constant comment, then studying the interaction and situation surrounding it, can lead to finding hidden meaning and key themes. One example of this was hearing the question: "What did you come for?" when studying the auction experience.

That question was heard by the investigator a number of times before its significance was intuitively grasped. Until it was understood, the investigator felt socially rebuffed as if a wrong answer had been given and was not privy to the central organizing concept underlying auction participation in small mid-western towns. Indeed, a wrong answer had been given; it was not an object for sale but a personally valued role that regular attenders expected to hear about. The question was heard repeatedly in an evening's conversation, and it took a number of months to realize the meaning underlying it.

Rational Approaches

One data analysis technique has gained recognition by numerous researchers in the field of recreation and leisure studies; that is the **constant comparison** method. As previous sections indicate, investigators are encouraged to develop their own useful systems for analyzing data, but none has yet gained the general acceptance that this particular one has achieved. Whenever a rational approach is used or adapted for use, the naturalistic investigator needs to be mindful of the guideline for reducing data units from naturally occurring whole units, into parts of those wholes, thus maintaining subjective integrity.

Constant Comparison

Analytic in nature, the constant comparison technique is attributed to Glaser and Strauss (1967). To prepare for this process, the investigative TRS breaks data down into the smallest chunks possible without rendering them meaningless. The data-bits may be whole statements, the interchange of several remarks between people, or action segments. Each data-bit is written on its own index card. After a large number of data-bits are acquired, the investigative TRS sorts the data into groups by reading each card and comparing it to the ideas represented on other cards. Each group of cards forms a concept or category of meaning that is different from the others in some way. It is common for some categories to be related and others to appear quite independent.

Waiting until all the data have been collected means this will be a tedious process, perhaps impossible in some cases. However, it is a useful way to examine data when the study is under way, searching for ideas or themes that may have been missed if analysis has been limited to intuitive approaches. The constant comparison technique forces the investigator to think about the data in a different way—a rational way. Until the themes uncovered by this method are made concrete by a coherent and cohesive narration grounded in the reality of the subjective experience, the subjective perspective is only vaguely known. So, constant comparison is best seen as one of several data analysis steps. For further information about constant comparison, see Lincoln and Guba (1985) for description and Howe (1990) for use in evaluating a community reintegration program.

Pattern Theories

All social research is concerned in some way with the idea that people tend to think and act in patterns. Naturalistic research allows the TRS to discover patterns which lead to uncovering the significance in the everyday experience of clients. Two views of how the naturalistic investigator should respond to the urge to typify are introduced in the following section.

In general, analysis of qualitative data involves taking the subjective perspective to understand and convey meaning authentically. It is up to the TRS to consider the implications created by adopting an outsider perspective when using subjective data to construct typologies. With practice and self-scrutiny, it is suggested that both approaches discussed below can enhance the outcome potential from any investigation. It is suggested that **constructed typologies** may be more appropriate for secondary analysis of data and generalization to other settings and situations; whereas, discovery of **indigenous typologies** are appropriate to authentic, in-depth knowledge of the subjective experience at hand.

Constructed Typologies

In the process of trying to understand the culture of the research participants being studied, naturalistic researchers quite often find themselves typifying people in some way—by their roles, their relationships, or some other complex pattern that has been uncovered. Situations, practices, and institutions are examples of other sorts of typologies. Patton (1987) explains that the constructed typology is a way "to look for patterns, categories, and themes that appear to exist but that are not a part of the participants' vocabulary" (p. 152). Lincoln and Guba (1985) and Bruyn (1966) are clear on the point that constructing typologies can lead the investigative TRS away from the real meaning or events transpiring. When typologies are constructed they impose the investigator's interpretation of data aggregated together and seldom do these represent reality to the subject.

As TRSs, it could seem natural to typify clients by disabilities, abilities, or by some other common attribute related to recovery or treatment. Using data to analyze the subjective experience, as if the clients thought of themselves as "Monday-Wednesday-Friday Bowlers" when they actually are not, could be misleading and result in false interpretations. If typologies are constructed in the analysis process, the investigative TRS should be careful to explain the limitations inherent in the findings and should use the ideas judiciously, perhaps as a way of unmasking or clarifying the *authentic* experience or generalizing and comparing to other studies.

Indigenous Typology/Folk Theory

To uncover the **themes** which research participants create to define themselves or to bring meaning to their activities requires the investigator to become familiar with the folk theories that operate in the situation. Gaining insight is gradual, starting with puzzles in the written record or constant comments and follow-up questions about what is meant (see also Patton, 1985). The learning process progresses as the investigative TRS becomes more and more intimate with the situation, the research participants, and the data (Glancy, in press). Holland (1985) describes four folk theory forms.[1]
- trait-driven—personal traits cause behavior
- emotion-driven—feelings cause behavior
- pathology-driven—some kind of sickness behavior
- goal-driven—ulterior motive causes behavior

---

1. See Glancy, M. (in press). Achieving intersubjectivity: The process of becoming the subject in leisure research. *Leisure Studies*, for an example of folk theories in use by auction players who attended the same weekly auction.

Clients are likely to think about themselves in terms that relate to an identity socially formed and understood by others who are important within the treatment setting and/or with whom they share a relationship. Referring to one's self as one of the "Clowns," the "Poker Gang," or "Cat's Brats" or even the reference "I'm your four o'clock appointment" suggest the way people learn to think about themselves. These examples could reflect self- or social-definition that results from what Holland labelled as trait-driven or pathology-driven folk theory.

The two approaches to typification were unexpectedly contrasted in the residential unit for older adults situation partially described earlier in this chapter. The staff observers adopted the outsider's view and created their own interpretation of the behavior they were watching. The student interns, on the other hand, took the subjective perspective, and adopted the interpretation used by the residents to describe themselves. Which was more appropriate?

In observing the geriatric residents at their luncheon, what appeared to be intoxicated behavior developed following the grape juice refreshment. How did the residents explain their behavior? To the interns, the residents gave sly smiles and whispered 'We're just having a high old time.' They talked about feeling released, free to let loose, and admitted knowing it was only grape juice. The staff, on the other hand, typified them as being so out of touch with reality that they didn't know the difference between grape juice and wine; they spoke of the residents as having 'no sense.' The interns reasoned that the party behavior was emotion-driven because that was how the residents explained it. The staff were of a different opinion, one that did not consider the subjective perspective.

Linking and Comparing

Construction of links between meanings and themes occurs later in the research project. At this point the investigative TRS is certain of some findings and has ideas about others. The test of worthiness of these findings is whether joined pieces can be found in other contexts. Showing such comparisons is an indication that findings are not limited strictly to the subject at hand, but that there is a more general cultural theme occurring. One asks, do the meanings and themes that link together in the Art Room or in the Geriatric Unit reflect comparable values, beliefs, norms, or customs in other life situations which the TRS knows, has read about, or studied? If comparisons can be made to other groups, times, situations, then the linkages being made in the study at hand are more likely to be true and more likely to reflect generalizable concepts. For example, the Geriatric Unit findings could be compared to Goffman's (1961) experience in a mental institution where he found residents had developed an elaborate informal social system that was meaningless to the staff. Describing the picture so the comparison is clear not only helps the investigative TRS feel more sure about the findings, but it also add great depth to the analysis so readers will grasp the concepts at play.

Rebuilding the Web—The Culture of Experience

The ultimate objective is to create a picture which makes an explanatory whole that is sensible, holds up in review by informants and other research participants, and links together the important elements found in the investigative process. Like displays, creating the web is a physical experience for many naturalistic researchers: they manipulate concepts and processes as labelled slips of paper and strings on the tabletop. This can also be a profoundly intuitive process, bringing together one's sense of knowing with one's sense of being there, feeling it as if it is real.

It is not until the culture has been reconstructed satisfactorily, that the naturalistic researcher is aware of the important essence of the study. Framing this picture are the theories of why and how; these are theories grounded in the subjective perspective. While previous summaries and oral reports have uncovered valuable information, compared to what is learned in this final stage of analysis, those earlier findings will generally be of comparatively less importance. Once the web has been sketched out, the major writing task follows. This is the comprehensive analysis in answer to the research question. It is a necessary step for the investigative TRS to synthesize thinking and to integrate the experience of the research participant into a comprehensible whole. This report usually goes into the files as a reference for shorter and more focused reports that are written later for other purposes.

Reanalysis of Findings

Having a volume of information and numerous focused and broad analyses available means that the investigative TRS has a continued opportunity to write and to learn from this study. Revisiting data often brings new insights. It is as if TRSs are blind to other possibilities until they have matured with their earlier findings. Be willing to follow new ideas as they occur. Since qualitative research analysis demands an intimate relationship between the researcher and the subjective data, changed thinking will occur and invite the investigative TRS on a continuing road of personal discovery and professional growth (Glancy, in press).

Ethics and Qualitative Data Analysis

Ethical considerations are not limited to the data collection or information dissemination phases of naturalistic inquiry as popularly discussed; they infuse the whole process. In reading this chapter, the investigative TRS should have a sense that authenticity, accuracy, and a personal motive to honor the truth in the client's perspective surrounds the qualitative data analysis process.

There are several ways to act which can be considered ethical when analyzing qualitative data. The most obvious is to use real data. Ensuring authenticity is important, so seeking informed verification by informally testing ideas with research participants is suggested, and allowing clients to read or hear the TRS's analysis is also appropriate. Both of these should be done after considering the possible impact of sharing research findings with clients in treatment. As long as the research purpose is altruistic, for improving professional services, clients whose psychological conditions permit are likely to be pleased to be of assistance to the TRS. Furthermore, they are apt to be impressed when the TRS's findings accurately reflect the client's perspective.

Protecting participant anonymity is more difficult with qualitative data analysis because so much information is created about the client(s) involved. Anyone tampering with the files can guess who the research participant is in most cases. Using fictitious names and keeping files locked and out of areas frequented by persons who should not have access to such data are logical precautions, though some researchers need reminders not to be too trusting.

The most important attitude to bring to the data analysis process is a willingness to question one's self; that is, to doubt one's intuition or finding. Reanalysis, discussion with appropriate others, collecting data and reviewing findings to the point of redundancy, and making searching comparisons to other situations and studies all contribute to the attitude that one undertakes this research with good intention and makes efforts to achieve the authenticity and accuracy expected.

Ethics also have to do with having courage. Perhaps engaging in qualitative data analysis as a different way of obtaining knowledge will threaten other personnel or colleagues. In this case, acting with courage may be the most ethical thing the TRS can do for the well-being of clients who are subjected to a treatment intervention system which too often is limited to the outsider perspective, relies on precision measurement, and creates inferred knowledge. Changing to analysis methods anchored in accuracy made possible by taking the subjective perspective is a way of acting with courage.

Discussion Questions

1. During a treatment plan meeting, staff training lecture, or recreation therapy session, mentally be aware of all that is going on. Jot down only a few field notes. Later, reconstruct the experience with as much detail (concrete description) as possible. When finished, reflect on the actual experience and your narrative of that experience. Have you captured the essence of the experience, making it seem real, or have you reported fact unaccompanied by the human experience perspective?

2. Describe your shoes or the top of your desk, using only analogies and negation. Give this to someone to read. Have you identified the essential meanings and themes properly from their perspective?

3. Write a letter to your best friend and tell that friend all about one of your clients (without name or jeopardizing confidentiality). Do not mail the letter. Instead, use a combination of rational and intuitive means to analyze the significant meanings and themes in the letter. Perhaps you will learn something about your client or yourself while practicing data analysis.

4. Discuss how a TRS or other professional can maintain a professional perspective while gaining intimate insight into a client's way of thinking. How can qualitative research be ethical in this regard?

5. If you have minutes from a meeting (or some other narrative document) that are fairly descriptive or complete, try analyzing them using an intuitive mode, then a rational mode. See what differences and similarities occur.

References

Bruyn, S. (1966). *The human perspective in sociology: The methodology of participant observation*. Englewood Cliffs, NJ: Prentice-Hall.

Glancy, M. (1986). Participant observation in the recreation setting. *Journal of Leisure Research, 18*(2), 59-80.

Glancy, M. (1988). The play-world setting of the auction. *Journal of Leisure Research. 20*(2), 135-153.

Glancy, M. (1990). Socially organized role-taking: Becoming an auction player. *Leisure Sciences, 12*(4), 349-366.

Glancy, M. (In press). Achieving intersubjectivity: The process of becoming the subject in leisure research. *Leisure Studies.*

Glaser, B. G., & Strauss, A. L. (1967). *The discovery of grounded theory: Strategies for qualitative research*. Hawthorne, New York, NY: Aldine.

Goffman, E. (1961). *Asylums*. Garden City, NY: Doubleday Book Club.

Holland, D. C. (1985). From situation to impression: How Americans get to know themselves and one another. In J. W. D. Dougherty (Ed.), *Directions in cognitive anthropology* (pp. 389-411). Urbana, IL: University of Illinois Press.

Howe, C. Z. (1990, May). *Phenomenology, naturalistic inquiry, and the analysis of qualitative data: An example from the evaluation of a community reintegration program*. Paper presented at the Sixth Canadian Congress on Leisure Research, University of Waterloo, Waterloo, Ontario, Canada.

Lincoln, Y. S., & Guba, E. G. (1985). *Naturalistic inquiry*. Beverly Hills, CA: Sage.

Miles, M. B., & Huberman, A. M. (1984). *Qualitative data analysis: A sourcebook of new methods*. Beverly Hills, CA: Sage.

Patton, M. Q. (1987). *How to use qualitative methods in evaluation*. Beverly Hills, CA: Sage.

Confirming, Interpreting and Reporting Naturalistic Research Findings
Norma J. Stumbo and Sandra L. Little

Confirmation is the process of verifying the accuracy or quality of the information obtained through data collection. **Interpretation** comes from examination of the data and brings meaning and insight to the behaviors and words of the individuals under study. The results of interpretation are then brought to intended audiences through a written and/or verbal report (Marshall & Rossman, 1989). The processes used to conduct these research functions differ between positivistic and naturalistic approaches, yet share the same basic mission of contributing to science through an enhanced understanding of the world and its players.

As first noted in Chapter 2, in studies using quantitative methods and a positivistic approach, it is possible to treat data collection, data analysis, and conclusions about the data as discrete, yet related, parts of the research process. In addition to being discrete, the relationship of these parts can be viewed as linear in nature. Data are first collected, then analyzed. Conclusions are then drawn and a report is written or given. The process is ideally completed one step after another.

Under the naturalistic paradigm, as indicated in Chapters 12 and 13, the researcher often uses qualitative methods and *is* the instrument for data collection. In naturalistic inquiry, the sense of discreteness among collection, analysis, and drawing conclusions is neither as segmented nor as linear. Rather than being linear, the inquiry processes for naturalistic studies are more cyclical in nature. Often the confirmation (or the verification of the data's accuracy or consistency) is intertwined with the interpretation of the meaning of the data. In this way, both functions take on formative and summative properties, occurring throughout the entire process. Miles and Huberman (1984) state that data analysis is a continuous, reiterative process involving movement back and forth between a number of elements including data collecting, reducing, displaying, reducing, drawing conclusions (interpreting), and reducing. Accuracy of interpretation depends upon the process preceding it—the research design, methods used, research participants, data collection, and the analysis process itself. Marshall and Rossman (1989) indicate that interpretation, along with data reduction, is a *part* of the data analysis process, not a separate function. Instead, interpretation can lead the researchers back into data collection for more information or at least point to further areas in which more analysis may need to occur. Just as there may be no clear point at which data collection ends and data analysis begins, there may be no clear separation of data interpretation from analysis (Patton, 1990).

This cyclical, reiterative process is necessary due to the general purpose of naturalistic inquiry—that of understanding people's behavior in their natural environments. So while debate continues about the strengths and weaknesses of using qualitative methods, as stated previously, they become appropriate when the purpose of the research dictates that they be used. Due to the settings in which it occurs and the individuals it involves, therapeutic recreation research may be in a position to more closely align with naturalistic approaches and qualitative methods.

The intent of this chapter is to provide information about the confirmation, interpretation, and reporting processes used in naturalistic research. Research conducted in a women's prison is used to illustrate the major points.

Application in TR Settings: Prison as a Case Study

The naturalistic perspective for research in TR settings can yield useful and meaningful information. A three-year study conducted in a women's prison is used in this chapter to illustrate how confirmation, interpretation, and reporting occur within a naturalistic inquiry. The project was part of a federal grant introducing overnight visitation in the form of a summer camping program for women who were incarcerated, and their children (Stumbo & Little, 1990). The intent of the program was to provide an opportunity for families, who had been separated since the time of the mother's incarceration, to be reunited using an overnight camping format. Children were brought to the prison grounds by family, friends, or social agencies, and remained for a 24 (first year) or 48 (second and third years) hour period with their mothers.

The purpose of this comprehensive field-based study was to observe and document human action concerning the camping program to determine its role, if any, with regard to mother-child interpersonal relationships and bonding processes. Two basic research strategies were used. One was positivistic in nature, suggesting a cause-and-effect relationship, using quasi-experimental design. Treatment and nontreatment groups were not randomly assigned. The second was based on naturalistic inquiry, and relied on qualitative data in the form of field notes, written records, and pictures/videos.

The first research strategy measured the possible impact of the camping program using structured personal interviews of both camping and noncamping mothers. The interview formats were based upon various knowledge, attitude, and perception scales and included other closed-ended questions. The interviews were conducted both pre- and postcamp. In addition, precamp written questionnaires were administered to prison administrators/staff and correctional officers in the first year. The majority of the data from both inmates and staff were quantitative and subjected to various descriptive and inferential statistical techniques (e.g., measures of central tendency, t-tests). The in-depth interviews with mothers did include some open-ended questions which allowed the interviewees to explain and expand upon the closed-ended items. All of the instruments were administered on the prison grounds in the "natural" environment of the research participants. Discussion of the quantitative data is limited to the extent that it confirmed or disconfirmed the naturalistic strategies of participant observation, focus groups, and review of written documents.

The second major research strategy used qualitative methods to document: (a) participant observation of the camping weekends, staff meetings, and orientations for mothers; (b) focus group interviews with mothers and camping staff; and (c) individual mothers' and staff's observations of the program. In addition, pictures and videotapes of the weekend experiences were taken by camping staff and inmates for post-camp review purposes. Videotapes were also used as part of the camping program and were shown to participants just before children left the grounds to go back to their caretakers.

Interviews with, and diaries by, the children were found to be intrusive to the camp environment when used in the first two years of the program. They were discontinued in the third year. Data concerning the children's experiences were documented through the observers' field notes, mothers' diaries, and videotapes.

Using criteria from Kidder (1981), naturalistic inquiry in this study meant observing and recording the behaviors of staff, administrators, and campers as they ordinarily and spontaneously occurred as part of the camp planning, implementation, and evaluation process. There were no interventions or treatments specifically designed within the camping program to "cause" bonding to take place between mother and child.

Rather, a typical program of camping activities, which could be found in many family camping settings outside the prison, was presented. The camp provided a "real life" situation for study in which natural behaviors occurred in a natural setting. A camp could be considered somewhat contrived inside a prison, and prisons themselves are contrived by governmental agencies and regulations. But, camps and prisons are both part of the human experience and condition, and, in this case, were part of the research participants' "reality."

Ethical Considerations

At the camp site, the researchers were introduced to the mothers and children as camp historians, whose purpose was to document how the camp functioned. A majority of the mothers had already met the research team as part of the precamp in-depth interviews and had been informed about the project. The pre/postcamp interviews were voluntary, and confidentiality and anonymity were ensured by the researchers.

The data were reported as group results or as anonymous quotations. All data were, and are, in the sole possession of the investigators. Permission had to be obtained from the mothers, children, and caretakers to participate in the camping program and to take pictures. Prior to release of photographs, permission was needed from mothers and prison officials. Chapter 6 provides further information on confidentiality and privacy as ethical issues in therapeutic recreation research.

In some instances, the researchers served as assistants for meal preparation, limited child care, transportation, and program implementation. These roles helped the research staff to integrate more fully into the operation and functioning of the camp and allowed fluidity between observer and participant roles.

Importance of Establishing Validity and Reliability in Naturalistic Research

Validity and reliability refer to the representativeness and consistency of the research data and results. In all research styles, the "scientist" is held accountable for systematic procedures and the degree of objectivity employed. With positivistic approaches, this is often measured by using statistical procedures; the often asked question is that of statistical significance. Using a correlational study as an example, one would report the coefficient, its statistical significance, and, if statistical significance was found, be able to generalize these findings to other similar sample groups. The matter is relatively simple because fairly concrete and well-known guidelines exist to aid the positivist researcher in determining the validity and reliability of the findings (Miles, 1983).

In naturalistic approaches, the use of statistics is often inappropriate because of the heavy reliance on words, descriptions, and meanings. However, the concepts of validity, reliability, and objectivity still apply. While the procedures for doing so may differ, validity and reliability in naturalistic studies also mean the ability to verify the consistency, accuracy, and generalizability of the information obtained from the research participants. This confirmation or verification process is what renders the results (of both positivistic and naturalistic research) credible (Miles, 1983; Patton, 1987).

In any research, external validity, internal validity and reliability are of major concern to the credibility of the research findings. **External validity** (or generalizability of the findings to other similar sample groups) is an area where naturalistic researchers are especially criticized. However, Yin (1984) notes that frequently those who criticize naturalistic inquiry's lack of external validity are comparing it to survey research designs whose criteria for external validity depend on statistical generalizations, as explained in Chapter 9. Studies relying on observation and description have a different set of criteria. They depend on **analytical generalizations**; that is, those in which the researcher strives to generalize a particular set of results to a broader theory (Patton, 1990).

Several authors have suggested ways to increase transferability of findings from one site to another, including triangulation (Marshall & Rossman, 1989), using both quantitative and qualitative methods (Jick, 1983), providing "thick descriptions" (Guba & Lincoln, 1989; Patton, 1990), and replicating studies to corroborate findings (Brewer & Hunter, 1989). The fact that naturalistic inquiry examines ordinary behavior rather than contrived behavior also helps researchers to naturalistically generalize the results outside the immediate research context (Kidder, 1981).

Internal validity is concerned with the match between the findings and reality. In the case of positivism, this means a match between the results and what is known about the sample. In naturalistic research, it means the match between the participants' words, behaviors, and feelings to those which the researcher attributes to them (Guba & Lincoln, 1989). Several techniques to increase the internal validity of studies using qualitative methods are reviewed in the remainder of this chapter.

Reliability is the degree to which the research results are consistent or accurate (Gronlund, 1981; Thorndike & Hagen, 1977). Quantitative methods research often uses correlations, such as Spearman-Brown, or Pearson's Product-Moment, to determine the reliability of the results. Again, since qualitative methods do not necessarily produce numbers, these are often not appropriate. The one exception to this is inter-rater or inter-observer reliability, which calculates the amount of agreement between two observers (Anastasi, 1968). For example, inter-rater reliability checks could be performed between two observers to determine whether they agreed on the frequency of certain camper behaviors, such as smiling, hugging, and initiating conversations. In other cases, where the concern is whether the data are stable over time, the **dependability** that behavior is being recorded the same way every time is important. While qualitative methods allow fluidity of changing focuses, inaccurate recording of similar behaviors over a specified time period would be problematic (Guba & Lincoln, 1989). Techniques to increase reliability and dependability are also discussed in the remainder of this chapter.

While being criticized for the lack of scientific rigor, investigators who use qualitative methods understand and attempt to address issues of validity, reliability, and objectivity. Although there is not total consensus in the field, several recent texts are beginning to develop a variety of methods and techniques to tackle these issues (cf. Guba & Lincoln, 1989; Marshall & Rossman, 1989; Miles & Huberman, 1984; Patton, 1987; 1990; Van Maanen, 1983). It will be through these efforts that qualitative methods and those who choose to use them will more clearly address the rigors of "science" and become more credible. It also should be noted that several authors advocate the simultaneous and complementary use of both quantitative and qualitative styles (Brewer & Hunter, 1989; Jick, 1983, 1987; Yin, 1984), and propose a continuum of methods (Patton, 1990).

Establishing Credibility in the Reduction, Confirmation, and Interpretation Process

Patton (1990) indicates that naturalistic studies depend on three elements for establishing **credibility** of the research process and results. These elements include:
1. rigorous techniques and methods for gathering high-quality data that are carefully analyzed, with attention to issues of validity, reliability and triangulation;
2. the credibility of the researcher, which depends on training; and
3. the philosophical belief in the phenomenological paradigm; that is, a fundamental appreciation of naturalistic inquiry, qualitative methods, inductive analysis, and holistic thinking. (p. 461)

These three elements of credibility point to the fact that naturalistic inquiry and positivistic research are equal in their demand for rigor. It is simply that the demands are different, and therefore may be more unfamiliar to the majority of researchers. Because of the limitations imposed within a book chapter, the major focus is placed on the first element of techniques and methods of naturalistic inquiry. The reader is referred to Guba and Lincoln (1989), Miles and Huberman (1984), and Patton (1990) as examples of texts that fully discuss the other issues in naturalistic research.

Methods and Techniques Used for Confirming and Interpreting Qualitative Data

A variety of methods and techniques have been suggested by Miles and Huberman (1984) and Patton (1990) to interpret and confirm the accuracy and quality of the data as they are analyzed and eventually reported. The reiterative interpretation and confirmation process is important because it is at this point where meaning and significance of the data are explained and verified. That is, the viability of the data is tested through offering alternative explanations, making inferences, building linkages, attaching meanings, imposing order, disconfirming ideas, drawing conclusions, and examining data irregularities. The responsibility of the researcher is to ensure the credibility and accuracy of the results through the continual process of description, interpretation, and confirmation. When these are subjected to systematic procedures, more confidence can be placed in the results.

Using the prison case study for illustration, some of the interpretation and confirmation techniques/methods suggested by Miles and Huberman (1984) and Patton (1990) are presented: (a) sampling and issues of representativeness; (b) triangulating; (c) seeking rival explanations and weighting the evidence; (d) searching for negative cases; and (e) getting feedback from informants. Included with the illustrations are highlights of problems encountered that threaten validity and reliability, and the actions that can be taken to counter those threats.

Sampling and Issues of Representativeness

According to Patton (1990) and Miles and Huberman (1984), sampling strategies or the time period in which the study was conducted are possible sources of distortion or inaccuracy. Decisions made during the research design and data collection phases can result in three types of sampling errors. The first involves the decision as to which *situations* to sample for observation. In the case of the women's prison study, error may have been introduced by sampling more heavily from the camp environment than the rest of the prison. It is quite likely that behavior observed at camp may have been very different than other areas within the prison. A tendency exists to draw inferences from what was observed and generalize these findings to other areas that were not observed. To overcome this tendency, one method to increase the validity of observations is to collect data from a variety of sources in a variety of environments.

The second kind of error results from the *timing* of the observations or the events that were observed; that is, the women's behavior may have differed during certain times of the day, days of the week, or weeks within the year. Observations during the prison study were limited to five hours on

Fridays and Sundays, and ten hours on Saturdays for approximately three months out of the year. Also, they were supplemented by informal observations during the approximate six weeks of pre- and postcamp interviewing. Obviously, other situations or events occurred that were not observed. Again, the tendency is to generalize these observations to periods that were not studied. While the duration and length of the observations helped alleviate this potential problem, observations during other times may have helped to increase the dependability of the results.

The third kind of sampling error involves the research *participants selected* for observations. Miles and Huberman (1984, p. 231) caution that often individuals who are "articulate, insightful, attractive and intellectually responsive" often become the focus of observations, but are atypical to the population under study. Certainly this may have been true for the first year of the study which focused on women from the Honors Cottage as the primary participants of the camping program. Although the researchers did not control the women who were selected to camp and the second and third years included women from all levels of security (minimum, medium, and maximum), caution is still warranted for generalizing the findings and conclusions beyond the sample group. Patton (1990, p. 471) cautions that "the evaluator-analyst must be careful to limit conclusions to those situations, time periods, persons, contexts, and purposes for which the data are applicable." This is especially true in naturalistic research in which the investigator has no or little control over the sample group's selection.

To overcome these types of sampling errors, Miles and Huberman (1984) suggest that the researcher *assume* that selective sampling and inaccurate generalizations are occurring. To counterbalance these effects and increase the reliability of the observations, they suggest four strategies. The first is simply to *increase* the size of the sample and the number of observations. In this way, atypical participants and situations have a better opportunity to come under study, and both the sample and the observations will become more representative of reality.

The second is to look for negative or contrasting cases, such as **outliers** or those who do not fit a normal pattern. Similar to the normal distribution chart used for statistics, in every situation there are individuals who fall into the outer extremes. Observations of these individuals is necessary to ensure representativeness along the entire spectrum of behavior.

The third way to counteract sampling error is to systematically sort cases into a **master matrix**. The matrix may be based on demographic characteristics, behavioral characteristics, and the like, and is similar to stratification in positivistic research. The point is to ensure that individuals from each section of the matrix are sampled, at least in proportion to their occurrence. When individuals from each section of the matrix are sampled, their likelihood of being representative of the entire sample or population is greatly enhanced.

The fourth solution is to sample randomly from the total universe of individuals or phenomena under study. **Randomization,** which is used extensively in experimental research, means that every individual in the population has an equal chance of being selected for study. In this way, the researcher's error (or bias) in focusing on certain types of individuals is reduced because randomization increases the chances for representativeness.

Observant readers will note that these strategies are also often used in well-designed experimental research studies. Miles and Huberman note that "while the experimental researcher uses the conventions early, as anticipatory controls against sampling and measurement error, the qualitative researcher typically uses them later, as verification devices" (1985, p. 232). Thus, in the cyclical process of reducing, interpreting, and confirming data, the investigative TRS continues these internal validity conventions to ensure the data and results will be representative.

Triangulating

In other types of research endeavors, the internal validity of the findings is often checked with other known sources through using concurrent validity techniques. For example, the results of a newly developed instrument on leisure satisfaction may be compared with results from other similar instruments on leisure satisfaction to confirm **concurrent validity** (the degree of overlap or correlation between the results of the instruments). In naturalistic research, this is not always possible because each study is unique in its mission, context, or duration. Therefore, other ways to ensure **convergent validity** (whether the measures converge on similar concepts) have been developed for naturalistic studies.

One of the most popular methods of increasing the convergent validity of such studies is to use **triangulation.** "Stripped to its basics, triangulation is supposed to support a finding by showing independent measures of it agree with it, or at least, don't contradict it" (Miles & Huberman, 1984, p. 234). Patton (1990, p. 464) explained that:

> [t]here are basically four kinds of triangulation that contribute to verification and validation of qualitative analysis: (1) checking out the consistency of the findings generated by different data-collection methods, that is, *methods triangulation*; (2) checking out the consistency of different data sources within the same method, that is, *triangulation of sources*; (3) using multiple analysts to review findings, that is, *analyst triangulation*; and (4) using multiple perspectives or theories to interpret the data, that is, *theory/perspective triangulation*.

Methods Triangulation

Methods triangulation usually involves the use of both quantitative and qualitative methods. The intent of this dual focus on both numbers and words implies that combination will allow for a fuller, complementary view of the phenomenon under study. Typically the use of quantitative data allows for increased breadth of the research and allows for the summarization of grouped results. The use of qualitative data results in more depth by targeting the meaning or explanation of the numbers, based on individual results. When used in tandem, this combination approach may seem at first like "data heaven," but Patton (1990, p. 466) cautions "that one ought to expect initial conflicts in findings from quantitative and qualitative data and expect those findings to be received with varying degrees of credibility." These conflicts call for further confirmation and interpretation probes, comparative analyses, and continual convergent validity checks (Patton, 1990).

Multiple Sources Triangulation

Using multiple sources of information is the second type of data triangulation. Patton broadly defines four categories of data source triangulation as comparisons between: (a) data from different data collection techniques (e.g., observations, interviews, and focus groups); (b) what research participants state in different settings; (c) what research participants state at different intervals of time; and (d) perspectives of people from different points of view.

Naturalistic inquiries often use a variety of data collection techniques. In the prison study, data were collected through personal interviews, written questionnaires, focus groups, and observations. The assumption behind using multiple procedures is that each may yield unique data from different perspectives. That is, in a follow-up personal interview the interviewee can reveal the meaning underlying his or her behavior viewed during an observation. This process results in a more holistic understanding of the phenomenon under study.

Comparing how research participants may differ in different settings or at different intervals is useful because individuals' behavior is not always consistent. For example, in prison it was observed that women acted differently in their housing units than they did on the grounds or at camp. They also acted differently with their children than when the children were not present. Observations, in order to be reliable and valid of the women's total behavior, would be required in a multitude of settings at varying intervals, and be of considerable duration. Thus, the validity and reliability of the data are increased when the researcher ensures that the "picture" of the behavior is both well-rounded and accurate.

The fourth category of source triangulation is the use of different kinds of people to gain information. Because of their experience, positions, and backgrounds, people within the same environment may see the experience quite differently. Because it was felt that this was the case in the prison environment, women from all levels of security (minimum, medium, and maximum) who did and did not camp, the children of the camping women, administrative officials, and correctional officers were all tapped as data sources. Interestingly enough, in the beginning of the research, the viewpoints were quite divergent, but over the three year span appeared to be converging more toward a consensual view of the effects of the camp.

Multiple Analyst Triangulation

The use of multiple analysts is the third type of data triangulation. The use of several investigators in the collection, reduction, confirmation, and interpretation of data is crucial in reducing the potential bias of a single individual. When a team approach is used, the chances of an individual researcher's perspective skewing the results is minimized. Conversations and meetings among the research team members help to confirm or contradict individual interpretations. These may be informal, such as when the research team spent an hour each way commuting to the prison grounds.

Multiple Theory/Perspective Triangulation

This type of data triangulation involves using different theoretical perspectives to explain the results. "The point of theory triangulation is to understand how findings are affected by different assumptions and fundamental premises" (Patton, 1990, p. 470). For example, two conflicting views of the weekend camp were present in the prison staff and general public. One view was that women, once incarcerated, lost rights of being mothers and, therefore, did not "deserve" to have their children visit. The opposing view was that women, regardless of past records, remained mothers, and if not given the opportunity to bond with their children, would lose an essential connection and motivation to return to the outside community. The reader can well imagine how the different assumptions might affect the confirmation, interpretation, and analysis of results.

Seeking Rival Explanations and Weighting the Evidence

One threat to the validity of the results is when the researcher continually seeks to find confirming data or begins to establish a mind-set about the potential explanations of the results. As with other types of research, the confidence placed in the results is strengthened by examining alternative forces and rival explanations. This balancing act requires that evidence is examined in light of its own viability and integrity, while inductive and logical explanations are explored. The balancing act reflects that "some ... data is [sic] 'better' than others" (Miles & Huberman, 1984, p. 235) while at the same time, "considering rival organizing schemes and competing explanations" (Patton, 1990, p. 462).

Two scenarios from the prison study highlight this balance. Since the intent was to examine the mother-child bond during the weekend experience, the primary focus was on the mothers' perspective. It was assumed that no one else (i.e., administrators and correctional officers) could possess that perspective. Additional confidence was put on the data from the women who were to remain in prison for a considerable time as their responses and behaviors were less likely to be influenced by the research. However, while this collection, confirmation, and interpretation process was occurring, additional explanations were sought from staff and short-term women to offset possible faulty conclusions. In this way, additional weight was given to some sources of information while the vigilance continued to gather rival descriptions. Miles and Huberman (1984) offer several suggestions for maintaining this balance in naturalistic research.

Searching for Outliers, Extreme, and Negative Cases

One major truth about the human experience is that "normal" is an elusive concept. "The human world is not perfectly ordered and human researchers are not omniscient" (Patton, 1990, p. 464). In trying to draw conclusions about the data, it seems reasonable to assume that individuals will differ, some very little, some greatly. While the purpose of the research may be to draw some conclusions and gain insight about human behavior, these conclusions and insights are strengthened by purposefully searching out those individuals who deviate from the norm. As with more positivistic research where the researcher will never probably achieve significance at the .000 level, naturalistic researchers should not assume that all individuals will fit into typecast categories (Guba & Lincoln, 1989, p. 238).

This search for deviant cases is one of the benefits of naturalistic inquiry and the cyclical reduction process. For example, there were a few women who chose not to have their children visit for the weekend, while the vast majority did. When asked for clarification, some of these nonparticipating women stated that they did not want their children to gain an unrealistic view that prison life was *fun*, as portrayed by a weekend filled with games activities. This, in turn, lead the camp staff to reevaluate some aspects of the program as well as for the researchers to focus on children's and mothers' comments that would reflect this perspective. The deviant cases led to another area for further exploration.

Getting Feedback from Informants

Another method of increasing the credibility of the research results and confirming that conclusions are logical and consistent is to have research participants review and evaluate the findings. Calling them "member checks," Guba and Lincoln (1989, p. 238-239) suggested that all major stakeholders in the research results participate in giving feedback. This action is necessitated by the fact that participants will almost always know more about the situation than the researcher and many participants are becoming part of the larger consumerism movement, extending rightful access to information to the research environment. Naturalistic researchers often see this as a challenging opportunity rather than a threatening situation.

While calling this feedback "the most crucial technique for establishing credibility," Guba and Lincoln (1989, p. 239) suggest that research participants' feedback be gathered throughout the design, collection, analysis, interpretation, and reporting stages. While Miles and Huberman (1984) caution about the timing of the feedback, it can be used to: (a) clarify a participant's intent of an action; (b) correct errors of fact, omission, or interpretation; (c) solicit additional information from the research participants; (d) ensure that written documentation is accurate from the participants' perspectives; (e) begin the circular process of interpretation; and (f) provide the participant with a summary of the research's purpose.

The intent in the prison project was to empower the research participants to the fullest extent possible; that is, "research that was with and for people rather than on people" (Reason, 1988, p. 1). Two methods of "empowerment" were used during the personal pre- and post-camp interviews. During these, the researchers not only used nonverbal behaviors (e.g., sitting on the same side of the table, and allowing women to sit in the "power" position facing the viewing window), but also showed the women what was being recorded and asked them if the information was accurately reflecting their comments. These strategies enhanced the concept of collaboration, reduced the chances for biased interpretations, and allowed for verbatim comments to be recorded. Thus, the interpretations and conclusions drawn from the research were able to capture more accurately the intent of the women.

Methods Used for Documenting and Reporting Qualitative Data

Unlike other styles of research, naturalistic inquiry has no universally accepted format for documenting and reporting findings. This comes as both a blessing and a curse. Where other styles may have preconceived and mandated sections (i.e., sample, instrumentation, data collection, data analysis, etc.), the form for reporting naturalistic findings may be as recursive as the study and methods themselves. Confinement to prescribed sections is an ill-sought end (Brewer & Hunter, 1989).

However, this is not to say that naturalistic reporting can be sloppy, partial, or inexact. As with all research, answers to basic questions must be addressed within the report. Marshall and Rossman (1989), citing Guba and Lincoln (1985), suggest that naturalistic research reports respond to the following questions: (a) How truthful are the findings and by what criteria can they be judged? (b) How applicable are these findings to other settings or groups of people? (c) What assurances are provided that, if replicated, similar findings would be found by other researchers? and (d) What assurances are provided that the findings reflect the research participants instead of the researcher's biases or prejudices?

Guba and Lincoln (1989) translated these four questions into areas of concern that reports of naturalistic findings must address to ensure applicability, consistency, and neutrality. **Credibility** refers to the accuracy with which the research participant was identified and described, and relates to internal validity. **Transferability**, seen as parallel to external validity or generalizability, refers to the extent that a future researcher would uncover the same phenomena. **Dependability**, much like conventional reliability, targets the stability of the data over time. **Confirmability** (or integrity) ensures that the data, interpretations, and outcomes of the study are grounded in the participants' reality, removing all possible personal distortion or bias by the researcher (Guba & Lincoln, 1989; Marshall & Rossman, 1989).

Miles and Huberman (1984) are strong advocates of the use of auditing procedures during the documentation and reporting process. Acknowledging that interpretation, confirmation, and documentation are interwoven processes, they suggest the use of specific recording forms to meet Guba and Lincoln's (1989) four criteria. Among the items that should be addressed in a naturalistic report include: (a) the research question or issue; (b) the basic intent of the analyses; (c) detailed descriptions of the analyses, including data sets, procedural steps, decision rules used to manage data, and analysis operations; and (d) preliminary conclusions and any concluding comments (Miles & Huberman, 1984).

Additional points are that the report should retain a clear focus of purpose, while allowing for "thick description" (Patton, 1990). That is, that enough description and direct quotations should be added to clarify and target readers' understanding of the study's primary purpose.

Facts also should be separated from the writer's interpretation. Interpretation, a cornerstone of naturalistic inquiry, is needed to help the reader distinguish between major and lesser points, much like what statistical tests of significance accomplish in positivistic reports. Interpretation may be interjected throughout the description of facts, as long as distinctions are noted. All of these considerations keep the audience or intended users in mind. The reduction of jargon, clear writing, and the provision of abstracts and executive summaries all assist in increasing readers' understanding and using of reports (Morris, Fitz-Gibbon, & Freeman, 1987). The focus of all report writing should focus on the intended audience(s), and their level of understanding about the nature of the study as well as the use of qualitative methods.

Methods Used to Reduce the Effects of the Researcher

One of the major dilemmas of naturalistic research is that the mere presence of the investigator may influence or change the behavior of the research participants. These changes may detract from the validity and reliability of the findings. Patton (1990, p. 473) outlines four ways in which changes or distortions may take place:

1. reactions of program participants and staff to the presence of the evaluator;
2. changes in the evaluator (the measuring instrument) during the course of the evaluation—that is, instrumentation effects;
3. the predispositions or biases of the evaluator; and
4. evaluator incompetence (including lack of sufficient training or preparation).

The first type often is called the "Hawthorne effect," in which the presence of the researcher influences the participants' actions from what would be seen under unobserved, natural conditions. These changes may work for and against the participant, in some cases increasing performance and in other cases decreasing it. Patton (1990) states that the investigator has the responsibility to consider the problem, make decisions to minimize it, and monitor and analyze observer effects throughout the study. One effort to reduce observer effects is to conduct long-term studies so that the researcher is no longer "new" to the research participants.

The second concern focuses on changes in the researcher as the measurement instrument. Sometimes called "observer drift," this phenomenon is most likely to occur when the researcher steps into the dual participant-observer role. Because of the need to be reiterative during the collection and analysis phases, the observer may begin to become "one of the gang" as well as begin to view situations unidimensionally. Since most naturalistic research requires intensive involvement, it is best to assume that the phenomenon under study will have an impact on the researcher, and to explicitly note these changes in field notes as they occur (Miles & Huberman, 1984; Patton, 1990).

The third concern deals with the biases and preconceived notions of the observer. No researcher is without biases and no research is value-free (Denzin, 1989; Keith-Speigel & Koocher, 1985; Miles & Huberman, 1984; Patton, 1987; 1990). "Numbers do not protect against bias; they sometimes merely disguise it. All statistical data are based on someone's definition of what to measure and how to measure it" (Patton, 1987). The fact that the researcher chose the topic and selected certain procedures for sampling and data collection point to the assumption that biases are present. However, Patton (1990) suggests that the researcher focus on maintaining objectivity, neutrality, and impartiality.

To counter the effects of these three concerns, several suggestions follow:

(a) perform long-term studies in which the participants are likely to revert to more natural behavior;

(b) perform in-depth observations to increase validity and mean ingful interpretations;

(c) use unobtrusive measures where possible;

(d) when possible, clearly inform participants of the purpose of the research;

(e) ask a reliable informant to observe for researcher effects;

(f) check with research participants and stakeholders about the accuracy of data recorded;

(g) include large samples of individuals and incidents;

(h) include negative case and outlier analysis;

(i) focus on the theoretical framework, not the interpersonal network for interpretation;

(j) use triangulation; and

(k) request an outsider to review field notes and interpretations through peer debriefing (Miles & Huberman, 1984; Patton, 1990).

All of these suggestions lead to the fourth concern of the researcher's competence. It is obvious that since judgment plays an integral role in the natural inquiry process, researchers must have a substantial background and training to perform competently. After all, when using qualitative methods, the investigator *is* the measurement instrument.

Researcher Competence and Credibility

Readers might notice that throughout the preceding discussions of methods and techniques, many comparisons have been made between positivistic and naturalistic inquiries. At least two common threads exist between the two styles: using *systematic methods* in the *search for meaning, value, and explanation*. Thus, both styles of research are based on "science" in that they involve rigorous study and analytical thinking. The more one knows about either style, the more one can become proficient in using either or both.

As a baseline in both naturalistic and positivistic research, a solid background in scientific theories or perspectives is needed to "ground" the research in an established perspective. One also must know about scientific rigor and how to select various methods or styles based on the purpose and anticipated outcomes of the study. In addition, understanding about various techniques for data collection and reduction is necessary to select the most appropriate and defensible option(s). Throughout these, the mandate for rigor, defensibility, and critical thinking is present.

However, naturalistic studies have fewer guidelines to follow because the search for meaning in each study is different. That is, while the concepts and principles are similar to those used in positivistic research, the procedures used in qualitative methods differ. The naturalistic investigator must understand the behavior of people, groups, and organizations, in order to appreciate and describe the context of their culture. Problem, theory, method, and the investigator are meshed in determining the direction, value, and worth of the study (Van Maanen, 1983).

"There are no simple formulas or clear-cut rules about how to do a credible, high-quality analysis. The task is to do one's best to make sense out of things ... Creativity, intellectual rigor, perseverance, insight—these are the intangibles that go beyond the routine application of scientific procedures" (Patton, 1990, p. 477).

So that while there is no "recipe" for conducting naturalistic inquiries (just as there really is no fail-proof formula for positivistic studies), the investigator must be able to justify the selection of theories, methods, techniques, and analyses used in the study. The ability to make these justifications comes from in-depth study of naturalistic techniques, a considerable amount of application and practice of those skills, and the ability to remain flexible and open as the data emerge (Patton, 1987; Strauss & Corbin, 1990).

> The requisite skills for doing qualitative research . . . are these: to step back and critically analyze situations, to recognize and avoid bias, to obtain valid and reliable data, and to think abstractly. To do these, a qualitative researcher requires theoretical and social sensitivity, the ability to maintain analytical distance while at the same time drawing upon past experience and theoretical knowledge to interpret what is seen, astute powers of observation, and good interaction skills. (Strauss & Corbin, 1990, p. 18)

Thus, the credibility of the researcher is paramount, and cannot occur before a considerable degree of skill is obtained. As Patton (1990, p. 476) suggests, the trustworthiness of the data depends directly on the trustworthiness of the investigator who collects and analyzes the data.

Similarly, the researcher's credibility is enhanced through the accurate and descriptive reporting of the procedures and results. The researcher's aim is to document these clearly enough so that the audience is able to arrive at the same interpretations and conclusions. The research has no value if the intended audiences (e.g., grant funders, presentation audiences, journal readers) are not clear about the process or outcomes.

Summary

The lines separating collection, confirmation, and interpretation of qualitative data are unclear at best. The beauty and attraction of naturalistic research is the ability to define and describe behavior as it occurs naturally in the setting of the research participant. However, participants' lives and realities are messy, and often defy the strict categorization of laboratory research. This messiness requires that the researcher develop and adopt detective-like behaviors in order to collect and synthesize qualitative research.

This chapter discusses validity, reliability, and objectivity which become the researcher's focus throughout the data collection, reduction, interpretation, and documentation phases. Illustrative examples of the application of these procedures are given from a project involving incarcerated women and their children. It is hoped that therapeutic recreation specialists will become involved as investigators who describe the subjective nature of research participants' lives through using processes similar to those that have been explained here.

Discussion Questions

1. Explain the similarities and differences in purposes and procedures used for positivistic and naturalistic inquiry. How do these relate to the concepts of validity, reliability, and objectivity of the findings? Develop a list of pros and cons for both types of research.
2. Briefly describe the relationship of confirmation, interpretation, and reporting to the overall process of engaging in naturalistic research.
3. Explain the importance of the researcher who chooses to use qualitative methods. That is, what role does the *researcher* play? How does this differ from roles in other types of research?
4. Provide an example where naturalistic inquiry could be used in TR settings. What would be the advantages and disadvantages of selecting this style for the example you give? What could it bring to this setting that other research styles could not?
5. Find an example in the literature which reports the results of a study using qualitative methodology. Cite examples throughout the report or article that provide evidence of credibility, transferability, dependability, and confirmability, of the findings as well as objectivity on the part of the researcher.

References

Anastasi, A. (1968). *Psychological testing* (3rd ed.). New York, NY: MacMillan

Brewer, J., & Hunter, A. (1989). *Multimethod research: A synthesis of styles.* Beverly Hills, CA: Sage.

Denzin, N. K. (1989). *Interpretive interactionism.* Newbury Park, CA: Sage.

Gronlund, N. E. (1981). *Measurement and evaluation in teaching.* (4th ed.). New York: MacMillan.

Guba, E. G., & Lincoln, Y. S. (1989). *Fourth generation evaluation.* Newbury Park, CA: Sage.

Jick, T. D. (1987). Triangulation in action. In J. Van Maanen (Ed.), *Qualitative methodology* (pp. 135-148). Beverly Hills, CA: Sage.

Keith-Speigel, P., & Koocher, G. P. (1985). *Ethics in psychology: Professional standards and cases.* New York, NY: Random House.

Kidder, L. H. (1981). *Sellitz, Wrightsman and Cook's research methods in social relations* (4th ed.). New York, NY: Holt, Rinehart & Winston.

Marshall, C., & Rossman, G. (1989). *Designing qualitative research.* Beverly Hills, CA: Sage.

Miles, M. B. (1983). Qualitative data as an attractive nuisance: The problem of analysis. In J. Van Maanen (Ed.), *Qualitative methodology* (pp. 117-134). Beverly Hills, CA: Sage.

Miles, M. B. & Huberman, A. M. (1984). *Qualitative data analysis: A sourcebook for new methods.* Beverly Hills, CA: Sage.

Morris, L. L., Fitz-Gibbon, C. T., & Freeman, M. E. (1987). *How to communicate evaluation findings.* Newbury Park, CA: Sage.

Patton, M. Q. (1987). *How to use qualitative methods in evaluation.* Newbury Park, CA: Sage.

Patton, M. Q. (1990). *Qualitative evaluation and research methods* (2nd ed.). Newbury Park, CA: Sage.

Strauss, A., & Corbin, J. (1990). *Basics of qualitative research: Grounded Theory procedures and techniques.* Newbury Park, CA: Sage.

Stumbo, N. J., & Little, S. L. (1991). *Research report 1990—Camp Celebration: Incarcerated mothers and their children camping together.* Springfield, IL: Illinois Department of Corrections.

Thorndike, R. L., & Hagen, E. P. (1977). *Measurement and evaluation in psychology and education* (4th ed.). New York, NY: Wiley.

Van Maanen, J. (Ed.). (1983). *Qualitative methodology.* Beverly Hills, CA: Sage.

Yin, R. K. (1984). *Case study research: Design and methods.* Beverly Hills, CA: Sage.

CHAPTER 15

Efficacy Studies in Therapeutic Recreation
Research: The Need, The State of the Art, and
Future Implications
*John W. Shank, W. B. (Terry) Kinney, and
Catherine P. Coyle*

Future Trends in TR Research

section IV

Section IV—Future Trends in TR Research

Within this concluding chapter, Shank, Kinney, and Coyle have complied a comprehensive and systematic analysis which reflects the body of knowledge regarding outcomes found in TR-related research as a result of the consensus building conference held at Temple University in the fall of 1991. Chapter 15 highlights the preexisting research that demonstrates the benefits of TR-related interventions for clients; identifies strategies for efficacy-oriented research in TR settings; and calls for future research in areas that are important to theory and practice. Finally, the authors suggest a way to interpret and integrate the two differing perspectives and definitions of TR into a cooperative venture.

Efficacy Studies in Therapeutic Recreation Research: The Need, The State of the Art, and Future Implications

John W. Shank, W. B. (Terry) Kinney, and Catherine P. Coyle

A major characteristic of a profession is a clearly established body of knowledge. This body of knowledge is something that is expected to change over time, grow with advances in discovery and understanding, and reflect a deliberate attempt by members to test the assumptions, theories, and the existing knowledge that guides their practice. Every member of the profession has a stake in the efforts to refine its body of knowledge, and must share the obligation to responsibly conduct and absorb empirical research.

Beyond our own professional duty to advance our body of knowledge through research, there are several outside groups pressing for definitive evidence regarding therapeutic recreation's contribution, particularly in health care. The insurance industry wants evidence that TR interventions are cost effective and will result in necessary and desirable outcomes. Accreditation bodies, such as the Joint Commission on Accreditation of Healthcare Organizations (JCAHO), are mandating an outcome focus in all quality improvement efforts. Also, in response to the unacceptably high costs of health care, the U.S. Congress has charged several federal agencies with the responsibility to determine the effectiveness of health care practices.

Two examples are particularly relevant to TR. In 1987 the National Institute on Disability and Rehabilitation Research (NIDRR), U.S. Department of Education, called for proposals to "assess definitively the merits of therapeutic recreation and to measure its impact on the rehabilitation of disabled persons" (*Federal Register*, p. 43302). The priorities included organizing a national conference to determine a consensus view of the benefits of therapeutic recreation in rehabilitation. Additionally, in 1989, Congress passed PL 101-239 which established the Agency for Health Care Policy and Research (AHCPR). The AHCPR created the Medical Treatment Effectiveness Program (MEDTEP) with the specific purpose of systematically studying the relationship between health care services and necessary and desirable outcomes. A division of Allied Health was created within the AHCPR (although it did not include TR). The activities of these two federal agencies depict a clearly established priority in health care today—the demonstration of treatment outcomes that have broad relevance beyond discipline specific interests. If therapeutic recreation wishes to operate within the health care arena, it must respond to the same pressure confronting all other disciplines; it must investigate the efficacy of its services and demonstrate beneficial outcomes.

Health care **outcomes**, or benefits, reflect varied perspectives on the meaning attached to the term "benefits." According to Driver, Brown and Peterson (1991), an economic perspective can be attached to the term **benefits** which suggests "economic gain, measured in monetary terms" (p. 4). Increasingly, health care administrators evaluate the effectiveness of various programs and treatments based upon cost/benefit ratios. Certainly, insurance companies use an economic perspective which evaluates the beneficial outcomes derived from various services when they consider whether that service is reimbursable in workmen's compensation cases.

In addition, benefits can be viewed generically. Driver and his colleagues (1991) also categorized **benefits** as "a change that is viewed to be advantageous—an improvement in condition, or a gain to an individual, a group, to society or to another entity" (p. 4). This more traditional and broader perspective of benefits is also well-established in health care today. For instance, the NIDRR-sponsored project referred to earlier in this chapter directed TR research toward investigating rehabilitation outcomes such as psychological well-being and community integration. Likewise, AHCPR's MEDTEP organizes outcomes and encourages research in such categories as satisfaction with care and quality of life, in addition to more objective and economic measures such as morbidity, mortality, and recidivism.

The likelihood of gaining long-term support for TR research will be increased to the extent that the outcomes or benefits relate to issues valued by the health care industry. This also increases the potential opportunities for collaborative research with other disciplines, which is strongly encouraged by funding agencies. For example, the research agenda established by the National Center for Medical Rehabilitation Research at the National Institutes of Health includes extensive reference to psychosocial concerns and quality of life issues which are purportedly addressed through TR intervention. While the central issue here is elaborated later in this chapter, the main point is that the TR discipline is challenged to document, in terms acceptable to the broader health care system, exactly what benefits TR contributes to health care and rehabilitation.

While there may be many individual factors that have hampered TR's attempt to build an outcomes-focused research agenda, as stated in Section I of this text, it appears that one of the more significant obstacles has been the lack of theory-driven practices within the discipline. Usually, the interventions or programs that result in outcomes/benefits for clients are developed based on a theoretical perspective; an example is Bandura's (1977) theory of social cognition. Because the interventions are designed from a theoretical perspective, the process by which the change or outcome will occur is suggested. For instance, Savell (1986) discussed the use of social cognition theory in designing TR programs. Within social cognition there are four information sources which a client can use to change his/her behavior. They include performance accomplishments, vicarious experiences, verbal persuasion, and emotional arousal. Savell suggested that TR practitioners who choose to work from a social cognition perspective develop interventions that contain all four of these sources of information in order to facilitate a change in their clients. The implementation and replication of this type of intervention is simpler because the theoretical framework and the derived process are clearly detailed. Unfortunately, it appears that contemplation of theoretical perspectives rarely occurs in TR. Analysis of the research and practice literature, as well as impressions drawn from a variety of TR conference presentations, would indicate that no *single* theoretical framework dominates the practice of TR and that theory is often not considered in developing interventions for TR practice.

Theories, however, pertaining to human development, cognition, social learning, and leisure are relevant to the discipline of TR, with many more theoretical perspectives becoming relevant when the disabling condition with which the TRS is working is considered. Because of the variety of theoretical perspectives relevant to TR, no single theoretical perspective dominates the discipline. In fact, the discipline often describes itself as operating from an **eclectic** perspective. An eclectic perspective is one in which the clinician evaluates all possible theoretical approaches to use with a client and chooses the approach which is most appropriate based upon research and clinical data.

Unfortunately, the eclectic perspective in TR is driven by an *intuitive practitioner-based eclecticism*. **Intuitive practitioner-based eclecticism** is derived from clinical trial and error that is often *situationally specific* (Barlow, Hayes, & Nelson, 1984). This means that similarly named TR services (e.g., leisure education) often differ according to the setting, therapist, and, most important, the client. This type of variation in practice is not a true *eclectic* perspective as it does not evolve from a ". . . consideration of all pertinent theories, methods, and standards for evaluating and manipulating clinical data according to the most advanced knowledge of time and place" (Barlow et al., p. 451). An **eclectic** approach implies a systematic evaluation of all pertinent theoretical perspectives which are not an intuitive response to a client.

The use of "**intuitive-eclecticism**" as suggested by Barlow et al. (1984), does not allow for systematic analysis of what interventions work in what settings and with what clients. "Intuitive-eclecticism" hampers research efforts within the discipline, causing difficulties in reproducing the actual intervention. Knowing *what works, with whom,* and *under what conditions* is the specific knowledge that the TR discipline is being challenged to document by MEDTEP's and other health care programs through empirical research (see "The Health Care Crisis," Chapter 1).

Research that attempts to document the outcome of services should therefore be driven by a theoretical framework. This theoretical perspective should be relevant to effecting changes in clients' behavior and result in the attainment of "benefits" or "outcomes" that are advantageous, cost-effective, and relevant to the health care system. The lack of theory-driven practice in TR has and will continue to hamper research efforts. Researchers and practitioners will have to work closely and intensely to identify common ground upon which practice can be systematically and scientifically tested and analyzed to determine the efficacy of various interventions. Nonetheless, some empirical evidence currently does exist which suggests that TR influences health care outcomes. The remainder of this chapter highlights some of the research literature which documents outcomes/benefits of TR involvement. It also provides suggestions for future efficacy research within the discipline of TR.

Developing a Typology of TR Benefits

In order to organize the research literature reviewed for this chapter into a coherent form, a typology of outcomes/benefits derived from TR involvement was developed. This typology needed to cut across disability groups and institutional settings. It should be noted that the material reviewed and reorganized in this section was first presented at "The National Conference on the Benefits of Therapeutic Recreation."[1] At this conference, disability-specific literature reviews were written for:

1. developmental disabilities by John Dattilo and Stuart Schleien;
2. geriatrics by Carol Riddick and Jean Keller;
3. mental health by Thomas Skalko, Glen Van Andel, and Gino DeSalvatore;

---

1. The National Conference on the Benefits of Therapeutic Recreation was sponsored by Temple University's Program in Therapeutic Recreation and NIDRR. Proceedings are available from the Therapeutic Recreation Program, Temple University, Box 062-62, Seltzer Hall, Philadelphia, PA 19122.

4. pediatrics by Viki Annand and Peggy Powers;
5. physical disabilities by Doris Berryman, Ann James, and Barb Trader; and
6. substance abuse by Ann Rancourt.

The typology derived from these papers contains six global "benefits." It categorizes research which is related to TR according to the following research outcomes: (a) *physical health and health maintenance; (b) cognitive functioning;* (c) *psychosocial health;* (d) *growth and personal development; (e) personal and life satisfaction;* and finally, (f) *societal and health care system outcomes.*

This typology should not be viewed as a comprehensive inventory; nor should it be perceived as the only areas in which benefits can be derived from TR involvement. Rather, it represents those areas in which some preliminary research evidence exists which indicates that TR or activities used within TR produce benefits for individuals with disabilities. Further systematic research is needed in each of these areas. The purpose in reviewing the present research studies is to provide readers of this chapter with:

1. a reference point for identifying existing research associated with TR;
2. direction for replication studies; and
3. an overview of research areas and appropriate research methods.

Research Documenting Physical Health and Health Maintenance Benefits[2]

Research in TR has been shown to improve cardiorespiratory functioning by reducing diastolic blood pressure, increasing work tolerance, and reducing asthmatic symptoms. TR has also been shown to reduce the percentage of body fat and body weight. TR has reduced the incidence of decubiti and urinary tract infections; improved functioning and rate of recovery from surgery and trauma; and significantly improved strength, agility, and perceptual motor abilities.

---

2.   Due to space constraints, a limited number of research studies are cited in this chapter. A more detailed listing of research in each of these areas is reported in the proceedings from the National Conference of the Benefits of Therapeutic Recreation.

Involvement in TR Reduces Cardiovascular and Respiratory Risk

- A water aerobics program two times a week for 16 weeks significantly reduced diastolic blood pressure, body fat, and body weight in 27 elderly community residents (Green, 1989). These findings were replicated in a second study with 24 elderly community residents (Keller, 1991).
- Research has indicated that involvement in exercise can significantly improve cardiorespiratory functioning among adults with physical disabilities (Figoni, Boileau, Massey, & Larsen, 1988; Hoffman, 1986; Jocheim & Strohkendle, 1973; Koch, Schlegel, Pirrwitz, Jaschke, & Schlegel, 1983; Miles, Sawka, Wilde, Durbin, & Gotshall, 1982; Santiago, Coyle, & Troupe, 1991; Van Loan, McCluer, Loftin, & Boileau, 1987; Zwiren, Huberman, & Bar-Or, 1973).
- A controlled study of exercise and asthma found that an exercise program involving physically active recreation (swimming and running) resulted in increased work tolerance and decreased heart rate for asthmatic children (Rothe, Kohl, & Mansfeld, 1990).
- Similarly, Szentagothai, Gyene, Szocska, and Osvath (1987) reported that long-term physical exercise programs (one to two years of regular swimming and gymnastic activities involving 121 children between 5 and 14 years of age) were effective in reducing asthmatic symptoms, frequency of hospitalization, and use of medication.
- Cerny (1989) found that an exercise program was as effective as a standard protocol of bronchial hygiene therapy in terms of the pulmonary function and exercise response of patients with cystic fibrosis.

Involvement in TR Reduces the Risk of Physical Complications Secondary to Disability

- Reduced incidences of decubiti and urinary tract infections were found among wheelchair athletes compared to wheelchair nonathletes (Stotts, 1986).
- Increased activity has been shown to reduce medical complications and increase survival rate of persons with spinal cord injuries (Anson & Shepherd, 1990; Krause & Crewe, 1987).

- Video games have been used to motivate young children with burns to exercise, thus maintaining mobility, enhancing healing, and counteracting the loss of function often associated with burns (Adriaenssens, Eggermont, Pyck, Boeckx & Gilles, 1988).
- Comparing 160 children (ages 3 to 13) in a control group with 68 children who received structured and comprehensive child life interventions, Wolfer, Gaynard, Goldberger, Laidley, and Thompson (1988) found that the treatment group had significantly greater rates of recovery from surgery.

Involvement in TR Improves the General Physical and Perceptual Motor Functioning of Individuals with a Disability

- A horseback riding program has been shown to improve coordination of individuals with physical disabilities (Brock, 1988); and improved perceptual-motor abilities, body perception, balance, locomotor agility, ball throwing, and tracking were reported among individuals with mental retardation who were involved in a physical recreation program (Marini, 1978).
- Strength and endurance of adults with disabilities have been shown to increase as a result of participation in physical recreation (Davis, Shephard, & Jackson, 1981).
- Increased flexibility, hand strength, and ambulation was demonstrated among older residents of a long term care facility through a developmental fitness program two times per week (Buettner, 1988); and range of motion was improved in a quasi-experimental design using a structured cooking group as the intervention (Yoder, Nelson, & Smith, 1989).

Research Documenting Cognitive Functioning

Cognitive benefits of TR involvement have been documented in a number of areas. They include improved reality orientation, short and long term memory, and general cognitive functioning, including attention span, strategizing, and control of impulses.

Involvement in TR Increases General Cognitive Functioning

- As measured on the Clifton Cognitive Ability Assessment, involvement in a comprehensive recreation program significantly improved cognitive abilities for 70% of the nursing home residents in the program (Conroy, Fincham, & Agard-Evans, 1988).
- In a quasi-experimental design using matched controls, elderly individuals who received dance and movement activities one hour per week for eight months showed significantly improved functioning on the Mini-Mental State exam (Osgood, Meyers, & Orchowsky, 1990).
- Peniston (1991), using an experimental prepost test research design, reported that elderly individuals with mild and moderate memory loss who participated in a six-week computer games program demonstrated significant improvement in cognitive strategies, attention, memory, and impulse control when compared to the control group who received no intervention.
- A unique program involving home visitations accompanied by rewards for seeking and remembering information between visits significantly improved both short- and long-term memory for nursing home residents in the randomly assigned treatment group (Beck, 1982).

Involvement in TR Decreases Confusion and Disorientation

- Reality orientation for disoriented nursing home residents significantly improved with a music-based reality orientation program, while randomly assigned controls who received a standard reality orientation program showed no improvement (Riegler, 1980).
- A music-based sensory stimulation program conducted 30 minutes per week, twice a week for 16 weeks significantly improved reality orientation of disoriented nursing home residents who were randomly assigned to treatment or control groups (Banziger & Rousch, 1983).

Research Documenting Psychosocial Health

Psychosocial benefits of TR encompass some of the strongest evidence of efficacy in the research literature. Strong evidence indicates reduction of depression, anxiety, and stress. Improved coping, self-control, self-concept, and self-esteem have also been documented. Some evidence shows an improved adjustment to disability and considerable evidence documents TR's effect on improving social skills and interpersonal relations. Other evidence indicates that TR plays a significant role in reducing various self-abusive and socially inappropriate behaviors.

Involvement in TR Reduces Depression

- Katz, Adler, Mazzarella, and Inck (1985) found that exercise reduced depression among individuals with a physical disability. Greenwood, Dzewattowski, and French (1990) found that tennis resulted in significant reductions in depression; and Weiss and Jamieson's (1988) study with the same population found that water exercise effectively reduced depression among individuals with a physical disability.
- Three separate experimental studies utilizing bibliotherapy with elderly who are depressed have significantly reduced depression—one for over six months (Scogin, Jamison, & Gochneaur, 1989); and one for over two years (Scogin, Jamison, & Davis, 1990). The third (Scogin, Hamblin, & Beutler, 1987) did not indicate the time period.
- In a quasi-experimental study with adults with physical disabilities, Santiago et al. (1991) using ANCOVA, found a lessening of depressive symptoms in the exercise experimental group's adjusted posttest mean score on the CES-D scale of 59.3% in comparison to an increase of 2.0% in the control group.
- A nine-week aerobic exercise intervention contributed to a significant reduction in depressive symptomatology such as inner tension, sleep disturbance, concentration difficulties, and depressive thinking in adults hospitalized for depression. These subjects were randomly assigned to either the treatment or control group (Martinsen, Medhus, & Sandvik, 1984).
- Sime (1987) found that adults with depression who completed an exercise treatment program not only had significantly lower depression scores compared to a control group, but those who

continued to exercise after the treatment program were also found to have lower depression scores at 6 and 21 month follow-up points.

- A structured activity treatment program has been found to be effective in reducing depressive symptomatology and can increase levels of active engagement with one's surroundings (Wassmann & Iso-Ahola, 1985).

Involvement in TR Reduces Anxiety

- Using a combination of behavioral indicators to create an overall anxiety score, Ipsa, Barrett, and Kim (1988) reported on an experimental study in which a supervised play program offered to children 5 to 10 years of age receiving medical treatment in an outpatient clinic resulted in less anxiety among the children and less irritability among the parents who were waiting with their children.
- The anxiety children normally experience due to hospitalization and related medical procedures can be significantly reduced through the provision of accurate, age appropriate information (Rasnake & Linscheid, 1989), although providing children with an opportunity to "play with" medical equipment and materials is more effective than merely providing information in reducing anxiety and helping children be prepared for surgery (Demarest, Hooke, & Erickson, 1984).
- A variety of studies have demonstrated the value of exercise in reducing anxiety associated with stress. Berger (1983/1984, 1986) reported that physical conditioning through swimming produces significant, short term reduction in stress, as does yoga and jogging (Long, 1984; Sachs, 1982).

Involvement in TR Improves Coping Behavior

- Hiking, camping, and adapted sports have produced significant increases in self-efficacy and self-confidence among individuals with a physical disability (Austin, 1987; Curtis, McClanahan, Hall, Dillon, & Brown, 1986; Robb & Evert, 1987; Stewart, 1981; Stuckey & Barkus, 1986).
- A music-based reality orientation intervention with disoriented nursing home residents significantly increased sensory and environmental awareness for the randomly assigned experimental group (Wolfe, 1983).

- In a quasi-experimental study with individuals hospitalized in a rehabilitation facility, Shank, Coyle, and Kinney (1991a) found that persons receiving individual TR services were significantly better able to use activities as a means of coping with the stress of hospitalization than were control subjects.

Involvement in TR Reduces Stress Level

- Individuals with physical disabilities who watch humorous videos have shown an increase in immune cell proliferation, which buffers stress (Berk et al., 1988a).
- In an experimental study using "matched controls," TR treatments were shown to strengthen the individual's immune response by acting as a catalyst for decreases in ACTH and increases in the growth hormone (Russoniello, 1991).
- Diversional recreation experiences have been shown to facilitate stress recovery, provided the experience is assessed positively by the individual (Heywood, 1978).

Involvement in TR Improves Self-Control

- Dattilo and Barnett (1985) have demonstrated that TR interventions lead to increased spontaneous initiation of activity, engagement with the environment, and self-assertiveness for individuals with mental retardation. Another study by Lanagan and Dattilo (1989) with the same population resulted in increased choice making and preference.
- An experimental design with 28 randomly assigned nursing home residents in a horticulture intervention resulted in significant improvement in perceived competence (Shary & Iso-Ahola, 1989).

Involvement in TR Increases Self-Concept, Self-Esteem, and Adjustment to Disability

- Sports and athletics have been shown to significantly increase body perception and body image in individuals with a physical disability (Hopper, 1988); hiking and camping have resulted in increased self-efficacy and self-confidence for individuals with a physical disability (Robb & Evert, 1987; Stuckey & Barkus,

1986). All four types of activities have resulted in increased acceptance of disability among individuals with a physical disability (Jackson & Davis, 1983; McAvoy, Shatz, Stutz, Schlein, & Lais, 1989; Sherrill & Rainbolt, 1988).

- Shank et al., (1991a) found that persons in a rehabilitation hospital who received individual TR services reported significantly higher levels of self-esteem at discharge when compared with individuals who did not receive any TR intervention. This difference remained significant when initial differences in the pretest levels of self-esteem were controlled.
- Comparing hospitalized children who received structured play programs with those who did not, Gillis (1989) found that structured play resulted in significantly more positive self-esteem.

Involvement in TR Improves General Psychological Health

- A comparison study showed improved psychological health on the Affect Balance Scale among the treatment group who received a music program 30 minutes per week for 12 weeks (Cutler Riddick & Dugan-Jendzejec, 1988).
- Involvement in a horticulture program showed significantly increased morale for nursing home residents randomly assigned to the treatment condition over those assigned to the control group (Shary & Iso-Ahola, 1989).
- Shank, Coyle, and Kinney (1991b) surveyed individuals with a variety of disabilities who were involved in special recreation programs across the United States. Benefits derived from recreation participation in the areas of positive feelings about themselves and maintaining and improving social and recreational activities were reported by these individuals.

Involvement in TR Improves Social Skills, Socialization, Cooperation, and Interpersonal Interactions

- Improvement in social skills has been demonstrated through a variety of studies conducted with individuals with developmental disabilities (Matson & Adkins, 1984; Rynders, Schleien, & Mustonen, 1990; Schleien, Cameron, Rynders, & Slick, 1988; Schleien, Krotee, Mustonen, Kelterborn & Schermer, 1987; Strain, 1975).

- Bullock and Howe (1991) have documented that a community transition program in North Carolina has decreased social isolation for adults with disabilities.
- Experimental studies by Banziger and Rousch (1983) and Beck (1982) have documented increased sociability (utilizing ratings by nursing staff) among nursing home residents using two separate TR interventions.
- Video game play has been shown to increase social affiliation among nursing home residents when compared to another control facility (Cutler Riddick, Spector, & Drogin, 1986).
- Rancourt (1991a, 1991b) has documented how individuals with substance abuse who were involved in a comprehensive leisure education program showed increased knowledge and skills in self-awareness, decision-making, social skills, and social interactions.
- Efficacy studies on adventure programs have determined this type of intervention to be effective in increasing communication skills (Roland, Summers, Friedman, Barton, & McCarthy, 1987), as well as social cooperativeness, and trust among adolescents and adults receiving inpatient treatment for psychiatric disorders (Witman, 1987).

Involvement in TR Reduces Self-Abusive and Inappropriate Behaviors

- Reductions in self-abusive and inappropriate behaviors in individuals with mental retardation were demonstrated as a result of a jogging program (Alajajian, 1981).
- Using case study methodology, it was demonstrated that systematic recreational therapy intervention reduced hallucinatory speech (Wong, Terranova, Bowen, et al., 1987; Wong, Terranova, Marshall, Banzett, & Liberman, 1983). Similarly, Liberman et al. (1986) determined that inappropriate laughter and bizarre behaviors were significantly reduced when psychiatric patients were engaged in structured recreational activities.

Research Documenting Growth and Development

A variety of developmental milestones and associated behaviors are related to TR involvement or similar interventions. These include communication skills, friendships and cooperation, and hearing and speech.

Involvement in Therapeutic Play Increases the Acquisition of Developmental Milestones

- Daily structured play interventions, beginning during hospitalization and continuing for two years after discharge, were found to significantly advance the developmental levels of severely malnourished children. The experimental group of malnourished children performed significantly better than the control group on locomotor, hearing and speech, and eye and hand coordination. In fact, the malnourished group receiving the play interventions actually scored higher than the healthy control group on hearing and speech, and reached the same levels of eye/hand coordination (Grantham-McGregor, Schofield, & Harris, 1983).

Involvement in TR Increases Communication and Language Skills

- In an experiment utilizing audio tapes with rehearsal of social skills, Matson and Adkins (1984) improved the social skills (i.e., initiating conversation, complementing one another, appropriate requests, appropriate responses) of individuals with a developmental disability.
- A quasi-experimental study in an integrated camp setting revealed increased social interaction, skill acquisition, and integrated friendships for individuals with a developmental disability who received the treatment program (Rynders et al., 1990).

Involvement in TR Reduces Inappropriate Behavior and Encourages Age-Appropriate Behavior

- Schleien et al. (1988) demonstrated that children with severe developmental disabilities could acquire and generalize recreation skills, social interactions, and cooperative play behavior. Eason, White, and Newsom (1982) documented that self-stimulatory behavior could be reduced in children with autism with instruction in appropriate play.
- A recreation skill training program, in addition to weekly counseling sessions on free time use, and reinforcement training resulted in reduced stereotypic and age-inappropriate behaviors for individuals who are moderately mentally retarded (Schleien, Kiernan, & Wehman, 1981).

Research Documenting Personal and Life Satisfaction

Considerable research evidence exists to document TR's benefits to personal and life satisfaction. Probably the greatest amount of research exists in the "quality of life" area, which is often measured by global scales which assess an individual's perceived satisfaction with life quality. Other evidence exists in improved happiness, morale, competence, and social affiliation. Some research documents a reduction in loneliness and social isolation as a result of TR involvement.

Involvement in TR Increases Life and Leisure Satisfaction and Perceived Quality of Life

- McGuire (1984), using residents of two wings of a nursing facility as treatment and control groups, demonstrated increased happiness with use of video games.
- A community transition program has proved to increase perceived quality of life for individuals with a physical disability (Bullock & Howe, 1991).
- Creative dance and movement activities resulted in significantly improved life satisfaction scores for the elderly individuals in the experimental group compared with the matched controls, according to Osgood et al. (1990).
- A horticulture program resulted in significantly improved morale and improved perception of competence for nursing home residents who were randomly assigned to the treatment condition compared to the control group (Shary & Iso-Ahola, 1989).
- Using a multiple baseline design, Skalko's (1990) research with adults with chronic mental illness indicated that leisure education and TR programming increased the quality of discretionary time use. Earlier research conducted by Skalko (1982) compared experimental and control groups of adults who are psychiatrically impaired and demonstrated that those receiving leisure education interventions reported significantly greater degrees of perceived leisure well-being.

Involvement in TR Increases Social Support

- Creative dance and movement activities for one hour per week for eight months have been shown to reduce loneliness and dissatisfaction in a matched control experiment with elderly individuals (Osgood et al., 1990).
- A community transition program for individuals with a physical disability proved to reduce social isolation (Bullock & Howe, 1991).
- An aquarium activity in houses for the elderly resulted in reduced loneliness among residents as measured on the UCLA Loneliness Scale in a randomly assigned experiment (Cutler Riddick, 1985).
- In two comparison group designs, a video game program resulted in increased affiliation (Cutler Riddick et al., 1986) and music sessions resulted in increased verbal interactions (Cutler Riddick & Dugan-Jendzejec, 1988) for nursing home residents.

Involvement in TR Increases Community Integration, Community Satisfaction, and Community Self-Efficacy

- Community outings have been shown to result in increased barrier management skills among individuals with spinal cord injury (Glass, Albright, Burns, Evans, & Apple, 1984).
- A sensitivity training program designed for personnel and nondisabled students in a community creative arts program resulted in improved community integration for the individuals with a developmental disability who participated (Schleien & Larson, 1986).
- A tennis activity resulted in increased self-efficacy in participants and increased wheelchair management skills according to Greenwood et al. (1990) and Hedrick (1985).

Involvement in TR Increases Family Unity and Communications

- Fink and Beddall Fink (1986) described a family leisure program on a psychiatric inpatient unit as offering opportunities for increased cooperative interaction skills and improved relationships between family members and staff.

- DeSalvatore and Roseman (1986) indicated that TR with families of emotionally disturbed hospitalized children resulted in increased self-esteem among family members, increased positive communication, and more effective parental skills in managing their children.

Research Documenting Benefits to the Health Care System

A limited amount of research presently exists which examines the benefits of TR in terms of health care system outcomes. The research that does exist has documented that TR is successful in preventing secondary complications related to disability, reduces the need for medication in some instances, and enhances patient compliance with discharge regimes.

Involvement in TR Helps Prevent Complications Secondary to Disability and Improves Patient Compliance with Treatment Regimens

- Reduced medical complications and enhanced survival have been positively correlated to activity level and community life in adults with physical disabilities (Anson & Shepherd, 1990; Krause & Crewe, 1987). Both of these (activity level and community life) are identified goals of TR.
- Trader and Anson (1991) reported significant health differences existed between individuals with a spinal cord injury who had a commitment to leisure involvement and those who did not. Individuals with a leisure commitment reported a higher mean score for sitting tolerance; had spent fewer days in the hospital in the previous year; and were two and one-half times less likely to have a pressure sore than individuals without a commitment to leisure involvement.
- Szentagothai et al. (1987) reported that long-term physical exercise programs (one to two years of regular swimming and gymnastic activities involving 121 children between 5 and 14 years of age) were effective in reducing asthmatic symptoms, frequency of hospitalization, and use of medication.
- Clients with dementia involved in TR programs showed reduction in need for medication (Schwab, Roder, & Doan, 1985).
- Simpson, Crandall, Savage, and Pavia-Krueser (1981) found positive changes in leisure functioning were related to favorable outcomes on drug use and criminality.

General Recommendations for Outcome Based Research in TR

This chapter has highlighted a number of research studies which provide evidence that TR influences the attainment of medical, rehabilitation, habilitation, and independent living outcomes. Although documented empirical evidence does exist which demonstrates the role of TR within health care, it is, frankly, scarce, often lacks scientific rigor, and is rarely systematically replicated within or across diagnostic groups or settings.

The TR literature contains more on professional issues (who we are) than it does on tested knowledge (what we do). However, it is getting better. For instance, in a review of articles published in the *Therapeutic Recreation Journal*, Austin and Kennedy (1982) found that nonresearch articles outnumbered research articles by a three to one margin during the 1970s. The relative number of research articles published in the *Therapeutic Recreation Journal* during the following decade rose by approximately 13% (to 36.7%), according to Voelkl, Austin, and Morris (1990).

Unfortunately, this percentage (36.7%) only represents 95 out of a total 259 articles published in the *Therapeutic Recreation Journal* in a 10-year period. Just as discouraging, in terms of efficacy research, is that this limited production of research articles occurred at a time when experts in the discipline were calling for an increase in research in TR (Austin, 1982; Compton, 1984; Iso-Ahola, 1988; Witt, 1988). Furthermore, only 51 (53.6%) of these 95 research articles reported using experimental (most typically quasi-experimental) designs. Tightly controlled experimental designs are needed to establish causal relationships between TR interventions and outcomes/benefits. Moreover, many of these 51 studies reported outcomes without making clear the connection these outcomes have to the larger health care arena. The discipline should move beyond using research only for discussion among its members. Investigative TRSs must make concerted efforts to report the outcomes of their research in ways that are seen as relevant to the broader health care system.

The research cited in this chapter was not limited to research articles found in the *Therapeutic Recreation Journal* nor to only experimental research designs. In fact, many studies cited do not directly examine TR interventions provided by C.T.R.S.s, nor do the outcomes that are included in these studies occur as a result of a TR interventions; rather, many of the studies document interventions and findings that are relevant to, but not specific to, the practice of TR.

It is clear from the preceding discussion that research efforts in TR still need to be intensified and focused to systematically document what works with whom and under what conditions. This is not an easy task and will require a collaborative effort among all those involved, as Chapter 5 suggested. What follows are some general research strategies and directions for future research in TR.

General Research Strategies

A number of general research strategies have emerged from the research literature and the discussions which occurred at the National Conference on the Benefits of Therapeutic Recreation. The strategies suggested were varied but can be grouped under the following headings: (a) *networking*, (b) *graduate programs*, (c) *research design*, (d) *values*, and (e) *research dissemination*.

Networking

A need exists for better communication and networking strategies directed at facilitating an efficacy-based research program in TR. Collaboration between academicians and practitioners in TR as well as interdisciplinary research endeavors are needed if TR is to increase the amount of efficacy-based research produced germane to this discipline.

Academicians to Practitioner

Research and its relevance to practice is viewed and valued differently between academicians and practitioners. For example, academicians are pleased when the results of their research suggest that significant differences exist between individuals randomly assigned to treatment and control groups. The fact that the TR intervention was administered in a highly controlled and systematic manner, across homogeneous groups of individuals only strengthens the validity and reliability of the findings. However, when practitioners read such research results, their response can be " ... that is absurd! When will these educators/researchers realize that the real world doesn't work that way! I'll never get a group of clients who all have experienced a right cerebral vascular accident, let alone see them for three scheduled 60-minute sessions each week for three weeks." Since practitioners frequently deal with unexpected discharges and individual clients rather than groups of clients, the results of research interventions are viewed as interesting but impractical. Strict adherence to intervention guidelines, which are necessities for rigorous research designs, are often viewed as impractical for the "real world" of TR practice (see Chapter 11).

The differing perspectives on research are further accentuated when one examines the opposing incentive system within the two environments. As Chapter 5 stated, academicians are typically rewarded for research productivity with recognition, tenure, promotion, and administrative support to assist with the research effort. Practitioners, in contrast, are asked to collect research data which are beyond that typically needed in the performance of their job with no decrease in work loads. Few agencies are able to justify a reduced client load because practitioners are involved in a research effort, and so research in the practice arena is often met with reservations. At the same time, all agencies are confronted with the need for tested knowledge and demonstrated outcomes in order to maintain their existence.

Equally apparent is the need for academicians and practitioners to collaborate and dialogue about efficacy research in new ways (see Chapter 5). Academicians are challenged to disseminate research findings in a manner that makes integration into practice feasible. Such a dissemination effort should include more than writing a discussion or implications section in a journal article or presenting findings at the Leisure Research Symposium. For example, if academicians presented research results in a new practice-based format in both journal articles and conference sessions with input and reaction from practitioners, existing barriers might be reduced (see Chapter 7).

Most important, a need exists for the establishment of a research directory in which academicians and practitioners in TR who are interested in collaborative efforts in efficacy research could identify their areas of interest. The establishment of such a directory would enable individuals with similar research interests to collaborate and begin to bolster the research data base that documents the clinical effectiveness of TR. The recent attempt by the ATRA Research Committee to develop such a directory is timely and potentially useful (see Malkin, *ATRA Newsletter*, January/February, 1992). The strengthening of the TR data base through collaborative research is imperative to the future of TR. Without it, " . . . others will determine when and how we practice and will control whether we are compensated for the services we deliver" (Seibert, 1991, p. 7).

Interdisciplinary Efforts

The urgent need for efficacy research in TR requires that cooperative efforts be forged with other disciplines. The need to conduct research studies from an interdisciplinary perspective is consistent with the research efforts in the larger health care arena. The utility of interdisciplinary research efforts is especially apparent in research studies which examine physiological changes as a result of TR involvement. Often TR researchers fail to use physiological measures for lack of knowledge regarding the techniques used to assess variables such as vital capacity, growth hormones, or choles- terol levels. Physiological outcomes of TR are an important area that has not received much attention, yet the few studies completed in this area (Berk et al., 1988; Russoniello, 1991; Santiago et al., 1991) have had extremely promising results. Because of the physiological outcomes assessed, this type of research is more consistent with and accepted by the larger medical community.

Graduate Training Programs

Graduate training programs at both the master's and doctoral levels can make significant contributions to efficacy research. Graduate programs need, first, to make a commitment to an efficacy research agenda and then encourage students to conduct research in one area of that agenda. If only one-third of the vast number of theses and dissertations produced each year contained efficacy research, we would be well on our way to creating a sizable data base.

Replication studies, which we give credence to in our discussions of the scientific method, usually receive lip service when it comes to student research. Students want, and are generally supported by faculty, to do original research. All too frequently, this original research turns out to be a survey on some benign issue that contributes little or nothing to our knowledge base. Graduate students, particularly at the master's level, should be encouraged to conduct replication research, and educators should encourage replication research by valuing it more.

Graduate programs at the doctoral level should intensify the research training experience in the curriculum. Students should be thoroughly familiar with various research methodologies that are amenable to the practical rigors of field settings, and they should be familiar and comfortable with the knowledge and use of a variety of statistical techniques. This is true even for those students who intend to focus on a phenomenological study for their dissertations. Even these students will eventually be in a position to consult with field settings where research questions are most suitably addressed by methodologies involving multivariate analysis.

Doctoral programs should consider adding a research apprenticeship to their curricular requirements where students run a small pilot of their intended dissertation design. They would thereby become aware of possible complications which require further thought before they proceeded with the dissertation. Such a requirement would add to the research expertise of the student and also produce stronger and more meaningful dissertations. TR educators should recognize that the doctoral degree is a research degree and put an end to the often heard statements that "I just want to be an advanced clinician . . . " or "I just want to be a good teacher, not a researcher." Practitioners generally consider someone with the doctorate to be an expert in research. It is time for university programs to deliver on that expectation by guaranteeing such expertise.

Variety of Research Designs

The selection of research methodology that is compatible with practice is an important consideration for all research conducted in TR. The investigative TRS needs to select research designs that: (a) will answer the research questions posed in a valid and reliable manner; (b) can be realistically implemented in the "real world" setting of TR practice; and, (c) contain interventions specific to TR conducted by TR specialists. Unfortunately, many of the studies summarized under the "benefits" section do not meet all of these criteria (see Chapter 11 for design and implementation of field-based TR research).

In particular, researchers and practitioners should consider single-subject (Chapter 10) and case study methods for research designs. Because of their individualistic focus, these designs are especially suited to clinical application as the emphasis is on the influence of a TR intervention on a particular client. Furthermore, the investigative TRS should consider the possibility of complementing quantitative research methods with qualitative methodologies (see Chapters 12-14 of this text). The combination of these two techniques within a research design often results in an enriched understanding of the phenomenon under study.

In addition to the use of alternate design strategies which are more suited for use in practice, research should be planned with a longitudinal perspective. It may not be until three to six months after discharge from a rehabilitation center that the influence of TR interventions surfaces and assists the client in maintaining independent functioning.

Valuing the Terms Leisure and Recreation

The terms "recreation" and "leisure" are concepts that continue to evoke strong opinions which influence the advancement of TR's body of knowledge. Some contend that TR research ought to preserve the discipline's claimed uniqueness—the emphasis on recreation and leisure. Individuals with this perspective believe that researchers should focus on outcomes directly related to leisure functioning and an autonomous leisure lifestyle regardless of the value others associate with these outcomes. These individuals argue that health care policy makers and service agencies need to be educated about the importance of recreation and leisure to the basic human right to a quality life. In short, some contend that recreation and leisure are important and valuable human endeavors and experiences in and of themselves, and TR researchers should not apologize for a leisure-outcome focus nor should they be compelled to establish the linkage of this leisure focus to health care concerns. All individuals, according to this perspective, are entitled to recreation and leisure and the provision of TR services in a health care setting is justifiable on the grounds that leisure expression reflects a basic human right to a quality life. This perspective reflects an internally relevant rationale for the inclusion of TR in health care and human service systems.

Others contend that research ought to demonstrate the contributions TR services make to larger outcomes widely valued by health care and human service systems. This view seems to best reflect the suggestion of AHCPR and MEDTEP (see Chapter 1). They urge the TR discipline to demonstrate outcomes that are valued by the agencies that employ TR practitioners and the entities that pay for health care services. Thus, documented benefits of TR, such as increased involvement in recreation and leisure pursuits, are researched in terms of their influence on overall services outcomes. These include the reduced likelihood of secondary health complications, the maintenance of sobriety, or the increased and continuous use of socially active community opportunities. This perspective promotes an externally relevant rationale for inclusion of TR services in health care and human service systems, and demonstrates a congruency between the discipline's outcome focus with that of other health care disciplines.

The enormity of the need for efficacy research supports both views. The discipline needs to demonstrate the contribution of recreation and leisure, both as treatment and as a human experience, and its relationship to regaining and maintaining overall health and well-being. Health care and social policy makers need to be educated to the importance of recreation and leisure in the total fabric of healthful living, including habilitation, rehabilitation, and independent living. The discipline of TR needs to be careful not to focus its research efforts within a narrow and restrictive range of outcomes but rather to fully understand the phenomenon of therapeutic recreation and the varied roles it plays in the lives of individuals with disabilities. As Iso-Ahola wrote in 1988 regarding the status of research in TR:

> It is surprising that empirical documentation of fundamental questions about *effects* of recreation on the well-being of various special population groups remain largely untapped and unstudied. Using recreation/leisure as an independent variable in research is particularly relevant to therapeutic recreation. Because many professionals work in various clinical settings they are faced with the challenge of demonstrating that therapeutic recreation programs are really therapeutic and make a difference in patients' care and rehabilitation. Among those who raise such questions are clinical psychologists or medical doctors. In addition, third party payers, insurance companies and accrediting bodies are increasingly demanding evidence of the impact of therapeutic recreation services, evidence that mainly comes from experimental studies (p. 9-10).

Regardless of the philosophical approach one chooses, the need for empirical experimental research was clear in 1988 and remains clear and desperately needed today.

Need for Dissemination to a Variety of Audiences

The knowledge and understanding created through TR research needs to be shared with other disciplines and agencies endeavoring to serve persons who are ill or have disabilities. It is particularly important to share this information in a context that is pertinent to others so that they are better able to see the relevance of TR services to *health status, functional capacity, and quality of life*. The discipline should make concerted and deliberate efforts to foster and stimulate more cross-disciplinary collaboration and cooperation within training, research, and dissemination of mutually useful information. It would be particularly useful to increase efforts to publish TR research and practice in journals external to the discipline. Also, it would be beneficial to have the *Therapeutic Recreation Journal* and the *Annual in Therapeutic Recreation* indexed in major health care indices (e.g., Psych Lit, Medline, Medlars, Index Medicus), and to explore similar possibilities with newer data base vendors such as DIALOG and BRS. Furthermore, TR representatives need to continue the work that they have begun under the auspices of the ATRA to cooperate with and educate important regulatory bodies in the rehabilitation field such as the Commission on the Accreditation of Rehabilitation Facilities (CARF), and the Joint Commission on the Accreditation of Healthcare Organizations (JCAHO). This type of liaison also needs to be nurtured with a variety of research agencies such as the U.S. Department of Education's National Institute on Disability and Rehabilitation Research (NIDRR), and the Public Health Service's National Center for Medical Rehabilitation Research, and agency for Healthcare Policy and Research (AHCPR).

Future Research Priorities in TR

It is our belief that future research in TR should address the six broad-based themes presented in the "benefits" section. Research in TR, therefore, should be designed to determine the benefits derived for the participant in the following areas: (a) *physical health and health maintenance*, (b) *cognitive functioning*, (c) *psychosocial health*, (d) *growth and personal development*, (e) *personal and life satisfaction*, and finally, (f) *societal and health care system outcomes*. Each of these research themes should be investigated in terms of the degree to which they influence/improve the *health status, functional capacity, and/or quality of life* for clients. Health status, functional capacity, and quality of life are the three main areas by which the efficacy of health care is evaluated. It is imperative that TR research be designed to examine not only the specific leisure/recreational outcomes derived from TR interventions but also how these outcomes affect a client's health status, functional capacity, and quality of life. Research of this nature is the only type that can respond to the challenge confronting all health care disciplines—demonstrating that what is delivered as interventions results in improved health for the consumers of these services. This is what TR must do if it is to remain a health care discipline.

Implementing such a research agenda will not be easy. It requires a **multiple tier approach to research**. This approach requires systematic efficacy evaluations of the direct results of TR interventions followed by a determination of how these outcomes influence broader health care system concerns. For instance, the consensus among those at the National Conference on The Benefits of Therapeutic Recreation in Rehabilitation was that the typical outcome areas that TR practitioners attempt to address (whether through treatment programs, leisure education/counseling programs or special recreation services) were enhancing the individual's *coping behavior, independent living skills, social skills* and *sense of affiliation,* and *health maintenance behaviors.* Determining that TR programs actually achieve these outcomes in tightly controlled research designs that are replicated in a variety of settings is the first level of research that is needed. Additional research at this level would also examine the differential effects associated with the timing of an intervention (i.e., whether it was provided as inpatient or outpatient) as well as the frequency, duration, and intensity of the treatment needed to bring about a change in client functioning.

The second level of research involves examining whether the attainment of these TR outcomes (e.g., coping behavior, social skills) have any influence on broader health concerns such as length of stay, medication compliance and use, motivation for and compliance with treatment programs, and decreasing incidence of secondary complications related to disability. Additional research at this level would examine in what ways (if any) the attainment of TR outcomes influenced the functional capacity of clients (i.e., their ability to function independently, vocational success) and the life quality of these individuals (i.e., psychological well-being, life satisfaction).

The challenge to the discipline is to conduct the research needed to answer these questions. Approximately ten years ago Park, Ellis, Eggert, and Goldstein (1980) edited a booklet entitled *Focus on Research: Recreation for Disabled Individuals* which identified priority research topics in recreation for differently abled individuals. Included in the chapter on "Treatment Implications of Therapeutic Recreation in Rehabilitation: A State-of-the-Art Paper" (Peterson, 1980), was a research agenda that suggested that research be conducted to determine the effects of recreation treatment and leisure education on successful community adjustment and living, and the effects of recreation treatment and leisure education on other primary treatment outcomes (p. 93). A minimal amount of research was done in this area in the past ten years and little of what was completed was done in a systematic manner. It appears, as Witt (1988) and Compton (1984) indicated previously, that most of the research conducted in TR is a "shot-gun" affair. Compton (1984) wrote:

> ... few individuals have produced research in a defined content area or expanded a base of knowledge. Although several individuals have proposed theories, models, or other paradigms, there is little longitudinal sense to their work. Follow-up studies and applications to other subjects under different conditions have rarely been undertaken as we move onto the next popular subject ... (p. 12).

Although a few exceptions exist, notably the research of Dattilo, Iso-Ahola, and Schleien, the situation is essentially the same a decade later. The discipline of TR was confronted with the need for efficacy research and a tentative framework to guide that research in 1980. We failed to meet that challenge in 1980. Will we and can we afford to do the same again?

Discussion Questions

1. Why should TR practitioners engage in research? What purposes do research findings serve?
2. List some of the possible physical and health maintenance benefits derived from TR services that are supported with empirical evidence. Suggest a possible research study which could be designed to enhance the research data in this area.
3. List some of the possible cognitive benefits derived from TR services that are supported with empirical evidence. Suggest a possible research study which could be designed to enhance the research data in this area.
4. List some of the possible psychosocial benefits derived from TR services that are supported with empirical evidence. Suggest a possible research study which could be designed to enhance the research data in this area.
5. List some of the possible human growth and development benefits derived from TR services that are supported with empirical evidence. Suggest a possible research study which could be designed to enhance the research data in this area.
6. List some of the possible health care system benefits derived from TR services that are supported with empirical evidence. Suggest a possible research study which could be designed to enhance the research data in this area.
7. In this chapter a number of research strategies were suggested that could enhance the amount of research conducted in TR. Discuss the strengths and weaknesses of these strategies and identify those which you believe would be most effective at increasing TR research efforts.
8. What is meant by a "multiple tier approach" to efficacy research in TR? Design a series of research questions which would reflect this approach.

References

Adriaenssens, P., Eggermont, E., Pyck, K., Boeckx, W., & Gilles, B. (1988). The video invasion of rehabilitation, *Burns, 14*, 417-419.

Alajajian, L. (1981). Jogging program for deaf-blind students improves condition and reduces self-stimulation. *News . . . About Deaf-Blind Student, Programmed Services in New England, 6*(1), 3-4.

Anson, C., & Shepherd, C. (1990, March). A survey of post-acute spinal cord patients: Medical, psychological, and social characteristics. *Trends: Research News From Shepherd Spinal Center.*

Austin, D. R. (1982). *Therapeutic recreation: Processes and techniques.* New York, NY: Wiley.

Austin, D. R. (1987). Recreation and persons with physical disabilities: A literature synthesis. *Therapeutic Recreation Journal, 21*(1), 36-44.

Austin, D., & Kennedy, D. (1982). Sources of articles published in the Therapeutic Recreation Journal during the 1970s. *Therapeutic Recreation Journal, 16*(3), 35-41.

Bandura, A. (1977). *Social learning theory.* Englewood Cliffs, NJ: Prentice-Hall.

Banziger, G., & Rousch, S. (1983). Nursing homes for the birds: A control-relevant intervention with bird feeders. *The Gerontologist, 23*, 527-531.

Barlow, D. H., Hayes, S. C., & Nelson, R. O. (1984). *The scientist practitioner.* Elmsford, NY: Pergamon Press.

Beck, P. (1982). The successful interventions in nursing homes: The therapeutic effects of cognitive activity. *The Gerontologist, 22*, 389-383.

Berger, B. G. (1983/1984). Stress reduction through exercise: The mind-body connection. *Motor Skills: Theory into Practice, 7*, 31-46.

Berger, B. G. (1986). Use of jogging and swimming as stress reduction techniques. In J. H. Humphrey (Ed.), *Current selected research in the psychology and sociology of sport, 1,* 97-113. New York, NY: AMS Press.

Berk, L. et al. (1988). Humor associated laughter decreases cortisol and increases spontaneous lymphocyte blastogenesis. *Clinical Research, 36,* 435.

Brock, B. J. (1988). Effects of horseback riding on physically disabled adults. *Therapeutic Recreation Journal, 22*(3), 34-43.

Buettner, L. (1988). Utilizing development theory and adaptive equipment with regressed geriatric patients in therapeutic recreation. *Therapeutic Recreation Journal, 22*(3), 72-79.

Bullock, C. C., & Howe, C. Z. (1991). A model therapeutic recreation program for the reintegration of persons with disabilities into the community. *Therapeutic Recreation Journal, 25*(1), 7-17.

Cerny, F. J. (1989). Relative effects of bronchial drainage and exercise for in-hospital care of patients with cystic fibrosis. *Physical Therapy, 69,* 633-638.

Compton, D. (1984). Research priorities in recreation for special populations. *Therapeutic Recreation Journal, 18*(1), 9-17.

Conroy, M., Fincham, F., & Agard-Evans, C. (1988). Can they do anything? Ten single-subject studies of the engagement level of hospitalized demented patients. *British Journal of Occupational Therapy, 51,* 129-132.

Cutler Riddick, C. (1985). Health, aquariums, and the non-institutionalized elderly. In M. Sussman (Ed.), *Pets and the family* (pp. 63-173). Binghamton, NY: Haworth Press.

Cutler Riddick, C., & Dugan-Jendzejec, M. (1988). Health related impacts of a music program on nursing home residents. In F. Humphrey and J. Humphrey (Eds.), *Recreation: Current selected research* (pp. 155-166). New York, NY: AMS Press.

Cutler Riddick, C., Spector, S., & Drogin, E. (1986). The effects of videogames play on the emotional states and affiliative behavior of nursing home residents. *Activities, Adaptation and Aging,, 8,* 95-108.

Curtis, K. A., McClanahan, S., Hall, K. M., Dillon, D., & Brown, K. F. (1986). Health, vocational, and functional status in spinal cord injured athletes and nonathletes. *Archives of Physical Medicine and Rehabilitation, 67,* 862-867.

Dattilo, J., & Barnett, L. (1985). Therapeutic recreation for individuals with severe handicaps: Implications of chosen participation. *Therapeutic Recreation Journal, 19*(3), 79-91.

Davis, G. M., Shephard, R. J., & Jackson, R. W. (1981). Cardiorespiratory fitness and muscular strength in the lower-limb disabled. *Canadian Journal of Applied Sport Sciences, 6,* 159-177.

Demarest, D. S., Hooke, J. F., & Erickson, M. T. (1984). Preoperative intervention for the reduction of anxiety in pediatric surgery patients. *Children's Health Care, 12,* 179-183.

DeSalvatore, G., & Roseman, D. (1986). The parent-child activity group: Using activities to work with children and their families in residential treatment. *Child Care Quarterly, 15*(4), 213-222.

Driver, B., Brown, P., & Peterson, G. (1991). *Benefits of leisure.* State College, PA: Venture.

Eason, L. J., White, M. J., & Newsom, C. (1982). Generalized reductions of self-stimulatory behavior: An effect of teaching appropriate play to autistic children. *Analysis and Intervention in Developmental Disabilities, 2,* 157-169.

Federal Register, 52(217), November 10, 1987.

Figoni, S., Boileau, R., Massey, B., & Larsen, J. R. (1988). Physiological responses of quadriplegic and able-bodied men during exercise at the same VO2. *Adapted Physical Activity Quarterly, 5,* 130-139.

Fink, J. B., & Beddall Fink, T. (1986). Implementation and rationale of family leisure programs for an inpatient psychiatric hospital. *Trends III: Therapeutic recreation expressions and new dimensions* (3rd ed.), pp. 52-59.

Gillis, A. (1989). The effect of play on immobilized children in hospital. *International Journal of Nursing Studies, 26,* 261-269.

Glass, J., Albright, C., Burns, C., Evans, J., & Apple, D. (1984, April). *Method and Outcome Analysis.* Paper presented at the American Spinal Injury Association.

Grantham-McGregor, S., Schofield, W., & Harris, L. (1983). Effect of psychosocial stimulation on mental development of severely malnourished children: An interim report. *Pediatrics, 72,* 239-243.

Green, J. (1989). Effects of a water aerobics program on the blood pressure, percentage of body fat, weight, and resting pulse rate of senior citizens. *Journal of Applied Gerontology, 8*(1), 132-138.

Greenwood, C. M., Dzewattowski, D. A., & French, R. (1990). Self-efficacy and psychological well-being of wheelchair tennis participants and wheelchair nontennis participants. *Adapted Physical Activity Quarterly, 7*(1), 12-21.

Hedrick, B. N. (1985). The effect of wheelchair tennis participation and mainstreaming upon the perceptions of competence of physically disabled adolescents. *Therapeutic Recreation Journal, 19*(2), 34-46.

Heywood, L. A. (1978). Perceived recreation experience and the relief of tension. *Journal of Leisure Research, 10,* 86-97.

Hoffman, M. D. (1986). Cardiorespiratory fitness and training in quadriplegics and paraplegics. *Sports Medicine, 3,* 312-330.

Hopper, C. (1988). Self-concept and motor performance of hearing impaired boys and girls. *Adapted Physical Activity Quarterly, 5,* 293-304.

Ipsa, J., Barrett, B., & Kim, Y. (1988). Effects of supervised play in a hospital waiting room. *Children's Health Care, 16,* 195-200.

Iso-Ahola, S. (1988). Research in therapeutic recreation. *Therapeutic Recreation Journal, 22*(1), 7-13.

Jackson, R. W., & Davis, G. M. (1983). The value of sports and recreation for the physically disabled. *Orthopedic Clinics of North America, 14,* 301-315.

Jocheim, K. A., & Strohkendle, H. (1973). Value of particular sports of the wheelchair disabled in maintaining health of the paraplegic. *Paraplegia, 11,* 173-178.

Katz, J. F., Adler, J. C., Mazzarella, N. J., & Inck, L. P. (1985). Psychological consequences of an exercise training program for a paraplegic man: A case study. *Rehabilitation Psychology, 30*(1), 53-58.

Keller, M. J. (1991). "The impact of a water aerobics program on older adults." Unpublished manuscript.

Koch, I., Schlegel, M., Pirrwitz, A., Jaschke, B., & Schlegel, K. (1983). On objectivizing the training effect of sport therapy in wheelchair-users (In German). *International Journal of Rehabilitation Research, 6*, 439-448.

Krause, J. S., & Crewe, M. M. (1987). Prediction of long-term survival of persons with spinal cord injury. *Rehabilitation Psychology, 32*(4), 205-213.

Lanagan, D., & Dattilo, J. (1989). The effects of a leisure education program on individuals with mental retardation. *Therapeutic Recreation Journal, 23*(4), 62-72.

Liberman, R. P., Mueser, K. T., Wallace, C. J., Jacobs, H. E., Eckman, T., & Massel, K. (1986). Training skills in the psychiatrically disabled: Learning coping and competence. *Schizophrenia Bulletin, 12*(4), 631-647.

Long, B. C. (1984). Aerobic conditioning and stress inoculation: A comparison of stress-management interventions. *Cognitive Therapy Research, 8*(5), 517-542.

Malkin, M. J. (1992, January/February). ATRACOM interest Survey. *ATRA Newsletter,* p. 6.

Marini, D. G. (1978). Effects of additional physical and recreational curriculum on selected perceptual-motor abilities of educable mentally retarded children. *Therapeutic Recreation Journal, 12*(3), 31-38.

Martinsen, E. W., Medhus, A., & Sandvik, L. (1984). The effect of aerobic exercise on depression: A controlled study. Unpublished manuscript.

Matson, J., & Adkins, J. (1984). A self-instructional social skills training program for mentally retarded persons. *Mental Retardation, 18*, 245-248.

McAvoy, L. H., Schatz, E. C., Stutz, M. E., Schlein, S. J., & Lais, G. (1989). Integrated wilderness adventure: Effects on personal and lifestyle traits of persons with and without disabilities. *Therapeutic Recreation Journal, 23*(3), 50-64.

McGuire, F. (1984). Improving the quality of life for residents of long term care facilities through video games. *Activities, Adaptation and Aging, 6*, 1-8.

Miles, D. S., Sawka, M. N., Wilde, S. W., Durbin, R. J., & Gotshall, R. W. (1982). Pulmonary function changes in wheelchair athletes subsequent to exercise training. *Ergonomics, 25*, 239-246.

Osgood, N., Meyers, B., & Orchowsky, S. (1990). The impact of creative dance and movement training on the life satisfaction of older adults. *Journal of Applied Gerontology, 9,* 255-265.

Park, D., Ellis, W., Eggert, D., & Goldstein, J. (1980). *Focus on research: Recreation for disabled individuals.* Washington, DC: George Washington University School of Education and Human Development.

Peniston, L. (1991, September). *The effects of a microcomputer training program on short-term memory in elderly individuals.* A paper presented at the Benefits of Therapeutic Recreation in Rehabilitation Conference, Lafayette Hill, PA.

Peterson, C. (1980). Treatment implications of therapeutic recreation in rehabilitation: A state-of-the-art paper. In D. Park, W. Ellis, D. Eggert, J. Goldstein (Eds.), *Focus on research: Recreation for disabled individuals* (pp. 77-94). Washington, DC: George Washington University School of Education and Human Development.

Rancourt, A. M. (1991a). An exploration of the relationships among substance abuse, recreation, and leisure for women who abuse substances. *Therapeutic Recreation Journal, 25*(3), 9-18

Rancourt, A. M. (1991b, April 7). *Results of a past discharge survey of women who participated in a six month comprehensive leisure education program while in substance abuse treatment.* Paper presented at the American Alliance of Health, Physical Education, Recreation, and Dance Symposium on Drugs and Drug Education, San Francisco, CA.

Rasnake, L. K,., & Linscheid, T. R. (1989). Anxiety reduction in children receiving medical care: Developmental considerations. *Developmental and Behavioral Pediatrics, 10,* 169-175.

Riegler, J. (1980). Comparison of a reality orientation program for geriatric patients with and without music. *Journal of Music Therapy, 17,* 26-33.

Robb, G. M., & Evert, A. (1987). Risk recreation and persons with disabilities. *Therapeutic Recreation Journal, 21*(1), 58-69.

Roland, C. C., Summers, S., Friedman, M. J., Barton, G. M., & McCarthy, K. (1987). Creation of an experiential challenge program. *Therapeutic Recreation Journal, 21*(2), 54-63.

Rothe, T., Kohl, C., & Mansfeld, H. J. (1990). Controlled study of the effect of sports training on cardiopulmonary functions in asthmatic children and adolescents. *Pneumologie, 44,* 1110-1114. (From Medline, 1991, UD 9104).

Russoniello, C. V. (1991, September). *An exploratory study of physiological and psychological changes in alcoholic patients after recreation therapy treatments.* Paper presented at the Benefits of Therapeutic Recreation in Rehabilitation Conference, Lafayette Hill, PA.

Rynders, J. E., Schleien, S. J., & Mustonen, T. (1990). Integrating children with severe disabilities for intensified outdoor education: Focus on feasibility. *Mental Retardation, 28,* 7-14.

Sachs, M. L. (1982). Running therapy: Change agent in anxiety and stress management. *Journal of Health, Physical Eduction, Recreation and Dance, 53*(7), 44-45.

Santiago, M. C., Coyle, C. P., & Troupe, J. T. (1991, November). *Effects of twelve weeks of aerobic exercise in individuals with physical disabilities.* Paper presented at 8th International Symposium on Adapted Physical Activity, Miami, FL.

Savell, K. (1986). Leisure efficacy: Theory and therapy implications for Therapeutic Recreation programming. *Therapeutic Recreation Journal, 20*(1), 43-52.

Schleien, S., Cameron, J., Rynders, J., & Slick, C. (1988). Acquisition and generalization of leisure skills from school to the home and community by learners with severe multihandicaps. *Therapeutic Recreation Journal, 22*(3), 53-71.

Schleien, S., Kiernan, J., & Wehman, P. (1981). Evaluation of an age-appropriate leisure skills program for moderately retarded adults. *Education and Training of the Mentally Retarded, 16*(1), 13-19.

Schleien, S. J., Krotee, M. L., Mustonen, T., Kelterborn, B., & Schermer, A. D. (1987). The effect of integrating children with autism into a physical activity and recreation setting. *Therapeutic Recreation Journal, 21*(4), 52-62.

Schleien, S. J., & Larson, A. (1986). Adult leisure education for the independent use of a community recreation center. *The Journal of the Association of Persons with Severe Handicaps, 11*(1), 39-44.

Schwab, M., Roder, J., & Doan, J. (1985). Relieving the anxiety and fear in dementia. *Journal of Gerontological Nursing, 11*(5), 8-15.

Scogin, F., Hamblin, D., & Beutler, L. (1987). Bibliotherapy for depressed older adults: A self-help alternative. *The Gerontologist, 27,* 383-387.

Scogin, F., Jamison, C., & Davis, N. (1990). Two-year follow-up of bibliotherapy for depression in older adults. *Journal of Consulting and Clinical Psychology, 58,* 665-667.

Scogin, F., Jamison, C., & Gochneaur, K. (1989). Comparative efficacy of cognitive and behavioral bibliotherapy for mildly and moderately depressed older adults. *Journal of Consulting and Clinical Psychology, 57,* 403-407.

Seibert, M. L. (1991). Chapter 2: Keynote. In Coyle, C., Kinney, W., Riley, B., & Shank, J. (Eds.). *Benefits of therapeutic recreation: A consensus view.* (pp. 5-15). Philadelphia, PA: Temple University Press.

Shank, J. W., Coyle, C. P., & Kinney, W. B. (1991a, September). *A comparison of the effects of clinical versus diversional therapeutic recreation involvement on rehabilitation outcomes.* Paper presented at Benefits of Therapeutic Recreation in Rehabilitation Conference, Lafayette Hill, PA.

Shank, J. W., Coyle, C. P., & Kinney, W. B. (1991b, September). *Comparative effects of segregated and integrated recreation on persons with disabilities.* Paper presented at Benefits of Therapeutic Recreation in Rehabilitation Conference, Lafayette Hill, PA.

Shary, J., & Iso-Ahola, S. (1989). Effects of a control relevant intervention program on nursing home residents' perceived competence and self-esteem. *Therapeutic Recreation Journal, 23*(1), 7-16.

Sherrill, C., & Rainbolt, W. (1988). Self-actualization profiles of male able-bodied and elite cerebral palsied athletes. *Adapted Physical Activity Quarterly, 5,* 108-119.

Sime, W. E. (1987). Exercise in the treatment and prevention of depression. In Morgan and Goldston (Eds.), *Exercise and mental health.* Washington, DC: Hemisphere Publishing Corporation.

Simpson, D. D., Crandall, R., Savage, L. J., & Pavia-Krueser, E. (1981). Leisure of opiate addicts at posttreatment follow-up. *Journal of Counseling Psychology, 28*(1), 36-39.

Skalko, T. K. (1982). *The effects of a leisure education program on the perceived leisure well-being of psychiatrically impaired active army personnel.* Unpublished doctoral dissertation, University of Maryland, College Park, MD.

Skalko, T. K. (1990). Discretionary time use and the chronically mentally ill. *Therapeutic Recreation Annual, 1,* 9-14.

Stotts, K. M. (1986). Health maintenance: Paraplegic athletes and nonathletes. *Archives of Physical Medicine and Rehabilitation, 67,* 109-114.

Strain, P. (1975). Increasing social play of severely retarded preschoolers with socio-dramatic activities. *Mental Retardation, 13,* 7-9.

Stuckey, K., & Barkus, C. (1986). Visually impaired scouts meet the Philmont challenge. *Journal of Visual Impairment and Blindness, 80*(5), 750-751.

Szentagothai, K., Gyene, I., Szocska, M., & Osvath, P. (1987). Physical exercise program for children with bronchial asthma. *Pediatric Pulmonology, 3,* 166-172.

Trader, B., & Anson, C. (1991, September). *The relationship of leisure commitment to health in individuals following spinal cord injury.* Paper presented at the Benefits of Therapeutic Recreation in Rehabilitation Conference, Lafayette Hill, PA.

Van Loan, M. D., McCluer, S., Loftin, J. M., & Boileau, R. A. (1987). Comparison of physiological responses to maximal arm exercise among able-bodied, paraplegics and quadriplegics. *International Medical Society of Paraplegia, 25,* 397-405.

Voelkl, J., Austin, D., & Morris, C. (1990, October). *Content analysis of articles published in Therapeutic Recreation Journal during the 1980s.* Paper presented at the National Recreation and Park Association's Leisure research Symposium, Phoenix, AZ.

Wassmann, K. B., & Iso-Ahola, S. E. (1985). The relationship between recreation participation and depression in psychiatric patients. *Therapeutic Recreation Journal, 19*(3), 63-70.

Weiss, C., & Jamieson, N. (1988). Hidden disabilities: A new enterprise for therapeutic recreation. *Therapeutic Recreation Journal, 22*(4), 9-17.

Witt, P. (1988). Therapeutic Recreation research: Past, present and future. *Therapeutic Recreation Journal, 22*(1), 14-23.

Witman, J. P. (1987). The efficacy of adventure programming in the development of cooperation and trust with adolescents in treatment. *Therapeutic Recreation Journal, 21*(3), 22-29.

Witt, P. A. (1988). Therapeutic recreation research: Past, present, and future. *Therapeutic Recreation Journal, 22*(1), 14-23.

Wolfe, J. (1983). The use of music in a group sensory training program for regressed geriatric patients. *Activities, Adaptation and Aging, 4*(1), 49-62.

Wolfer, J., Gaynard, L., Goldberger, J., Laidley, L. N., & Thompson, R. (1988). An experimental evaluation of a model child life program. *Children's Health Care, 16,* 244-254.

Wong, S. E., Terranova, M. D., Bowen, L., et al. (1987). Providing independent recreational activities to reduce stereotypic vocalizations in chronic schizophrenics. *Journal of Applied Behavior Analysis, 20,* 77-81.

Wong, S. E., Terranova, M. D., Marshall, B. D., Banzett, L. K., & Liberman, R. P. (1983, May). *Reducing bizarre stereotypic behavior in chronic psychiatric patients: Effects of supervised and independent recreational activities,* presented at the Ninth Annual Convention of the Association of Behavior Analysis, Milwaukee, WI.

Yoder, R., Nelson, D., & Smith, D. (1989). Added purpose versus rote exercise in female nursing home residents. *American Journal of Occupational Therapy, 43*(9), 581-586.

Zwiren, L., Huberman, G., & Bar-Or, O. (1973). Cardiopulmonary functions of sedentary and highly active paraplegics. *Medicine and Science in Sport, 5,* 683-686.

Alphabetical Index

veracity   103
visual analysis   190
visual inspection   190

W
withdrawal designs   193

Often Referred to Names

INDEX

*See references and suggested readings for Chapter 7 and 8

Kratochwill
McReynolds
Thompson
Murphy
Pelegrino
McCormick
Scott

Chapter 11
Campbell
Stanley
Cook
McMillan
Schumacher

Chapter 12
Howe
Rancourt
Scott
Godbey
Weissinger
Guba
Lincoln
Hultsman
Anderson
Miles
Huberman
Stones
Bruyn
McCormick
Chillcott
Glaser
Strauss
Bullock
Douglas

Chapter 13
Glancy
Lincoln
Guba
Miles

Huberman
Bruyn
Patton

Chapter 14
Miles
Huberman
Marshall
Rossman
Patton
Yin
Lincoln
Guba
Kidder
Jick
Brewer
Hunter
Strauss
Corbin
Van Maanen

Chapter 15**
JCAHO
NIDRR
AHCPR
Driver
Brown
Peterson
Barlow
Hayes
Nelson

**See Chapter 15 references for additional authors cited.

Marjorie J. Malkin Ed.D., C.T.R.S., is currently serving as an Assistant Professor in the Department of Recreation, Southern Illinois University, in Carbondale, IL., teaching primarily within the therapeutic recreation curriculum. She is coeditor and contributor to this text. Malkin received her bachelor's degree in Philosophy from Mt. Holyoke College, and her master's degree (Recreation) and doctoral degree (Therapeutic Recreation) from the University of Georgia. She has served as the Chair of the ATRA Research committee 1990-92 and has recently been elected to the ATRA Board of Directors. Research areas include: leisure attitudes of depressed, suicidal women; family leisure education for adolescents in substance abuse treatment programs; and third party reimbursement for therapeutic recreation services. Prior to accepting a full-time teaching position, Malkin had four and one-half years of clinical experience, both as a C.T.R.S., and as head of Activity Therapy Departments in inpatient psychiatric and substance abuse treatment programs.

Christine Z. Howe is a coeditor of and contributor to this book. Howe received her Ph.D. in Leisure Studies from the University of Illinois at Urbana-Champaign. Since then her positions have been in university-based recreation and leisure studies departments. Her contacts with professional practice have been through research, consulting, and volunteering. Howe is currently Professor and Graduate Coordinator in the Recreation and Leisure Studies Program at the State University of New York College at Brockport. Howe's teaching interests lie in research methods, programming, social scientific concepts of leisure, and service delivery systems. Her research interests have focused on assessment, evaluation, and research methods (particularly naturalistic inquiry); understanding leisure as a subjective phenomenon; and investigating community, transitional, and clinical leisure service delivery systems.

Charles C. (Charlie) Bullock, Ph.D., is an Associate Professor in the Curriculum in Leisure Studies and Recreation Administration at the University of North Carolina at Chapel Hill. Bullock has a bachelor's degree in Religion and master's degree in Recreation Administration with an emphasis in Therapeutic Recreation from the University of North Carolina at Chapel Hill. He received his Ph.D. in Leisure Studies from the University of Illinois, Urbana-

Champaign. He joined the faculty at the University of North Carolina at Chapel Hill in 1979. He is the Director of the Curriculum's Center for Recreation and Disability Studies which conceives and conducts exemplary training, research and demonstration projects. Bullock is currently the Project Director of a research and demonstration project entitled Reintegration Through Recreation, the Project Director of a training project entitled LIFE: Leisure is for Everyone, and Principal Investigator of two research projects to determine the effectiveness of leisure education in the transition of special education students from secondary schools to adult life. During his professional career, he has written, presented, and consulted extensively in the areas of integration, reintegration, transition, and leisure education. Although trained in positivistic research initially, his major research interest and expertise is in phenomenological/interpretive research.

Linda L. Caldwell received her B.S. from The Pennsylvania State University, her M.S. from North Carolina State University, and her Ph.D. from the University of Maryland. Highlights of Caldwell's employment in therapeutic recreation include directing recreation in a 500 bed nursing home and providing recreation to persons in the psychiatric unit of a general hospital. She has also led a two-county project that provided community living for adults with mental retardation. Caldwell's contacts with professional practice have been maintained through extensive research, training programs, and consulting in Maryland, the Province of Ontario, and North Carolina. Caldwell is also an active leader in professional societies and associations in Canada and the U.S. She is currently an Assistant Professor in the Department of Leisure Studies at the University of North Carolina–Greensboro and Senior Cochair of NRPA's Leisure Research Symposium. Caldwell teaches research methods, advanced concepts of recreation and leisure, and leisure in modern society. Her present research interests include zoo studies, leisure and health, at-risk adolescents, and boredom.

Catherine P. Coyle, Ph.D., C.T.R.S., has been a member of the Department of Sport Management and Leisure Studies at Temple University for over six years as a professional research manager directing two major research grants in therapeutic recreation. She is also an Assistant Professor, teaching graduate and undergraduate courses in research methods and TR. Coyle received her bachelor's and master's degrees in TR and her Ph.D. in Educational Psychology. As a C.T.R.S. Coyle has over six years of professional practice in psychiatric care, physical rehabilitation, and service to individuals with developmental disabilities. Among Coyle's many achievements are her numerous articles and her presentations at major conferences and symposia. She is particularly interested in pursuing research in the areas of self-efficacy, depression, learning theory, and the application of TR as a clinical intervention in rehabilitation.

John Dattilo is an Associate Professor in the Department of Recreation and Leisure Studies at the University of Georgia. He is a C.T.R.S. who has been examining effects of interventions on leisure patterns of people with disabilities. Dattilo has published extensively on the topic including coauthoring two text books, *Leisure Education Program Programming: A Systematic Approach* (1991) and *Behavior Modification in Therapeutic Recreation* (1987). He received his Ph.D. in Leisure Studies at the University of Illinois at Urbana–Champaign and has taught therapeutic recreation at University of Nebraska and The Pennsylvania State University.

Julia (Julie) Kennon Dunn is an Associate Professor in the Department of Human Services and Studies at Florida State University in Tallahassee. She is a graduate of Florida State University and holds a doctorate degree from the University of Illinois at Urbana–Champaign. She is currently certified as a C.T.R.S. and has worked in mental health settings. In addition to teaching therapeutic recreation courses she has also taught recreation programming, leisure education, and research. Her research interests include: client assessment validation, creativity, and program design and evaluation.

Gary D. Ellis is a Professor, Director of Graduate Studies, and Director of the Western Laboratory for Leisure Research at the University of Utah. Prior to this position, he served as Assistant Professor at Western Kentucky University and as Project Coordinator and Research Associate on the Leisure Diagnostic Battery Project at North Texas State University. He holds a doctorate in Higher Education (College Teaching major) from North Texas State University, a master's degree in Recreation and Park Administration from the University of Kentucky, and a bachelor of science degree, also in Recreation and Park Administration, from Eastern Kentucky University. His teaching areas include measurement and research design and his research interests are in measurement of leisure related phenomena, leisure assessment, and, more recently, in applications of self-efficacy theory in therapeutic recreation.

David L. Gast is a Professor of Special Education in the Division of Exceptional Children at the University of Georgia. He received his Ph.D. in Child Psychology and Child Development from the University of Kansas. He regularly publishes in the areas of single subject research methodology, errorless teaching strategies and observational learning with students with moderate to severe intellectual disabilities.

Maureen Glancy, Ph.D., is an Associate Professor on the faculty in Recreation and Leisure studies at San Jose State University. Her experience includes administration, teaching, and consulting in higher education, business and industry, social agencies, organized camping, and environmental education. Her principal efforts in working with persons with disabilities have been in mainstreaming and adaptive solutions. She was certified to teach physical education to children with physical and developmental disabilities, and also combines counseling and activity therapy in group therapy and team building for persons with emotional and social dysfunctions. Taking research into the natural setting has become a focal interest in order to study social and psychological processes in action and to build a grounded theory of leisure experience.

Ann D. Huston, presently the Chief of Recreation Therapy Service at the Department of Veterans Affairs Medical Center at Palo Alto, California, received her bachelor's degree in Recreation (with a therapeutic emphasis) from the University of Nebraska–Lincoln in 1980. In 1991, she completed her master's degree in Public Administration (in Health Services) from the University of San Francisco. She maintains active certification with the National Council for Therapeutic Recreation Certification and serves on the Council's Exam Review Committee. Ann has served the American Therapeutic Recreation Association in a variety of leadership capacities including president. Ann also serves as an Adjunct Professor at San Jose State University teaching graduate level Therapeutic Recreation practice courses. Her interests in research include treatment effectiveness, mental health, and homelessness.

W. B. (Terry) Kinney, Ph.D. is an Associate Professor and Chairperson of the Department of Sport Management and Leisure Science at Temple University. He is a successful grant recipient, author, presenter, and consultant. Kinney is particularly recognized for contributions in the area of efficacy research in TR, and he is active in TR and rehabilitation-related professional associations. He earned his Ph.D. in Therapeutic Recreation at New York University. His research interests focus on determining the outcomes of TR interventions in the habilitation and rehabilitation of individuals with disabilities, psycho-social aspects of disability, and TR assessment.

Douglas A. Kleiber is currently a Professor in the Department of Recreation and Leisure Studies at the University of Georgia. He has published extensively on the impact of sport and leisure on developmental processes and on the psychological concomitants of various leisure experiences and orientations. Kleiber received a Ph.D. in Educational Psychology from the University of Texas and has held teaching and research positions at Cornell University, St. Cloud State University, and the University of Illinois at Urbana–Champaign.

Sandra L. Little, Ph.D., CLP, is an Associate Professor and Coordinator of the Graduate Program in HPERD at Illinois State University. She received her Ph.D. in Recreation and Park Administration from The Pennsylvania State University. In addition to extensive experience as a practitioner, Little has taught previously at the University of Oregon, Penn State, and Triton College. Her research interests include: recreation program development and evaluation, administration, and the social-psychological aspects of leisure.

Keith Savell, Ph.D., C.T.R.S., RTR (CA), consultant, formally served as an Assistant Professor in the Department of Recreation and Leisure Studies at San Jose State University. He received his Ph.D. from the University of Illinois at Urbana–Champaign, focusing on TR and Gerontology. Savell has been a member and committee officer in ATRA. In addition to his teaching and research, Savell has been an active presenter, nationally and internationally. His research interests lie in TR, gerontology, self-efficacy and self-determination. Savell has had clinical experience in physical medicine and rehabilitation and gerontology.

Stuart J. Schleien is an Associate Professor in the School of Kinesiology and Leisure Studies, with a joint appointment in Special Education Programs, at the University of Minnesota. He is a C.T.R.S. who has published extensively on the social integration of individuals with developmental disabilities in community settings. He has written four books and over 60 journal articles and book chapters. Since receiving his Ph.D. at the University of Maryland, he has presented his research throughout the U.S. and Canada, and in Israel, England, Sweden, and Australia.

John W. Shank, Ed.D., C.T.R.S., is an associate professor in the Department of Sport Management and Leisure Studies, and coordinator of Temple University's program in Therapeutic Recreation. His primary research interests are psychosocial issues of illness, disability, and health care and human services, and the social psychology of leisure. Prior to joining the faculty at Temple, Shank practiced for seven years as a TRS in mental health and mental retardation programs, and taught at Northwestern University. He has directed or co-directed several federally funded research, special recreation demonstration, and personnel preparation grants. He served as the co-principal investigator of a three-year "efficacy of therapeutic recreation" grant funded by the National Institutes of Disability and Rehabilitation Research. Shank has served as a member of the NTRS Board of Directors and the NCTRC Appeals Board. He received his Ed.D. from Boston University.

Norma J. Stumbo, Ph.D., C.T.R.S., received her bachelor's and master's degrees at the University of Missouri–Columbia in Recreation and Park Administration/Therapeutic Recreation; and her doctorate from the University of Illinois at Urbana–Champaign in Leisure Studies/Therapeutic Recreation. Her practical experience has focused on adults with physical disabilities. She is currently an Associate Professor and Coordinator of Therapeutic

Recreation at Illinois State University in Normal. Her primary teaching responsibilities include both undergraduate and graduate therapeutic recreation, as well as core recreation, coursework. Her research interests include applied studies in entry-level knowledge, credentialing, assessment, and evaluation. She has served on state and national boards, as well as an Associate Editor of the *Therapeutic Recreation Journal*.

Ellen Weissinger is an Associate Professor in the Quantitative and Qualitative Methods in Education Program in the Department of Educational Psychology at the University of Nebraska. She earned a Ph.D. in Recreation and Leisure Studies at the University of Maryland, and a master's in Leisure Studies at the University of Iowa. Her research has focused on the psychological antecedents and consequences of leisure behavior, and measurement issues relevant to leisure-related variables. She teaches research methodology, thinks research is cool, and is committed to the notion that research is a meaningful process.